THE
THEATER
EXPERIENCE

THE THEATER EXPERIENCE

EDWIN WILSON
Hunter College
The City University of New York

THIRD EDITION

McGRAW-HILL BOOK COMPANY
New York St. Louis San Francisco Auckland Bogotá
Hamburg Johannesburg London Madrid Mexico
Montreal New Delhi Panama Paris São Paulo
Singapore Sydney Tokyo Toronto

THE
THEATER
EXPERIENCE

1 2 3 4 5 6 7 8 9 0 D O C D O C 8 9 8 7 6 5 4

ISBN 0-07-070671-9 SC

ISBN 0-07-070673-5 HC

Library of Congress Cataloging in Publication Data

Wilson, Edwin.
The theater experience.

Bibliography: p.
Includes index.
1. Theater.   2. Drama.   I. Title.
PN1655.W57   1985   792   84-10038
ISBN 0-07-070673-5
ISBN 0-07-070671-9 (pbk.)

This book was set in Optima by Black Dot, Inc. (ECU).
The editors were Marian D. Provenzano, Allan Forsyth, and Susan Gamer;
the designer was Joan E. O'Connor;
the production supervisor was Leroy A. Young.
The photo editor was Inge King.
New drawings were done by Fine Line Illustrations, Inc.
R. R. Donnelley & Sons Company was printer and binder.

Soft cover photograph credits
Front cover photograph by Richard Howard.
Back cover photograph from *Sganarelle*,
American Repertory Theatre,
photo by Richard Feldman.

The part-opening illustrations were done by Al Hirschfeld, reproduced by
special arrangement with his exclusive representative,
The Margo Feiden Galleries, New York.

The passage from *Death of a Salesman* by Arthur Miller which appears on pages
215-217 is reprinted by permission of Viking, New York, 1968; copyright 1949
by Arthur Miller.

The passage from *Long Day's Journey into Night* by Eugene O'Neill which
appears on page 6 is reprinted by permission of Yale University Press; copyright
© 1955 by Carlotta Monterey O'Neill.

To my wife, Catherine

CONTENTS

LIST OF SYNOPSES OF PLAYS

PREFACE

The third edition of *The Theater Experience* retains the many features that have won wide acceptance for the first two editions. These include a nonhistorical approach to theater; an informal writing style; frequent analogies to everyday experience; a clear organization; abundant illustrations tied directly to the text; and a series of informative appendixes. At the same time, the third edition includes a number of significant changes and additions that it is hoped will make the book even more helpful to both teachers and students.

One important change is in the sequence of chapters and sections. As in both previous editions, the book begins with three chapters on the audience. One of the innovations of the first edition of *The Theater Experience* was its emphasis on the audience and on the key role that the audience plays in a theater event. By putting this first, students—who will become audience members in college and in the years after—are put at the center of the experience. Important additions, however, have been made to these chapters. A section on the critic, for example (formerly in Chapter 18) has been moved ahead to Chapter 3, The Background of the Audience. Thus, students can incorporate the role of the critic in their theatergoing at an early stage of the course.

Even more significant are shifts in major sections. Because students begin attending and reading plays early in the course, it was felt advisable to move material on genre and dramatic structure to an earlier position in the book.

This will give students a better grasp of the material they are reading and viewing from the outset.

In this newest edition, the section on purpose and point of view—Part Two—has been placed immediately after the chapters on the audience. The concepts of tragedy, comedy, farce, tragicomedy, and so forth, are introduced at this point. Also, these chapters have been reworked to eliminate repetitious sections that existed before. Following genre comes the section on the playwright and dramatic structure—Part Three—again, to prepare students for understanding plays.

The section on the performers and the director—Part Four—comes next. It is followed by the section on environment and the visual elements—Part Five—and, finally, by the section on the total experience, Part Six.

For this edition, individual chapters have also been revised. The chapters on acting, for example, have been extensively reworked to show even more than before the discipline, training, and experience required of performers, and to put less stress on differences between realistic and nonrealistic techniques.

One important point should be made about the rearrangement of the sequence of chapters. In conversations with a number of teachers who use the text, and in written responses to inquiries, I have discovered that teachers often develop their own order of progression. They teach the book out of sequence, and it works well for them. If, therefore, a teacher wishes to use this edition in the same sequence as the second edition—or the first edition, for that matter—it can be done easily and satisfactorily.

Two appendixes have been added to the three that appeared in previous editions. The material on theories of tragedy and comedy has been taken out of the chapters on genre and has been made Appendix 1. A table contrasting realism and nonrealism has been moved from the text to become Appendix 5. Three appendixes remain from earlier editions: one on common technical terms, a second on the chief types and genres of theater, and a third featuring a brief historical survey. All five appendixes can be used for reference, or can be integrated into a course as part of an assignment. It is also possible to devote separate class sessions to the appendixes.

Another new feature of the third edition is a series of plot summaries set apart from the text in boxes. The plays thus summarized are *King Oedipus, King Lear, Tartuffe, The Way of the World, Ghosts, The Cherry Orchard, Mother Courage and Her Children, Death of a Salesman, A Streetcar Named Desire, A Raisin in the Sun,* and *Waiting for Godot.* Naturally, it is better for students to see or read the plays than to consult a summary, but many times this is difficult; certainly students could not be asked to read all eleven plays. By providing separate summaries, the plays can be referred to along with the text. Also, when plays have been seen or read, the summaries provide a convenient review.

A trademark of *The Theater Experience* has been the use of carefully selected and clearly reproduced illustrations. This feature has been expanded in the third edition to include sixteen pages of full-color photographs. All the photographs in the book are closely tied to the material being discussed and provide further elaboration of key concepts. Ninety percent of the photographs are new to this edition. The photographs are drawn from a wide range of productions—Broadway, regional theater, and college. In addition, there are expanded illustrations of scenic devices and materials, provided by Harry Lines; and charts on the duties of the director and producer, courtesy of Paul Antonie Distler and George Thorn.

Before *The Theater Experience,* most theater texts adopted either a historical or a genre approach to the subject. Historically oriented texts begin where western theater began—with the Greeks. Those texts adopting a historical approach generally devote half of the book to a chronological treatment of theater, with subsequent chapters on the actor, designer, and director, among others. In the genre approach, chapters on tragedy, comedy, farce, and so forth, are substituted for the history. In both of these, theater tends to be treated as a frozen artifact divided into discrete units of history or genre: tragedy, Restoration drama, the Spanish golden age, and so on.

In his book *The Empty Space,* Peter Brook speaks of the "immediate theater." In a sense, all theater is immediate—an experience given and received. Treated as a set entity, a remote body of knowledge divorced from the lives of those who view it, theater loses any chance of immediacy. The aim of this text is to analyze and explain what theater is about—what goes on in theater and what it means to the viewer. The experience begins for the audience when it comes into the theater, confronts the environment, and, following that, encounters the performance. The crucial role of the audience—its importance in the dynamic encounter between creators and viewers in theater—is dealt with throughout this text.

Every effort has been made to relate theater to experiences already familiar to the student. Certain elements in theater have analogues in daily life; where possible, these analogues are used to provide a key, or bridge, to the theater experience. Interior decoration, for example, used to create an atmosphere or ambience in a restaurant or a room, is a form of "scene design." In this way a familiar experience becomes the basis for understanding the more specialized art of stage design.

The Theater Experience is intended as a text for the introductory theater course offered by most colleges and universities. Generally, such courses are aimed at those not intending to major in theater, and the book has been written with that in mind. While it is neither a history nor a "how to" book, there is an abundance of solid information in it. It can serve equally well as the text for a prerequisite course leading to advanced work in theater or for the theater component in a combined arts course. Those students who plan to concentrate on theater can begin in no better way than by examining the actor-audience exchange, learning the spectator's side of the equation as well as the creator's.

Because the book stresses the encounter between audience and performers, it is assumed that anyone using it will make attendance at performances an integral part of the course. Though the text deals with specific plays, the approach can easily be adapted to any current production readily available to students. Any Shakespearean play, for example, can prove beneficial, as can any Greek play, a work by Ibsen, or a more modern piece.

From the beginning—in the approach, the writing style, and the organization—the aim has been to provide both teachers and students with a book which is not only informative and incisive but also pleasurable.

ACKNOWLEDGMENTS

I developed many of the ideas in this book while teaching a course in introduction to theater at Hunter College of the City University of New York. To my colleagues and students at Hunter, I express my deep appreciation.

Certain teachers who have used the book have contributed specific material which I have incorporated in the text. James Monos furnished important new material in the chapter on acting, and Harry Lines furnished new design illustrations; Alvin Goldfarb wrote the special sections on the theories of tragedy and comedy, and Mira Felner wrote "A Note on Women and Greek and Elizabethan Theater"; and Daniel Koetting provided material on lighting, special effects, and sound. From the first two editions, repeated here, there are three appendixes prepared by Stuart Baker. The third and fourth appendixes particularly, which are entirely his work, have been enthusiastically received.

I express special appreciation to the artist Al Hirschfeld, who allowed us to use his incomparable drawings for part openings.

I also wish to thank Sally Small, who provided all the material for the plot summaries of plays, prepared the index, and assisted in many other ways, including typing the instructor's manual and the manuscript.

The following teachers read the manuscript and made helpful suggestions, many of which are included in this edition: Bruce Coblentz, Oregon State University; Paul A. Distler, Virginia Tech; Philip G. Hill, Furman University; Justin Lombardo, OSB, College of St. Benedict; Tice Miller, University of Nebraska; Robert Morgan, William Patterson College; and George Thorn, Virginia Tech.

I have been fortunate to work closely with two people, on all three editions of *The Theater Experience:* Inge King, the perceptive and knowledgeable photograph editior, and Joan O'Connor, the exceptionally talented art director. In addition, my three editors at McGraw-Hill have been enormously helpful: Allan Forsyth, Marian Provenzano, and Susan Gamer.

Edwin Wilson

THE
THEATER
EXPERIENCE

INTRODUCTION

Theater: A unique experience.
Masks, costumes, lights, scenery—these combine with the actions of the performers and the words of the script to create a special moment of theater. When we go to the theater, we experience a series of such moments, like the one shown here in a production of the PAF Playhouse, Huntington Station, New York, of Friedrich Duerrenmatt's *An Angel Comes to Babylon*.

The impulse toward theater is universal. It has occurred wherever human society has developed: in Europe and Asia, throughout Africa, and among American Indians. In virtually every culture recorded in history or studied by anthropologists, we find rituals, religious ceremonies, and celebrations that include elements of theater.

One of these elements is a presentation by *performers* in front of an *audience*—a ceremony, for example, by priests before members of a community.

Storytelling is another element. In many cultures there are strong traditions of storytellers who recite myths or legends from the past, or teach lessons by means of stories, to a group of listeners.

Another recurring element is the wearing of costumes, such as those worn by priests or tribal chiefs. In many rituals or ceremonies, animals or gods are impersonated by people.

Exactly how and at what point these rituals, ceremonies, or stories move into the separate realm of theater is a matter of conjecture. Disputes among authorities over these questions need not concern us here. It is enough to know that theater as a distinct art form has emerged in many different cultures. In India, for instance, theater had become well established nearly 2000 years ago. In Greece, a fully developed theater had emerged almost 2500 years ago.

Wherever theater has become a separate art form, it has certain essential qualities: an action or story (the play) is presented by one group (the performers) to another group (the audience). Theater thus becomes an experience—a shared, indivisible event that includes both those who perform and those who observe. Like other experiences—falling in love, riding a bicycle, attending a football game—theater requires a personal presence: in this case, the presence of the audience.

THEATER IS TRANSITORY

A theater performance changes from moment to moment as the audience encounters a series of shifting impressions and stimuli. It is a kaleidoscopic adventure through which the audience passes, with each instant a direct, immediate experience.

The transitory nature of theater—a quality it shares with all performing arts—sets it apart in a significant way from literature and the visual arts. A painting, a piece of sculpture, a novel, and a book of poems are fixed objects. When they leave the artist's hands (or in the case of a book, when they leave the printer's shop), they are complete. They exist as finished products, and their tangible, unchangeable quality is one reason we value them, in the same way that we value historic buildings or antique automobiles. In a world of change and uncertainty, they remain the same.

A theatrical ceremony in Africa.
Cultures throughout the world have rituals, ceremonies, and dances that include theatrical elements like masks, costumes, and acting impersonations. In this picture, natives of New Guinea are performing at the Mount Hagen Festival.

(Malcolm Kirk—Peter Arnold, Inc.)

We can go back to them again and again; and, if they have been preserved, they will always be there and always be the same. Bernini's sculpture of the Blessed Ludovica Albertoni is the same work of art today that it was the day it was completed in 1674, over 300 years ago.

The essence of literature and the visual arts is to catch something at a moment in time and freeze it. With the performing arts, however, this is impossible, because they are not objects but events. Music provides a good illustration. Music may have timbre, pitch, and volume, but none of these registers except as it moves through time. A note in a melody cannot be held forever as a line in a drawing is forever fixed. Instead, music is created by the perpetual shift of notes, through repetition, variation, and an accumulation of effects. Similarly, theater occurs through time. A cumulative series of sights, sounds, and impressions creates theater.

Bernini's statue of the Blessed Ludovica Albertoni.
This masterpiece of sculpture, completed in 1674, is the same today as when it was created more than 300 years ago. Paintings and sculptures—unlike theater—are permanent, unchanging works of art.

Objects are a part of theater—costumes, props, scenery, a script—but none of these constitutes the art. Bernard Beckerman explains the difference:

> Theater is nothing if not spontaneous. It occurs. It happens. The novel can be put away, taken up, reread. Not theater. It keeps slipping between one's fingers. Stopping, it stops being theater. Its permanent features, facets of activity, such as scenery, script, stage, people, are no more theater than the two poles of a generator are electricity. Theater is what goes on between the parts.[1]

The distinction between reading a novel and attending a theatrical performance reminds us that drama is sometimes looked on as a branch of literature. The confusion is understandable. On the one hand, plays are often printed in book form, like literature; on the other hand, many novels and short stories contain extensive passages of dialogue that could easily be scenes in a play.

Although scenes of dialogue in a novel resemble drama—and plays appear in book form—there is an important difference between the two forms. Unlike a novel, a play is written to be performed. In some respects a script is to a stage production as a musical score is to a concert, or an architectural blueprint to a building: it is an outline for a performance.

Playwrights understand this distinction quite well. They know that what occurs on stage may be different from what we imagine when we read a script. Certainly the *experience* will be different. The physical production—the environment, scenery, and costumes—will affect the performance; so will the performers. The *ways* actors and actresses interpret their roles—such things as facial expressions, gestures, and vocal inflections—have much to do with a play's ultimate effect on the audience.

Because of this, some playwrights go to great lengths in their stage directions to tell performers how to play their parts. Look, for example, at the stage direction given by the American playwright Eugene O'Neill (1888–1953) in the third act of *Long Day's Journey into Night*. Tyrone, the father, and Edmund, his son, have been drinking. As they approach their

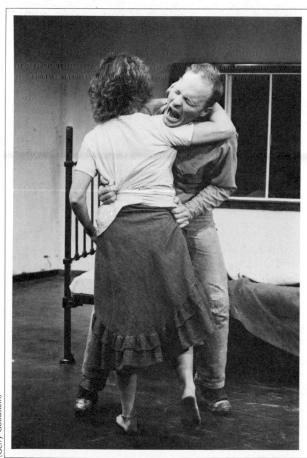

(Gerry Goodstein)

Theater is action.
In contrast to sculpture, painting, or literature, theater is a dynamic art, changing from moment to moment as performers interact with one another—and with the audience. Here we see Kathy Whitton Baker and Ed Harris struggle in the Circle Repertory Theater production of Sam Shepard's *Fool for Love*, directed by the playwright.

home they are fearful that Mary, the mother, has begun taking drugs again, as she had done in the past. The following are O'Neill's instructions:

> Tyrone comes in through the front parlor. Edmund is behind him. Tyrone has had a lot to drink but beyond a slightly glazed look in his eyes and a trace of blur in his speech, he does not show it. Edmund has also had more than a few drinks without much apparent effect, except that his sunken cheeks are flushed and his eyes look bright and feverish. They stop in the doorway to stare appraisingly at her [Mary]. What they see fulfills their worst expectations. But for the moment Mary is unconscious of their condemning eyes. She kisses her husband and then Edmund. Her manner is unnaturally effusive. They submit shrinkingly. She talks excitedly.[2]

Drama can be studied in a classroom for imagery, character, and theme, just as we study a novel; but study of this sort takes place *before* the event. It is a form of preparation for the experience; the experience is the performance itself. Obviously, we have more opportunities to read plays in book form than to see them produced; but when we read a play, we should always attempt to visualize the other aspects of a production in our mind's eye. We should be aware constantly that theater is performance.

One special quality of a theater performance is its immediacy. In the theater we live in what the playwright Thornton Wilder (1897–1975) called the *perpetual present tense*. Contained in the present is the fresh remembrance of the past and the anticipation of what is to come. Robert Edmond Jones (1887–1954), an American scene designer and critic, describes it this way:

> All that has ever been is in this moment; all that will be is in this moment. Both are meeting in one living flame in this unique instant of time. This is drama; this is theater—*to be aware of the now*.[3]

As Jones suggests, the theater experience has a quality all its own; it is like other experiences—the other arts in particular—but it is also unique.

The nature of the theater experience and the elements which make up that experience will be the subject of this book.

THE ELEMENTS OF THEATER

A performance is the result of many forces coming together—some tangible, some intangible—including the physical presence of the performers, the colors and shapes of the costumes and scenery, and the ideas and emotions expressed in the words of the playwright. Each element of theater is varied and complex, and to understand theater we must study the elements separately.

Altogether, we will examine the following basic elements of theater:

1   The audience: its function, its general makeup, and the background which each spectator brings to a performance.
2   The purpose of a theater piece and the point of view adopted by those who create it. Is the work intended to entertain or to provoke thought? Is it serious or comic?
3   The work of the playwright in creating dramatic structure and dramatic characters.
4   The performances of the actors and actresses and the director's supervision of the production.
5   The environment in which a production occurs—in a small space or a large one, indoors or outdoors—together with the visual effects created by costumes, lighting, and scenery.

At every point during a performance, these elements intersect; they fuse and combine to produce theater. In addition to studying the elements separately, we will look at the ways in which they join together to form the whole.

When an audience comes to witness a performance, an exchange takes place between performers and spectators; the two groups engage in a form of communication or a celebration. At its best, theater affords members of the audience an opportunity to be transported outside themselves or to look deep inside themselves. In the following pages we will attempt to discover what makes this profound and magical experience possible.

PART 1
THE
AUDIENCE

The performer meets the audience.

In the drawing by the artist Al Hirschfeld on the following pages, the actress Julie Andrews is applauded by a theater audience. The audience is an essential part of every theater event. The three chapters of Part One will examine the ways in which the audience participates in the theater experience.

1

THE ROLE
OF THE
AUDIENCE

The audience plays a key role.
The audience and the performers are the two basic elements in the theater equation; both are essential. Here, performers in a French production of Giraudoux's *The Trojan War Will Not Take Place* take a curtain call before a receptive audience.

Throughout the twentieth century, theater has faced a series of unprecedented challenges. For nearly 2500 years, theater was the means by which drama was presented to audiences. Beginning around 1900, however, a succession of mechanical and electronic devices threatened to replace theater. In the early part of the twentieth century, silent movies became popular. With comedians like Charlie Chaplin and Buster Keaton, and melodramas like *The Birth of a Nation,* it was predicted that theater would soon be a thing of the past. Movies, after all, were much cheaper and could be seen in many more places.

In the 1920s, radio appeared; and again it was predicted that theater would be eclipsed. With radio, people did not even need to leave their homes to hear a good suspense story or an amusing comedy. In the late 1920s and early 1930s, when talking movies arrived, it was argued that theater stood no possible chance of survival. The talkies, after all, combined sight and sound; they could do everything theater could. In fact, because they are able to move around to show vast outdoor panoramas and chases on horseback or by car, movies could do things theater could not do.

Despite these grave challenges, theater did not disappear. But more was to come. After World War II, television arrived, first black-and-white television and then color. This seemed the ultimate challenge—one it would be impossible for theater to meet; plays with first-rate actors and actresses, with full color and good sound, could now be seen free in the home.

How could theater match that? Theater did, though. It has met each one of these threats and survived very much intact. In fact, theater is as healthy today as it has been in some time. In the United States, for example, there is an amazing diversity of theater activity—not only in New York, with Broadway, off-Broadway and off-off-Broadway theaters, but throughout the country, with permanent professional companies in major cities and college and university theaters in every state. (The full range of theaters in the United States will be described in Chapter 3.)

THE ACTOR-AUDIENCE RELATIONSHIP

How has theater been able to meet so many challenges and not only survive but emerge in some ways stronger than ever? There are several answers; but the most important has to do with the "live" nature of theater. Theater is an event in which the performers are in the presence of the audience.

A Contrast with Film

The special nature of theater will be more apparent if we contrast a drama seen in a theater with one shown on film or television. In many ways the two

14

Television is different from theater.
When audiences watch television—or a film—they see images, or pictures, of people on a screen rather than the people themselves. The experience, therefore, is once removed from personal contact.

forms are alike. Both present a story told in dramatic form—a reenactment of scenes played by performers who speak and act as if they were the people they represent. The same actress can play Juliet in *Romeo and Juliet* by William Shakespeare (1564–1616) on both stage and screen. Not only the dramatization and the acting but also other elements, such as scenery and costume, are often similar on stage and screen. In fact, many films or television specials have been based on stage productions: *Grease, Annie, The Wiz, A Streetcar Named Desire,* and numerous Shakespeare plays. Unquestionably one can learn a great deal about theater from watching a play on film or television—and have some of the same experiences.

Despite this, there is a fundamental difference of which we become aware when we contrast theater with movies. This does not have to do with technical matters, such as, the way films can show outdoor shots made from helicopters or can cut instantaneously from one scene to another. The most significant difference between films and theater is the *actor-audience relationship.* The experience of being in the presence of the performer is more important to theater than anything else. No matter how closely a film follows the story of a play, no matter how involved we are with the people on the screen, we are always in the presence of an image, never a person.

We all know the difference between an image of someone and the

THE ROLE OF THE AUDIENCE

15

flesh-and-blood reality. How often we rehearse a speech we plan to make to someone we love or fear. We run through the scene in our mind, picturing ourselves in conversation with the other person; but when we meet face to face, it is seldom the same. We freeze or find ourselves unable to speak; sometimes the words gush forth incoherently. Seldom is the encounter the way we planned.

The American playwright Jean-Claude van Itallie (1936–) explained the importance of the actor-audience relationship in the theater, and how theater differs from films and television. In the introduction to one of his plays, he wrote:

> Theater is not electronic. Unlike movies and unlike television, it does require the live presence of both audience and actors in a single space. This is the theater's uniquely important advantage and function, its original religious function of bringing people together in a community ceremony where the actors are in some sense priests or celebrants, and the audience is drawn to participate with the actors in a kind of eucharist.[1]

The Chemistry of Actor-Audience Contact

The drama critic Walter Kerr elaborated on the idea of what it means for the audience and actors to be together:

> It doesn't just mean that we are in the personal presence of performers. It means that they are in *our* presence, conscious of us, speaking to us, working for and with us until a circuit that is not mechanical becomes established between us, a circuit that is fluid, unpredictable, ever-changing in its impulses, crackling, intimate. *Our* presence, the way we respond, flows back to the performer and alters what he does, to some degree and sometimes astonishingly, so, every single night. We are contenders, making the play and the evening and the emotion together. We are playmates, building a structure.
>
> This never happens at a film because the film is already built, finished, sealed, incapable of responding to us in any way. The actors can't hear us or feel our presence; nothing *we* do, in our liveness, counts. We could be dead and the film would purr out its appointed course, flawlessly, indifferently.[2]

Like films, television seems very close to theater; sometimes it seems closer than film. Television programs often begin with such words as "This program comes to you live from Burbank, California." But the word *live* must be qualified; in one sense, television distorts the meaning we have customarily assigned to the term. Prior to television, *live* in the entertainment or theatrical world meant "in person": not only was the event taking place at that moment, it was taking place before the spectator's eyes. *Live television* means that the event is taking place at that moment, but not in the presence of the viewer. In fact, it is generally far removed from any member of the television audience, possibly half a world away. With television we see an image on a tube; we are free to look or not look, or even to leave the room. But the effect of a personal encounter, so vital to theater, is missing.

The fascination of being in the presence of a person is difficult to explain, but not difficult to verify. No matter how often fans have seen their favorite stars on television or in the movies, they will go to any lengths to see them in person. As another example, at one time or another, each of us has braved bad weather and shoving crowds to see celebrities at a parade or a political rally. The same pull of personal contact draws us to the theater.

At the heart of the theater experience, therefore, is the actor-audience relationship: the immediate, personal exchange whose chemistry and magic give theater its special quality. At a stage performance the actresses and actors can hear the laughter, can sense the silence, and can feel the tension in the audience. In short, the audience can affect, and in subtle ways change, the performance. At the same time, those in the audience watch the performers closely, asking a number of unconscious questions: Are the performers unusually skilled? Have they learned their parts well? Are they convincing in their roles? Will they do something surprising? Will they make a mistake? Each moment, in every stage performance, these remain unanswered questions.

It is important to understand, too, that for the audience, theater is a group experience as the following section will discuss.

THE GROUP EXPERIENCE

Some of the arts—painting, sculpture, literature—provide solitary experiences. The viewer or reader contemplates the work alone, at her or his own pace. This is true even in a museum, where people may flock to look at a single painting; they are with other people, but they respond as individuals, one at a time. In theater, however, as in the other performing arts, the group experience is indispensable; the performing arts in turn share this with other communal events: religious services, sports, and celebrations. Before the event can take place, a group must assemble—at one time in one place. When people are gathered together in this way, something mysterious happens to them. Though still individuals, with their own personalities and backgrounds, they take on other qualities as well, qualities which often overshadow their independent responses.

Psychology of Groups

Gustav Le Bon, a forerunner of social psychology and one of the first to study the phenomenon of crowds, wrote that a collection of people "presents new characteristics very different from those of the individuals composing it. The sentiments and ideas of all the persons in the gathering

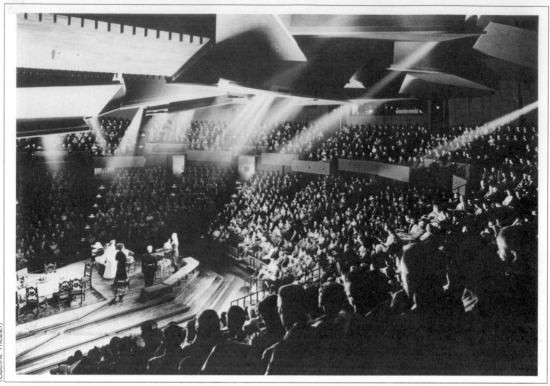

Theater is a group experience.
A large audience attends a performance at the Tyrone Guthrie Theater in Minneapolis.
In the theater, the size, attitude, and makeup of the audience affect the overall
experience.

take one and the same direction, and their conscious personality vanishes."[3] Le Bon went on to say that the most striking peculiarity of a crowd is
that although the individuals who compose it are quite different as individuals, once they have been transformed into a crowd, they develop a
"collective mind which makes them feel, think, and act in a manner quite
different from that in which each individual of them would feel, think, and
act were he in a state of isolation."[4]

In his book *Social Psychology*, Lawrence S. Wrightsman points to a
number of recent studies that confirm the ways in which a crowd or group
can influence the thoughts and actions of individuals. "Groups can be
swayed by a 'groupthink' process," he writes.[5] Elsewhere he affirms that
"the awareness of others watching us has an impact on virtually every
component of behavior."[6]

Not all crowds are alike. Some are aggressive—groups of people on the
street who decide to riot or terrorize a neighborhood. Others are docile—
the passengers on an airline flight, for example. The crowd at a football

game is different from a gathering at a religious observance; and a theater crowd is distinct from all these. In spite of being different, however, the theater audience shares with all such groups the special characteristics of the collective mind.

As an example, when sitting alone in a theater, we are reluctant to clap and laugh out loud. In a group, however, we feel free to do so. One explanation for this is what behaviorist B. F. Skinner calls *reinforcement*.

> If it is always the individual who behaves, it is nevertheless the group which has the more powerful effect. By joining a group the individual increases his power to achieve reinforcement. . . . The reinforcing consequences generated by the group easily exceed the sums of the consequences which could be achieved by members acting separately. The total reinforcing effect is enormously increased.[7]

This is a complicated subject, of course, and Skinner deals with only one aspect of it. Also, this is not the place to try to fathom the mysteries of the group mind or crowd behavior. It is important, however, to note its existence and, beyond that, to emphasize the importance of group behavior to theater. Becoming part of an audience is a crucial element of the theater experience. For a time we share a common undertaking; we are members of a group focused on one activity—the performance of a play. Not only do we laugh or cry in a way we might not otherwise; we also sense an intangible communion with those around us.

When a collection of individuals responds more or less in unison to what is occurring on stage, their relationship to one another is reaffirmed. If there is a display of cruelty at which we shudder, or sorrow by which we are moved, or pomposity at which we laugh, it is reassuring to have others respond as we do. For a moment we are part of a group sharing a common experience; and our sorrow or joy, which we might have feared was idiosyncratic, is found to be part of a broad human response.

Audience Makeup Affects the Experience

Being part of a group is an essential element of theater. But groups vary, and this will alter the occasion. Some audiences are general—for instance, the thousands who attend outdoor productions each summer such as *Unto These Hills,* the play about the Cherokee Indians presented on the Cherokee Reservation in western North Carolina. These audiences include people of all ages, from all parts of the country, and from all socioeconomic levels. Other audiences are more homogeneous, such as spectators at a high school play, a children's theater production, a Broadway opening night, a political play, or a performance in a prison.

Still another factor affecting our experience in the theater is our relationship to the other members of the audience. If we are among friends or people of a like mind, we are likely to feel comfortable and relaxed; we readily give in to the group experience. On the other hand, if we feel alien—for example, a young person with an older group, a radical with conservatives, or a naive person with sophisticates—we will be estranged from the group as a whole. The people with whom we attend the theater—their relative homogeneity and our relation to them—strongly influence our response to the total event.

THE SEPARATE ROLES
OF PERFORMERS AND SPECTATORS

In recent years numerous attempts have been made to involve members of the audience in the action of the play. Performers have come into the audience to make contact with spectators—shaking hands, touching them, arguing face to face. Spectators, too, have been encouraged to come on stage and join the action. At certain performances of the Living Theater, a group that flourished in the late 1960s, the stage sometimes became so crowded with spectators that a space had to be cleared so the performers could get on with the play.

How Should the Audience Be Involved?

This attempt to involve audience members directly springs from a worthwhile impulse: the desire to make theater more immediate and intense. But it ignores the manner in which art functions.

Art is not life but a reflection of life—a special creation that abstracts or mirrors life. Often, as we shall see in Chapter 2, it comes closer than our everyday observations to portraying the truth of life; but it remains a separate process and creation. One essential element of this process is a degree of separation between the object or event an artist creates—a painting, a sculpture, a dance, a musical performance, a theater production —and the audience that observes it.

One can imagine trying to get the full effect of a large landscape painting when standing a few inches from it. One would see only the brushstrokes of a single tree or a small patch of blue sky. We need distance in order to take in and appreciate works of art. This separation, which is called *aesthetic distance,* is necessary in theater just as it is in the other arts.

On the question of separation between actors and audience, Bernard Beckerman made the following observations:

> The performers and spectators must be separated from each other so that the spectators can observe what is happening. But this isolation is not merely utilitarian; it is both physical and psychological. A sacred grove may be selected, a dancing circle may be circumscribed, a platform may be erected.

Somehow, an area is defined, which then becomes the servant of the performer. It is manipulable, both as actual and imaginative space; it is the place where presentations can be made. Recently, in drama, we have had instances in productions such as *The Connection* and *The Blacks,* in the work of Jerzy Grotowski, and in novelties such as Happenings, where a breakdown of isolation is sought. Frequently, roles are reversed, and the spectator, instead of being god, becomes scapegoat. Such attempts to erase the line between presenter and presentee only define it more sharply. The auditor becomes acutely aware that he has been cast in the role of a particular kind of spectator. Isolation is not eliminated, merely recharacterized.[8]

Participation through Direct Action

The question of actor-audience separation has been complicated in recent years by the rapid growth of theatrical activities in which ordinary people play roles and improvise dramatic scenes. Most theater events offer an experience to an audience observing what happens on stage. But a theater event can be set up as a workshop or laboratory in which everyone present is expected to take part. Both types of theater involve participation, but of different kinds.

In observed theater the audience participates vicariously or empathically with what is happening on stage. *Empathy* means that we mentally enter into the feelings or spirit of another person—in this case, a character on stage. Sometimes an audience will not be in tune with the characters on stage but will react violently against them. In either case members of the audience are participating. They might shed tears, laugh, pass judgment, sit frozen in their seats, or literally tremble with fear. But this is done through the imagination while separated from the action: sitting in a seat or, in the case of street theater, standing around the edge of the playing area.

The theater of direct participation works differently. Those who take part are not actors in the usual sense, and there is no attempt to follow a written script. Rather, the emphasis is on education, personal development, and therapy: fields in which theater techniques have opened up new possibilities. In schools, for example, creative dramatics, theater games, and group improvisations have proved invaluable in aiding self-discovery and developing healthy group attitudes. By acting out hypothetical situations or giving free rein to their imaginations, children build confidence, discover creative potential, and overcome inhibitions. In some cases creative dramatics teaches lessons which are difficult to teach by conventional means.

For adults as well as children, sociodrama and psychodrama are coming more and more to the forefront as therapeutic techniques. In sociodrama, the members of the participating groups, such as parents and children, students and teachers, or legal authorities and ordinary citizens, explore their own attitudes and prejudices. When young people, for instance, take the part of the parents, and adults assume the roles of the children, both

Participatory theater: A different experience.
A group enacting a sociodrama in Prof. Patricia Sternberg's class at Hunter College—
CUNY. Participatory theater is for the benefit of those taking part, not for an audience.
Education or personal satisfaction is the object, rather than a polished performance.

groups become aware of deep-seated feelings and arrive at a better understanding of one another.

Psychodrama uses some of the same techniques as sociodrama, but is more private and interpersonal; in fact, it can become so intense that it should be carried out only under the supervision of a carefully trained therapist. In psychodrama, individual fears, anxieties, and frustrations are explored. A person might reenact a particularly traumatic scene from childhood, for example.

The various fields of participatory theater are fascinating, and their full potential has only recently begun to be explored; but our purpose here is to draw the distinction between participatory drama and observed drama. In participatory drama, theater is a means to another end: education, therapy, group development, and the like. The aim is not public performance, and so there is little emphasis—in fact, quite the reverse—on a carefully prepared, expertly performed presentation before an audience. In observed drama there must always be a separation between the performers and the audience. This is the aesthetic distance referred to earlier.

At times in the contemporary theater, as has been noted, spectators go on stage to be part of the action; at other times, performers come into the audience to engage in repartee with a spectator. If the spectator takes part, he or she is no longer an observer, but a participant. For those moments the observer has changed roles and becomes what Bernard Beckerman calls the *presenter* rather than the *presentee*.

Our concern in this study is primarily with those who observe theater. By definition, the experience of the observer is not one of direct, physical contact. How, then, does this experience occur? If we are not involved physically, how can those of us who are spectators be so affected by what happens on a stage? What can cause us to laugh out loud, to become so frightened that we break out in goosebumps, to cry, to become enraged? The answer is the human imagination—the power of the mind and heart—and in Chapter 2 we will look at how it operates.

SUMMARY

1   During this century theater has been challenged by silent movies, radio, talking pictures, and television. It has survived these challenges partly because of the special nature of the actor-audience relationship.
2   The actor-audience relationship is a "live" relationship: each is in the other's presence, in the same place at the same time. It is the exchange between the two which gives theater its unique quality.
3   Theater—like other performing arts—is a group experience. Also, the makeup of the audience has a direct bearing on the effect of the experience.
4   Participants and spectators play different roles in the theater experience, the latter's role being to observe and respond.
5   There is a difference between participating in theater by direct action and by observation. In the former, nonactors take part, usually for the purpose of personal growth and self-development. In the latter, a presentation is made by one group to another, and the spectators do not participate physically in the experience.

2
THE
IMAGINATION
OF THE
AUDIENCE

The audience uses its imagination.
The play *Crossing Niagara* by Alonso Alegria concerns a man who crosses Niagara Falls on a tightrope with a young man on his back. In this production at the Manhattan Theater Club, Paul McCrane plays the boy and Alvin Epstein the tightrope walker. By using the power of its imagination, the audience accepts this as if it were actually happening.

For those who take part in it, theater is a direct experience: a stage carpenter builds scenery, a scene designer paints it, an actress wears a costume and stands on stage in a spotlight. Theirs is the experience of someone who cuts a finger or is held in an embrace: the pain or the warmth is felt directly and physically.

As members of the audience, we feel a different kind of pain or warmth: a no less immediate, but separate sensation. As spectators in the theater we are presented with a number of stimuli—we sense the presence of other audience members; we observe the movements and gestures of performers and hear the words they speak; and we see costumes, scenery, and lighting. From these we form mental images or make imaginative connections which provoke joy, laughter, anger, sorrow, or pain. As I noted in the previous chapter, however, all this occurs without our moving from our seats.

THE DRAMATIC IMAGINATION OF SPECTATORS

We naturally assume that those who create theater are highly imaginative people and that their minds are full of vivid, exciting ideas which may not occur to the rest of us. If we carry this idea too far, however, and conclude that we in the audience have limited or nonexistent theatrical imaginations, we are doing ourselves a great injustice. As we saw earlier, theater is a two-way street—an exchange between actors and audience—and this is nowhere more evident than in the creation of *illusion*. Illusion may be initiated by the creators of theater, but it is completed by the audience.

In the musical *Cats*, the stage setting resembles a back alley filled with junk. Old rubber tires and empty toothpaste tubes are made three times life-size so that they will look the way they would to a cat. The performers are dressed to represent various kinds of cats, with tails, whiskers, and fur. And they sing and dance. One sings a song describing his life as a man about town, and another a song explaining his life as a theater cat. We in the audience know that this is not real; people are not cats, and cats do not sing or dance about the stage. We accept such unreal behavior without question, though, in a musical comedy. Something similar happens in other forms of theater.

In the eerie world of *Macbeth*, by William Shakespeare, when three witches appear out of the mist, or Banquo's ghost interrupts Macbeth's banquet, we know it is fantasy; witches and ghosts like those in *Macbeth* do not appear in everyday life. Again, we take such fantasy at face value. In Shakespeare's own day, a convention readily accepted by Elizabethan audiences was having women's parts played by boy actors. All of Shakespeare's heroines—Juliet, Desdemona, Lady Macbeth—were played not by women, as they are today, but by young boys. Everyone in the audience at

In theater, fantasy becomes real.
We know that witches such as those from Shakespeare's *Macbeth* do not actually exist, but through the power of the imagination they become completely believable. In this scene, Patricia Hayes, Anne Dyson, and Sheila Kelley cast a spell as the three witches.

an Elizabethan theater knew that the young boys were not actually women but accepted without question the notion that a boy actor was presenting an impression or an imitation of a woman. In a symbolic sense, the boy *was* the female character portrayed.

The main character of the expressionistic play *The Adding Machine* by Elmer Rice (1892–1967) is called Mr. Zero. The play, written in 1923 and depicting the loss of identity and individuality in the machine age, continues to be prophetic even now. Mr. Zero, however, is not a name from a telephone book—it is not meant to be. Rather, it is symbolic of the character: he is nothing—a cipher, zero. His friends do not have ordinary names either. They are Mr. One, Mr. Two, Mr. Three, and so forth. An example in *The Adding Machine* of our acceptance of the fantastic in theater occurs when Mr. Zero dies and goes to heaven; he is shown in the afterlife carrying on conversations with two people who have worked with him in his office for many years.

Among the adjustments in the theater accepted by audiences are drastic shifts in time and space. Someone on stage dressed in a Revolutionary

THE IMAGINATION OF THE AUDIENCE

A dead man comes to life.

In the play *Foxfire*, by Hume Cronyn and Susan Cooper, the ghost of a dead man appears as if the man were alive. The play also has a series of flashbacks—scenes from the past interspersed with the present. Such apparitions and jumps in time are readily accepted in the theater, as in this scene between Hume Cronyn, as the man who has returned to life, and William Newman.

uniform says, "It is the winter of 1778, at Valley Forge," and we do not question it. What is more, we accept rapid movements back and forth in time. *Flashbacks*—abrupt movements from the present to the past and back again—are commonplace in modern drama.

A similar device often used in drama is the *anachronism*. This means placing a person or an event outside the proper time sequence: for example, having characters from the past speak and act as if they were living today. Medieval mystery and morality plays frequently contained anachronisms. The medieval play *Abraham and Isaac*, for instance, is set in Old Testament days, but it contains several references to the Christian trinity, obviously a religious concept introduced centuries later. The medieval audience accepted the shift in time as a matter of course, just as we do in theater today.

Eugène Ionesco (1912–   ), a Rumanian-born French dramatist, fills his plays with bizarre and fantastic concepts. In his play *Rhinoceros*, a man turns into a rhinoceros. Another play, *A Stroll in the Air*, features a man who rises from the stage floor each time he speaks; at times he walks several feet off the ground. In Ionesco's *Amédée*, a corpse, dead many years, continues to grow; it is in the next room, and during the play it pushes through the wall of the apartment on stage.

In the theater, our imagination allows us to conceive of people and events we have never seen or experienced and to transcend our physical circumstances to the point where we forget who we are, where we are, or what time it is. How is this possible? It works in the same way that our imagination works for us in everyday life. Perhaps we can understand this process better if we look closely at two tools of our imagination, usually considered poetic devices, but actually potent forces in real life: symbol and metaphor.

FUNCTIONS OF SYMBOL AND METAPHOR

Symbol

In general terms, a *symbol* is a sign, token, or emblem that signifies something else. A simple form of symbol is a sign. Some signs stand for a single uncomplicated idea or action. In everyday life we are surrounded by them: road signs, such as an S-shaped curve; audible signals, like sirens or fog horns; and a host of mathematical and typographical symbols: −, +, $, ¼, %, &. We sometimes forget that language itself—both written and spoken language—is symbolic. In written language, the letters of the alphabet are only lines and curves on a page. And words are an arrangement of letters which by common agreement represent something else. The same four letters mean different things, depending on the order in which they are placed: *pear, reap, rape*. They set three different imaginative wheels in motion and signal a response which varies greatly from word to word.

In the commercial world, the power of the symbol is acknowledged in the value placed on a trademark. As an example, in 1972 Standard Oil Company of New Jersey changed its name; but before doing so it had spent five years of computer research to find what it considered the best one and finally came up with "Exxon." The company then spent $125 million changing its stationery, service station signs, etc., to the new name. The term *status symbol* is a frank recognition of the importance of personal possessions in conferring status on the owner. The kinds of cars people drive, the way they dress, the furnishings of their homes: these indicate what kind of people they are—at least that is the theory.

Flags are symbols: lines, shapes, and colors which in given combinations become immediately recognizable. At times, symbols exhibit an incredible emotional power; and flags are a good example, embodying a nation's passions, fears, and ambitions. Like flags, some symbols signify ideas or emotions that are far more complex and profound than the symbols itself. The cross, for example, is a symbol of Christ and, beyond that, of Christianity as a whole. The peace or victory symbol, a V formed by two fingers, and the black power salute of the raised clenched fist are both powerful symbols.

The famous psychologist Carl Jung (1875–1961) makes a distinction between symbols and simple signs such as product trademarks. Jung reserves the term symbol for an emblem, word, or picture that has a special, even mystical, meaning. Examples are religious symbols or those suggested in dreams or by the unconscious. As the mind explores such a symbol, he says "it is led to ideas beyond the grasp of reason." Jung goes on to explain: "Because there are innumerable things beyond the range of human understanding, we constantly use symbolic terms to represent concepts that we cannot define or fully comprehend."[1]

Whatever form a symbol takes—language, flags, or religious emblems—it can embody the total meaning of a religion, nation, or idea.

Metaphor

A similar transformation takes place with *metaphor,* another form of imaginative substitution. With metaphor we announce that one thing is another, in order to describe it or point up its meaning more clearly. (In poetry, you will remember, a simile says that one thing is *like* another; metaphor simply states that one thing *is* another.) Calling the government "the ship of state" or a religious leader a "shepherd" involves the use of a metaphor.

Like symbols, metaphors are part of the fabric of life, as the following common expressions suggest.

"Everything's coming up roses."

"It's raining cats and dogs."

"He's really out to lunch."

"That's off the wall."

"What a rip-off."

"Give me the bottom line."

These are metaphors; we are saying one thing but describing another. Everyone knows, for instance, that the statement "everything's coming up roses" does not mean that a field of flowers is suddenly springing up. The person saying it might be standing on a concrete pavement in the dead of winter. Still, the meaning is unmistakably clear: everything is working well, things are looking up. We can see from this, and from the other examples above, that metaphor, like symbol, is part of everyday life.

"REALITY" OF THE IMAGINATION

Some people believe—or think they believe—only the tangible and objective. They want an object they can see, touch, and measure; for them, anything which defies this test has an air of fakery about it. In modern society, this has been a widely held attitude.

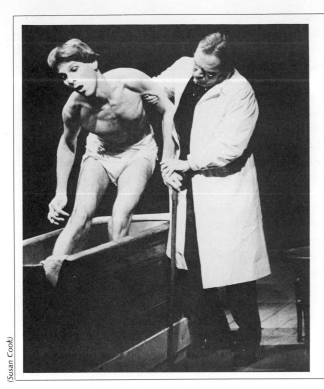

(Susan Cook)

The audience imagines an ugly man. The title character of *The Elephant Man* is based on a man named Merrick who lived in London in the nineteenth century. In real life Merrick was a grotesque figure, with large protuberances of flesh hanging from his body. In the New York production of Bernard Pomerance's play, the actor Philip Anglim, on the left, played Merrick without attempting to duplicate his appearance. Merrick's abnormalities were suggested by Anglim's posture and his voice. In this scene, the actor Kevin Conway, playing a doctor, assists Merrick.

Our use of symbol and metaphor, however, shows how large a part imagination plays in our lives. Soldiers go to battle inspired by a flag or slogan; and the millions of automobiles in the United States can be brought to a halt, not by concrete walls, but by a small colored light changing from green to red. Imagine attempting to control traffic, or virtually any type of human activity, without symbols. Beyond being a matter of convenience, symbols are necessary to our survival.

The same holds true for metaphor. Frequently we find that we cannot express fear, anxiety, hope, or joy—any of the deep human feelings—in descriptive language. That is why we sometimes scream. It is also why we have poetry and use metaphors.

Even scientists, the men and women we presume to be superrealists, turn to metaphor at crucial times. They discuss the "big bang" theory of creation, and talk of "black holes" in outer space. Neither description is a scientific formulation, but both communicate what scientists have in mind in a way that equations and logical language cannot.

Dreams provide another example of the power of the imagination. You dream that you are falling off a cliff, then suddenly you wake up and find you are not flying through the air but lying in bed. Significantly, however, the dream means more to you than the objective fact of your lying in bed.

Though people have long recognized the importance of dreams in human affairs, in the modern period interest in dreams has been intensified as a result of the monumental work of Sigmund Freud (1856–1939) on the subconscious. Despite variations and corrections of his theories, no one today disputes Freud's notion of the importance and "reality" of dreams, nightmares, or symbols in the human mind.

Even when a product of the imagination cannot be verified by outside observation or proved scientifically, it nevertheless exists in the mind and in that sense is entirely real. A young woman feeling alienated and alone is told she cannot feel lonely because she is not alone: she is sitting elbow-to-elbow in a football stadium or on a crowded bus. But in her mind she knows she is alone. And she is.

Theater functions in precisely the same way. Though not real in a literal sense, it can be painfully real in an emotional or intellectual sense. The critic and director Harold Clurman (1901–1980) named one of his books on the theater *Lies Like Truth*. Theater—like dreams or fantasies—can sometimes be more truthful about life than a mundane, objective description. This is a paradox of dreams, fantasies, and art, including theater: by probing deep into our psyches to reveal inner truths, they can be more real than outward reality.

THEATER IS A METAPHOR

Theater operates on the level of symbol, metaphor, and dreams. Mr. Zero, for example, is a symbol. So are virtually all dramatic characters, as well as much scene and costume design. In later chapters we will study in detail the ways in which theater makes use of these elements of the imagination. Beyond using symbols and metaphors, however, one could say that theater itself is a metaphor. When an actress stands on stage dressed as Joan of Arc, she does not say, "I am going to act *like* Joan of Arc," as in a simile; rather, by her presence she proclaims, "I *am* Joan of Arc." In the same way, the theater program does not say, "A room designed to look like the Dauphin's palace." It says simply, "The Dauphin's palace." Everything we see in a theater—an entire performance, including the action and the scenery—can be viewed as a giant metaphor.

When the metaphor succeeds, we see before us a complex creation which mirrors life. It takes us inside our subconscious and lets us either laugh at ourselves or learn to look at our deepest fears. At such moments we suspend disbelief; theater is undeniably real even though we are not in the action at all, but sitting still. Such is the power of the imagination.

REALISTIC AND NONREALISTIC THEATER

In theater, the audience is called on to accept many kinds of imaginary worlds. One way we divide these imaginary realms is into realistic and nonrealistic theater. At the outset, it is essential to know that in the theater the term *realistic* denotes a special application of what we call genuine or real. A realistic element is not necessarily more genuine or truthful than a nonrealistic element. Rather, in the theater, *realistic* and *nonrealistic* denote different ways of presenting reality.

Realistic Elements

A realistic element in the theater is one that resembles *observable* reality. It is a kind of photographic truth. We apply the term *realistic* to those elements of theater that conform to our observation of people, places, and events. Realistic theater follows the predictable logic of everyday life: the law of gravity, the time it takes a person to travel from one place to another, the way a room in a house looks, the way a person dresses. With a realistic approach these conform to our normal expectations. The act of imagination the audience is called on to exercise in realism is the acceptance of the notion that what is seen on stage is not make-believe but real life.

Theater has always had realistic elements. Every type of theater that is not pure fantasy has realistic aspects. For example, characters who are supposed to represent real people must be rooted in a human truth that audiences can recognize.

During the latter part of the nineteenth century, however, realistic elements became increasingly predominant. In Chapter 3, we will examine the relationship between theater and society. The rise of realistic elements in the theater of the late nineteenth century offers a good example of this.

In the wake of the discoveries and writings of Charles Darwin in science, Karl Marx in politics and economics, and Sigmund Freud in psychology, life was to be looked at squarely and uncompromisingly; people would see life as it was, without the embellishments of "art."

In the theater this trend led to an attempt to avoid any kind of formal, exaggerated drama and to depict people and events as "real." The emphasis was not to be on fairy tales or make-believe, on kings or knights in armor in faraway places, but on what was happening to ordinary people in familiar surroundings. Dialogue would not be poetry or elevated prose but normal conversation, and the actors would behave like people we know and recognize from life around us.

Although there had always been aspects of realistic theater in European drama, it became a dominant form in the late nineteenth century when three playwrights—Henrik Ibsen (1828–1906) of Norway, August Strindberg (1848–1912) of Sweden, and Anton Chekhov (1860–1904) of Russia—produced a series of strongly realistic plays. Together they set the pattern for the next century in this type of theater. Their dramas presented characters with life histories, with motives and anxieties, which audiences could immediately identify as truthful from their own experiences or observations. The housewives of Ibsen's plays, the quarreling couples of Strindberg's, and

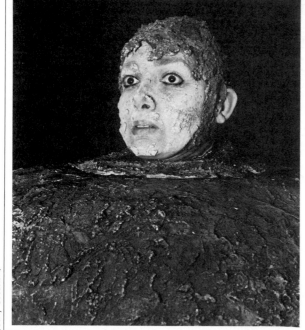

Realistic and nonrealistic theater contrasted.

These scenes illustrate the difference between two approaches to the make-believe of theater. The photograph at the top shows a junk shop which is the setting for the play *American Buffalo* by David Mamet. The table, the chairs, and the many other objects resemble those in real life, as do the clothes, the mannerisms, and the conversation of the characters in the play, performed here by Al Pacino (on the left) and J. J. Johnson (on the right). The scene below shows a character covered with mud who lives in an urn. This unreal situation is a poetic fantasy found in *Play*, by Samuel Beckett, as performed by the Manhattan Theater Club.

the dispossessed families of Chekhov's: here were characters who spoke, dressed, and behaved as one expected people to; and because the characters and situations were so easily recognizable, they seemed truer.

This kind of theater resembles life so closely that one assumes it must *be* life. When we are so readily able to verify what we see before us from our own observations and experience, we are likely to accept its authenticity more quickly. Because of this direct appeal, realistic theater has become firmly established in the past 100 years, and it seems likely to remain so.

Nonrealistic Elements

Nonrealistic elements of theater consist of everything that does not conform to our observations of surface reality—poetry instead of prose, ghosts rather than believable people, abstract forms for scenery, and so forth.

The argument for nonrealism is that the surface of life—a real conversation or a real room in a house—can never convey the whole truth of life, because so much of life occurs in our heads, in our imagination. If we are deeply depressed and we tell a friend that we feel "lousy" or "awful," we do not begin to communicate the depths of our feelings. It is because of the inadequacy of ordinary words that people turn to poetry, and because of the inadequacy of other forms of daily communication that they turn to music, dance, art, sculpture, and the entire range of symbols and metaphors discussed earlier.

In theater, symbolic expression takes the form of nonrealistic techniques. The chorus in a Greek play can express ideas, feelings, and emotions which could never be included in a strictly realistic presentation. The feeling of being haunted by the past can never be as vividly portrayed in a simple description as it can by a figure like the ghost of Hamlet's father, or Banquo's ghost appearing before Macbeth. The opportunity for the presentation of these inner truths—of the reality that is "realer than real"—is what nonrealistic theater offers.

A wide range of techniques and devices in the theater fall into the nonrealistic category. A good example is the *soliloquy,* in which a character speaks alone to the audience, expressing in words a hidden thought. In real life, we might confess some of our inner fears or hopes to a priest, a psychiatrist, or our best friend; but we do not announce such fears out loud for the world to hear as Hamlet does when he says, "To be, or not to be . . ." Another example is *pantomime,* in which performers pretend to be using articles that do not actually exist, such as pouring a cup of coffee or opening an umbrella. Many aspects of musical comedy are nonrealistic. People in the streets do not break into song or dance on the pavements as they do in musicals like *Guys and Dolls* or *West Side Story.* Nor do people burst into song in someone's living room or in a classroom. One could say that any activity or scenic device which transcends or symbolizes reality tends to be nonrealistic. (For a detailed contrast between realism and nonrealism, see Appendix 5.)

Combining the Realistic and the Nonrealistic

In discussing the realistic and nonrealistic elements of theater, it is a mistake to assume that these two approaches are mutually exclusive. They are simply a convenient way to separate those parts of theater that correspond to our observations and experiences of everyday life from those that do not.

Most performances and theater events contain a mixture of realistic and nonrealistic elements. In acting, for example, the performance of a Shakespearean play calls for a number of nonrealistic qualities or techniques. At the same time, any performer playing the part of a Shakespearean character must convince the audience that he or she represents a real human being. To take a more modern example, in *The Glass Menagerie,* by Tennessee Williams (1912–1983), and Thornton Wilder's *Our Town,* one performer serves as a narrator and also participates in the action. When the person playing this part is speaking directly to the audience, the action is nonrealistic; when he is taking part in a scene with other characters, he is realistic.

SEPARATING STAGE REALITY FROM FACT

Whether theater is realistic or nonrealistic, and no matter how strong the "reality" of theater is, it is different from the physical reality of everyday life. In recent years there have been attempts to make theater less remote from our daily lives. Partly as a result of this trend, theater and life have become deeply intertwined. There are "staged" political demonstrations, for instance, and we hear of "staged news." Such confusion and interaction have been heightened, of course, by the emergence of television and film documentaries, which cover real events but are also edited. How "real," we may ask, are the news films we see? In the last few years, plays have been presented which were largely transcripts of court trials or congressional hearings. This was part of a movement called the *theater of fact,* with reenactments of material gathered from actual events. When the news becomes "staged" and theater becomes "fact," it is difficult to separate the two.

While this points up rather vividly the close relationship between theater and life, nevertheless, when we see a performance, even of events which have actually occurred, we are always aware on some level that we are in the theater. No matter how authentic the reenactment, we know it is a replay and not the original. Most of us have seen plays with a stage setting so real we marvel at its authenticity: a kitchen, for instance, in which the appliances actually work, with running water in the faucets, ice in the refrigerator, and a stove on which an actor or actress can cook. What we

Theater of fact.
Shown here is a scene from *In the Matter of J. Robert Oppenheimer*, a play based on actual testimony at a hearing before the board of the Atomic Energy Commission investigating the loyalty of Dr. Oppenheimer, the atomic scientist. This type of theater recreates on stage scenes based on transcripts of court trials and other legal proceedings.

stand in awe of, though, is that the room *appears* so real when we know, in truth, it is not. We admire the fact that, not being a real kitchen, it looks as if it were.

We are reminded quite abruptly of the distinction between stage reality and physical reality when the two lines cross. If an actor unintentionally trips and falls on stage, we suddenly shift our attention from the character to the person playing the part. Has he hurt himself? Will he be able to continue? A similar reaction occurs when a performer forgets lines, or a sword falls accidentally in a duel, or a dancer slips in a musical number.

We remember the distinction, also, at the moment when someone else *fails* to remember it. Children frequently mistake actions on stage for the real thing, warning the heroine of the villain's plan or assuming that the blows on the head of a puppet actually hurt. There is a famous story of a production of

THE IMAGINATION OF THE AUDIENCE

King Lear comforts the blinded Gloucester.
Because theater is a product of the imagination and is not actually happening, audiences are able to accept such horrible enactments as the blinding of Gloucester in Shakespeare's *King Lear*. In this scene, Morris Carnovsky, on the right, is Lear and William Larsen is Gloucester.

Othello in which a spectator ran on stage to prevent the actor playing Othello from strangling Desdemona. Another instance of this audience involvement was a production of the Street Theater of Ossining, New York, of *Street Sounds* by the black playwright Ed Bullins (1935–   ). The play opens with two black policemen beating a fifteen-year-old black youth. At one performance a spectator ran on stage in the midst of the beating to stop the actors playing the policemen. In each of these cases, the distinction between fantasy and reality disappeared for the spectator, who mistook the imagined event for a real one.

There have been instances where people considered a symbol or a fantasy as the fact itself. J. A. Hadfield reports that this was frequently the case with the dreams of primitive people. A "primitive man . . . considered that if in his dream he saw himself in a neighboring hostile village, he had actually been in that village, and if he saw the villagers in his dream

THE AUDIENCE

preparing for battle, this would be quite enough for him to report the fact, and his tribe would immediately prepare to meet the onslaught."[2]

One manifestation of insanity occurs when a person cannot separate the real from the imagined. Most people, however, are always aware of the difference. The result is that our minds manage two seemingly contradictory feats simultaneously: we know on the one hand that an imagined event is not objectively real, but at the same time we go along with it completely as fantasy.

In a scene from *King Lear*, Cornwall, one of Lear's evil sons-in-law, stands over the elderly, helpless nobleman, Gloucester. He puts his thumbs in the old man's eyes and, with the words, "Out vile jelly! Where is thy lustre now?" pushes his thumbs into the sockets, and blinds him. Meanwhile we remain seated. We are struck dumb; we identify with the pain and agony of the old man, and we watch horrified at the level to which his enemies have sunk. And yet we do not intervene—we sit in our seats, and the reason is that we know this is not actually happening to the actor playing Gloucester. We could not stand to watch one person treat another so cruelly if it were.

We accept all kinds of theater, the most realistic as well as the most fantastic, because of a "willing suspension of disbelief." This is the term the poet and critic Samuel Taylor Coleridge (1772–1834) used to explain the phenomenon of our accepting so completely the products of our imaginations, particularly as they occur in art. The aesthetic distance mentioned earlier makes this possible. Having separated at the outset the reality of art from the reality of everyday life, the mind is prepared to go along with the former without reservation.

In this chapter we have looked at what goes on inside the minds of spectators at a play: how they use their imaginations to conjure up images that deeply affect their ideas and emotions. When we turn from the inside to the outside, there are other factors, surrounding the theater event, that also have a bearing on how we view the experience and how well we understand it. These include the circumstances under which a play was created and the expectations we have when we attend a performance; and they will be the subject to which we turn next, in Chapter 3.

SUMMARY

1 For the observer, theater is an experience of the imagination and the mind, which seems capable of accepting almost any illusion as to what is taking place, who the characters are, and when and where the action occurs.

2 Our minds are capable of leaps of the imagination not just in the theater, but in our everyday lives, where we employ symbol and metaphor to communicate with one another and to explain the world around us.

3 The world of the imagination—symbols, metaphors, dreams, fantasies, and various expressions of art—is "real" even though it is intangible and has no objective reality. Frequently it tells us more about our true feelings than any form of logical discourse.

4 Theater makes frequent use of symbols and metaphors—in writing, acting, design, etc.—and theater itself can be viewed as a metaphor.

5 In theater, audiences are called on to imagine two kinds of worlds: the realistic and the nonrealistic. The first depicts things on stage that conform to observable reality; the second is in the realm of dreams, fantasy, symbol, and metaphor. Frequently in theater, realism and nonrealism are mixed.

6 In order to take part in theater as an observer, it is important to keep the "reality" of fantasies and dreams separate from the real world. By making this separation, we open our imagination to the full range of possibilities in the theater.

3

THE BACKGROUND OF THE AUDIENCE

3

THE
BACKGROUND
OF THE
AUDIENCE

(William B. Carter)

Audiences identify with contemporary theater. The background and experience an audience member brings to a theater production will affect his or her response to the event. With Lorraine Hansberry's *A Raisin in the Sun*, anyone who is part of a family trying to better its situation—especially a black family seeking a better life—will closely identify with family in the play. Here we see Troy Streeter as a young boy, Mary Alice as his mother, and Beah Richards as his grandmother, the matriarch of the family, in the play's twenty-fifth-anniversary production by the Yale Repertory Theater.

43

Audiences bring more to a performance than their mere presence; they bring a background of personal knowledge and experience which helps to form the impressions they receive from a production. The individual experiences of the members of an audience at a performance will be significantly affected by several important factors.

The first factor is their knowledge about the social, political, and philosophical world in which the play was written or produced: the link between theater and society.

Second is their expectations about theater experiences. As we will see, misconceptions about what the theater experience is or should be can lead to confusion and disappointment.

Third is their specific information about the play and playwright.

The fourth factor is closely related to the third: it is the role of the theater critic, who may be considered a source of background information.

Fifth and finally, the personal memories and experiences of each member of the audience affect the theater experience.

THE LINK BETWEEN THEATER AND SOCIETY

All art, including theater, is related to the society in which it is produced. Charges are sometimes made against artists that they are "antisocial," "subversive," or "enemies of the state," with the strong suggestion that artists are outsiders or invaders of a culture. To be sure, art frequently challenges society and is sometimes on the leading edge of history, appearing to forecast the future. But more often than not such art simply recognizes what is already present in society but has not yet surfaced. A good example is the abstract art which emerged in Europe in the early part of the twentieth century. At first it was considered an aberration or freak: an unattractive series of jagged lines and patches of color with no relation to nature, truth, or anything human. In time, however, abstract art came to be recognized as a genuine movement whose disjointed and fragmentary lines reflect the quality of much of modern life.

Art grows in the soil of a specific society. It must in order to take root. With very few exceptions—and those soon forgotten—art is a mirror of its age, revealing the prevailing attitudes, underlying assumptions, and deep-seated beliefs of a particular group of people. Art may question society's views or reaffirm them, but it cannot escape them; the two are indissolubly linked like a person and his or her shadow. When we speak of art as being "universal," we mean that the art of one age has so defined the characteristics of human beings that it can speak eloquently to another age; but it should never be forgotten that every work of art first emerges at a given time and place and can never be adequately understood unless the conditions surrounding its birth are also understood.

The symmetry of the Parthenon.
The formalism and sense of order of Greece in the fifth century B.C. are reflected in the Parthenon, located atop the Acropolis in Athens. All art, including theater, reflects the attitudes and values of the society in which it is created.

Greek Theater and Culture

A study of theater in significant periods of history confirms the close link between art and society. In ancient Greece, for example, civilization reached a high point during the time of Pericles in the latter part of the fifth century B.C. This was the golden age of Greece; when politics, art, architecture, and theater thrived as they never had before, and rarely have since. As the Greeks of that period gained control over the world around them and took new pride in human achievements, they developed ideals of beauty, order, symmetry, and moderation which permeated their entire culture, including theater.

By the fifth century B.C., standard forms of drama had emerged in Greece for both tragedy such as *King Oedipus* and comedy. Playwrights introduced innovations—but essentially they adhered to prescribed conventions. One of these conventions required a limited number of scenes in each play, usually five scenes interspersed with choral sections. The drama took place in one locale—often in front of a palace—and covered a limited amount of time. Another convention reflected the society's sense of propriety.

King Oedipus (ca. 430 B.C.)

SOPHOCLES (ca. 496–406 B.C.)

CHIEF CHARACTERS:

Oedipus—King of Thebes
Jocasta—wife of Oedipus
Creon—brother-in-law of Oedipus
Teiresias—a blind seer
A shepherd
A priest
Chorus

SETTING: The entire play takes place in front of the palace at Thebes in Greece.

BACKGROUND: When Oedipus was born, an oracle told his parents, the king and queen of Thebes, that their son would kill his father and marry his mother. Fearing this prophecy, they gave Oedipus to a shepherd to be killed. But the shepherd pitied the child and sent him to Corinth, where he was adopted by the king and queen. Oedipus grew up, learned of the oracle's prediction, and fled Corinth. On the journey toward Thebes, at a place where three roads met, Oedipus argued with a man and killed him—not knowing that the man was his natural father, Laius. When Oedipus arrived in Thebes, the city was plagued by a Sphinx who killed anyone who could not answer her rid-

dle. Oedipus answered the riddle correctly and the Sphinx died. Oedipus then became king and married Jocasta, not realizing she was his mother. Years later, the city was struck by another plague; this is the point at which the play begins.

PROLOGUE: The priest describes the plague and the people beg Oedipus to help. Creon enters and reports that the oracle has said that the plague will end when Laius' murderer is discovered; whereupon Oedipus vows to find the murderer.

PARADOS: The chorus prays to the gods to end the plague.

SCENE 1: Oedipus swears to track down the murderer and puts a curse on him. The blind prophet Teiresias is brought in; he knows the truth, but does not want to tell Oedipus, who rages at him. Oedipus accuses Teiresias of plotting with Creon to gain power, but Teiresias vehemently denies this and leaves.

ODE 1: The chorus confirms their belief in Oedipus and refuses to accept the idea that he murdered Laius.

SCENE 2: Creon answers the charges brought against him by Oedipus; the two men argue until Jocasta makes peace between them. Jocasta discredits the oracle, saying that long ago it had proved false: it had said that Laius would be killed by his son, but he was not—he was killed by a stranger where three roads meet. Oedipus becomes fearful that perhaps he did kill Laius after all, and he sends for the only witness to the murder.

ODE 2: The chorus speaks of the evils of pride, recklessness, and vanity. Their faith in the oracle of the gods is shaken.

SCENE 3: A messenger tells Jocasta that the king of Corinth is dead and the people there want Oedipus to be their new king. Oedipus is informed, but he is still concerned because his "mother" yet lives. The messenger tries to allay his fears by telling him that Merope, in Corinth, is not his mother—Oedipus was brought from Thebes by a shepherd when he was very young. Jocasta sees the truth, and tries unsuccessfully to dissuade Oedipus from continuing his search.

ODE 3: The chorus prays to the gods to help Oedipus find out about his true birth.

SCENE 4: The old shepherd enters with the messenger and Oedipus forces the hesitant man to speak. He finally admits that Jocasta told him to kill the baby because he would eventually kill his father, but he pitied the child, and took him far away, to Corinth; Oedipus was that boy. In despair, Oedipus rushes into the palace.

ODE 4: The chorus repeats the tale of the fall of the great man, Oedipus, and expresses their sorrow about the tragedy.

EXODOS: The second messenger enters from the palace to say that the queen has killed herself. He describes how Oedipus burst into Jocasta's room, to find her hanging, dead. He pulled her down, took a brooch from her dress, and blinded himself. The doors to the palace open to reveal the blinded Oedipus. Oedipus blames the god Apollo for leading him to his fate. When Creon enters, Oedipus begs him to exile him, to give Jocasta a proper funeral, and to take care of his daughters, who say a last farewell to their father. The chorus warns that man should take nothing for granted.

Although bloody deeds occurred in the myths on which most Greek plays were based, these deeds never took place in sight of the audience; murders, suicides, and other acts of violence occurred offstage. To reinforce the Greek notion of moderation, another feature of most Greek tragedies was that any character in a play who acted in an excess of passion was generally punished or pursued by avenging furies.

Elizabethan Theater and Culture

Another example of the strong link between theater and society—one which stands in contrast to the classic Greek period—is the Elizabethan age in England. Named after Queen Elizabeth I, who reigned from 1558 to 1603, this period saw England become a dominant force in the world. Under Elizabeth's rule England was forged into a unified country; trade and commerce flourished, and with the defeat of the Spanish Armada in 1588, an age of exploration for England was in full bloom. England was expanding on all fronts and feeling self-confident in the process; these characteristics were reflected in the drama of the period. The plays of Shakespeare, Christopher Marlowe (1564–1593), and their contemporaries are quite different from the restrained, formal drama of the Greeks. A single play might move from place to place and cover a period of many years. The plays have an expansiveness of characters and action, and there is no hesitancy whatsoever about showing murder and bloodshed on stage. At the end of an Elizabethan play, corpses frequently cover the stage in full view of the audience.

A Note on Women and Greek and Elizabethan Theater

In considering the link between theater and society, it is worth noting that in neither Greek nor Elizabethan theater were there women playwrights or women performers. This is a result of the place women were accorded in these two cultures.

Classical Greek theater was intrinsically linked to the well-being of the state. Its themes reflect the necessity for order and control and were intended to serve a didactic purpose, assuring the continuation of democratic government. In Athenian society, where women were excluded from all political roles and were not even considered citizens, it followed logically that they could not participate in the theater's creative processes. In fact, we do not even know if women were permitted to attend performances. It is interesting to note that the most persuasive evidence given by classical scholars for women's presence at theatrical events is that men were allowed to bring their male slaves: If slaves could attend, why not free women? We do know that women often acted in wandering mime troupes. These popular entertainers performed songs, dance numbers, acrobatics, juggling, and brief comic sketches. Because of the bawdy nature of these acts, women mimes were often thought to be of low moral character. This unfortunate label was to remain with women performers for hundreds of years and is at least partly responsible for an exclusionary attitude which eliminated the contribution of women from legitimate theater activity.

In Elizabethan England, despite the presence of a powerful female monarch, theater practices continued to reflect long-standing prejudices against women. Although during the reign of Elizabeth actors were raised from vagabond status, actresses were still considered little better than prostitutes—a result of medieval and Puritan thinking. Women were thus barred from performing on the legitimate stage, and female roles were played by young boys who did much to affect feminine beauty and grace. It was not until 1660 that women were allowed to appear on the stage of licensed theaters in England.

Modern Theater and Culture

Moving to a more contemporary period, we find once again a tie between theater and society. Modern society, especially in the United States, is heterogenuous. We have people of many races, religions, and national

Theater and modern life.
Theater reflects society. A recent play that focuses on the twentieth-century conflict between psychiatry and religion is *Agnes of God*, by John Pielmeier. In this scene, Elizabeth Ashley (on the right), playing a psychiatrist, is attempting to work with a young nun, played by Maryann Plunkett.

backgrounds living side by side. Moreover, the twentieth century has been marked by increasingly swift global communications. By means of radio and television, events that occur on one side of the globe are instantaneously flashed to other parts of the world. By this means, too, people are constantly made aware of cultures other than their own.

When cultures and societies are brought together, we are reminded of the many things people have in common, but also of the differences among us. At the same time, our view of other aspects of life has become increasingly fragmented in recent years. A number of institutions that held fairly constant through many centuries—organized religion, the family, marriage—have been seriously challenged in the past 100 years. Discoveries by Charles Darwin about evolution raised fundamental questions about views of creation held at that time: Were human beings special creatures created by God, or were they subject to the same process of evolution that other forms of life had gone through? People of the nineteenth century feared that if human beings had evolved, they might not occupy the unique place in the universe that had always been assumed for them.

Further, at the end of the nineteenth century, Sigmund Freud (referred to in Chapter 2) cast doubt on the ability of human beings to exercise total rational control over their activities. Later, Albert Einstein's discoveries about relativity questioned long-held views of the universe. The net effect of these discoveries was to make human beings much less certain of their place in the cosmos and of their mastery of events. Life now appears to be much less unified and ordered than it once seemed.

These two developments—the bringing together of cultures by population shifts and communication, and the challenges to long-held beliefs—are reflected in today's theater. It is a theater of *eclecticism* (a blending of different strains) and of fragmentation. The typical theater company today performs a wide range of plays side by side. In a given season, the same company may present a tragedy by Shakespeare, a farce by the Frenchman Molière (1622–1673), a modern drama by the Spanish writer Federico García Lorca (1898–1936), and a new play by an American playwright. Moreover, the dramatists of today write on many subjects and in a wide range of styles.

The two societies discussed earlier—Greek and Elizabethan—were homogeneous; each contained people of a similar racial and religious background. Theatergoing in each society was a uniform experience. In the modern world, by contrast, the variety and types of drama reflects the complex and heterogeneous nature of society.

The three periods we have looked at are only examples, illustrating the close relationship between a given society and the art and theater it produces. One could find comparable links in virtually every culture. Whatever the period in which it was first produced, drama is woven into the fabric of the time.

(German Information Center)

Theater of protest.
Typical of the diversity of theater in recent years are theatrical events taking a strong political stand or making a political statement. Often these "theater" events are not on a regular stage but in the streets—as is this protest by a group of Germans against the deployment of American nuclear weapons in West Germany.

The Audience and the Cultural Background

When we as spectators see a play that has been written in our own day, we automatically bring with us a deep awareness of the world from which the play comes because we come from the same world. Through the books we read, through newspapers and television, through discussions with friends, we have a background of common information and beliefs. Our shared knowledge and experience is much larger than most of us realize, and this forms a crucial ingredient in our theater experience.

In the case of plays from the past, however, we have to compensate for a lack of this kind of knowledge. To understand fully a play written many years ago, we have to become acquainted with the history, the culture, the psychology, and the philosophy of the period in which it was produced. We can appreciate a classic without such knowledge, but this kind of background information makes our experience much richer.

EXPECTATIONS: THE VARIETY OF EXPERIENCES IN MODERN THEATER

One misconception frequently held by spectators—which can lead to confusion and disappointment in the contemporary theater—is the expectation that all theater experiences are alike. Just as audiences must be prepared to see plays from many different periods and cultures, so must they be prepared to see plays in different settings. (The variety of places where drama can be seen is further evidence that theater reflects life in our diverse society.) Fifty years ago the theater was synonymous with one kind of experience: Broadway. To see how that has changed, we will look briefly at developments of recent decades.

The Broadway Theater

Broadway is the name given to the professional theater in New York City: it refers specifically to plays performed in the large theaters in the district near Times Square. From 1920 until the early 1950s, most new plays written in the United States originated there, and productions in other areas were usually copies of Broadway productions. Broadway itself was confined and standardized; it consisted of an area in Manhattan roughly six blocks long and a block and a half wide. The thirty or more theaters located in these few

The formality of the traditional Broadway theater.
All Broadway theaters have the same style and interior layout, except for one or two that have been altered in recent years. The Majestic Theater, shown here, typifies the elaborate, formal architecture of the picture-frame stage. This type of theater prevailed throughout the United States for most of the nineteenth and early twentieth centuries.

blocks were the same size, seating between 700 and 1400 people, and had the same style of architecture as well as the same type of stage: a picture-frame stage.

Productions sent on tour from Broadway to the rest of the country were exact replicas of the original. Scenery was duplicated down to the last detail, and New York actors and actresses often played roles they had played on Broadway. Nonprofessional theaters copied Broadway as well; acting versions of successful plays were published for colleges, schools, and community theaters, providing precise instructions for the movements of the actors and the placement of scenery on stage.

The Broadway concept gave the theater a yardstick of excellence and produced outstanding work; but in the period just after World War II the realization grew that there were large numbers of people in the United States from whom Broadway was remote—not just geographically, but spiritually.

Because our society is diverse and complex, and because theater reflects society, it is difficult to see how any one form of theater today—however profound—can speak equally to all of us. As if in response to the complexity of the modern world, in the years immediately after World War II people began searching for new forms in theater and for alternative locations in which to present drama. Let us now look at some of these developments.

Resident Professional Theaters

A significant development which began in the 1950s and has since spread across the country is the resident professional theater movement. In a number of cities around the United States, theater companies have been formed, and theater facilities have been built, for the continuing presentation of high-quality professional productions to local residents. The performers, directors, and designers are generally high-caliber artists who make theater their full-time profession.

A few of these theaters are repertory in the European tradition. *Repertory* means that several plays are performed on alternate nights rather than a single play's being performed night after night for the length of its run. For example, in repertory a Molière play will appear on Monday night, a Beckett play on Tuesday night, a Shakespearean play on Wednesday, and so forth. Two successful repertory theaters in the United States are the American Conservatory Theater in San Francisco and the American Repertory Theater in Boston.

Many other cities have developed theaters that present a series of plays over a given time, with each play being performed for from four to twelve weeks. Among the best known of these theaters are the Arena Stage in Washington, D.C., the Long Wharf in New Haven, the Mark Taper Forum in Los Angeles, the Alley Theater in Houston, the Goodman Theater in Chicago, the Milwaukee Repertory Theater, and the Seattle Repertory

Resident professional theater.
One of the most important developments in theater in the past few decades has been the establishment of resident professional theaters in cities throughout the United States. Here we see a scene from *The Splintered Wood*, a play about World War I, performed by the Milwaukee Repertory Theater.

Theater. A season of plays in these theaters will usually consist of a mixture of new plays and classics, and audiences are encouraged to buy a season subscription.

In addition to resident companies, there are now a number of permanent summer theater festivals throughout the United States and Canada. Among the best known are the Shakespeare festivals at Stratford, Ontario; San Diego, California; and Ashland, Oregon.

College and University Theaters

In the last few decades, college and university theater departments have become increasingly important too, not only in teaching the theater arts but in presenting plays. In some localities, college productions offer virtually the only form of theater to local residents. In other areas they are a significant supplement to professional theater programs.

The theater facilities in many colleges are excellent. Most large colleges and universities have two or three theater spaces—a full-size theater, a

College and university theater.
A vital segment of theater in the United States consists of the many productions mounted by theater departments in colleges and universities. This scene is from a production of Oliver Goldsmith's *She Stoops to Conquer* by Illinois State University.

medium-size theater, and a smaller space for experimental dramas—as well as extensive scene shops, costume rooms, dressing rooms, and rehearsal halls. Productions are usually scheduled throughout the school year.

The quality and the elaborateness of these productions vary. In some localities productions are extremely elaborate, with full-scale scenery, costumes, lighting, and sound. Colleges vary, too, in their level of professionalism in acting. Many colleges use only performers from the undergraduate theater program. If the college has a masters' degree program, it will utilize both graduate and undergraduate performers. Colleges or universities may bring in outside professionals to perform along with student actors. Most college and university theaters offer a variety of plays, including classics and experimental plays rarely done by professional theaters.

Alternative Theaters

In New York City the *off-Broadway theater* began in the 1950s as an alternative to Broadway, which was becoming increasingly costly. Off-Broadway theaters were smaller than Broadway theaters—most of them under 200 seats—and were located outside the Times Square area in places like Greenwich Village. Because off-Broadway was less expensive than

Alternative theater.
Aside from Broadway and other professional theaters, many smaller theaters offer a wide variety of new plays and revivals. One such theater is The Source in Washington, D.C., located in a part of the city where theater had not been produced before. The production shown here is *The Queen and the Rebels* by Ugo Betti.

Broadway, it offered more opportunity for producing serious classics and experimental works.

Off-Broadway itself, however, became expensive and institutionalized in the 1960s and 1970s. As a result, small independent groups wishing to produce plays had to develop another forum. The result was off-off-Broadway.

Under an arrangement with the actors' union, Actors Equity Association, professionals were allowed to perform for little or no salary for short runs in workshop productions, and for minimal salaries in longer-running productions. *Off-off-Broadway* shows are produced wherever inexpensive space is available—churches, lofts, warehouses, large basements—and are characterized by low-priced productions and a wide variety of offerings. It is in these theaters, too, that experimental work takes place (see Chapter 9). These include productions in which performers create their own work, and in which theater is combined with painting, dance, or television.

An important development in the American theater is that an equivalent of the off-off-Broadway movement has sprung up in other major cities across

Experimental theater.
Many experimental or avant-garde theaters offer theater of a special nature: feminist, political, black, Hispanic, and so forth. This scene, from a production by the SoHo rep in New York, is from *Subject to Fits* by Robert Montgomery.

the United States—Washington, Atlanta, Chicago, Minneapolis, Los Angeles, San Francisco, Seattle—where small theater groups perform as alternatives to large organizations.

One virtue of these small theater groups is that they can present productions of interest to special groups. The kinds of plays they offer include classics, new plays, and experimental work. Other theaters aim their productions at particular groups; for example, feminist theater, labor theater, black theater.

In addition, all across the country there are cabaret and dinner theaters in which the atmosphere of a nightclub or restaurant is combined with that of a theater; in an informal setting guests eat and drink before watching a performance.

Still another growing theater movement is theater for children. Theaters across the country have developed programs of theater training and full-scale productions for young people. Some children's theater operations, like those in Minneapolis and Nashville, occupy impressive building complexes and produce an extensive season of plays.

Today there is theater for almost everyone, in many kinds of places, under widely varying conditions, and for very different purposes. With theater taking so many forms, it is important in approaching the subject not to have a preconceived or rigidly fixed notion of what it is.

BACKGROUND INFORMATION ON A PLAY OR PLAYWRIGHT

In some cases it is not only the period or other conditions surrounding the play about which we need additional knowledge but also the play itself. In plays from the past as well as contemporary plays, there are sometimes difficult passages or obscure references which it is helpful to know before we see a performance of the play.

As an example, we can take a segment from Shakespeare's *King Lear:* the scene in the third act when Lear appears on the heath in the midst of a terrible storm. Earlier in the play Lear had divided his kingdom between two of his daughters, Goneril and Regan, who he thought loved him, but who he discovered had deceived him. Gradually they stripped him of everything: his possessions, his soldiers, even his dignity. Finally they send him out from their homes to face the wind and rain in open country. As the storm begins, Lear speaks the following lines:

> Blow, winds, and crack your cheeks! Rage! Blow!
> You cataracts and hurricanoes, spout
> Till you have drenched our steeples, drowned the cocks!
> You sulphurous and thought-executing fires,
> Vaunt-curriers of oak-cleaving thunderbolts,
> Singe my white head! And thou all-shaking thunder,
> Strike flat the thick rotundity o' the world . . .

Even if we do not understand every reference, we realize that Lear is invoking the heavens to bring on a terrifying storm. The sounds of the words alone—the music of the language in its combinations of vowels, rhythm, and inflections—convey the sense of a raging storm. But how much more the passage will mean if in addition we understand the meanings of key words and phrases. Let us examine the passage more closely: In the first line, the expression "crack your cheeks" refers to pictures in the corners of old maps showing a face puffed out at the cheeks, blowing the wind.[1] Shakespeare is saying that the face of the wind should blow so hard that its cheeks will crack. In the second line, "cataracts and hurricanoes" refer to water from both the heavens and the seas. In line three, the word "cocks" refers to weathercocks on the tops of steeples; Lear wants there to be so much rain that even the weather cocks on the steepletops will be covered with water. In line four, "thought-executing" means as quick as thought; in other words, fires should ignite instantaneously. "Vaunt-curriers" of line five suggests that lightning is followed by thunderbolt; first the fire comes and then a bolt which can split an oak tree. Line seven, "strike flat the thick rotundity o' the world," conveys the image of a storm so powerful that the round earth will be flattened. If we are aware of these meanings, we can join them with the sounds of the words and the rage which the actor expresses in his voice and gestures to get the full impact of the scene.

In the contemporary theater, playwrights frequently employ special techniques which will confuse us if we do not understand them. The German playwright Bertolt Brecht (1898–1956), who lived and wrote in the United States during the 1940s, wished to provoke his audience into thinking about what it was seeing. To do this, he interrupted the story with a song or a speech by a narrator. The theory is that when a story is stopped in this manner, the audience has an opportunity to consider more carefully what it has seen and to relate the drama onstage to other aspects of life. If one is not aware that this is Brecht's purpose in interrupting the action, one might conclude that he was simply a careless or inferior playwright. In this, as in similar cases, knowledge of the play or playwright is indispensable to a complete theater experience.

THE THEATER CRITIC

One source of background information on a play or a production is the *critic*. The critic, loosely defined, is someone who observes theater and then analyzes and comments on it. In a sense the critic stands between the theater event and the audience, serving as a knowledgeable and highly sensitive audience member. Critics fall into several categories.

The Reviewer and the Critic

A distinction is frequently made between *reviewers* and *critics*. The reviewer, who usually works for a television station, a newspaper, or a magazine, reports on what has occurred at the theater. He or she will tell briefly what the theater event is about, perhaps describing the plot and explaining whether it is a musical, a comedy, or a serious play. The reviewer might also offer an opinion as to whether the event is worth seeing or not. (Everyone has seen newspaper ads with quotations from reviewers saying such things as "A play not to be missed," "A laugh riot; the whole family will enjoy it," etc.) The reviewer is usually restricted by either time or space. The television reviewer, for instance, will have only a minute or two on the air to describe a play and offer a reaction. The newspaper reviewer similarly is restricted by the space available in the newspaper.

In contrast to the reviewer stands the critic, who attempts to go into greater detail in describing and analyzing a theater event. Critics generally work for magazines or scholarly journals. At times they write entire books about a playwright, a group of plays, or a particular movement in the theater. The critic generally has more time to write his or her piece—perhaps several days or weeks rather than the few hours allotted to the reviewer. The critic also attempts to put the theater event into a larger context, relating the play to a category such as nonrealism or realism, for instance. The critic will try to explain how the theater event fits into this framework or into the body of the work of the playwright. The critic might also put the theater event into a social, political, or cultural context. For example, plays by minority playwrights of the 1960s and 1970s could be looked at in terms of their relationship to the civil rights movement.

The critic attempts to analyze the theater event very closely, looking carefully at the purpose and point of view of the author, the dramatic structure, and the acting and directing, to determine how these elements fit together. Ideally, the critic has developed a personal point of view about various aspects of theater. He or she has arrived at an idea of how plays are put together, what constitutes good acting, what is expected of a realistic play as opposed to an experimental play, and so forth.

Ideally, too, the critic has the proper background on which to base opinions. This background should consist of a thorough knowledge of theater history. It should also consist of an awareness of all aspects of theater—production elements as well as dramaturgy. The critic should be familiar with plays written in various styles and modes and should know the body of the work of individual writers. Also, the critic should be able to relate what is happening in theater to what is happening in the other arts, and beyond that, to events in society generally.

Admittedly, this is asking a great deal, and very few critics come to their jobs as well prepared as they should be; there is a wide variation in the backgrounds and abilities of critics, just as there is among actors, directors, and playwrights.

Critical Criteria

The great German playwright and commentator Johann Wolfgang von Goethe (1749–1832) said that the critic should address a theater event in terms of three questions: (1) What is the playwright or the production attempting to do? (2) How well has it been done? (3) Is it worth doing? In asking these fundamental questions, critics often take different approaches.

Two of the earliest theater critics established different, but basic, approaches to theater criticism. The Greek philosopher Aristotle (384–322 B.C.) undertook to analyze the tragedies of playwrights like Aeschylus (525–456 B.C.), Sophocles (ca. 496–406 B.C.), and Euripides (ca. 484–406 B.C.). Aristotle was also a scientist, and his method was one chiefly of describing tragedy: he attempted to break tragedy down into its component parts, and to describe the way it worked and the effect it had on spectators.

The Roman writer Horace (65–8 B.C.), on the other hand, attempted not just to describe but to *prescribe* what theater should be. In other words, Horace attempted to establish rules for theater. Horace said, for example, that tragedy and comedy should never be mixed in the same play and that poetry should instruct as well as please the members of the audience.

Since the time of Aristotle and Horace, critics have tended to fall into one category or the other: those who analyze and describe theater, and those who set down rules and say exactly what form plays and theater productions should follow. The second approach can sometimes lead to a moralistic or overly rigid viewpoint about theater which restricts both the creativity of theater artists and the enjoyment of audiences.

The Audience's Independent Judgment

One word of caution regarding critics. Quite often they state authoritatively that a certain play is extremely well written or badly written, beautifully performed or atrociously performed, and so on. Because critics often speak so confidently and because their opinions appear on television or in print,

"Tell me, sir. Is it good or bad?"

THE BACKGROUND OF THE AUDIENCE

their words have the ring of authority. But theatergoers should not be intimidated by this. In New York City, where a number of reviewers in various media comment on each Broadway production, there is a wide range of opinion. It is not unusual for half a dozen critics to find a certain play admirable, another half-dozen to find the same play highly objectionable, and still other reviewers or critics to find a mixture of good and bad in it. What this means is that there is no absolute authority among the critics, and audience members should make up their own minds. If a critic dislikes a certain play, for example, because he or she feels that it is too sentimental, and you happen to like that kind of sentiment, you should not be dissuaded from your own preferences.

In reading the works of critics it is important to distinguish between *fact* and *opinion*. Opinion, as suggested above, should be carefully weighed. On the other hand, the facts or insights presented by a critic can be extremely helpful. Many times critics can make us aware of facts that we might not otherwise have known—for example, by explaining a point that was confusing to the audience or noting how a particular scene relates to an earlier scene in the play. The critic might also offer background information about the playwright, the subject matter of the play, or the style of the production. Such information should broaden the audience's understanding and appreciation of theater. The more we know about why a playwright arranges scenes in a given manner or what a playwright is attempting to do, the better we will be able to judge the value of a theater event.

THE BACKGROUND OF INDIVIDUAL SPECTATORS

One background element which every member of the audience brings to a theater experience without additional study is his or her own individual memories and experiences. Each one of us has a personal catalog of emotional scars, childhood memories, and private fantasies; and anything we see on stage which reminds us of them will have a strong impact on us.

In the story of Antigone, treated in a play by Sophocles in Greece in the fifth century B.C., and more recently by the French playwright Jean Anouilh (1910–) during World War II, the young woman Antigone adamantly opposes her uncle Creon, the ruler of the state, because he is a political pragmatist making compromises and she is an idealist who believes in higher principles. Anyone, especially a young woman, who has ever tried to oppose corruption or complacency in an entrenched political regime will find much to recognize in Antigone. The individual will feel a special affinity for the character, and the performance will have a more personal meaning than for someone who has no direct relationship to the situation. Any activity on stage which reminds us of something in our own lives will trigger deep personal responses which become part of the equation of our theater experience.

Personal identification with theatrical characters.
When a person has personal experience that provides a point of reference with what he or she sees on stage, the play will have a great deal more meaning. A young woman who has had to stand up to authority—of any kind—will better understand the character of Antigone (Lisa Banes), seen here on the right, who defies her uncle Creon (F. Murray Abraham) in the play by Sophocles.

Chapters 1, 2, and 3 have dealt with the part the audience plays in the theater experience. We have looked at their vital role in the actor-audience equation, in the way the audience uses its imagination to participate in theater, and at the background knowledge and experience that affect the experience. In Part Two, we turn from the audience to the event itself, to what happens on stage. The primary encounter, as we have seen, is between the audience and the performers; but the performers offer a special type of presentation. They are actors and actresses putting on a play; and in Chapters 4, 5, and 6, we turn to the nature of the plays they perform.

SUMMARY

1   Theater—like other arts—is closely linked to the society in which it is produced; it mirrors and reflects the attitudes, philosophy, and basic assumptions of its time.

2 Spectators attending a play written in their own day bring to it an awareness of the society's values and beliefs, and this background information forms an important part of the overall experience.

3 A play from the past can be understood better if the spectator is aware of the culture from which it came.

4 In the past, theater experiences were relatively uniform within a given society, but in contemporary society their time, place, content, and purpose are far more varied. Expectations about the nature of the theater experience affect our reaction to it.

5 For any play which presents difficulties in language, style, or meaning, familiarity with the work itself can add immeasurably to a spectator's understanding and appreciation of the play in performance.

6 The critic analyzes and reports on the theater and can provide audiences with information and understanding about a theater event.

7 Those commenting on theater can be divided into *reviewers,* who report briefly on a theater event on TV or in newspapers and magazines; and *critics,* who write longer articles analyzing in depth a script, a theater event, or the work of a playwright.

8 Audience members must realize that critics, too, have their prejudices and weaknesses and that ultimately each individual spectator must arrive at his or her own judgment regarding a theater event.

9 All individuals attending a theater event bring to it a personal background of experience which becomes a vital ingredient in their response to the event.

PART 2

PURPOSE AND PERSPECTIVE: THEATRICAL GENRES

A modern play with a tragic point of view.

Every theater event serves a purpose, and every play has a point of view—serious, comic, or some combination of the two. In *Death of a Salesman,* the playwright Arthur Miller takes a tragic view of the salesman Willy Loman and his family. On the following pages the artist Al Hirschfeld shows a production of the play with Dustin Hoffman as Willy at the center surrounded by his wife, his two sons, and others who played a part in his life.

4

PURPOSE
AND
POINT OF VIEW

Different views of Electra, a Greek heroine. Playwrights establish a point of view about their subject and their characters. The same event can be seen as tragic by one writer and comic by another. An action can be considered admirable or despicable, depending on the point of view. An interesting example of differing points of view is the way in which the three great Greek tragic dramatists—Aeschylus, Sophocles, and Euripides —treated the story of Electra. Electra and her brother Orestes conspire to kill their mother Clytemnestra, who had killed their father Agamemnon. Aeschylus, the first dramatist to tell the story, saw the murder of the mother as unfortunate, a terrible deed in a cycle of retribution that had to be eliminated. Sophocles saw the murder as a noble deed, carrying out the will of the gods. Euripides reduced Electra to a lowly status; instead of living in a palace as a princess, she was married to a peasant and living in a hut. The murder of Clytemnestra in this version was a cowardly act. The heroine is seen here as played by Harriet Harris in a play called *The Greeks* that draws from several Greek sources. It was produced by A Contemporary Theater (ACT) of Seattle.

Theater is art, and as such it mirrors or reflects life. It does not try to encompass the whole of life at one time, but rather selects a part of the total picture on which it focuses. In this way it can achieve a clarity, an order, and a beauty that is rarely found in life.

The selection process of art occurs in several ways. To begin with, all art forms use certain elements while eliminating others. Music, for instance, focuses on the sounds produced by musical instruments and the human voice. Painting uses only visual elements: the colors, shapes, and designs that can be put on a canvas. Dance focuses on the movements of the human body made to the accompaniment of music. Part of the force and effectiveness of art is this selectivity: when we look at a painting we concentrate the full force of our attention on the visual—on the single surface of the canvas—and are not distracted by other considerations.

The means by which an art form presents its material is often referred to as the *medium*. Thus, sound is the medium of music. For theater, the medium is a story enacted by performers: theater always involves actresses and actors on a stage playing characters. We saw previously that the basic encounter in theater is between the performers and the audience; but this is a special type of encounter: the performers are playing other people. Moreover, the people are part of a human story that has been written by a dramatist. This combination sets theater apart from other art forms. The focus of the story in a drama is always the same: human concerns. This chapter begins with that focus and goes on to examine purpose and point of view.

HUMAN BEINGS: THE SUBJECT OF THEATER

Throughout history theater has concentrated or focused, on one subject: human beings. This is true even though different human concerns are emphasized in different plays: the pretenses of men and women in society in *The Way of the World* by William Congreve (1670–1729); the conflict between high principle and expediency in *Antigone* by Sophocles; the terrible way in which members of one family can drive one another into desperation and despair in *Long Day's Journey into Night* by Eugene O'Neill; the alternating hope and futility of men waiting for salvation in *Waiting for Godot* by Samuel Beckett (1906–   ); the celebration of life in a small town in Thornton Wilder's *Our Town*.

Drama focuses on human concerns even when performers play animals, inanimate objects, or abstract ideas. The medieval morality play *Everyman* is a good example. Although some of the roles are abstract ideas such as Fellowship, Knowledge, Good Deeds, Beauty, and Strength, the central character is Everyman, a human character if there ever was one. And the

Art is selective.

Each art form focuses on certain elements to the exclusion of others. Painting, for example, concentrates on color, line, and design. Among performing arts, ballet deals exclusively with movement set to music; no words or dialogue are used. An example of ballet is this leap by Baryshnikov in *The Nutcracker*.

problem of the play—death coming to human beings before they want it to come—is a universal human theme.

The way in which gods are depicted provides a further illustration of the person-centered quality of theater. In Greek drama, the gods sometimes appeared at the end of the play to intervene and tie up loose ends of the plot. The manner of their entrance is noteworthy: they were lowered to the orchestra level from the top of the stage house by a large lever or crane, called a *machine*. The term *deus ex machina,* which means literally "god from the machine," has come to stand for any device, divine or otherwise, brought in to solve problems arbitrarily. The gods were introduced, however, at the end, after the main characters—all human beings—had been through the anguish and struggle of the play. The emphasis was on the human problem, and the appearance of a god was almost an afterthought.

In the modern world, human beings have lost the central place they once occupied in the universe. In the Ptolemaic view of the universe, which prevailed until the sixteenth century—when Copernicus discovered that the earth revolved around the sun—it was assumed that the earth, ruled by human beings, was the center of everything. Today, we have long since

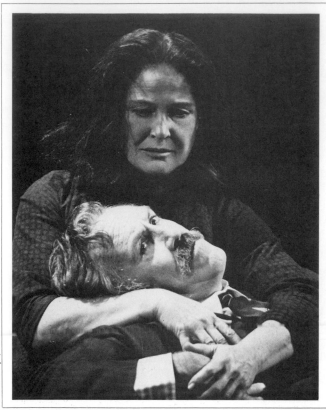

The focus of theater: Human concerns. Unlike art forms that concentrate on colors and shapes (painting), movement (dance), or sound (music), theater focuses on the encounter between human beings. Performers impersonate characters who engage in a series of personal exchanges. An example can be found in Eugene O'Neill's *A Moon for the Misbegotten*. In the scene shown here, Colleen Dewhurst plays a mother figure who comforts the guilt-ridden hero, played by Jason Robards.

given up that notion, particularly in light of recent explorations in outer space. The human being has become less and less significant, and less and less at the center of things. But not in theater. Theater is one area where the preoccupations of men and women, for better or worse, are still the core, the center of gravity around which other elements orbit—the center, in other words, of the dramatic universe.

In films, by contrast, the frame of reference may be quite different: an aerial shot from a helicopter will present a panorama of a whole countryside; the scale is vast and the human being hardly figures in it at all. In theater this could never happen; the human being is always center stage, literally and figuratively.

THE PURPOSE OF A THEATER EVENT

Art goes further in its selectivity than using one medium as opposed to another. An artist can paint with special purpose; one painter, for example, simply wishes to reproduce a landscape, while another wishes to make a political statement. In a similar fashion, a theater event can be performed for a special *purpose* and can be viewed from a unique angle of vision. Again, this results in the clarity and the power that such selectivity can achieve.

Every theater event is intended to serve some purpose. It may be a casual, unconscious purpose—much as someone says, "Let's go to the movies tonight," or "Let's watch television." Even in these seemingly casual decisions, however, there is a purpose; movies or television are seen primarily as entertainment or "escape." In Chapter 3, it was noted that various types of contemporary theater are presented for a specific purpose: feminist theater, Hispanic theater, black theater. In theater of this kind, both those who create the event—playwright, director, performers—and members of the audience have a definite purpose in mind.

The Playwright's Purpose

Historically, the creators of theater—playwrights and others—have intended it to serve different purposes.

There have been times, for example, when the purpose of a theater event was religious. In the medieval period, theater performances were employed to teach people stories from the Bible, to instruct them in religious precepts, and so forth. At times theater serves a civic function. A pageant will be arranged to present a play telling the history of a community. This kind of play is frequently given on the anniversary of a town. In 1976, when the United States celebrated its bicentennial, many dramas were presented depicting events surrounding the founding of the nation.

In the seventeenth century playwrights in England frequently wrote plays for the purpose of entertaining royalty as a part of a celebration. In France, Molière wrote several of his plays as part of an entertainment at some château, or for Louis XIV. The play would be only one of several activities—a banquet, a dance, a fireworks display—arranged for an evening, or for a celebration of several days' duration.

Throughout history some playwrights have written primarily to entertain their audiences, and others have written with a serious purpose in mind: to call attention to injustice, to make a statement against war, to raise moral or philosophical questions.

In the present-day theater, when a playwright begins work on a play, he or she may not have a clear purpose in mind. The purpose may emerge only as the script goes through several revisions. Before a play goes into production, however, the playwright should know where it is headed.

Once the purpose is clear, the director, the performers, and the designers join the playwright in working toward achieving it. One of the tasks of those developing a production is to make certain that all those concerned are moving toward the same goal. If they are not, various elements will be in conflict. If the playwright intends his or her work to be serious and the performers make fun of it, the two are at cross-purposes.

One of the tasks of an alert audience member is to understand what purpose the work is intended to serve. The writer and the actors and actresses should make this clear as early as possible in a performance so that the audience will know on what basis to judge the production.

Purposes of the Audience

Audiences, too, go to the theater for different purposes. Some, like those who enjoy the escape offered by movies and television, are interested primarily in light entertainment. Audiences at dinner theaters or Broadway musicals frequently do not want to be faced with troublesome problems or serious moral issues. They are tired from hard work and want some relief from the job and from tensions at home. Consequently they seek an "escape" from everyday cares. They look, therefore, for something which will be amusing and perhaps will include music, dancing, and beautiful costumes.

There are other audiences, however, that want to be stimulated and challenged, both intellectually and emotionally. For these audiences a situation comedy or a light musical will seem to be frivolous or sentimental.

It must be remembered, too, that many people like both kinds of theater. The situation and the audience member's frame of mind are the determining factors. At times a person may seek light entertainment; at other times, meaningful drama.

In understanding a theater event it is important to understand the social context in which it occurs and the demands of the audiences. A theater event can entertain, offer an escape, provoke thought, inspire, educate, challenge, delight. Often several of these purposes are combined. A production might be intended, for instance, to amuse but also to teach a lesson. Another production may challenge the audience to think and, beyond that, to take action.

POINT OF VIEW

Closely related to purpose is *point of view*. Point of view is the way we look at things.

People and events can always be interpreted in widely different ways. How we perceive them depends on our point of view. There is the familiar story of two people looking at a bottle half-filled with wine; the optimist will say that the bottle is half-full, but the pessimist will note that the same bottle is half-empty.

Anyone familiar with the giving of evidence in a court trial—one involving an automobile accident, for instance—knows that different witnesses, each of whom may be honest and straightforward, will describe the same incident differently. One will say that she saw a yellow car go through a stoplight and hit a blue car; another will say that he remembers clearly that the blue car pulled out before the light had changed and blocked the path of the yellow car. The same variation In viewpoint affects our assessment of politicians and other public figures. To some people, a certain politician will be a dedicated, sincere public servant, interested only in what is best for the people. But to others, the very same politician will be a hypocrite and a charlatan—that is, a fake concerned exclusively with personal gain.

Point of view influences the way we look at virtually everything in life, but it plays a particularly important role in the arts. Under ordinary circumstances, those who attempt to determine our point of view, such as advertisers and politicians, frequently disguise their motives, employing subtle and indirect techniques to convince us that they are not trying to impose their views on us; but we know that that is exactly what they are trying to do. In the arts, on the other hand, the imposition of a point of view is direct and deliberate. Rather than being disguised, it is emphasized. The artist makes it clear that he or she is looking at the world from a highly personal point of view, perhaps turning the world upside down, or looking at it from an unusual angle.

A good example can be found in films, where we have become familiar with the various points of view, angles of vision, and perspectives which the camera selects for us. In a close-up we do not see an entire room or even an entire person; we see one small detail: a hand putting out a cigarette or a finger on the trigger of a gun. In a medium shot we see more—a couple embracing, perhaps—but still only part of their bodies. In an exterior scene we might view a panorama of the vast Russian steppes or a full military parade. The camera also predetermines the angle from which we see the action. In a scene emphasizing the strength of a figure, the camera will look up from below to show a person looming from the top of a flight of stairs. In another scene we might look down on the action. The camera might be tilted so that a scene looks off balance; a scene might be shot out of focus so that it is hazy or blurred; or it might be filmed through a special filter.

Whereas in everyday life we resist having someone tell us how to look at things, greeting an advertisement or a political speech with a certain skepticism, in the arts our reaction is just the opposite. We value art precisely because it presents its own point of view, giving us a fresh look at ourselves and the world around us.

As with the other arts, point of view is an important ingredient of theater. It tells us how to interpret the words and actions of the characters we see on stage; it provides a key to understanding the entire experience. In a successful theater production, point of view is reflected in the script, in the actions of the performers, and in the design of the costumes, scenery, and lighting. So strong is it that it takes us inside the work and permits us to see the subject through the artists' eyes. Their world becomes our world.

Serious or Comic Point of View:
The Dramatist's Attitude

"There is nothing either good or bad, but thinking makes it so," Shakespeare wrote in *Hamlet,* to which could be added a parallel statement: "There is nothing either funny or sad, but thinking makes it so." One's point of view determines whether one takes a subject seriously or laughs at it, whether it is an object of pity or of ridicule.

Horace Walpole (1717–1797), an English author of the eighteenth century, wrote: "This world is a comedy to those that think, a tragedy to those that feel." There may or may not be truth in Walpole's epigram, but the chief point it underlines is that people see the world differently. Just why some people look at the world and weep, and others look at it and laugh, is difficult to say; but there is no question that they do.

Once adopted, a point of view is transmitted to others in innumerable ways. In everyday life, for instance, we telegraph to those around us the relative seriousness of a situation by the way we behave. Anyone coming into a scene where a person has been hurt in an accident will immediately sense that the situation is no laughing matter. The people looking on will have concerned expressions on their faces, and their voices and actions will reflect tension and urgency. In contrast, a person coming into a group where a joke is being told will notice an air of pleasurable expectancy among the spectators and a teasing, conspiratorial tone on the part of the storyteller.

A similar thing happens in the theater. Point of view begins when a dramatist takes a strong personal view of a subject, deciding that it is grave, heroic, or humorous. In theater, as in other art forms, the opportunities for selectivity are greater than in everyday life; and hence the adoption of a point of view can be included in drama in a quite conscious and deliberate way. In a serious play, for instance, the playwright says: "I know the world is not always somber; there are pleasant moments. Life is not made up exclusively of violence, treachery, and alienation. But at times it seems that way, and so for the duration of this play I will deal only with the serious side of life and put everything else aside."

Having taken this point of view, the dramatist then incorporates it in the play itself, giving the characters words to speak and actions to perform which convey that attitude. In a serious work the writer will choose language and actions suggesting sobriety and sincerity. Take the lines spoken by Othello:

O, Now for ever
Farewell the tranquil mind! Farewell content!
Farewell the plumed troop and the big wars
That make ambition virtue!

These words express Othello's profound sense of loss in unmistakable fashion.

Another writer might take what is ordinarily a serious subject and treat it humorously. A good example is Arthur Kopit (1937–   ), who, in his play *Oh, Dad. Poor Dad. Mama's Hung You in the Closet, and I'm Feelin' So Sad,* gave a comic twist to a man who has hanged himself. The title itself, with its mocking tone and its unusual length, makes it clear from the beginning that Kopit wants us to laugh at his subject.

Once the playwright's intentions are known, the director and the performers must transmit them to the audience. The actor playing Othello, for example, must deliver his lines in a straightforward manner and move with dignity, that is, without the exaggerations or excesses of comedy. When a series of gestures, vocal inflections, and activities on the part of performers are combined with the words and ideas of the dramatist—and set in an appropriate visual environment established by the designers—a world is created in a theatrical production. It might be a sad world, a bittersweet world, a hopeful world, or a tragic world. If it is fully and properly created, however, the audience becomes aware of it instantly, enters it, and lives in it for the duration of the performance. Entering and inhabiting a world which reflects a particular point of view is an indispensable part of the theater experience.

Society's Point of View

In discussing this subject, we cannot overlook the role that society plays in adopting a point of view. We saw earlier that there is a close relationship between theater and society. This relationship manifests itself particularly in the point of view artists adopt toward their subject matter.

Tragedy, for example, occurs only in periods when society as a whole assumes a certain attitude toward people and the universe in which they live. Two periods conducive to the creation of tragedy were the golden age of Greece in the fifth century B.C. and the Renaissance. Both periods incorporated two ideas essential to tragic drama: on the one hand, the notion that human beings are capable of extraordinary accomplishments; and on the other, the notion that the world is potentially cruel and unjust. A closer look at these two periods will demonstrate how they reflected these two viewpoints.

In both the fifth century B.C., in Greece, and the Renaissance (the fourteenth through the sixteenth century) in Europe and England, human beings were exalted above everything else; the gods and nature were given a much less prominent place in the scheme of things. A look at the history of the two periods shows that men and women of the time considered the horizons for human achievement unlimited. In the fifth century B.C., Greece was enjoying its golden age in commerce, politics, science, and art; nothing seemed impossible in the way of architecture, mathematics, trade, or philosophy. The same was true in Europe and England during the Renaissance. Columbus had discovered the new world in 1492, and the possibili-

A climate for tragedy.
The world-view of a society is one factor that determines whether it will embrace and encourage tragedy. Some societies, such as Greece in the fifth century B.C., had a cultural atmosphere in which tragic drama could develop. An example is the trilogy of *The Oresteia* by Aeschylus, about the aftermath of the Trojan war. Here Orestes is seen with the furies who pursue him after he has murdered his mother.

ties for trade and exploration appeared infinite. Science and the arts were on the threshold of a new day as well.

In sculpture in the two periods, the human figure was glorified as it rarely had been before or has been since. Fifth-century Greece abounded in statues—on friezes, in temples, in public buildings—of heroes, athletes, and warriors. And during the Renaissance, Michelangelo was only one of many who gave inimitable grace and distinction to the human form.

The celebration of the individual was apparent in all the arts, including drama. The Greek dramatist Sophocles exclaimed:

Numberless are the wonders of the world.
but none
More wonderful than man

And in the Renaissance, Shakespeare has Hamlet say:

What a piece of work is man! How noble
in reason! how infinite in faculty!
in form, in moving, how express and
admirable! in action how like an angel!
in apprehension how like a god!

PURPOSE AND PERSPECTIVE: THEATRICAL GENRES

Shakespearean tragedy.
Like the classic Greek period, the Elizabethan era in England was also conducive to the creation of tragedy. The best known tragic dramatist of the era was Shakespeare, one of whose tragic heroes is Hamlet, played here by William Hurt at the Circle Repertory Theater.

The credo of both ages was expressed by Protagoras, a Greek philosopher of the fifth century B.C.:

Man is the measure of all things.

But there is another side to the tragic coin. Along with this optimistic and highly humanistic view, there was a simultaneous awareness of what life can do to men and women: a faculty for admitting, unflinchingly, that life can be—and in fact frequently is—cruel and unjust. Shakespeare put it this way in *King Lear:*

As flies to wanton boys, are we to the gods;
They kill us for their sport.

And in *Macbeth,* he expressed it in these words:

Out, out brief candle!
Life's but a walking shadow, a poor player
That struts and frets his hour upon the stage
And then is heard no more; it is a tale
Told by an idiot, full of sound and fury,
Signifying nothing.

PURPOSE AND POINT OF VIEW

These periods of history—the Greek golden age and the Renaissance—were expansive enough to encompass both strains: the greatness of human beings on the one hand, and the cruelty of life on the other. These two attitudes form two indispensable sides of the tragic equation; without them, the possibilities for traditional tragedy are virtually nonexistent.

To clarify the distinction between tragic and other points of view, we need only examine other periods in history when one or both of the attitudes forming the tragic equation were absent or expressed in a quite different way. In Europe and Great Britain, the eighteenth century was known as the age of enlightenment, and the nineteenth century as the century of progress. The French and American revolutions were under way, and the industrial revolution as well; the merchant class and the middle class were in the ascendancy. The glorification was not of single men and women—alone and unafraid—but of groups, or masses, beginning to stir and throw off the yokes of the past. Enlightenment and progress: together they express the philosophy that men and women can analyze any problem—poverty, violence, disease, injustice—and by applying their intelligence to it, solve it. In general, it was an age of unbounded optimism, in which no problem was thought insurmountable and feelings of moral justice ran strong. This is not the soil in which tragedy can grow.

Such an age can have a profound effect on art. For example, in 1681 a man named Nahum Tate (1652–1715) rewrote the ending of Shakespeare's *King Lear* so that Lear's daughter does not die as she does in Shakespeare's play, but remains alive, thus softening the tragic effect. This version of the play was performed in England throughout the eighteenth century and much of the nineteenth. The critic Dr. Samuel Johnson (1709–1784), a cold-eyed realist in many respects, preferred the Tate version and wrote in 1765 that he found the death of Cordelia in Shakespeare so painful that he had been unable to bring himself to read the original play for many years. In times such as the eighteenth and nineteenth centuries it is difficult for any dramatist, no matter what his or her personal inclinations, to produce tragedy.

Personal Vision

As important as it is, however, the outlook of society serves only as the background in creating theater. In the foreground stands the point of view of the individual artist: that highly personal outlook referred to above. Proof of this is the variation among playwrights within the same area. At the same time that Euripides was writing tragedies in ancient Greece, Aristophanes (ca. 450–ca. 388 B.C.) was writing satirical farces. In France in the seventeenth century, Molière was writing comedies when Jean Racine (1639–1699) was writing tragedies. In the modern period particularly, we have a multiplicity of individual viewpoints expressed in drama.

(Charles P. Ford)

(Joan Marcus)

The individual point of view.

In addition to the social and cultural climate of an age, the individual artist's outlook also determines whether a work will be serious or comic. Two people writing in the same place at the same time will view the world differently. A good example is seventeenth-century France. Racine wrote mostly tragedies, such as *Phaedra*, seen above at the bottom in a production at the Catholic University of America. Racine's contemporary Molière, however, wrote comedies like *The Imaginary Invalid*, shown at the top in a production at the Arena Stage in Washington, D.C.

The Problem of Categories

By combining the two elements—the view of society and the individual outlook of the artist—a wide range of serious and comic points of view are incorporated in individual plays. For the sake of convenience people often classify plays according to point of view: tragedy, comedy, and so forth. A group of plays which forms a single type is called a *genre,* after a French word which means "category" or "type."

In Chapter 5, we will study tragedy and other serious drama; and in Chapter 6, comedy. Before we turn to these subjects, however, I should express a word of caution about the question of genre, or categories of drama. The attempt to separate and organize plays according to categories can present problems in developing a free and open understanding of theater. Shakespeare made fun of this problem in *Hamlet* when he had Polonius announce that the players who had come to court could perform anything: "tragedy, comedy, history, pastoral, pastoral-comical, historical-pastoral, tragical-historical, tragical-comical-historical-pastoral." In spite of the absurdity of this, there are those who continue to try to pigeonhole or label every play that comes along.

The attempt to assign plays to given categories can be a dangerous pursuit. In the first place, more often than not, plays do not fit neatly into categories. As the quotation from Polonius suggests, different dramas intersect and overlap: a few plays are pure tragedy, but some are heroic drama with tragic elements, and others are serious drama with no elements of tragedy. Also, the serious and the comic are often combined.

Dramatists do not write categories or types of drama; they write individual plays. The dramatist, as well as everyone else concerned with producing a theater event, deals with a specific play—and so should members of the audience. A preoccupation with establishing categories diverts our attention from the main purpose of theater: to *experience the play in performance.*

The reason we learn the various forms of drama is not to spend our time pinning labels on plays, but to understand that writers, as well as those responsible for the production of a play, take a point of view with regard to their material. Members of the audience must be aware of that point of view if they are to understand a performance properly. A play which aims at a purely melodramatic effect, for instance, should be looked at differently from one which aspires to tragedy. A lighthearted comedy should not be judged by the same standards as a philosophical play. It is to understand these differences, and to grasp the various ways in which playwrights have traditionally approached their material, that we study the categories into which groups of plays frequently fall.

The category we will examine in Chapter 5 is serious drama. In Chapter 6, we will consider comedy and tragicomedy.

SUMMARY

1 Drama is written and produced for different purposes: to move us, to involve us, to amuse us, to entertain us, to inform us, to shock us, to raise our awareness, to inspire us. Audiences, too, go to the theater for different purposes.

2 Point of view is the way we look at things: the perspective or angle of vision from which we view people, places, and events.

3 In the arts, the establishment of a point of view is direct and deliberate; it is an integral part of a performance or work of art, providing a clue to the audience as to how to interpret and understand what is being seen and heard.

4 Whether a theater piece is serious, comic, or some combination of the two depends on the point of view of the artists who create it.

5 The viewpoint of society also affects the outlook of individual artists in terms of tragedy, comedy, etc.

6 In studying various types of drama—tragedy, comedy, farce—an over-emphasis of labels and categories must be avoided; otherwise, theater is robbed of its immediacy and spontaneity.

5
TRAGEDY
AND OTHER
SERIOUS DRAMA

The tragic hero.
Serious drama emphasizes the somber aspects of life, and generally the highest form of such drama is considered to be tragedy. An example is the play *Othello* by William Shakespeare. The leading character becomes enmeshed in circumstances that lead to his murdering his wife and killing himself. Shown here is James Earl Jones portraying the character in a Broadway production.

A wide range of theater experiences fall under the heading of serious theater. These experiences include the inspiration and lofty feelings of high tragedy, the intellectual challenge of plays of ideas, and the fright and horror induced by melodrama.

Serious drama takes a thoughtful, sober attitude toward its subject matter. It puts the audience in a frame of mind to think carefully about what it sees and to become involved with the characters on stage: to love what they love, fear what they fear, and suffer what they suffer. The best known form of serious drama, to which we turn first, is *tragedy*. (For a discussion of theories of tragedy, turn to Appendix 1.) Other forms are *heroic drama, melodrama,* and *domestic drama.*

TRAGEDY

Tragedy asks the most basic questions about human existence. Why is the world sometimes so unjust? Why are men and women called on to endure such suffering in their lives? What are the limits of human suffering and endurance? In the midst of cruelty and despair, what are the possibilities of human achievement? To what heights of courage, strength, generosity, and integrity can human beings rise?

Tragedy assumes that the universe is indifferent to human concerns, and often cruel or malevolent. Sometimes the innocent appear to suffer while the evil prosper. In the face of this, some human beings are capable of despicable deeds, but others can confront and overcome adversity, attaining a nobility which places them "a little lower than the angels." We can divide tragedy into two basic kinds: traditional and modern. Modern tragedy generally includes plays of the last one hundred years. Traditional tragedy includes works from several significant periods of the past.

Traditional Tragedy

Three noteworthy periods of history in which tragic drama was produced are Greece in the fifth century B.C., England in the late sixteenth and early seventeenth centuries, and France in the seventeenth century. The tragedies which appear in these three ages had several characteristics in common, characteristics which help define traditional tragedy. They include the following:

1 Generally the hero or heroine of the play is an extraordinary person: a king, a queen, a general, or a nobleman—that is, a person of stature. In Greek drama, Antigone, Electra, Oedipus, Agamemnon, Creon, and Orestes are members of royal families. In Shakespeare, Hamlet, Claudius,

Extraordinary characters
caught in the web of tragedy.
The heroes and heroines of traditional tragedy
are generally extraordinary people, because
of a combination of their personalities and
their position. When tragic heroes or heroines
fall, it has a special significance. An example
of an extraordinary tragic heroine is Lady
Macbeth in Shakespeare's play *Macbeth*. She
is depicted here in the sleepwalking scene in
which she acknowledges her guilt for the
crimes she and her husband have committed.

Gertrude, Lear, and Cordelia also are royalty; Julius Caesar, Macbeth, and
Othello are generals; and others—Ophelia, Romeo, and Juliet—are members of the nobility. Because the heroes and heroines are important, the
plays in which they appear have added importance; the characters of
tragedy stand not only as individuals, but as symbols for an entire culture or
society. The idea is expressed in *Julius Caesar* as follows:

> Great Caesar fell
> O! what a fall was there my countrymen
> Then I, and you, and all of us fell down . . .

2   The central figures of the play are caught in a series of tragic circumstances: Oedipus, without realizing it, murders his father and marries his
mother; Phaedra falls hopelessly and fatally in love with her stepson,
Hippolytus; Othello is completely duped by Iago; and Lear is cast out by the
very daughters he benefited. In traditional tragedy, the universe seems
determined to trap the hero or heroine in a fateful web.
3   The situation becomes irretrievable: there is no turning back, no way
out. The figures of tragedy find themselves in a situation from which there is

TRAGEDY AND OTHER SERIOUS DRAMA

no honorable avenue of escape; they face a tragic fate and must go forward to meet it.

4 The hero or heroine accepts responsibility for his or her actions and also shows a willingness and an immense capacity to suffer. This is true whether the characters are praiseworthy or villainous; they endure the calamities suffered and fight back. Heroic figures accept their fate: Oedipus puts out his eyes; Antigone dies; Othello kills himself. One who suffers immensely, King Lear, lives through personal humiliation, a raging storm on a heath, partial insanity, and the death of his daughter, and finally faces his own death. A statement by Edgar in *King Lear* applies to all tragic figures: "Men must endure their going hence even as their coming hither."

5 The language of traditional tragedy is verse. Because it deals with lofty and profound ideas—with men and women at the outer limits of their lives—tragedy soars to the heights and descends to the depths of human experience; and many feel that such thoughts and emotions can best be expressed in poetry. Look at Cleopatra's lament upon the death of Mark Antony; the sense of admiration for Antony, and of desolation now that he is gone, could never be conveyed so tellingly in less poetic terms:

> O, wither'd is the garland of war,
> The soldier's pole is fall'n! Young boys and girls
> Are level now with men. The odds is gone,
> And there is nothing left remarkable
> Beneath the visiting moon.

When the above elements of traditional tragedy are combined, they appear to produce two contradictory reactions simultaneously. One is pessimistic: the heroes or heroines are "damned if they do and damned if they don't," and the world is a cruel, uncompromising place, a world of despair. When one sees *Hamlet,* for instance, one can only conclude that people are avaricious and corrupt, and the world unjust. Claudius, Gertrude, Polonius, Rosencrantz, Guildenstern, and even Ophelia, are part of a web of deception, in which Hamlet is irrevocably caught. And yet, in the bleakest tragedy—whether *Hamlet, Medea, Macbeth,* or *King Lear*—there is affirmation: the other side of the tragic coin. One source of this positive feeling is the drama itself. It has been pointed out that Sophocles, Euripides, Shakespeare, and Racine, though telling us that the world is in chaos and utterly lost, at the same time affirmed just the opposite by creating such carefully shaped and brilliant works of art. Why bother, if all is hopeless, to create a work of art at all? The answer must be some residual hope in the midst of the gloom.

Another positive element resides in the persons of the tragic heroes and heroines. They meet their fates with such dignity and such determination that they defy the gods. They say: "Come and get me; throw your worst at me and I will not only absorb it, but fight back. Whatever happens, I will not surrender my individuality and my dignity." In Aeschylus's play *Prometheus,* the title character, one of the first tragic heroes, says: "On me the tempest falls. It does not make me tremble." In defeat, the men and women of tragedy triumph. They lose; but in losing, they win. This paradox gives traditional tragedy much of its resonance and meaning, and explains why we are both devastated and exhilarated by it.

As for the deeper meanings of individual tragedies, there is a vast literature on the subject, and each play has to be looked at and experienced in detail to obtain the full measure of its meaning. Certain tragedies seem to hold so much meaning, to contain so much in substance, in echoes and reverberations, that one can spend a lifetime studying them.

Modern Tragedy

Tragedies of the modern period—that is, of the last hundred years—do not have queens or kings as central figures, and they are written in prose rather than poetry. For these reasons, as well as more philosophical ones, a debate has raged for some time over whether they are true tragedies. Small men and women, the argument runs, lack the stature of tragic figures. A traveling salesman, such as Hickey in *The Iceman Cometh* by O'Neill or Willy Loman in *Death of a Salesman* by Arthur Miller (1915–   ); a nymphomaniac southern woman like Blanche DuBois in *A Streetcar Named Desire* by Williams; and a housewife who shoots herself, like Hedda Gabler by Ibsen, lack the grandeur of princely rulers.

Similarly, it is argued that the present world view, in our industrialized, computerized age, looks on the individual human being as a helpless victim of society. How can a hero or heroine show defiance of the gods when people are not free to act on their own, but are controlled by social or mechanical forces?

In answer to these questions, the playwright Arthur Miller argues that it is not necessary to have people of noble birth as tragic heroes and furthermore that modern characters do have an element of choice in determining their lives. In an essay entitled "Tragedy and the Common Man," Miller states: "Insistence upon the rank of the tragic hero, or the so-called nobility of his character, is really but a clinging to the outward form of tragedy." He adds: "I believe that the common man is as apt a subject for tragedy in its highest sense as kings were." Regarding the tragic feeling experienced by the audience, Miller has this to say: "The tragic feeling is evoked in us when we are in the presence of a character who is ready to lay down his life, if need be, to secure one thing—his sense of personal dignity. . . . Tragedy, then, is the consequence of a man's total compulsion to evaluate himself justly."[1]

With regard to Miller's ideas about noble figures in tragedy, it should be pointed out that today we have no kings or queens—neither in a mythology nor, for all practical purposes, in real life. Does this mean that no one can

A modern tragic figure.
Commentators debate whether modern tragedy is possible. Arthur Miller, who wrote *Death of a Salesman,* argues that there can be a tragedy of common people. Certainly many figures in modern drama bear the marks of tragedy. Shown here is the central figure in *Death of a Salesman,* Willy Loman the salesman, whose ideas for himself and his sons did not work out as he had hoped. In this revival on Broadway, Dustin Hoffman plays Willy and Kate Reid, at the table, is his wife Linda.

stand for other people, or be symbolic of a whole group or culture? In the sense of mythical figures like Oedipus and Antigone in ancient Greece, or kings and queens in Renaissance England, the answer is, probably not. At the same time, many would agree that we have characters today who can stand as symbolic figures for important segments of society.

Another argument against modern tragedy holds that the lofty ideas of tragedy can never be adequately expressed in the language of ordinary conversation. There is no doubt that poetry can convey thoughts and feelings to which prose can never aspire. Some prose, however, approaches the level of poetry; and beyond that, there is nonverbal expression: the structure of the plot, the movements and gestures of actors and actresses, the elements of sound and light. These have a way of communicating meanings below the surface of the words themselves.

Speaking of the importance of nonverbal elements in theater, Friedrich Nietzsche (1844–1900), in *The Birth of Tragedy*, wrote:

The myth by no means finds its adequate objectification in the spoken word. The structure of the scenes and the visible imagery reveal a deeper wisdom than the poet himself is able to put into words and concepts.[2]

The director Constantin Stanislavski (1863–1938), who will be discussed in Chapter 12, stressed what he called the *subtext* of a play, by which he meant emotions, tensions, and thoughts not expressed directly in the text. These often appear much stronger than the surface expressions, and when properly presented are abundantly clear to the audience.

Some modern dramatists have attempted to recreate Greek or Elizabethan tragedy in works featuring royal figures and written in blank verse. But the results are often archaic. They tend to be imitations, rather than fresh creations. These attempts provide a strong argument against imitation of the classics as a means of achieving modern tragedy, but this method is not the only way to go about it.

(Martha Swope)

Trapped by circumstances. Frequently the characters in serious drama are made to suffer as a result of outside forces, their own personalities, or some combination of the two. Nora, the heroine of Henrik Ibsen's *A Doll's House*, is such a figure. Nora is a naive woman who forges a signature to get a loan for her sick husband. Krogstad—a desperate, vindictive man—attempts to blackmail her. She is caught in a terrible predicament which makes for strong drama. In this scene Claire Bloom is Nora and Robert Gerringer is Krogstad.

A modern tragic family.
The family in Arthur Miller's *A View from the Bridge* lack the scale and grandeur of figures from the past, but their suffering has meaning for us today and speaks more directly to us. It becomes, therefore, a form of modern tragedy. In *A View from the Bridge* the man in the center, played by Tony Lo Bianco, is in love with his niece (on the left, played by Saundra Santiago). He does not acknowledge his feelings, however, or understand his jealousy of the young boarder in his house (James Hayden), whom his niece is in love with.

In attempting to create modern tragedy, the question is not whether we view the human condition in the same way as the French in the seventeenth century or the Greeks in the fifth century B.C.—the truth is that those two societies did not view life in the same way either—but whether our age allows for a tragic view on its own terms. The answer seems to be yes. Compared with either the eighteenth or the nineteenth century—the ages of enlightenment, progress, and unbounded optimism—our age has its own tragic vision. Despite a supposedly mechanistic approach to life, our dramatic heroes and heroines fight to the end. If there is sometimes less exaltation or exhilaration at the end of a modern tragedy than at the end of some classic tragedies, this does not negate the total effect.

(Martha Swope)

Modern tragic dramatists probe the same depths and ask the same questions as their predecessors: Why do men and women suffer? Why is there cruelty and injustice in the world? And perhaps most fundamental of all: What is the meaning of our lives? Naturally they do it on their own terms; but many dramatists of the recent past have looked at life with the same level gaze, and the same sense of awe, as those who came before.

It is on this basis that many commentators would argue that writers like Ibsen, Strindberg, García Lorca, O'Neill, Williams, and Miller can lay claim to writing legitimate modern tragedy. Part of this, of course, is a question of definition, perhaps even of semantics. The ultimate test of a play is not whether it meets someone's definition of tragedy, but the effect it produces in the theater and the way in which it subsequently stands up to continued scrutiny. Eugene O'Neill's *Long Day's Journey into Night* takes as bleak a look at the human condition, with, at the same time, as compassionate a view of human striving and dignity, as it seems possible to take in our day.

HEROIC DRAMA

The term *heroic drama* is not a commonly used term like *tragedy* or *comedy*, but there is a wide range of plays with common characteristics which are not tragedies and for which heroic drama seems an appropriate name. I use the term specifically to indicate serious drama of any period which features heroic or noble figures and includes other traits of traditional tragedy— dialogue in verse or elevated language, extreme situations, etc.—but differs from tragedy in important respects. Such serious drama may differ on the one hand in having a happy ending, and on the other in assuming a basically optimistic world view, even when the ending is sad. If there is a happy ending, the chief characters go through many trials and tribulations but emerge victorious at the end. The threatening events of the play turn out to have been narrow escapes, but escapes nevertheless. We agonize with the hero or heroine, knowing all the time that the play will end well.

Several Greek plays, ordinarily classified as tragedies, are actually closer to what we are calling heroic drama. In Sophocles's *Electra,* for instance, Electra suffers grievously, but at the end of the play she and her brother Orestes triumph. *The Cid,* written by Pierre Corneille (1606–1684) in France in the seventeenth century, has a hero who leads his men to victory in battle and in the end, rather than being killed, wins a duel over his rival, Don Sanchez. In *Life Is a Dream,* by the Spanish playwright Pablo Calderón de la Barca (1600–1681), Prince Segismundo, after numerous misfortunes, emerges as a generous and dignified king. In the late seventeenth century in

England, a form of drama developed which was called specifically *heroic drama*, or *heroic tragedy*, and it was precisely the type of which we are now speaking—the serious play with the happy ending for the hero or heroine.

Many plays in Asian drama—from India, China, and Japan—though resisting the usual classifications and involving a great deal of dance and music as part of the presentation, bear a close resemblance to heroic drama. Frequently, for example, a hero goes through a series of dangerous adventures, emerging victorious at the end. The vast majority of Asian dramas end happily.

A second type of heroic drama involves the death of the hero or heroine, but neither the events along the way nor the final conclusion could be thought of as tragic. Several of Goethe's plays follow this pattern. *Egmont* depicts a much-loved count who fights for freedom and justice. He is imprisoned and dies, but not before he sees a vision of a better world to which he is going, to be a free man. In *Goetz von Berlichingen,* the leading character wages war against an unjust bishop and the emperor; and though he dies, he dies in triumph, with the word "freedom" on his lips. Many of Goethe's plays, along with those of his contemporaries in the late eighteenth and early nineteenth centuries, form a subdivision of heroic drama, referred to as *romantic drama*. Romanticism was a literary movement which took hold in Germany at the time and spread to France and throughout much of Europe. It celebrated the spirit of hope, personal freedom, and natural instincts.

A number of plays in the modern period fall into the category of heroic drama. *Cyrano de Bergerac,* written in 1897 by Edmond Rostand (1868–1918), is a good example. The title character of the play dies at the end, but only after the truth of his love for Roxanne, hidden for fifteen years, is revealed. He dies a happy man, declaring his opposition to oppression and secure in the knowledge that he did not love in vain. Some might find the play sentimental, but it could not be called tragic. *Saint Joan,* by George Bernard Shaw (1856–1950), is another example: Joan's death at the stake is actually a form of triumph; and as if that were not enough, Shaw provides an epilogue to the play in which Joan appears alive after her death.

History plays, such as Shakespeare's *Richard II; Henry IV, Parts 1 and 2;* and *Henry V,* also fall into the genre of heroic drama. In the modern period the Swedish dramatist August Strindberg wrote a number of history plays about his native land; and there have been others by modern writers about historical figures in a similar vein.

In the history of theater, the group of plays we are calling heroic drama occupies a large and important niche, cutting, as it does, across Asia and Western civilization, and across periods from the Greek golden age to the present.

Melodrama.
The stress in melodrama is on suspense and excitement. The good characters and bad characters are clearly delineated. This scene is from a nineteenth-century melodrama called *Under the Gaslight*, by Augustin Daly. The heroine, on the left—a good character— is taken by surprise by an evil one.

MELODRAMA

The word *melodrama* means "music drama" or "song drama." It comes from the Greek, but its modern form was introduced by the French in the late eighteenth century and applied to plays which employed background music of the kind we hear in movies: ominous chords underscoring a scene of suspense, and lyrical music underscoring a love scene.

Melodrama is exaggerated theater, and we have come to use the term *melodramatic* as an expression of disdain or disapproval. When taken to extremes, melodrama is laughable; we have all seen silent movies where a heroine with curly blond hair, pure as the driven snow, is being pursued by a heartless villain, a man with a sinister moustache and penetrating eyes who will foreclose the mortgage on the home of the girl and her mother unless she will let him have his way with her. This is a caricature, however, for melodrama is an ancient and honorable form of serious drama. It does have a measure of exaggeration, but so does most theater. Actually, melodrama has much in common with all forms of serious drama, and in many cases the difference lies more in degree and emphasis than anything else.

Melodrama puts a premium on effects, particularly the element of suspense. Will the heroine escape? Will the bad guys be punished? Melodrama is dedicated to results and will sacrifice reality and logic in order to achieve them; but it should be made clear that there is nothing inherently wrong with this.

Among the effects for which melodrama generally strives is fright or horror. It has been said that melodrama speaks to the paranoia in all of us: the fear that someone is pursuing us or that disaster is about to overtake us. How often do we have the sense that others are ganging up on us or the premonition that we have a deadly disease? Melodrama brings these fears to life; we see innocent victims tortured, or people terrorized, as in *The Desperate Hours,* a play of the 1950s in which a family is held captive by a group of escaped convicts. Murder mysteries and detective stories almost invariably are melodramas because they stress suspense and a close brush with danger. This type of melodrama usually ends in one of two ways: either the victims are maimed or murdered (in which case our worst paranoid fears are confirmed); or, after a series of dangerous episodes, they are finally rescued (in which case the play is like a nightmare or a bad dream from which we awaken the following morning to realize we are safe in bed and everything is all right).

Although the term was not used at the time, many plays written in England during the Jacobean period (the reign of James 1, 1603–1625) were melodramas. *The White Devil* and *The Duchess of Malfi,* by John Webster (ca. 1580–1625); *The Malcontent,* by John Marston (1576–1634); and *The Revenger's Tragedy,* by Cyril Tourneur (1575–1626) could well qualify as revenge or horror melodramas.

Melodrama finds its modern equivalent in television soap operas, suspense dramas, science fiction fantasies, and the westerns that have been a staple of movies for so many years. In each of these, the audience is drawn into the action, the issues are clear-cut, and the characters are easily identified as good or bad.

Still another form of melodrama argues a case or presents a strong point of view. One of the hallmarks of melodrama is that the characters tend to be simple and whole rather than complex and divided, as they are in tragedy. Melodrama invariably shows us the good guys against the bad guys. When a playwright, therefore, wishes to make a case, he or she will often write a melodrama in which the good characters represent the author's point of view.

Didactic melodrama: *The Little Foxes*.

Some melodramas are intended to convince or persuade an audience to adopt a particular viewpoint toward an idea or the characters in a play. Lillian Hellman's *The Little Foxes* is a condemnation of the ruthless behavior of the members of a southern family determined to seize control of a small business empire. By extension, the play condemns all such predators. This scene, from a Broadway revival, shows Elizabeth Taylor as Regina, the most avaricious of the family members.

Lillian Hellman (1905–1984), in order to depict the predatoriness of greedy southern materialists, wrote a forceful melodrama called *The Little Foxes*. The play takes place at the close of the Civil War, when the leading character, Regina Giddens, wishes to take control of the family cotton mills so that she can have wealth and move to Chicago. She will do anything to obtain her objectives: flirt with a prospective buyer, blackmail her own brothers, and even allow her husband to die. In a terrible scene, she stands by while her husband has a heart attack, refusing to go for the medicine which would save his life.

As with horror or suspense, melodramas arguing strongly for a point of view employ striking dramatic devices like the scene noted above. Hellman exaggerated the good qualities of the good people and the bad qualities of the bad. This technique is characteristic of all melodrama. To put it in gambling terms, those who write melodrama "load the dice" or "stack the deck."

A list of significant melodramas would range over most of theatrical history and would include writers from Euripides through Shakespeare and his contemporaries to dramatists throughout Europe and America in the modern period. Other types of serious drama, tragic and nontragic, frequently have strong melodramatic elements as well.

BOURGEOIS OR DOMESTIC DRAMA

Another important group of serious works are known as *bourgeois* or *domestic* dramas. Although they have neither the profundity of tragedy, the loftiness of heroic drama, nor the sensationalism of melodrama, they often prove to be extremely powerful. *Bourgeois* refers to people of the middle or lower-middle class rather than the aristocracy, and *domestic* means that the plays often deal with the problems of the family or the home rather than great affairs of state. In the Greek, Roman, and Renaissance periods, ordinary people serve as the main characters only in comedies; they rarely appeared as the heroes or heroines of serious plays. Beginning in the eighteenth century, however, as society changed, there was a call for serious drama about men and women with whom members of the audience could identify and who were like themselves.

In England in 1731, George Lillo (1693–1739) wrote *The London Merchant,* a story of a merchant's apprentice who was led astray by a prostitute and who betrayed his good-hearted employer. This play, like others after it, overstated the case for simple working-class virtues; but it dealt with recognizable people from the daily life of Britain, and audiences welcomed it. In Germany, Gotthold Ephraim Lessing (1729–1781) followed the same ideas in *Miss Sara Sampson,* a play which takes the Medea legend and translates it into commonplace terms, focusing on a young girl who is the victim of an older woman's anger. From these beginnings, bourgeois or domestic drama developed through the balance of the eighteenth century and the whole of the nineteenth, until it achieved a place of prominence in the works of Ibsen.

A typical modern domestic drama is *A Raisin in the Sun,* by Lorraine Hansberry (1930–1965). The play concerns a black family living in a poor

A modern domestic drama.
Lorraine Hansberry's *A Raisin in the Sun* is a good example of a contemporary drama
dealing with the problems of a typical family. In this case, it is a black family in Chicago
just after World War II. The son wants to become successful, and the family wants to
move to a better neighborhood. Shown here are Sidney Poitier and Claudia McNeil in
the original Broadway production.

section of Chicago. The son, on whom both his mother and his wife pin
their hopes, falls prey to the scheme of a con man who takes from him the
money with which the family had planned to buy a new home. The family
seems defeated; but in the end the son, having matured, determines to lead
them to a better life. Problems with society, struggles within a family,
dashed hopes, and renewed determination are frequent characteristics of
domestic drama.

Included in the general category of bourgeois dramas are plays in which
the hero is not one person but an entire group, such as the people in a
village or those forming their own small society. Examples include *The*

A Raisin in the Sun (1959)

LORRAINE HANSBERRY (1930–1965)

CHIEF CHARACTERS:

Lena Younger—Mama
Walter Lee Younger—her son
Ruth Younger—Walter's wife
Travis Younger—Ruth and Walter's son
Beneatha Younger—Walter's sister
Joseph Asagai—Beneatha's friend
George Murchison—Beneatha's friend
Karl Lindner—representative of white
  neighborhood

SETTING: The Younger apartment in a poor section of Chicago, sometime after World War II.

BACKGROUND: The Youngers are a hard-working black family with dreams of improving their lives. The father had worked hard all his life. Now that he is dead, his only legacy is a $10,000 life-insurance policy which the family is about to receive. He and Mama wanted to own a house but could never afford one.

ACT I, Scene 1: It is Friday morning and Ruth wakes the family. All of them are looking forward to the arrival of the insurance check, which promises an escape from poverty. After their son Travis goes to school, Walter tells Ruth that he has a chance to buy a liquor store with some friends. Walter wants Ruth to persuade Mama to give him the insurance money for this new venture, but Ruth is not supportive. Walter's sister Beneatha, an aspiring doctor, enters and tells him that the insurance money is Mama's, not theirs. After Walter goes to work, Mama enters. Her grandmotherly concern for Travis is a source of conflict between her and Ruth. Ruth talks to Mama about Walter's liquor store: Ruth believes that Walter needs a purpose in life which the store could provide, but Mama, a god-fearing woman, doesn't like the idea of selling liquor. Mama wants to put some money aside for Beneatha's education and to buy a house in a nice neighborhood with the remainder of the money. Ruth suddenly becomes ill, and Mama expresses concern for her condition.

Scene 2: The following morning, Saturday, is cleaning day. As Mama works at home, Walter goes out to talk with his friend Willy about the liquor store deal. Ruth comes back from the doctor very upset and tells Mama she is pregnant. Beneatha's friend Asagai arrives with an African outfit for her to wear. Beneatha is always trying new things, like playing the guitar and pursuing her African roots. Asagai is from Africa; he is an intellectual taken with Beneatha, but his attentions frighten her because she wants to find her own identity. Meanwhile, the insurance check arrives and Mama becomes upset. It acts as a reminder that instead of the warm, loving husband whom she has lost, now all she has is a piece of paper. Walter enters excitedly talking about the liquor store deal, and Ruth storms out. Mama tries to understand Walter's frustration, but explains to him that Ruth is pregnant and wants an abortion.

ACT II, Scene 1: Later the same day. Ruth is ironing when Beneatha enters, ready for a date with George, a wealthy, successful black man. Walter is obviously jealous of George's success. Mama enters and tells everyone that she has made a down payment on a house. Ruth and Travis are happy with the news, but Walter is depressed. He believes it is another setback to his dream of owning the liquor store. When the family discovers that the house Mama plans to buy is in an all-white section, they wonder how they will be accepted.

Scene 2: Friday night a few weeks later. The house is strewn with packing crates in anticipation of the move to the new house. Walter has not gone to work for three days; he is spending his time in a bar. This dismays Mama, who has always worked for her children and now fears that she may be destroying her son. She therefore decides to give Walter the remainder of the insurance money to invest as he chooses. She tells Walter that he should finally become the head of the family. He excitedly begins to talk to his son about his dreams.

Scene 3: Saturday, moving day, one week later. Ruth tells Beneatha that her relationship with Walter is better because he seems to have a new lease on life. Walter enters, followed by Mr. Lindner, a middle-aged white man who has come to discourage the black family from moving into their new house. Walter throws him out, and when Mama comes back they tell her about this "welcoming committee" from the new neighborhood. Mama is greatly moved when the others give her some presents for the new house. In the midst of the celebration, Walter's friend Bobo enters with the bad news: their "friend" Willy has run off with all their money. Walter breaks down, and tells the family that he had invested the whole $6500 with Willy. Mama is distraught, remembering all the suffering and sacrifices the family has made for the money.

ACT III: An hour later. The mood is despairing. Beneatha fears it is the end of all her plans. She attacks Walter bitterly, and he exits. Mama starts unpacking because now they must stay in the old house. Walter returns and tells them he has called Lindner to make a deal. Mama is against it: "We ain't never been that poor." Walter is about to sell out to "The Man" when his pride stops him; he tells Lindner that they have decided to move into the new house because his father earned it. The family members bustle into activity. After everyone else has left, Mama stands alone for a short while, and then exits into the future.

Sheep Well by the Spanish playwright Lope de Vega (1562–1635); and in the modern period, *The Weavers,* by the German writer Gerhart Hauptmann (1862–1946), and *The Lower Depths,* by the Russian dramatist Maxim Gorki (1868–1936). In one form or another, bourgeois or domestic drama has become the predominant form of serious drama throughout Europe and America during the last hundred years.

Although tragedy is the best-known type of serious drama, it should be clear that other forms, including domestic drama, are significant in their own ways. In terms of a variety of theater experience, we are more likely to encounter domestic drama—or heroic drama or melodrama—than pure tragedy. It is hoped, however, that in our theatergoing we will have the opportunity to encounter them all.

In this chapter we have seen that within the realm of serious drama, many different theater experiences are open to us. We observe people very much like ourselves and people far removed from our own lives; we see characters to admire and characters to abhor; we become deeply involved emotionally with the action on stage, or we probe the philosophical depths of what we see. As always, the direction the experience takes depends on the point of view established in the theater event itself by the playwright and those who implement the script on stage.

In Chapter 6, when we turn to the points of view reflected in comedy and tragicomedy, we will find a variety of experiences as well.

SUMMARY

1   Tragedy attempts to ask the most basic questions about human existence: Why do men and women suffer? Is there justice in the world? What are the limits of human endurance and achievement? Tragedy presupposes an indifferent and sometimes malevolent universe in which the innocent suffer and there is inexplicable cruelty. It also assumes that certain men and women will confront and defy fate, even if they are overcome in the process.

2   Tragedy can be divided into traditional and modern. In traditional tragedy the chief characters are kings, queens, persons of stature, and nobility; the central figure is caught in a series of tragic circumstances which are irrevocable; the hero or heroine is willing to fight and die for a cause. The language of the play is verse.

3   Modern tragedy involves ordinary people, not the nobility, and is written generally in prose rather than verse. The deeper meanings of tragedy are explored in its modern form by nonverbal elements and by the cumulative or overall effect of events as well as by verbal means.

4 There are several kinds of nontragic serious plays, the most notable being heroic drama, melodrama, and bourgeois or domestic drama.

5 Heroic drama has many of the same elements as traditional tragedy frequently dealing with highborn characters and being written in verse. In contrast to tragedy, it is marked by a happy ending, or an ending in which the deaths of the main characters are considered a triumph and not a defeat.

6 Melodrama features exaggerated characters and events arranged to create horror or suspense or to present a didactic argument for some political, moral, or social point of view.

7 Bourgeois or domestic drama deals with ordinary people in a serious but nontragic manner. It stresses the problems of the middle and lower classes, and has become a particularly prominent form in the past century.

6
COMEDY AND TRAGICOMEDY

Comedy: Mostly for fun.
In pure comedy no one gets hurt too seriously, but human foibles are exposed. An example is Molière's *Tartuffe*, a play about a hypocritical man who claims to be pious but is actually trying to seduce another man's wife. In this scene, John Wood is Tartuffe, on the floor on top of the wife, played by Tammy Grimes.

Aside from a basically serious point of view, there are two other fundamental approaches to dramatic material. One is *comedy*, with its many forms and variations; the other is a mixture of the serious and the comic, usually called *tragicomedy*. (For a discussion of theories of comedy, see Appendix 1.)

COMEDY

Those who create comedy are not necessarily more frivolous or less concerned with important matters than those who create serious works; they may be extremely serious in their own way. Aristophanes, Molière, and George Bernard Shaw cared passionately about human affairs and the problems of men and women. But those with a comic view look at the world differently: with a smile or a deep laugh or an arched eyebrow. They perceive the follies and excesses of human behavior and develop a keen sense of the ridiculous, with the result that they show us things which make us laugh. How does comedy work? In the following pages, we will attempt to find out.

Characteristics of Comedy

Contrast between the social order and the individual   The comic viewpoint stems from a basic assumption about society against which the writer places other factors, such as the characters' behavior or the events of the play. Comedy develops when these two elements—the basic assumption about society and the events of the play—cut against each other like the blades on a pair of scissors. Most traditional comic writers accept the notion of a clear social and moral order in their society. They appear to believe that it is not the laws of society which are at fault when something goes wrong, but the defiance of those laws by individuals. In their comedies, the excesses, the frauds, the hypocrisies, and the follies of men and women are laughed at mercilessly; but they are laughed at against a background of normality and moderation. The comic writer (or the comic performer) is saying, in effect, "These characters I show you are amusing because they are eccentric; they go beyond the bounds of common sense and turn ordinary moral values upside down." This view, we should note, is in contrast to the view of many serious plays, particularly tragedies, which assume that society itself is upside down, or that "the time is out of joint."

In Molière's comedy *Tartuffe,* the chief character is a charlatan and hypocrite who pretends to be pious and holy, going so far as to wear clerical garb. He lives in the house of Orgon, a foolish man who trusts Tartuffe implicitly. The truth is that Tartuffe is trying to possess Orgon's wife as well as his money; but Orgon, blind to Tartuffe's true nature, is completely taken in by him. The audience and the other members of Orgon's family are aware of what is going on; they can see how ludicrous these two characters are, and in the end both Tartuffe's hypocrisy and Orgon's gullibility are exposed. But it is the individual who is held up to ridicule; neither religion nor marriage is assailed by Molière. Rather, it is the abuse of these two basic institutions which is criticized.

Many modern comedies, especially those of the *theater of the absurd,* reverse the positions of the scissor blades: the basic assumption is that the world is not orderly but absurd or ridiculous. Society, rather than providing a moral or social framework, offers only chaos. Against this background, ordinary people—like the husband and wife in Ionesco's *The Bald Soprano* (described in Chapter 9)—are set at odds with the world around them. The comedy in this case results from normal people being thrust into an abnormal world.

Suspension of natural laws A characteristic of most comedy, both traditional and modern, is the temporary suspension of the natural laws of probability and logic. Actions do not have the consequences they do in real life. In comedy, when a haughty man walking down the street steps on a child's roller skate and goes sprawling on the sidewalk, we do not fear for his safety or wonder if he has any bruises. The focus in comedy is on the man's being tripped up and getting his comeuppance. In burlesque, a comic character can be hit on the backside with a fierce thwack and we laugh, because we know it does not hurt anything but pride. At one point in stage history a special stick made of two thin slats of wood held close together was developed to make the sound of hitting even more fearsome. When this stick hits someone, the two pieces of wood slap together, making the whack sound twice as loud as normal. The stick is known as a *slapstick,* a name which came to describe all kinds of raucous, knockabout comedy.

Prime examples of the suspension of natural laws in comedy are film cartoons and silent movies. Characters falling from buildings are flattened temporarily, but soon get up, with little more than a shake of the head. There are no thoughts in the audience of real injury, of cuts or bruises, because the cause-and-effect chain of everyday life is not in effect.

Under these conditions, murder itself can be viewed as comic. In *Arsenic and Old Lace,* by Joseph Kesselring (1902–   ), two sweet old women, thinking they are being helpful, give elderberry wine containing arsenic to lonely old men, resulting, of course, in the men's deaths. The two sisters let their brother, who thinks he is Teddy Roosevelt, bury the bodies in the cellar, where the brother is digging his own version of the Panama Canal. Altogether, these innocent-seeming ladies murder twelve men before their scheme is uncovered. But we watch these proceedings with amusement; we do not really think of it as murder, and we have none of the feelings one

Tartuffe (1664)

MOLIERE (JEAN-BAPTISTE POQUELIN; 1622–1673)

CHIEF CHARACTERS:

Tartuffe—a hypocrite
Mme. Pernelle—Orgon's mother
Orgon—Elmire's husband
Elmire—Orgon's wife
Damis—Orgon's son; Elmire's stepson
Mariane—Orgon's daughter, in love
  with Valere
Valere—in love with Mariane
Cleante—Orgon's brother-in-law
Dorine—Mariane's lady's maid

SETTING: Orgon's house in Paris in the 1600s.

BACKGROUND: Tartuffe, a hypocrite who dresses in religious clothes, is staying at Orgon's home. He has completely fooled Orgon by feigning a virtuous lifestyle.

ACT I: When Orgon's mother, Mme. Pernelle, tells the family that they should be virtuous like Tartuffe, they try to persuade her that he is a fraud. The maid, Dorine, enters and tells Orgon's brother-in-law Cleante that Tartuffe has bewitched Orgon who shows more affection toward Tartuffe than toward his own family. We learn that Orgon opposes the wedding of his daughter Mariane to Valere. This is distressing to her brother Damis because he wants to marry Valere's sister. When Dorine tells Orgon

that his wife was sick while he was away, Orgon, instead of pitying his wife, commiserates with Tartuffe, who is perfectly healthy. Cleante tells Orgon that he is being deceived by Tartuffe, but Orgon continues to believe in Tartuffe's virtuousness.

ACT 2: Orgon tells his daughter Mariane that she should marry Tartuffe. Mariane is outraged. When Dorine tries to persuade Orgon that Tartuffe and Mariane are ill-suited, Orgon defends the hypocrite despite Dorine's insults. After Orgon leaves, Dorine tries to persuade Mariane to stand up to her father, but Mariane is weak-willed. Her fiancé Valere confronts Mariane with the rumor that Mariane doesn't love him and is planning to marry Tartuffe instead. The two quarrel until Dorine gets them to make up.

ACT 3: Dorine tells Damis that his stepmother Elmire might persuade Tartuffe not to marry Mariane. As Damis hides in a closet, Dorine tells Tartuffe that Elmire wants a word with him. When she is alone with Tartuffe, Elmire raises questions about her husband's plan to have Tartuffe marry Mariane. Tartuffe replies that he is not interested in the daughter but rather in Elmire herself, whereupon he tries to seduce her. Elmire says that she will not tell

Orgon of Tartuffe's advances if he agrees not to marry Mariane. The stepson, Damis, who has overheard the conversation, tells Tartuffe that he will reveal all. When Damis tells Orgon of Tartuffe's adulterous offer, Tartuffe very cleverly admits the truth and begs Orgon to drive him out. Orgon, however, disbelieves Damis, thinking that he is merely trying to slander Tartuffe. When Tartuffe says that he should leave because he is upsetting the household, Orgon insists that he stay and, furthermore, disinherits his children and makes Tartuffe his sole heir.

ACT 4: Cleante asks Tartuffe to help Damis regain his father's love, but Tartuffe says that if Damis comes back, he will go. Cleante then accuses Tartuffe of exerting influence on Orgon in order to get Damis' inheritance. The maid Dorine tries to enlist Cleante's aid in helping Mariane get out of marrying Tartuffe, but Orgon enters with a marriage contract. After the family vainly begs Orgon not to insist on the marriage, Elmire develops a plan to expose Tartuffe. She decides that Orgon should hide in the room while she is alone with Tartuffe. As Orgon hides under the table, she warns him that he should not be shocked by her attempts to trap Tartuffe. When Tartuffe enters, Elmire expresses her passion for him.

Tartuffe says he will not believe her until he receives a "palpable assurance" of her favor. Elmire expresses concern that her husband might be around, but Tartuffe says, "Why worry about the man! Each day he grows more gullible; one can lead him by the nose." On hearing this, Orgon jumps out from under the table and confronts Tartuffe, who boldly replies that he now owns everything and that Orgon will have to leave. In desperation Orgon goes to find his strongbox.

ACT 5: Orgon tells Cleante that, among other things, he had a friend's libelous papers in the strongbox and he fears they are now in Tartuffe's possession. Orgon now laments that he was taken in by Tartuffe, but his mother still defends the hypocrite. M. Loyal, a bailiff, enters with an eviction notice ordering the family to leave the house, because everything now belongs to Tartuffe. At this point, the mother is finally convinced of Tartuffe's hypocrisy. Orgon expects to be arrested because of the libelous papers, but when Tartuffe and an officer enter, the officer arrests Tartuffe instead. The prince of the realm has realized the sham, invalidated the deed, and pardoned Orgon. Orgon thanks the prince, and all ends happily as Orgon gives his blessing to Valere and Mariane's marriage.

usually has for victims. The idea of suffering and harm has been suspended, and we are free to enjoy the irony and incongruity of the situation.

The comic premise   The suspension of natural laws in comedy—together with the scissors effect of setting a ridiculous person in a normal world or a normal person in a ridiculous world—makes possible the development of a *comic premise.* The comic premise is an idea or concept which turns the accepted notion of things upside down and makes this inverted notion the basis of a play. As an example, in *Arms and the Man,* George Bernard Shaw gave a complete twist to the idea that the most important attributes in war are courage and honor. Shaw says that survival is more important and that the smart soldier leaves behind some of his ammunition in order to carry chocolate into battle—after all, if a soldier does not eat, he will not be around to fight. The comic playwright uses the comic premise as the foundation on which to build the entire play. It can provide thematic and structural unity for the play and can serve as the springboard from which comic dialogue, comic characters, and comic situations develop.

Aristophanes, the Greek satiric dramatist, was a master at developing a comic premise on which to build a play. There are times when he seems to know no bounds in creating ridiculous situations. In *The Clouds,* Aristophanes pictures Socrates as a man who can think only when perched in a basket suspended in the air. In *The Birds,* two ordinary men convince a chorus of birds to build a city between heaven and earth. The birds comply, calling the place Cloudcuckoo Land, and the two men sprout wings to join them. In another play, *Lysistrata,* Aristophanes has the women of Greece agree to go on a sex strike: they will not make love to their husbands until the husbands stop fighting and sign a peace treaty with their opponents.

The comic premise of *The Madwoman of Chaillot,* by Jean Giraudoux (1882–1944), is that a group of impractical madwomen—three in all—are smarter than hardheaded businessmen and bankers; as a corollary, Giraudoux develops a further premise that the fantasy world of the madwomen and their friends is more realistic than the workaday world of everyday life.

Techniques of Comedy

The suspension of natural laws and the establishment of a comic premise in comedy involve exaggeration and incongruity. In a way uniquely its own, comedy emphasizes the discrepancy between a norm and some aberration or excess. The contradictions of comedy arising from exaggeration and incongruity show up in several areas—in verbal humor, in characterization, and in comic situations.

Verbal humor   Verbal humor can be anything from a pun to the most sophisticated verbal discourse. A *pun*—the simplest form of wit—is a

The fun of farce.
In farce, serious matters often become hilarious because of the way they are treated. An example is the farce *Noises Off,* by the British playwright Michael Frayn. In this scene, note the exaggerated acting and the comic attitude conveyed by the performers.

humorous use of words with the same sound but different meanings. A man who says he is going to start a bakery if he can "raise the dough" is making a pun. Close to the pun is the *malaprop*—a word which sounds like the right word but actually is something quite different. The term comes from Mrs. Malaprop, a character in *The Rivals* by the English playwright Richard Brinsley Sheridan (1751–1816). Mrs. Malaprop wishes to impress everyone with her education and erudition but ends up doing just the opposite because she constantly misuses long words. As an example, she uses "supercilious" when she means "superficial," and she insists that her daughter is not "illegible" for marriage, meaning that her daughter is not "ineligible" for marriage.

Frequently a character who wishes to appear to be more learned than he or she really is uses the malaprop. In *Juno and the Paycock,* by Sean O'Casey (1880–1964), the chief character is Captain Boyle, a man always pronouncing the last word on any subject. Throughout the play he complains that the world is "in a state of chassis," using the word "chassis" when he means "chaos." The more pompous the speaker who uses the wrong word in this way, the more humorous the effect.

A man devoted to verbal humor, Oscar Wilde (1854–1900) often turned

Comedy of manners.
Verbal wit, plot complications, and sharply etched characters are hallmarks of high comedy, or comedy of manners. Historically, such plays have been concerned with the mores and the immorality of the upper classes. Typical of the genre is *The Way of the World* by William Congreve. In this scene, a lady is being deceived into thinking that a butler disguised as a nobleman, on the right, is in love with her. Note the costumes and wigs of the English upper class.

accepted values upside down in his epigrams. "I can resist anything except temptation," says one of his characters; and "A man cannot be too careful in the choice of his enemies," says another. Displays of verbal virtuosity are hallmarks of comedy from various periods: English *Restoration comedy* of the late seventeenth century such as *The Country Wife,* by William Wycherley (1640–1716), and *The Way of the World,* by William Congreve; *comedies of manners* of the eighteenth century in England such as *She Stoops to Conquer,* by Oliver Goldsmith (1730–1774), and *The Rivals,* by Richard Brinsley Sheridan; and, more recently, George Bernard Shaw's plays. Modern French playwrights like Anouilh and Giraudoux also use verbal wit extensively in their plays.

Comedy of character   In comedy of character the discrepancy or incongruity lies in the way characters see themselves or pretend to be, as opposed to the way they actually are. A good example is a person who pretends to be a doctor—using obscure medicines, hypodermic needles, and Latin jargon—but who is actually a fake; such a person is the chief character in Molière's *The Doctor in Spite of Himself.* Another example of incongruity of character is Molière's *The Would-Be Gentleman,* in which the title character, Monsieur Jourdain, a man of wealth, but without refinement, is determined to learn courtly behavior. He hires a fencing master, a dancing master, and a teacher of literature (the last tells him, to his great delight, that he has been speaking prose all his life). In every case Jourdain is made a fool of: he dances and fences awkwardly and even gets involved in a ridiculous courtship with a noblewoman. All along he is blind to what a ridiculous figure he makes, until the end, when his follies and pretenses are exposed. Comedy of character is a basic ingredient of Italian *commedia dell'arte* and all forms of comedy where stock characters, stereotypes, and characters with dominant traits are emphasized.

Plot complications   Still another way in which the contradictory or the ludicrous manifests itself in comedy is in plot complications, including coincidences and mistaken identity. A time-honored comic plot is Shakespeare's *The Comedy of Errors,* based on *The Menaechmi,* a play of the late third century B.C. by the Roman writer Titus Maccius Plautus (ca. 254–184 B.C.). *The Comedy of Errors* in turn was the basis of a successful American musical comedy, *The Boys from Syracuse,* with songs by Richard Rodgers (1902–1979) and Lorenz Hart (1895–1943).

In *The Comedy of Errors,* identical twins and their identical twin servants were separated when young, with one master and servant growing up in Syracuse and the other growing up in Ephesus. As the play opens, however, both sets of masters and servants—unknown to one another—are in Ephesus. The wife and mistress of one master, as well as a host of others, mistake the second master and his servant for their counterparts in a series of comic encounters (with people making romantic advances to the wrong person, etc.) leading to ever-increasing confusion, until all four principals appear on stage at one time to clear up the situation.

A classic scene of plot complication occurs in Sheridan's *The School for Scandal,* written in 1777. Surface, the main character in the play, is thought to be an upstanding man but is really a charlatan, whereas Charles, his brother, is mistakenly considered a reprobate. In the scene called the "screen scene," the popular images are reversed and the truth comes out. As the scene opens, Lady Teazle, a married woman, is visiting Surface secretly. When her husband, Sir Peter Teazle, unexpectedly appears, she quickly hides behind a floor screen, but shortly after Sir Peter's arrival, Surface's brother Charles turns up as well, and in order not to be seen by Charles, Sir Peter starts for the screen. Sir Peter notices a woman's skirts behind the screen, but before he can discover it is his wife, Surface sends him into a closet. Once Charles enters the room, he learns that Sir Peter is in the closet and flings it open. As if this discovery were not enough, he also throws down the screen and in one climactic moment reveals both the infidelity of Lady Teazle and the treachery of Surface. The double, even

In farce, everything happens at once.

Plot complications are at the heart of bedroom farce, which was carried to a high art by the French dramatist Feydeau. In this scene from *A Flea in Her Ear*, discoveries, intrigues, and disasters are occurring on several fronts simultaneously. This was a Hilberry Theatre Repertory Company production, directed by Richard Spear, designed by William Rowe, with costumes by Stephanie Schoelzel and lights by Gary M. Witt.

triple, comic effect is due to the coincidence of the wrong people being in the wrong place at the wrong time.

A master of the device of characters hiding in closets and under beds was Georges Feydeau (1862–1921), a French dramatist who wrote over sixty farces in his lifetime. Variations of this form—complications and revelations arising from coincidences and mistaken identity—are found in plays from Roman times to the present; and this device, along with verbal wit and exaggerated characters, has been used as a major weapon of the comic dramatist.

Forms of Comedy

Comedy takes various forms, depending on the dramatist's intent and on the comic techniques emphasized.

Most plays discussed in the section on plot complications are *farces*. Farce has no intellectual pretensions but aims rather at entertainment and

A 1930s farce.
A number of modern farces were written in the United States in the 1920s and 1930s. A good example is *Room Service*, by John Murray and Allen Boretz. Shown here peering from a closet into a hotel room are, top to bottom, Danny Sewell, Richard Howard, Ken Ruta, Seth Allen, and Warren Pincus.

provoking laughter. In addition to excessive plot complications, its humor results from ridiculous situations and strong physical humor, such as pratfalls and horseplay. It relies less on verbal wit than the more intellectual forms of comedy do. Mock violence, rapid movement, and accelerating pace are hallmarks of farce. Marriage and sex are the objects of fun in *bedroom farce;* but medicine, law, and business can also be the subject matter.

Burlesque also relies on knockabout, physical humor, as well as gross exaggerations and occasionally vulgarity. Historically, burlesque was a ludicrous imitation of other forms of drama or of an individual play. A modern musical like *The Boy Friend* is a burlesque of the boy-meets-girl musicals popular earlier in the twentieth century. In the United States, the term *burlesque* has come to describe a type of variety show featuring low comedy skits and attractive women.

A form related to traditional burlesque, but with more intellectual and moral content, is *satire.* Satire employs wit, irony, and exaggeration to attack or expose evil and foolishness. Satire can attack one figure, as *Macbird* attacked the late President Lyndon Johnson; or it can be more inclusive, as in the case of Molière's *Tartuffe,* which ridicules religious hypocrisy generally. Satire that attacks an entire society is an exception to the notion (discussed above) that comedy usually exposes individuals who are foolish and excessive rather than criticizes society.

Comedy of manners is concerned with pointing up the foibles and peculiarities of the upper classes. Against a cultivated, sophisticated background, it uses verbal wit to depict the charm and expose the social pretensions of its characters. Rather than horseplay, witty phrases and clever barbs are at a premium in the comedy of manners. In England a line of comedies of manners runs from Wycherley, Congreve, and Goldsmith in the seventeenth and eighteenth centuries to Oscar Wilde in the nineteenth century and Noël Coward (1899–1973) in the twentieth.

Many plays of George Bernard Shaw could be put under a special heading, *comedy of ideas,* for Shaw used comic techniques to debate intellectual propositions and further his own moral and social viewpoint.

In all its forms, comedy remains a way of looking at the world in which basic values are asserted but natural laws are suspended in order to underline the follies and foolishness of men and women—sometimes with a rueful look, sometimes with a wry smile, and sometimes with an uproarious laugh.

TRAGICOMEDY

What Is Tragicomedy?

Comedy is usually set in juxtaposition to tragedy or serious drama: serious drama is sad, comedy is funny; serious drama makes people cry, comedy makes them laugh; serious drama arouses anger, comedy causes a smile.

True, the comic view of life differs from the serious, but the two are not always as clearly separated as this polarity suggests. As we saw earlier, many comic dramatists are serious people; "I laugh to keep from crying" applies to many comic writers as well as to certain clowns and comedians. A great deal of serious drama has comic elements in it. Shakespeare, for instance, employed comic characters in several of his serious plays. The drunken porter in *Macbeth*, the gravedigger in *Hamlet*, and Falstaff in *Henry IV, Part 1* are examples.

In medieval plays, comic scenes are interpolated in the basically religious subject matter. In a play about Noah and the ark, Noah and his wife argue like a bickering couple on television, with Mrs. Noah refusing to go aboard the ark with all those animals. Finally, when the flood comes, she relents, but only after she has firmly established herself as a shrewish, independent wife. One of the best known of all medieval plays, *The Second Shepherds' Play*, concerns the visit of the shepherds to the manger of the newborn Christ child. While they stop in a field to spend the night, Mak, a comic character, steals a sheep and takes it to his house, where he and his wife put it in a crib, pretending that it is their baby (a parody of Christ lying in the manger). When the shepherds discover what Mak has done, they toss him in a blanket, and after this horseplay the serious part of the story resumes.

The alternation of serious and comic elements is a practice of long standing, particularly in episodic plays; but *tragicomedy* does not refer to plays which shift from serious to comic and back again. In such cases the plays are predominantly one or the other—comic or serious—and the change from one point of view to the other is clearly delineated. In tragicomedy the point of view is itself mixed—the overview, or the prevailing attitude, is a synthesis or fusion of the serious and the comic. It is a view in which one eye looks with a comic lens and the other with a serious lens; and the two points of view are so intermingled as to be one, like food which tastes sweet and sour at the same time.

In addition to his basically serious plays and his basically comic ones, Shakespeare wrote three plays which seem to be a combination of tragedy and comedy: *Measure for Measure, All's Well That Ends Well,* and *Troilus and Cressida*. Because they do not fit neatly into one category or the other, these plays have proved troublesome to critics—so troublesome that they have been officially dubbed *problem plays*. The "problem," however, arises largely because of the difficulty in accepting the tragicomic point of view, for these plays have many of the attributes of the fusion of the tragic and the comic. In all three, there is a sense of comedy pervading the play, the idea that all will end well and that much of what happens is ludicrous or ridiculous; at the same time, the serious effects of a character's actions are not dismissed. Unlike true comedy, in which the fall on the sidewalk or the temporary threat of danger has no serious consequences, the actions in these plays appear quite serious. And so we have tragicomedy. In *Measure for Measure*, for instance, a man named Angelo—a puritanical, austere creature—condemns young Claudio to death for having made his fiancée pregnant. When Claudio's sister, Isabella, comes to plead for her brother, Angelo is overcome by passion and tries to make the lady his mistress. Angelo's sentencing of Claudio is deadly serious, but the bitter irony, which arises when he proves to be guilty of even worse "sins of the flesh" than Claudio, is comic. The result is that we have tragic and comic situations simultaneously.

Modern Tragicomedy

It is in the modern period—during the last hundred years or so—that tragicomedy has become a predominant form, the primary approach, in fact, of many of the best playwrights of our day. As suggested before, these writers are not creating in a vacuum; they are part of the world in which they live, and ours is an age which has adopted a tragicomic viewpoint more extensively than most previous ages. As if to keynote this attitude and set the tone, the Danish philosopher Søren Kierkegaard made the following statement in 1842: "Existence itself, the act of existence, is a striving and is both pathetic and comic in the same degree." The plays of Anton Chekhov,

A tragicomic scene from
The Cherry Orchard.
In Chekhov's play about life in Russia at the turn of the century, a student, played by Stephen Keep, has a serious confrontation with Madame Akardina (Kim Stanley). Only moments later the seriousness evaporates as the student falls down a flight of steps.

written at the end of the nineteenth century, reflect the spirit described by Kierkegaard. Chekhov labeled two of his major plays comedies; but Stanislavski, who directed them, called them tragedies, an indication of the confusion arising from Chekhov's mixture of the serious and the comic.

As an illustration of Chekhov's approach, there is a scene in the third act of *The Cherry Orchard,* written in 1904, in which Madame Renevsky, the owner of the orchard, talks to an intense young graduate student about love and truth. She tells him that people should be charitable and understanding of those in love; no one is perfect and truth is not absolute, she argues. The student, however, insists that reason is all and that feelings must be put aside. She retorts that he is motivated not by purity but by "simple prudery." He is not above love, as he claims, but is actually avoiding it, and she insists that he should have a mistress at his age. He is incensed. Declaring that he cannot listen to such talk, he runs offstage. The stage directions say that a moment later he is heard falling down a flight of stairs. A crash is heard, women scream, and then, after a pause, they laugh. The women scream because they fear he is hurt—not the spirit of comedy—but once they learn he is all right, they laugh, realizing that the fall of this pompous lad is extremely comic. Here we have the perfect blend: a part of the scene is deadly serious; another part, genuinely comic.

A comparable, and even more significant, scene occurs at the end of the third act of Chekhov's *Uncle Vanya,* first produced in 1899. Vanya and his niece, Sonya, have worked and sacrificed for years to keep an estate going to support her father, a professor. At the worst possible moment, just when Vanya and Sonya have both been rebuffed by people they love, the professor announces that he wants to sell the estate, leaving Vanya and Sonya with nothing. Sonya explains how cruel and thoughtless this is, and a few moments later Vanya comes in to shoot the professor. He waves his gun in the air like a madman and shoots twice, but misses both times, and then collapses on the floor. In this scene, Vanya and Sonya are condemned to a lifetime of drudgery and despair—a serious fate—but Vanya's behavior with the gun (there is doubt that he honestly means to kill the professor) is wildly comic. Once again, the serious and comic elements are inextricably bound together.

Sean O'Casey, an Irish playwright, wrote plays with a similar outlook. In his *Juno and the Paycock,* mentioned above, Captain Boyle and his friend Joxer are complete comic figures, bragging about imaginary exploits, pretending bravery where none exists, and promising to go to work with no real intention of doing so. During the play, Boyle thinks he has received an inheritance and begins spending money with abandon, only to find it is a hoax. Other misfortunes strike: his daughter is abandoned by her fiancé, his son is dragged away to be shot as a traitor to the Irish cause, and the family is destitute. But since Boyle has never made provisions for his family or taken the problems of life seriously, he is of no help in this crisis. Instead, he comes in at the end of the play with his buddy, Joxer, drinking and carrying

The Cherry Orchard (1904)

ANTON CHEKHOV (1860–1904)

CHIEF CHARACTERS:

Lyubov Andreyevna—owner of the estate
Anya—her daughter, 17 years old
Varya—her adopted daughter, 24 years old
Gaev—her brother
Lopahin—a merchant
Trofimov—a student
Charlotta—a governess
Firs—an old servant
Yasha—a young servant

ACT I: Lyubov Andreyevna, owner of an ancestral estate in Russia, returns from a self-imposed exile in Paris to seek peace in her girlhood home. She is accompanied by her daughter, Anya, age seventeen, who had gone to Paris to make the return trip with her mother, and her brother, Gaev, an ineffectual aristocrat whose chief interests are playing billiards and eating caramels. Madame Lyubov's estate, with its famous cherry orchard, is heavily mortgaged and is about to be foreclosed, leaving the family virtually penniless. Lyubov, absent since the death of her husband seven years ago, laments her past. Among those who have come to greet her is Lopahin, a merchant who recalls Lyubov as a splendid, kind-hearted woman who befriended him when he was a peasant child. Lopahin's father had been a serf on the estate.

Varya, Lyubov's adopted daughter, is the housekeeper of the estate. Anya tells Varya that her mother simply cannot understand the change in their fortunes. Although they had only enough money for the trip from Paris, Lyubov brought her young valet, Yasha, with her, and insisted upon the most expensive meals for the party, which included Charlotta, Anya's governess. The merchant, Lopahin, is supposed to marry Varya, but Varya tells Anya that Lopahin still has failed to propose to her, despite a neighborhood assumption that they are to marry.

ACT II: In a meadow near an old chapel not far from the house. Lopahin tells Madame Lyubov that he will always be grateful to her for her kindness to him when his father and grandfather were serfs of her family. He tells her that she can avert the forced sale of the estate, set for August, if she will raze the house and cherry orchard and develop the land for summer villas. He offers a loan to help, but Lyubov and Gaev cannot bear the thought of destroying the beautiful old orchard. Trofimov, a student, makes a speech about the lazy intelligensia of Russia and says that they should work. He, however, does not work himself.

Later, Lopahin persists, but Lyubov chatters of a telegram from her lover, demanding that she return to Paris; she talks of summoning an orchestra for a dance some evening and laments the drabness of the peasants' lives. She promptly discourages Gaev's plan to work in a bank. In other words, she does nothing to save the estate. Although the servants and the family have only soup to eat, she gives a beggar a gold piece and calls for another loan from Lopahin.

ACT III: It is an evening in August in the drawing room of the house. Lyubov has engaged an orchestra for a dance, although it is the evening of the sale of the estate. Her daughter Varya comforts her with the assurance that Gaev, who has attended the sale, probably has bought the estate with money to be sent by a wealthy great-aunt, but Lyubov knows that the sum is not enough. She tells Trofimov, a penniless student who has won the heart of Anya, that she cannot conceive of life without the house and orchard. Madame Lyubov also tells Trofimov that he should experience more of life, perhaps even have a mistress. He angrily stamps out of the room. Gaev and Lopahin, the latter giddy with joy, return. Lyubov demands to know at once if the home is lost. Lopahin cries: "I have bought it! . . .Now the cherry orchard's mine! Mine! . . .I have bought the estate where my father and grandfather were slaves." Lyubov sits down, crushed and weeping.

ACT IV: The scene is the same as Act I, the nursery. The nursery is now stripped bare and the time for leave-taking has come. Lyubov, her face pale and quivering, has given her purse to the peasants. Gaev is to work in a bank; Lyubov is going to Paris to live as long as possible on the money sent by the great-aunt; Varya, still waiting in vain for Lopahin's proposal, is to be a housekeeper in a distant town; Anya is to remain in school while Trofimov, her betrothed, completes his studies in Moscow. Lopahin has brought a bottle of champagne, but only Yasha drinks. An ax is heard in the distance, and Anya pleads for the workers chopping down the cherry trees to wait until Madame Lyubov has gone. Lyubov, gallantly courageous now, says her farewells and speaks of only two cares: the health of the old butler Firs and the future of her daughter Varya. She is assured that Firs has been sent to the hospital, and is promised by Lopahin that he will marry Varya; but Lopahin is left alone with Varya, and again he fails to propose to the weeping girl.

Everyone leaves. Lyubov and Gaev, the last to go, wait until they are alone and fall into each other's arms in smothered sobs, afraid of being overheard. Lyubov weeps: "Oh, my orchard!—my sweet, beautiful orchard! My life, my youth, my happiness, good-bye! Good-bye!" They leave, and the ancient servant Firs, who has not been sent to a hospital and is deathly ill, totters in and lies down on a sofa; he has been left behind. A sound like that of a breaking harp string is heard, dying away mournfully. Then there is only the sound of the ax cutting down the trees of the cherry orchard.

Tragicomedy:
Funny and sad at the same time.
Richard Riehl and Traber Burns play Captain Boyle and his friend Joxer in Sean O'Casey's tragicomedy *Juno and the Paycock*. These characters are comic but also pathetic because their lack of responsibility brings about great misery for others.

on just as they did earlier in the play—but it is not funny now. Their jokes ring hollow and serve only to underline the sadness of what has occurred.

About a century after Kierkegaard wrote about the pathetic and the comic, the French philosopher and writer Albert Camus (1915–1960) described the "divorce between man and his life, the actor and his setting," and "the feeling of Absurdity." Many plays in the category of *theater of the absurd,* whose name came from this notion, are tragicomic. They probe deeply into human problems and cast a dark eye on the world, and yet they are also imbued with a comic spirit, containing juggling, acrobatics, clowning, and verbal nonsense, among other traditional manifestations of humor.

Samuel Beckett has given us one of the finest expressions of human loneliness and futility ever written, in *Waiting for Godot*. There is nothing bleaker or more desolate than two tramps waiting on a barren plain every night for a supreme being called Godot, who they think will come but never does. But they themselves are comic. They wear the baggy pants of burlesque comedians, and they engage in any number of vaudeville routines, including one in which they grab each other's hats in an exchange where the confusion becomes increasingly compounded.

The plays of Harold Pinter (1930–   ) another writer associated with the theater of the absurd, have been called *comedies of menace,* a phrase indicating the idea of a theater simultaneously terrifying and entertaining.

Eugene Ionesco's plays afford a third example. In *The Lesson,* a professor victimizes a young woman pupil. The play contains a great deal of nonsense about words and their meanings, with elements of slapstick as well; but in the end, the professor, with an authoritarian fanaticism, plunges a knife into the pupil, making it a macabre farce, humorous but thoroughly unsettling.

Not only Beckett, Pinter, and Ionesco, but Jean Genet, (1910–   ), Arthur

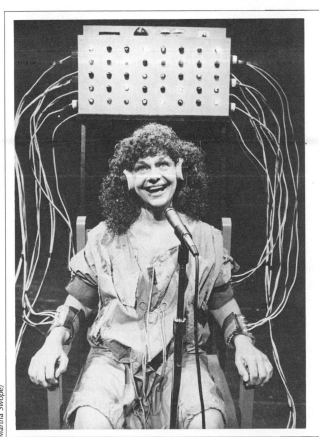

Political farce.
Some forms of tragicomedy are didactic—that is, intended to teach a lesson. One type is satirical farce; a good example is *Orgasmo Adulto,* by the Italian playwrights Franca Rame and Dario Fo. *Orgasmo Adulto* is a series of short plays dealing with the political, social, and cultural repression of women. Shown here is Estelle Parsons as a woman suffering from the problems of modern technology.

Adamov (1908–1971), Fernando Arrabal (1932–), Edward Albee (1928–), Günter Grass (1927–)—all of whom are included in the theater of the absurd—have written plays in a similar vein. But there are other recent writers, too, not considered absurdists, who adopt the tragicomic attitude. *The Visit,* by Friedrich Duerrenmatt (1921–), a Swiss dramatist, is an example. A wealthy woman returns to her birthplace, a small village which is poverty-stricken. She offers money—a billion marks —to the town on the condition that the citizens murder a storekeeper in the village who wronged her when she was young. The townspeople express horror at the idea, but at the same time they begin buying expensive objects on credit, some buying from the man's own store. There is a comic quality to these scenes: the man's wife, for instance, shows up in a flashy fur coat. The conclusion, however, is not funny, for the man is eventually murdered by his greedy neighbors.

In tragicomedy, a smile is frequently cynical, chuckles may be tinged with a threat, and laughter is sometimes bitter. Whereas in the past the attitude which produced these combinations was the exception and not the rule, in our day it seems far more prevalent, not to say relevant. As a result, tragicomedy has taken its place as a major form alongside the more traditional approaches.

THE SIGNIFICANCE OF GENRE

The combination of forms in tragicomedy reminds us that individual plays rarely fall completely into one category. Some plays are pure examples of their form, but many have characteristics of two genres, and some include more than two. Frequently melodrama overlaps with tragedy or heroic drama. In tragicomedies, the serious and the humorous intersect; and within comedy, burlesque crosses into farce, and farce into satire.

In considering the major forms of theater, we end where we began, with the notion that we should never rush to pigeonhole or label a play. Genre can be an aid or guide telling us how to interpret and understand a play, but it should never be an end in itself. The struggle should be less to discover what genre a play belongs to than to understand it. The important lesson of genre is that in a worthwhile production, a world is created which reflects a definite point of view. For spectators, entering and living in the world is central to the theater experience.

Unlike certain arts in which point of view is established largely by a single device—the brushstrokes of the artist in painting, or the use of the camera in films—in theater, point of view results from a collaborative effort of many artists. The creation of a viewpoint in theater is the responsibility not only of the dramatist, who establishes it and incorporates it in the script, but of a director, designers, and performers who must add to, reinforce, and underline the dramatist's point of view. As an example, in a production of Molière's comedy *Tartuffe*, the designers must strike just the right note of exaggeration and comment in the costumes and the scenery. There should be wit as well as elegance in the lines of the costumes and in the shapes and forms of the scenery. The color of the lighting, as well as the colors of the costumes and scenery, should be warm and bright—except, of course, for Tartuffe's black clerical costume, which stands in somber contrast to everything else and emphasizes his hypocrisy. The performances, too, must capture the dead seriousness of Molière's words, but with an awareness of the underlying humor and comment the words imply. The actions of the performers should be exaggerated without being excessive, comic without being ludicrous. The total effect of script, performances, and visual effects will be a comic world, with undertones of seriousness.

If any segment of a production fails to maintain a consistent viewpoint, the result will be confusion on the part of the audience. If the scene design suggests comedy when the play is serious, or if a performer is too realistic in a nonrealistic play, the spectators will lose their sense of direction. It is the responsibility of every artist working on a production to understand and follow through on the intentions and perspective of the playwright and director. Like structure, point of view is not visible to the audience in the way that a piece of scenery is, but it is an essential element of theater. Without a point of view which permeates and informs a production, members of the audience have no compass to tell them where they are headed and no key to let them unlock the play's meaning. Whatever world we are introduced to in a theatrical production—a real world or a make-believe world, a despondent world or a carefree world—the point of view which produces it must color and illuminate everything on stage. It must cut across the production like a giant spotlight cutting across the stage, throwing on every object the same light and shadow.

In Part Two we have looked at the purpose a theater experience is intended to serve: to provide an escape from daily cares, to make us laugh, to make us think, to make us feel deeply. We have also examined the point of view—tragic, comic, tragicomic—that informs the experience. The person who initially gives a theater experience a point of view is the playwright. He or she incorporates in the script the language, the attitudes of the characters, and the chain of events that determine the nature of the play. The way the playwright develops structure and creates characters will be the subject of Part Three.

SUMMARY

1   Comedy takes a different approach from serious forms of drama. It sees the humor and incongruity in people and situations. Comic dramatists accept a social and moral order and suspend natural laws (the man who falls flat on his face but does not really hurt himself).

2   Comedy is developed by means of several techniques. *Verbal humor* turns words upside down and creates puns, malapropisms, and inversions of meaning. *Comedy of character* creates men and women who take extreme positions, make fools of themselves, or contradict themselves. *Plot complications* create mistaken identity, coincidences, and people who turn up unexpectedly in the wrong house or the wrong bedroom. There are also physical aspects to comedy: slapstick and horseplay.

3   From the foregoing, the dramatist fashions various kinds of comedy. Depending on the degree of exaggeration, a comedy can be *farce* or *comedy of manners;* the former, for instance, features strong physical humor, while the latter relies more on verbal wit. Depending on its intent, comedy can be designed to entertain, as with *farce* or *burlesque,* or to correct vices, in which case it becomes *satire.* Many of Shaw's plays represent *comedy of ideas.*

4   Serious and comic elements can be mixed in theater. Many tragedies have comic relief: humorous scenes and characters interspersed in serious material.

5   Authentic tragicomedy fuses, or synthesizes, two elements—one serious, the other comic. We laugh and cry at the same time. Plays by Chekhov, Beckett, Duerrenmatt, and writers of the theater of the absurd employ tragicomedy. Some commentators feel that it is the form most truly characteristic of our time.

6   Many plays have elements of more than one genre; therefore genre should not be overstressed. It is a guide or an aid to understanding a theater experience.

7   Ideally, a clear point of view should inform and permeate every aspect of a theatrical production. It should create in each play a world which the spectators can enter and inhabit. Point of view tells the audience how to approach what they are seeing and how to assess its meaning.

PART 3

THE PLAYWRIGHT: DRAMATIC STRUCTURE AND DRAMATIC CHARACTERS

Ghosts: Strong characters and a powerful structure.

Along with the story, the playwright develops a structure and creates dramatic characters. A good example is *Ghosts*, by Henrik Ibsen, shown on the following pages in a drawing by Al Hirschfeld. The play has a climactic structure and is filled with vivid characters, such as Mrs. Alving on the right, played by Liv Ullmann; her son, played by Kevin Spacey, in the center; and Pastor Manders, played by John Neville. The work of the playwright in creating structure and characters will be the subject of the four chapters in Part Three.

7
CONVENTIONS OF DRAMATIC STRUCTURE

A character caught in a conflict.
In *Cat on a Hot Tin Roof* by Tennessee Williams, the heroine, Maggie, is in conflict with her husband Brick and also with her in-laws. The antagonism between Maggie, portrayed here by Elizabeth Ashley, and others is an important part of the play's structure.

In theater, the person who provides the blueprint for a production—the words, the mood, the tone, the sequence of events—is the playwright. The first task of the playwright is to *dramatize* the story, to transform it into action and conversation which is called *dialogue,* since ultimately everything on stage must be acted or spoken by a performer. In addition, the playwright conceives of the situation, constructs the plot, creates the characters, and determines how realistic or nonrealistic the play will be. In short, he or she provides the vision that guides the production.

There are instances in theatrical production where a collective group of performers develops a theatrical piece through improvisations. This was the case with organizations such as the Living Theater and the Open Theater in the late 1960s and early 1970s. There have also been cases where a director has determined what appears on stage. Avant-garde directors like Robert Wilson and Richard Foreman are good examples. This does not mean, however, that the function of the playwright can be dispensed with; it simply means that in the cases cited, the playwrighting function has been taken over by performers or a director. The indispensable role of the playwright remains.

In this chapter and in Chapters 8, 9, and 10, we will be examining the work of the playwright in developing dramatic structure and creating dramatic characters.

ESSENTIALS OF DRAMATIC STRUCTURE

The Subject and Verb of Drama

The subject of theater is always people—their hopes, their joys, their foibles, their fears. In other words, if we were to construct a grammar of theater, the *subject* would be people, the dramatic characters that represent human concerns. Just as in grammar every subject needs a verb, so in theater dramatic characters need a verb—some form of action—to define them. A noun standing alone can mean many things, or it can mean very little. By itself, a word like *telephone* or *box* or *toothbrush* has a limited meaning. When we add a verb, however, we know a great deal more: the telephone *rang* or *fell off the table,* or *went dead.* With people even more than with objects, a verb is necessary to tell us who they are and what they are about. We do not get to know people by seeing them in a tableau or still-life picture; we get to know them from what they do and say.

The words *to act* and *to perform* are used in theater to denote the impersonation of a character by an actor or an actress, but the words also mean "to do something," "to be active." Professor Alvin B. Kernan has pointed out that the word *drama* derives from a Greek root, the verb *dran,* meaning "to do" or "to act."[1] At its heart, theater involves action. Characters in plays "act" or "do something"; they do not stand on stage like statues.

Conflict

One theory of history maintains that the growth and well-being of a civilization lie in its ability to respond successfully to environmental and human challenges. Without speculating on the accuracy of this as a theory of history, we can say that *people* often define themselves by the way they handle challenge and response. If they cannot face up to a challenge, it tells us one thing; if they meet it with dignity, even though defeated, it tells us another; if they triumph, it tells us something else. It is the same in our own lives. We get to know the members of our family, our friends, and our enemies by being with them over a period of time. We see how they respond to us and to other people; we see how they meet crises in their own lives and in ours.

In life this process can take years—in fact, it continues to unfold for as long as we know a person. But in the theater we have only a few hours. The playwright, therefore, must devise means by which the characters will face challenges and be tested in a short space of time. The American playwright Arthur Miller named one of his plays *The Crucible.* Literally, a *crucible* is a vessel in which metal is tested by being exposed to extreme heat. Figuratively, a crucible has come to stand for any severe test of human worth and endurance—a trial by fire. In a sense, every play provides a crucible: a test devised by the playwright to show how the characters behave under conditions of stress. Through this test the meaning of the play is brought out.

The crucible of a play can vary enormously: it might be a fight for a kingdom, or in modern terms a fight for "turf," but it can just as easily be a fight over a person. It can be an intellectual or moral confrontation. There may be no overt clash at all, as in Samuel Beckett's *Waiting for Godot;* but there must be tension of some sort. In *Waiting for Godot,* for instance, there are several sources of tension or conflict: the ever-present question whether the mysterious Godot will come or not; the friction between the two main characters, who get on one another's nerves but desperately need each other; the unfolding revelation of men deluding themselves, over and over again; and on top of these, a constant probing of religious and philosophical ideas in a series of questions posed by Beckett.

A play might even consist of a series of apparently disconnected events, which rub against one another, producing a jarring effect and challenging the spectator to make his or her own pattern out of the events.

Though the conflict or tension in drama may take a number of forms, its presence is essential. Every play must have "kinetic energy," a "magnetic field," a "flow of electrical current"—use whatever figure of speech you choose. This is the only way we come to know dramatic characters, to experience a play, and ultimately to absorb its meaning.

Plot versus Story

Traditionally, the most widely employed means of providing the dynamics of theater has been the dramatization of a story: a character or a group of characters move through a series of episodes seeking goals, facing obstacles, and making choices. Stories, being narrative accounts of what people do, are as old as the human race: they form the substance of daily conversation, of newspapers and television, of novels and films. However, every medium presents a story in a different form.

In theater, the story must be presented by living actors and actresses on a stage in a limited period of time, and this requires selectivity. In presenting a play about Abraham Lincoln, for example, the playwright must make choices. Does the dramatist include scenes in Springfield, Illinois, where Lincoln served as a lawyer and held his famous debates with Stephen A. Douglas? Or does everything take place in Washington after Lincoln became president? Are there scenes with Lincoln's wife, Mary Todd, or only with government and military officials?

The selection and order of scenes in a play is the *plot*. It is important to remember that plot differs from story. A *story* is a full account of an event, or series of events, usually told in chronological order. The story of Abraham Lincoln begins with his being born in a log cabin and continues to the day he was shot at Ford's Theater in Washington. *Plot,* as opposed to story, is a selection and arrangement of scenes taken from a story for presentation on the stage. Plot is what actually happens on stage and the *way* it is made to happen. The plot of a play about Abraham Lincoln and his wife, Mary Todd, would include scenes and characters related primarily to their lives. The plot of a play about the Lincoln-Douglas debates would include scenes relating chiefly to that subject.

Even when a story is fictional, its plot is more restricted and structured than the imaginary story. A good example is Henrik Ibsen's *Ghosts* (which will be discussed in Chapter 8). In such a story, invented by the playwright, the characters and scenes must still be selected and the sequence determined.

Plot is the responsibility of the playwright; he or she decides at what point in the story the plot will begin, what characters will participate, what scenes will be included, and in what sequence they will occur.

Plot complications in *Ghosts*.

In traditional plot structure a series of problems confronting the characters prolongs the action and increases tension. In Ibsen's *Ghosts*, the mother, shown here on the left, thinks that things will work out for her and her son; but during the course of the play her plans are upset when the son falls in love with his half-sister. Then, a terrible fire occurs and the son goes blind. In the scene here, the actress Liv Ullmann plays the mother and Kevin Spacey the son.

Significance of Structure

Every work of art has some kind of *structure*. Whether it is loosely connected or tightly knit is not important; what is important is that a framework exists. There is a loose analogy or parallel between the structure of a play and that of a building. An architect and an engineer are like a playwright and a director. The architect and engineer plan a skeleton or substructure which will provide the inner strength for the building. They determine the depth of the foundation, the weight of the support beams, and the stress on the side walls. In a similar fashion the playwright and director establish a premise for the play which serves as its foundation; they introduce various stresses and strains in the form of conflicts; they establish boundaries and outer limits to contain the play; they calculate the dynamics of the action. In short, they "construct" a play.

Buildings vary enormously in size and shape: they can be as diverse as a skyscraper, a cathedral, and a small cottage. Buildings can come in clusters, such as the homes in a suburban development or the buildings on a college campus. And engineering requirements will vary according to the needs of individual structures: a gymnasium roof must span a vast open area, and this calls for a different construction from that of a sixty-story skyscraper. These in turn call for something different from a ski lodge on the side of a mountain. Plays, too, vary; they can be tightly constructed or loosely arranged. The important point is that each play, like each piece of architecture, has its own internal laws, its own framework, which give it its shape, strength, and meaning. Without structure, a theater event falls apart, just as a building collapses which has been put together improperly.

Naturally, structure manifests itself differently in theater from the way it manifests itself in architecture. A play is not a building. It unfolds through time rather than occupying space. It evolves and develops like a living organism, and we become aware of its structure as we sense the underlying pattern and rhythm of the production. The repeated impulses of two characters in conflict or the tension which mounts as the pace quickens— these insinuate themselves into our subconsciousness like the throb of a silent drum beat. Moment by moment we see what is happening on stage; but below the surface we sense a substructure, giving the event meaning and purpose.

Underscoring the significance of structure are the problems that arise when it is not developed satisfactorily. Frequently we see a production in which most elements—the acting, the costumes, the scenery, the words, even the situation—appear correct. But somehow the play does not seem to progress; it becomes dull and repetitious. Or perhaps the play becomes confusing and diffuse, going off in several directions at once. When this happens, the chances are that the problems are structural. Either no clear structure existed to begin with, or the structure which did exist was violated along the way. This suggests two principles of dramatic structure: (1) every theatrical event must have an underlying pattern or organization, and (2) once the pattern or organization is established, it must be true to itself—it must be organic and have integrity. A plot in the climactic form which suddenly becomes episodic two-thirds of the way through the play will cause confusion. Conversely, a play cast in a random mold which suddenly takes on the rigid structure of a climactic drama becomes overly artificial and contrived.

Sometimes a basically acceptable pattern is repeated too often and becomes repetitious. *La Ronde,* by the Austrian playwright Arthur Schnitzler (1862–1931), is a clever theater piece in ten scenes, each of which is a seduction scene. As the play progresses, one person from a preceding scene is paired with a new partner in the next scene in a kind of "round dance." In spite of its originality, however, the play eventually is predictable because the action underlying each scene remains the same. Quite often, plays with a less obvious pattern than *La Ronde* have a similar problem: though the characters and events appear to change and develop, underneath they remain essentially the same.

Although sometimes less apparent than the performances of the actors and actresses or less obvious than the words and actions of the play, structure is no less important.

We saw earlier that for the audience theater is an experience of the imagination and that it involves particularly the encounter between spectators and performers. But no matter how stimulating a performance on stage might be, it is not a complete theater experience if it has no form or shape. Structure provides the necessary shape and form, the profile or contour into which the experience can fit.

CREATING A DRAMATIC STRUCTURE

In developing a dramatic structure for a play, the dramatist must keep a number of factors in mind; we now look at these. From the audience's point of view, dramatic structure begins with the opening scene of the play.

The Opening Scene

The formation of a play's structure begins with the first scene, which sets the tone and style of the play. It tells us whether we are going to see a serious play or a comic one, and whether the play will deal with affairs of everyday life or some fantasy. The opening scene is a cue or signal as to what lies ahead; it also sets the wheels of action in motion, giving the characters a shove and hurtling them toward their destination.

The playwright provides this initial shove by posing a problem to the characters, establishing an imbalance of forces or a disturbance in their equilibrium which compels the characters to respond. Generally this imbalance occurs just before the play begins or arises immediately after it opens. In *King Oedipus,* for example, a plague has hit the city just before the opening of the play. In *Hamlet,* "something is rotten in the state of Denmark" before the play opens; and early in the play the ghost of Hamlet's father appears to tell Hamlet that he must seek revenge. At the beginning of *Romeo and Juliet,* the Capulets and the Montagues are at one another's throats in a street fight. Strindberg's *Miss Julie* is set on midsummer's eve and opens with Miss Julie acting "wildly," obviously on the verge of some precipitous act. In the opening of *A Streetcar Named Desire,* Blanche DuBois arrives in the apartment of her sister and brother-in-law, where she is an unwanted guest.

As these examples suggest, the opening scene initiates the action. Characters are presented with a challenge and thrust into a situation which provides the starting point for the entire play.

Obstacles and Complications

Having met the initial challenge of the play, the characters then move through a series of steps alternating between achievement and defeat, between hope and despair. The moment they seem to accomplish one goal or reach a plateau of satisfaction, something cuts across the play to upset the balance and start them on another path. A series of hurdles or challenges is thrown up before them. In theater these are referred to as *obstacles* or *complications*. The former are impediments put in a character's way; the latter are outside forces, or new twists in the plot, introduced at an inopportune moment.

Shakespeare's *Hamlet* provides numerous examples of obstacles and complications. Hamlet stages a play-within-the-play in order to confirm that Claudius has killed his father. Once Claudius's reaction to the play makes it certain that he is guilty, Hamlet's way to revenge seems clear. But when Hamlet goes to kill Claudius, he discovers him at prayer. An obstacle has been thrown in Hamlet's path: if Claudius dies while praying, he may go to heaven rather than to hell. Since Hamlet does not wish Claudius to go to heaven, he does not kill him. Later, Hamlet is in his mother's bedroom when he hears a noise behind a curtain. Surely Claudius is lurking there, and Hamlet can kill him instantly. But when Hamlet puts his sword through the curtain, he finds that he has killed Polonius instead. This complicates matters because it provides Claudius with an excuse to send Hamlet to England with Rosencrantz and Guildenstern, whom Claudius has instructed to murder Hamlet. Hamlet gets out of that trap and returns to Denmark. Now, at last, he can carry out his revenge. But upon his return he discovers that Ophelia has killed herself while he was away, and her brother, Laertes, is seeking revenge on Hamlet. This complicates the situation once again; Hamlet is prevented from meeting Claudius head-on because he must also deal with Laertes. In the end Hamlet does carry out his mission, but only after many interruptions.

Dramatic characters have objectives or goals that they are strongly motivated to obtain. Macbeth wants to become king; Miss Julie wants to conquer the servant, Jean; Blanche DuBois wants to find a safe haven. But there are obstacles to achieving these goals, and other characters oppose the main characters' wishes and interfere with their plans. The result is inevitable tension and conflict.

Crisis and Climax

As a result of conflicts, obstacles, and complications in a play, characters become involved in a series of *crises*—some less complicated than those in *Hamlet,* some more complicated. A play in the traditional mode builds from one crisis to another. The first crisis will be resolved only to have the action lead to a subsequent crisis. The final and most significant crisis is referred to as the *climax*. Sometimes there is a minor climax earlier in the play and a major climax near the conclusion. In the final climax the issues of the play are resolved, either happily or in the case of tragedies usually with the death of the hero or heroine.

In facing the initial challenge, moving past obstacles and complications, and living through crises, the characters in a play provide members of the audience with an experience of their own. By identification or association, the audience lives through the adventures of the characters.

STRUCTURAL CONVENTIONS: THE RULES OF THE GAME

In order to ensure that the events on stage will be dynamic and that the characters will face a meaningful test, a series of conventions or "ground rules" have evolved in dramatic structure. A good analogy is the rules in sports, developed to ensure lively contests. There are several obvious similarities between theater and sports: many sports have a playing area similar to the stage, and spectators at a sporting event are comparable to the audience in a theater. More important, however, is the parallel in the events themselves. In sports the spectators want to see a strong, sustained contest. To achieve this end, each sport has a set of rules, designed to test to the maximum the ability and finesse of the participants. Theater is more varied and complex than most sports events, and its rules are not so clearly defined or consciously imposed. Nevertheless, there are similarities which point up the ways in which a play achieves maximum impact.

Limited Space

Most sports have a limited playing area. In some cases this consists of a confined space: a boxing ring, a basketball court, a baseball field. Invariably there is some kind of "out of bounds." The combatants cannot run away; they must stand there and face one another. The playing area is clearly defined, and both players and spectators know a fair ball from a foul.

Theater is, of course, usually limited to a stage; but there is also a limit within the play itself. The action of a play is generally confined to a "world" of its own—that is, to a fictional universe which contains all the characters and events of the play—and none of the characters or actions moves outside the orbit of that world. Sometimes the world of a play is restricted to a single room. In his play *No Exit,* Jean-Paul Sartre (1905–1980), a French existentialist, confines three characters to one room, from which, as the title suggests, there is no escape. The room is supposed to be Hell, and the three characters—a man, Garcin; and two women, Estelle and Inez—are confined there forever. Estelle loves Garcin, Garcin loves Inez, and Inez (a lesbian) loves Estelle. Each one, in short, loves the one who will not reciprocate; and by being confined to the one room, they face a form of permanent torture—in other words, a form of Hell.

The neoclassical writers in France, such as Jean Racine, a great tragic dramatist, set their plays in one room, generally the hall or vestibule of a palace. Writers like Ibsen and Strindberg frequently confined their plays to one room as well. Among modern plays, there are numerous instances in which the action takes place in a single room. Even plays that are not so closely contained usually occupy a restricted area. The action might take place in one castle and its environs, as in *Hamlet,* or in the general area of a battlefield, as in Bertolt Brecht's *Mother Courage.* But the sense of a private universe, with outer limits, is always there.

A Time Limit

Sporting events put some limit on the duration of action. In football and basketball, there is a definite time limit. In golf, there is a given number of holes; and in baseball or tennis, there is a limited number of innings or games. Theoretically, sports which are open-ended, such as baseball and tennis, can go on forever; but fans get impatient with this arrangement, as is indicated by the move in tennis in recent years to establish a "sudden death" or tie-breaker playoff when a set reaches six-all. A time or score limit ensures that the spectators can see a complete event; they can live through a total experience in miniature, with a clear winner and loser and no loose ends.

The notion of a time limit in theater can be looked at in two ways: first, as the length of time it takes a performance to be completed; second, as the time limit placed on the characters within the framework of the play itself. Let us look at each of these.

Most theatrical performances last anywhere from one to three hours. The longest theatrical productions about which we have records are medieval cycle plays. A series usually lasted several days; and one, at Valenciennes, France, in 1547, went on for twenty-five days. Generally, however, these presentations comprise a group of separate plays—one on Adam, another on Noah, a third on Abraham and Isaac, etc.—each one complete in itself, with the series strung together like beads on a chain.

In the ancient Greek drama festivals, plays were presented for several days in a row. On a single day there might be a trilogy of three connecting plays followed by a short comic play. Even if we count a Greek trilogy as one play, it lasted only the better part of a day. These examples are exceptions, though; most performances are limited to two or three hours.

More important than the actual playing time of a performance is the time limit or deadline which the characters within a play must face. Frequently one finds in a play a fixed period within which the characters must complete an action. At the end of the second act of Ibsen's *A Doll's House,* the heroine, Nora, is trying desperately to get her husband to put off until the following evening the opening of a letter which she fears will establish her as a forger and will threaten their marriage. When he agrees, Nora says to herself, "Thirty-one hours to live." In Thornton Wilder's *Our Town*, the young girl, Emily, is given one day to return to earth to relive her experiences.

Strongly Opposed Forces

Most sports involve two teams, or two individuals, opposing each other. This ensures clear lines of force: the good guys and the bad guys, the home team and the visitors. The contest is straight and simple, like a shoot-out on Main Street at high noon between the sheriff and the outlaw. (Imagine what a hockey game would be like if there were five teams playing in one game.) The musical *West Side Story* (which is based on *Romeo and Juliet*) features two opposing gangs, not unlike opposing teams in sports. In the simplest dramatic situations, one character directly opposes another—the *protagonist* against the *antagonist*.

(Martha Swope)

Opposing factions in *Romeo and Juliet*.
Traditional plot structure calls for strongly opposing forces in a play—the antagonist opposes the protagonist; one group opposes another. In the production shown here, the families of the Capulets and the Montagues oppose one another in Shakespeare's *Romeo and Juliet*.

CONVENTIONS OF DRAMATIC STRUCTURE

141

In a manual on playwrighting, the critic Kenneth MacGowan emphasized that "characters must be so selected and developed that they include people who are bound to react upon each other, bound to clash."[2] In the vast majority of dramas, playwrights have followed this approach. A perfect example of characters bound to clash are the man and woman, Julie and Jean, in Strindberg's *Miss Julie*. Julie, an aristocrat, is the daughter of the owner of an estate. She has had an unhappy engagement and is deeply suspicious of men but at the same time sexually attracted to them. Jean, an aggressive male, is a servant with dreams of escaping his life of servitude and becoming a hotel owner. These two, drawn together by strong forces of repulsion and attraction, meet on midsummer's eve in a climactic encounter.

A similar confrontation occurs in Tennessee Williams's *A Streetcar Named Desire* between Blanche DuBois and Stanley Kowalski. Stanley, crude and outspoken, is the person most inimical to Blanche, a faded southern belle trying desperately to hold on to her gentility. On his side, Stanley is insecure about his lack of education and refinement, and Blanche with her superior airs provokes him almost to the breaking point.

A Balance of Forces

Rules ensuring that the contest will be as equal as possible without coming to a dead draw are a feature of most sports. We all want our team to win, but we would rather see a close, exciting contest than a runaway; nothing is duller to a sports fan than a lopsided game. The struggle, as much as the outcome, is the source of pleasure. And so rules are set up, with handicaps or other devices to equalize the forces. In basketball or football, the moment one team scores, the other team gets the ball so that it will have an opportunity to even the score.

In theater, a hard-fought and relatively equal contest is implicit in what has been said about opposing forces: Jean stands opposite Miss Julie, and Blanche opposite Stanley. Even in the somewhat muted, low-key plays of Anton Chekhov, there is a balance of forces among various groups. In *The Cherry Orchard,* those who own the orchard are pitted against the man who will acquire it; in *The Three Sisters,* the sisters of the title are opposed in the possession of their home by their acquisitive sister-in-law.

A device frequently used by dramatists to guarantee friction or tension between forces is the restriction of characters to members of one family. Relatives have built-in rivalries and affinities: parents versus children, sisters versus brothers. Being members of the same family, they have no avenue of escape. Mythology, on which so much drama is based, abounds with familial relationships. The story of Agamemnon, the basis of a trilogy by the Greek playwright Aeschylus, is a good example. In simple outline, Agamemnon sacrifices his daughter Iphigenia, believing that the gods have ordered it. Later, when he returns home from the Trojan war, his wife, Clytemnestra, and her lover, Aegisthus, slay him to avenge the daughter's

(Martha Swope)

Members of a family in conflict. Drama frequently puts members of the same family in confrontation with one another. The family shown here is in Sam Shepard's *Buried Child;* the father (Richard Hamilton), on the left, is at odds with his wife (Mary Louise Wilson), in the center. The sons also oppose their parents as well as each other.

death. Following that, Clytemnestra's children, Electra and Orestes, murder their mother to avenge their father's death. Because family pride and honor run so strong, one member after another feels compelled to commit murder in a chain reaction of revenge.

Shakespeare frequently set members of one family against each other: Hamlet opposes his mother; Lear opposes his daughters; Jessica opposes her father, Shylock, in *The Merchant of Venice.* In modern drama, virtually every writer of note has dealt with close family situations: Ibsen, Strindberg, Chekhov, Williams, Miller, and Albee, to mention a few. The American dramatist Eugene O'Neill—who used the Agamemnon myth in his *Mourning Becomes Electra*—wrote what many consider his finest play, *Long Day's Journey into Night,* about the four members of his own family. A powerful play about a black family, *The River Niger* by Joseph Walker (1935–   ), concerns a son and his father, mother, fiancée, and old friends. In plays not directly involving families, the characters are usually in close proximity, fighting for the same turf, the same throne, the same woman or man.

Incentive or Motivation

In sports, to guarantee that the participants will give their best in an intense, hard-fought contest, a prize is offered. In professional sports it is money; in amateur sports, a cup. In addition, there is the glory of winning, the accolades of television and the press, and the plaudits of family and friends.

For its part, good drama never lacks incentive or motivation for its characters: Macbeth wishes desperately to be king; Antigone fights for her family's honor; St. Joan wishes to save France; and Blanche DuBois must find protection and preserve her dignity in order to survive.

DEVELOPING A PLOT

The playwright uses the tools we have examined—the initial imbalance of forces in a play, the motivations and goals of the characters, obstacles and complications, crisis and climax, and the conventions of dramatic construction—to develop a plot. In developing a dramatic plot, however, the playwright has something specific in mind. He or she wants to show us a special world, to portray an unusual character, to emphasize a particular point of view, to underscore a theme. In short, the playwright wants to provide a specific experience for the audience.

A playwright decides, for example, to focus on one character, as Edmond Rostand did in *Cyrano de Bergerac;* or on a group of characters, as Anton Chekhov did in such plays as *The Three Sisters* and *The Cherry Orchard.* A playwright can emphasize a particular character trait in one play and its opposite in another. This is what Henrik Ibsen often did. In his *Brand* the leading character is a stark, uncompromising figure who will sacrifice everything—family, friends, love—for his principles. "I am stern in my demands," Brand says. "I require all or nothing. No half-measures." On the other hand, Ibsen's Peer Gynt, from the play of the same name, is always compromising, always running away. In the dark forest Peer meets an unseen force called the Boyg, which advises him not to meet life directly. "Go roundabout, Peer," the voice says over and over again, advice which he follows throughout his life.

It is up to the playwright to determine how to interpret the characters or story, and in doing so he or she sometimes even changes the order of events. A good example is the way the three prominent tragic dramatists of Greece in the fifth century B.C. treated the Electra myth. The story, referred to above, concerns Electra's revenge on her mother, Clytemnestra, and her stepfather, Aegisthus, for having murdered her natural father, Agamemnon. In carrying out her revenge, Electra enlists the help of Orestes, her brother, who has just returned from exile. In the versions by Aeschylus and Euripides, the stepfather is murdered first, and the mother, Clytemnestra, murdered last. This puts emphasis on the terror of murdering one's own mother. But Sophocles saw the story differently. He wished to emphasize that Electra and her brother were acting honorably and to play down the mother's murder. And so he reversed the order of the murders and had the mother killed first, then built up to the righteous murder of the stepfather as the final deed. The change made by Sophocles indicates the latitude writers have in altering events to suit their artistic purposes. The manner in which a play unfolds is up to the playwright and is controlled by his or her individual approach.

Whatever the approach, however, playwrights make choices aimed at providing the maximum dramatic impact. A playwright selects the scenes, characters, words, and actions to engage the spectator, excite the imagination, and communicate a total experience. The goal is a plot which will be the ultimate crucible, or *verb*, for that particular play.

In this chapter we have been looking at the development of plot, which thrusts characters into action. So far we have examined general principles; when we look at dramatic construction more closely, we discover that certain forms have recurred throughout theater history. In Chapters 8 and 9, we will examine specific forms of dramatic structure.

SUMMARY

1 We learn about dramatic characters by what they do and say, just as we learn about people in everyday life.

2 The action of a play frequently consists of a test or crucible for the characters in which their true nature is defined.

3 The usual test for a character is being enmeshed in activities or events—a dramatic plot.

4 A dramatic plot is not the same as a story. A *story* is a complete account of an episode or sequence of events, but a *plot* is what we see on stage. In a plot the events have been selected from a story and arranged in a certain sequence.

5 A play generally begins with an imbalance of forces, or a loss of equilibrium by one of the characters; this propels the characters to action.

6 As a play progresses, the characters meet a series of complications as they attempt to fulfill their objectives or realize their goals. These encounters produce the tension and conflict of drama.

7 Dramatic conventions, ensuring a strong plot and continuation of tension, are analogous to rules in sports. In both sports and theater there are limited spaces or playing areas, time limits imposed on the action, strongly opposing forces, evenly matched contestants, and prizes or goals for the participants.

8 In developing a plot, the playwright uses the conventions and tools of dramatic construction to emphasize specific characters or other elements. The same story can be told in different ways, an example being the three different versions of the Electra myth as told by Aeschylus, Sophocles, and Euripides.

8

DRAMATIC STRUCTURE: CLIMACTIC AND EPISODIC

(Roundabout Theater—Martha Swope)

Climactic structure in *Miss Julie*.
Strindberg's play *Miss Julie* is an excellent example of a modern play written in the climactic form. The play has only three characters: Miss Julie, shown here on the left (played by Giulia Pagnano); the servant Jean, on the right (portrayed by Stephen Schnetzer); and a maid named Bertha. The play concerns one main action. Julie is the daughter of the owner of an estate in Sweden, but she is drawn to Jean, her father's valet. Jean, on the other hand, wants to improve his situation and sees Miss Julie as the means. Jean seduces Miss Julie, which leads to tragic consequences for them both, especially Miss Julie. Other characteristics of climactic structure are that it occurs in a limited space—in this case the kitchen of the estate—and that the play begins near the climax of the story.

Throughout theater history, whatever the country or period, we find basic dramatic forms reappearing. In western civilization, a form adopted in Greece in the fifth century B.C. emerges, somewhat altered, in France in the seventeenth century. The same form shows up once more, again with variations, in Norway in the late nineteenth century. This form, which will be discussed shortly, can be referred to as *climactic*. Another, contrasting form, best illustrated by the plays of Shakespeare, can be called *episodic*. One or the other of these forms—or some combination of the two—has been the predominant dramatic structure through most of the history of western theater. Another approach, in which dramatic episodes are strung together without any apparent connection, has emerged in a new guise in recent times. The absurdist approach is a more modern phenomenon. Finally, the structure based on a ritual or pattern is both old and new.

The characteristics of the basic types will be clearer when we look at each separately, and in its purest forms. This chapter begins with the climactic form and goes on to examine the episodic form; Chapter 9 takes up additional forms.

CHARACTERISTICS OF THE CLIMACTIC PLOT

The Plot Begins Late in the Story

The first hallmark of climactic drama is that the plot begins quite late in the story. Ibsen's *Ghosts,* written in 1881, affords a example. Before the play begins, the following has occurred: Mrs. Alving has married a dissolute husband who fathers an illegitimate child by another woman and contracts a venereal disease. Discovering this early in her marriage, she visits the family minister, Pastor Manders, to try to get out of the marriage. Though she is attracted to Manders and he to her, and though he realizes that she is wronged and miserable, he sends her back to her husband. She stays with her husband out of a Victorian sense of duty, sending her own son away to escape the father's influence. When her husband dies, Mrs. Alving builds an orphanage in his honor to camouflage his true character.

As is typical with a climactic plot structure, the play still has not begun; it begins later, when the son returns home and the facts of the past are unearthed, precipitating the crisis of the play. Thus, in climactic structure the play begins when all the roads of the past converge at one crucial intersection of the present—at the climax, in other words.

The fact that the plot begins so late in climactic drama has at least two consequences.

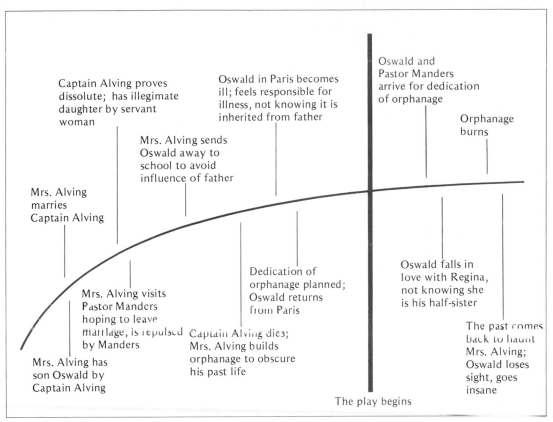

Captain Alving proves dissolute; has illegimate daughter by servant woman

Oswald in Paris becomes ill; feels responsible for illness, not knowing it is inherited from father

Oswald and Pastor Manders arrive for dedication of orphanage

Orphanage burns

Mrs. Alving sends Oswald away to school to avoid influence of father

Mrs. Alving marries Captain Alving

Mrs. Alving visits Pastor Manders hoping to leave marriage, is repulsed by Manders

Dedication of orphanage planned; Oswald returns from Paris

Oswald falls in love with Regina, not knowing she is his half-sister

Mrs. Alving has son Oswald by Captain Alving

Captain Alving dies; Mrs. Alving builds orphanage to obscure his past life

The past comes back to haunt Mrs. Alving; Oswald loses sight, goes insane

The play begins

Climactic structure in *Ghosts*.
Henrik Ibsen's play follows the climactic form, in which the play begins toward the very end—or climax—of the sequence of events. The parts of the story that occur before the play begins are to the left of the vertical line. Only the events to the right occur in the play; the ones before them must be described in exposition.

First, it is frequently necessary to explain what has gone before by having one character report the information to another. The technical term for this revelation of background information is *exposition*.

Second, the time span in a climactic play is usually brief. The action of Racine's plays, for example, takes place in a few hours. At the most, events in a climactic play cover a few days. Some playwrights, attempting to push events as near the climax as possible, have stage time (the time we imagine is passing when we are watching a play) coincide with real time (that is, clock time). An example is Tennessee Williams's *Cat on a Hot Tin Roof:* the events depicted in the story last the same 2½ hours as the play itself.

Ghosts (1881)

HENRIK IBSEN (1828–1906)

CHIEF CHARACTERS:

Mrs. Alving—a widow
Oswald Alving—her son, an artist
Manders—a pastor
Engstrand—a carpenter
Regina Engstrand—his daughter, Mrs. Alving's
maid

SETTING: The sitting room of Mrs. Alving's
house on a large fjord in western Norway.

TIME: The late nineteenth century.

BACKGROUND: Mr. Alving, a prominent
local businessman, was also a womanizer.
Because of this Mrs. Alving left him once and
went to seek advice from Pastor Manders; but
she was persuaded by Pastor Manders to return
to her "duty." She returned to Mr. Alving.
Although Mr. Alving did not change, Mrs.
Alving covered up for him. Their son Oswald
was sent away to school by Mrs. Alving so that
he would not be under his father's influence.
The maid, Regina, is Mr. Alving's daughter
from a union with Mrs. Alving's first maid,
Joanna, who later married the carpenter
Engstrand.

ACT I: Engstrand tries to convince his step-
daughter Regina to live with him instead of at
Mrs. Alving's house. Engstrand is a carpenter
at the orphanage Mrs. Alving has built in
memory of Alving and, now that it is finished,
Engstrand wants to open a sailors' home for

which he claims to need Regina's help. She
becomes angry and tells him to leave. Pastor
Manders arrives and tries to convince Regina
to go with Engstrand as a "daughter's duty."

Mrs. Alving is building an orphanage to
obliterate the memory of Mr. Alving's dissolute
life. Manders has come for the dedication of
the orphanage, but when Mrs. Alving asks him
to stay at her home rather than in town, he
refuses, fearing for his reputation. He also
advises her not to take out insurance on the
new orphanage because people would think
he and Mrs. Alving had a lack of faith. She tells
him there was a small fire the day before, most
likely caused by Engstrand, who is careless.
Mrs. Alving also tells him she is against Regina's moving to the sailors' home Engstrand has
planned. A weary Oswald, who had arrived
from Paris the night before enters. Manders
says that it is too bad that Oswald never
learned what a well-regulated home means,
but Oswald replies that he lived with couples
who were not married but who were, nevertheless, hard-working and principled. Manders
is scandalized, but Mrs. Alving thinks Oswald
is right in everything. After Oswald leaves the
room, Manders reminds Mrs. Alving that when
she left her husband, he made her "do her
duty" and return home. She then tells Manders
the truth about everything: that her husband
died a profligate, that he had a child by her
maid, Joanna, and that it was then that she sent
Oswald away to escape his father's influence.
She is building the orphanage not to honor

Alving but to silence all rumors. Meanwhile, Oswald makes advances to Regina in the dining room; when Mrs. Alving hears this, she is agitated because she sees the "ghost" of her dead husband in Oswald's actions.

ACT II: After dinner, Mrs. Alving tells Manders that now that Oswald is pursuing Regina, she must find another place for Regina. She also tells him that after Alving got Joanna pregnant, Engstrand married her and took responsibility for the child, Regina. Manders is shocked that Engstrand would marry a "fallen woman." Mrs. Alving points out that she was married to a "fallen man." When Engstrand comes to ask Manders to lead the workers at the orphanage in prayer, Manders questions him about his relationship with Regina and tells him that he knows the truth. The clever Engstrand says that he raised Joanna's morals and that he used the money he was given by Alving for Regina's welfare. Engstrand sways Manders into thinking that he is repentant.

After Manders leaves, Oswald tells his mother that he thinks his mind is going; he has violent headaches which have been interfering with his work. A doctor has told him that he has inherited a venereal disease: "The sins of the fathers are visited on the children," he says. Oswald has assumed that he had contracted the disease himself because he did not think it could have come from his righteous father. Now Oswald looks upon Regina as his chance for happiness and he wants to take her to Paris. Mrs. Alving is about to tell the whole truth when Manders enters. A moment later they look out the window and discover that the orphanage is on fire.

ACT III: Manders is lamenting the ruined orphanage when Engstrand says that the fire was caused because Manders was careless with a candle. This may not be true, but Engstrand plans to blackmail Manders with it. Engstrand then tells Manders that he will take the blame if Manders will give him some financial help for his sailors' home. Manders is relieved and promises to help him, but Oswald says that the sailors' home will be destroyed also, that nothing will be left in his father's memory. At this point, Mrs. Alving reveals to Regina and Oswals who Regina's true father is.

Mrs. Alving and Oswald talk about the bleak prospects for the future. Oswald is desperate with fear. He had thought that Regina could help him, but she has decided to leave. Mrs. Alving assures him that she will always be there. Oswald makes his mother promise that when he can no longer take care of himself, she will give him some pills so that he can die peacefully. When dawn comes, Oswald has gone blind; the disease has taken over. As the curtain falls, Mrs. Alving is trying to decide whether or not to take her son's life.

True West: A recent climactic drama. The entire action in Sam Shepard's *True West* takes place in the kitchen and an adjoining alcove in the home of one of the characters. The play, which is also limited in characters and action, concerns two brothers, one of whom is shown here played by Bruce Lyons.

Scenes, Locales, and Characters Are Limited

A limited number of long segments, or acts, mark climactic drama. In Greek plays there are generally five episodes separated by choral interludes. The French neoclassicists invariably used five acts. For much of the nineteenth and twentieth centuries, three acts were standard.

Limited scenes in a play usually entail a restricted locale as well. In the discussion of the "rules" of drama, we saw that the action can be confined to a single room, as in Sartre's *No Exit*. Such close confinement is a hallmark of climactic drama.

Along with restriction of locale, there is a restriction of characters. Aside from the chorus, Greek drama generally has four or five principal characters. Racine never had more than seven or eight, and the modern realistic dramatists rarely go above that number.

Construction Is Tight

Because it is carefully constructed, a climactic play fits tightly together, with no loose ends. It is like a chain indissolubly linked in a cause-and-effect relationship. As in a detective story, A leads to B, B to C, which causes D, leading in turn to E, and so on. Just as the space and the time frame afford no exit, so the chain of events is locked in; once action begins, there is no stopping it.

To give an illustration: in Racine's *Phaedra,* the heroine, Phaedra, is secretly in love with her stepson, Hippolytus. When she hears (A) that her husband, Theseus, is dead, she (B) confesses her love to Hippolytus, causing him (C) to react in horror and disgust. Theseus, unknown to Phaedra, is not dead, however; and when he returns home, Phaedra, fearing disclosure of her incestuous love, (D) allows her nurse to tell Theseus that Hippolytus has made advances to her. Thereupon, Theseus (E) invokes a god to punish Hippolytus. Hippolytus (F) is slain, leading Phaedra (G) to poison herself, confessing the truth to Theseus before she dies.

Anouilh, in his *Antigone,* compares tragedy to the workings of a machine.

> The spring is wound up tight. It will uncoil of itself. That is what is so convenient in tragedy. The least little turn of the wrist will do the job. . . . The rest is automatic. You don't need to lift a finger. The machine is in perfect order; it has been oiled ever since time began and it runs without friction.[1]

Anouilh claims that this notion applies only to tragedy, but in fact it fits every play in the climactic form; the aim always is to make events so inevitable that there is no escape—at least not until the very last moment, when a *deus ex machina* may intervene to untangle the knot. Because a climactic drama is so carefully and tightly constructed, in the modern period it has frequently been referred to as a *well-made* play.

Clearly, the method of climactic drama is one of compression. Every element—characters, locale, events—is severely restricted. As if by centripetal motion, everything is forced to the center, in a tighter and tighter nucleus, making the ultimate eruption that much more explosive. It is like the cylinder in an automobile engine: a mixture of gasoline and air is compressed by the piston in the cylinder to such extreme intensity that when a spark is introduced, the resulting detonation pushes the piston out, thereby providing power for the car. And so it is with climactic drama; since the story begins near its conclusion, people and events are forced together in a sort of compression chamber, making an explosive confrontation inevitable.

The climactic plot is a popular form of structure. The countries and periods (together with the names of a few well-known playwrights) in which it has been the dominant form include Greece, fifth century B.C. (Aeschylus, Sophocles, Euripides); Rome, third to first centuries B.C. (Plautus, Terence [ca. 185–ca. 159 B.C.]); France, seventeenth century (Corneille, Racine, Molière); France, nineteenth century (Augustin-Eugène Scribe [1791–1861], Victorien Sardou [1831–1908]); Europe and the United States, late nineteenth and twentieth centuries (Ibsen, Strindberg, O'Neill, Williams, Miller).

Episodic drama: Many characters, places, and events.
All of Shakespeare's plays are episodic in structure. One characteristic of this form is the presence of many characters, such as we see in this scene from the American Shakespeare Theater production of *The Comedy of Errors*.

CHARACTERISTICS OF THE EPISODIC PLOT

When we turn to examples of the episodic plot, we see a contrast in construction. Episodic drama begins relatively early in the story and does not compress the action but expands it.

People, Places, and Events Proliferate

The typical episodic play covers an extensive period of time, sometimes many years, and ranges over a number of locations. In one play we can go anywhere: to a small antechamber, a large banquet hall, the open countryside, and mountaintops. Short scenes, some only a half-page or so in length, alternate with longer ones. The following examples, giving the number of characters and scenes in each play, indicate the extended nature of episodic drama:

Shakespeare's *Antony and Cleopatra:* thirty-four characters, forty-plus scenes

Lope de Vega's *The Sheep Well:* twenty-six characters, seventeen scenes

Goethe's *Goetz von Berlichingen:* forty-plus characters, fifty-six scenes

Ibsen's *Peer Gynt:* forty-plus characters, thirty-nine scenes

Brecht's *The Caucasian Chalk Circle:* fifty-plus characters, approximately seventeen scenes.

Unlike climactic drama, episodic plays do not necessarily follow a close cause-and-effect development. Both the methods and the effects of episodic drama are different from those of climactic. The forces are centrifugal rather than centripetal, moving out to embrace additional elements. The possibilities of the episodic or extended approach are discussed by John Gassner in the following description of Bertolt Brecht's work.

> He favors a type of dramatic composition that grasps the various facets of man's life in society without limiting itself to unity of time, place, and action. Some of his plays . . . even have the extensiveness of an Elizabethan chronicle such as *Henry IV, Parts I* and *II* and as much variety of action and tone. One scene may convey a realistic situation while another may symbolize it; or the scene may take the form of a debate or narration; or there may be no scene at all, only a song or recitation, at points in the play. But the episodes, combined with narrative and lyrical passages; and augmented with pantomime, dance, signs or placards, slides and motion-picture sequences if necessary—all following one another in rapid succession or alternation—will form one rich tumultuous play.[2]

There May Be a Parallel Plot or Subplot

In place of compression, as Gassner suggests, episodic drama offers other techniques. One is the *parallel plot* or *subplot.* In *King Lear,* by Shakespeare, Lear has three daughters, two evil and one good. The two evil daughters have convinced their father that they are good and that their sister is wicked. In the subplot—a counterpart of the main plot—the Earl of Gloucester has two sons, and one son has deceived his father into thinking he is the loyal son when the reverse is true. In both cases the old men have misunderstood their children's true worth, and in the end they are punished for their mistakes: Lear is bereft of his kingdom and his sanity, Gloucester loses his eyes. The Gloucester plot, with complications and developments of its own, is a parallel and reinforcement of the Lear plot.

In Brecht's *The Caucasian Chalk Circle,* we are two-thirds into the play when what appears to be a brand-new drama begins. In the first portion, we follow the story of Grusha, a peasant girl who, in the midst of a revolution,

(Oregon Shakespeare Festival—Hank Kranzler)

Mother Courage

The Caucasian Chalk Circle

(Denver Center Theater Company—Christopher D. Kirkland)

THE PLAYWRIGHT: DRAMATIC STRUCTURE AND DRAMATIC CHARACTERS

156

The episodic plays of Bertolt Brecht.

The dramatist Bertolt Brecht generally uses the loose, multiscene structure referred to as *episodic*. In *Mother Courage*, shown above on the opposite page, the title character, played here by the actress Margaret Rubin, goes through many adventures in a series of scenes. This form contrasts with the more compressed climactic structure.

In Brecht's *The Caucasian Chalk Circle* (below on the opposite page), the heroine, Grusha, has gone through many adventures. Then for a time the focus of the play shifts to a completely different set of characters, including Asdak, who becomes a judge. The two-plot threads come together in the scene shown here, when the child raised by Grusha is put in a circle at the order of judge Asdak, in the rear. He orders the neglectful natural mother (on the left) and Grusha (on the right) to pull for the child. When Grusha refuses to harm him, Judge Asdak awards the child to her.

flees to the mountains with an abandoned child, who happens to be a prince. After following Grusha through several episodes, we suddenly leave her entirely and shift back in time to the point where the play began. We pick up the story of a reprobate named Asdak and trace his misadventures to the point where he becomes an enlightened judge. Although their stories are seemingly unrelated, Grusha and Asdak are two sides of the same coin: one is a rascal, the other a simple peasant; but both are decent people caught in the injustices of a corrupt political system. In the end their stories come together when Asdak presides at the trial which allows Grusha to keep the child and marry her fiancée. The plot is not nearly so tidy as in a climactic drama, but the tapestry is richer. Two plots running side by side provide the kind of strength which results when strands of steel cable or threads in a rope are intertwined.

Juxtaposition and Contrast Occur

Another technique of episodic drama is *juxtaposition* or *contrast*. Rather than moving in linear fashion, the action alternates between elements. We identify colors by relating one color to other colors, and in music we identify notes by relating one note to another. We determine size in the same way: a man 6 feet tall is of no particular significance unless he is surrounded by other men who are shorter by contrast—then he stands out.

To develop its theme and story and to provide contrast, episodic drama employs a number of alternations and juxtapositions:

1 Short scenes alternate with longer ones. *King Lear* begins with a short scene between Kent and Gloucester, goes to a long scene in which Lear divides his kingdom, then returns to a brief scene in which Edmund declares his intention to deceive his father.

2 Public scenes alternate with private ones. In *Romeo and Juliet*, full-blown scenes, such as the street fight between the Capulets and Montagues, and the Capulets' ball, stand in contrast to the intimate scenes between

KING LEAR by William Shakespeare

I-1 **Lear's Palace.** Kent and Gloucester discuss the division of the kingdom and Gloucester's sons. Lear comes. The division of the kingdom: first Goneril and then Regan praise Lear. Cordelia cannot. Kent intercedes and is banished. Gloucester enters with Burgundy and France. Burgundy will not have her without dowry. France takes her. Goneril and Regan began plotting. (305 lines)

I-2 **Gloucester's Castle.** Edmund's soliloquy and scheme. Letter and plan against Edgar begins. Gloucester leaves, Edgar comes, scheme furthered. (173 lines)

I-3 **Albany's Palace.** Goneril and Oswald scheming. (26 lines)

I-4 **The same.** Kent enters disguised; Lear comes, then Oswald, Kent trips him. Fool enters and talks to Lear. Goneril comes, chides Lear. He curses her and leaves. Goneril, Albany and Oswald conspire further, then leave. (336 lines)

I-5 **In Front of Palace.** Lear, Kent, Fool. Lear sends letters to Gloucester, starts to Regan. (46 lines)

II-1 **A Court in Gloucester's Castle.** Edmund and Curan. Edgar comes, then leaves. Edmund stabs himself; Gloucester comes, Edmund blames Edgar, Gloucester finds letter. Cornwall and Regan enter. (The forces of evil join in.) (129 lines)

II-2 **Before Gloucester's Castle.** Kent confronts Oswald, Cornwall comes; Kent put in stocks. (168 lines)

II-3 **The Open Country.** Edgar's soliloquy: he will disguise and abase himself. (21 lines)

II-4 **Before Gloucester's Castle.** Lear comes, sees Kent; confronts Regan. She is stubborn too. Goneril comes. He sees a league. Begs; leaves as storm begins. (306 lines)

III-1 **A Heath.** Kent with a Gentleman. (55 lines)

III-2 **Another Part of Heath.** Lear comes with Fool. Storm and insanity begin. Kent comes. (95 lines)

III-3 **Gloucester's Castle.** Gloucester tells Edmund of divisions between Dukes and of letter from France. (23 lines)

III-4 **The Heath Before a Hovel.** Lear, Kent, Fool - Storm. Lear's madness and beginning self-realization. Edgar joins them, then Gloucester with a torch. (172 lines)

III-5 **Gloucester's Castle.** Cornwall and Edmund scheming. (22 lines)

III-6 **A Farmhouse Near Glouster's Castle.** The mock trial for Lear. Kent, Gloucester, Fool, Edgar. All leave but Edgar. (112 lines)

III-7 **Gloucester's Castle.** Cornwall, Regan, Goneril, Edmund. They send for Gloucester (the "traitor"), prepare to blind him. Servant is killed, they pluck out Gloucester's eyes. (106 lines)

IV-1 **The Heath.** Edgar. Enter Gloucester, blind. Edgar prepares cliff scene. (79 lines)

IV-2 **Before Albany's Palace.** Goneril and Edmund. Enter Oswald. Intrigue of Goneril and Edmund. Albany comes, she chides him. Servant comes telling of Cornwall's death. (979 lines)

IV-3 **The French Camp Near Dover.** Kent and Gentleman – reports Lear ashamed to see Cordelia. (55 lines)

IV-4 **The French Camp.** Cordelia and Doctor enter; plan to go to England. (29 lines)

IV-5 **Gloucester's Castle.** Regan and Oswald. She says Edmund is for her. (40 lines)

IV-6 **Country Near Dover.** Gloucester and Edgar – jumping scene. Lear comes, mad. The two wronged, mad men together. Gentleman comes, then Oswald attacks him. Edgar kills Oswald, finds lette's to Edmund – Goneril is plotting Albany's death to marry Edmund. (283 lines)

IV-7 **Tent in French Camp.** Cordelia and Kent. Lear brought in. The awakening and reconciliation. (96 lines)

V-1 **British Camp Near Dover.** Edmund, Regan, etc. Goneril comes, also Albany. Edgar enters, leaves. (69 lines)

V-2 **A Field Between Camps.** Cordelia and Lear cross. Edgar and Gloucester come. (11 lines)

V-3 **British Camp.** Edmund comes, Lear and Cordelia are prisoners; are sent away. Edmund sends note with guard. Enter Albany, Goneril and Regan, who quarrel. Edgar comes; challenges Edmund and wounds him. Truth about Goneril's plan comes out; she leaves. Edgar talks. Goneril and Regan are brought in dead. Edmund dies. Lear enters with the dead Cordelia; then he dies. Kent and Albany pronounce the end. (326 lines)

Episodic structure in *King Lear.*

Shakespeare's play sets up a juxtaposition of scenes. Note how the scenes move from place to place and alternate from one group of characters to another. Note, too, that the scenes move back and forth from intimate scenes to those involving a number of characters (an alternation of public and private scenes) and how the length of the scenes varies, with short scenes followed by longer ones and so forth. This structure gives the play its dynamic, its rhythm, and its meaning.

Romeo and Juliet. In Brecht's *The Caucasian Chalk Circle,* the first bustling scene of revolution in the town square contrasts with a quiet scene between the two lovers, Grusha and Simon, which follows immediately.

3 We move from one group to an opposing group. In the early sections of Goethe's *Goetz von Berlichingen,* the hero is waging war against the bishop of Bamberg, and the scenes move from Goetz to the bishop and back again. We can view both sides as they prepare for a confrontation.

4 Comic scenes alternate with serious scenes. In *Macbeth,* just after Macbeth has murdered King Duncan, there is a knock on the door of the castle. It is one of the most serious moments of the play, but the man who goes to open the door is a comical character, a drunken porter, whose speech is a humorous interlude in the grim business of the play. In *Hamlet,* the gravedigger and his assistant are preparing the grave for Ophelia when Hamlet comes on the scene. The gravediggers are joking about death; but for Hamlet, who soon learns that the grave is Ophelia's, it is a somber moment. This juxtaposition of the comic with the serious may seem incongruous; but properly handled, it can bring out the irony and poignancy of an event in a way rarely achieved by other means.

There are, of course, other forms of alternation in episodic drama, but the above illustrations give an indication of the ways in which this technique can be used to create dramatic effects.

The Overall Effect Is Cumulative

As for cause and effect in episodic drama, the impression created is of events piling up: a tidal wave of circumstances and emotions sweeping over the characters. Rarely does one letter, one telephone call, or one piece of information determine the fate of a character. Time and again, Hamlet has proof that Claudius has killed his father; but it is a rush of events which eventually leads him to kill Claudius, not a single piece of hard evidence. The corruption in the court of Denmark is pervasive, and it is the combined weight of incidents and atmosphere, rather than a single precipitating incident, that makes the outcome inevitable. Episodic drama, by developing a series of extensions, parallels, contrasts, juxtapositions—in fact a whole web or network of characters and events—achieves a cumulative effect all its own, at its best creating what Gassner referred to as a "tumultuous play."

The countries and periods in which the episodic form has predominated include England, late sixteenth and early seventeenth centuries (Shakespeare, Marlowe); Spain, late sixteenth and early seventeenth centuries (Lope de Vega, Calderón); Germany, late eighteenth and early nineteenth centuries (Goethe, Lessing, Friedrich von Schiller [1759–1805], Georg Büchner [1813–1837]); and Europe and the United States, late nineteenth and twentieth centuries (Ibsen, Brecht, Genet).

It will be noted that in modern theater both climactic and episodic forms have been adopted, sometimes by one playwright. This is characteristic of the diversity of our age. Ibsen, for example, wrote a number of well-made plays—*Ghosts, Hedda Gabler,* and others—but also several episodic plays, such as *Brand* and *Peer Gynt.*

COMPARING THE CLIMACTIC AND EPISODIC FORMS

The following table outlines the chief characteristics of the two major forms and illustrates the differences between them:

CLIMACTIC	EPISODIC
1 Plot begins late in the story, toward the very end or climax.	Plot begins relatively early in the story and moves through a series of episodes.
2 Covers a short space of time, perhaps a few hours, or at most a few days.	Covers a longer period of time: weeks, months, and sometimes many years.
3 Contains a few solid, extended scenes, such as three acts with each act comprising one long scene.	Many short, fragmented scenes; sometimes an alternation of short and long scenes.
4 Occurs in a restricted locale, one room or one house.	May range over an entire city or even several countries.
5 Number of characters severely limited, usually no more than six or eight.	Profusion of characters, sometimes several dozen.
6 Plot is linear and moves in a single line with few subplots or counterplots.	Frequently marked by several threads of action, such as two parallel plots, or scenes of comic relief in a serious play.
7 Line of action proceeds in a cause-and-effect chain. The characters and events are closely linked in a sequence of logical, almost inevitable development.	Scenes are juxtaposed to one another. An event may result from several causes, or no apparent cause, but arises in a network or web of circumstances.

It is clear that the climactic and episodic forms differ from each other in their fundamental approaches. The one emphasizes constriction and compression on all fronts; the other takes a far broader view and aims at a cumulative effect, piling up people, places, and events.

COMBINING THE CLIMACTIC AND EPISODIC FORMS

There is no law which says that a play must be exclusively episodic or climactic. These forms are not watertight compartments. It is true that during certain periods, one form or the other has been predominant. And it is not easy to mix the two, because as we have seen, each has its own laws and its own inner logic. In various periods, however, they have been successfully integrated.

For example, I have been referring to Greek drama as conforming to climactic structure. In the case of the main drama of the play, this is true. In *King Oedipus* by Sophocles, for instance, the plot begins late in the story, the action takes place in one location, and there are very few characters. There is an element in Greek drama, though, that gives it an added dimension, and this is the *chorus*. By the time of Sophocles, the chorus consisted of fifteen performers who sang, danced, chanted, and sometimes interacted with the principal characters. The choral sections, which alternated with the episodes of the main plot, make Greek drama less rigidly climactic than a play like *Ghosts* or classical French plays like those by Racine. The Greek chorus stands outside the action, arguing with the main characters, making connections between present events and the past, warning the main characters of impending danger, and drawing conclusions from what has occurred.

A group of plays that combine elements of the climactic and episodic forms are the comedies of the Restoration period in England (from 1660, when the English monarchy was restored, to 1700). These comedies usually had large casts, a subplot as well as a main plot, and several changes of scene. They did not, however, cover extended periods of time or move rapidly from place to place as the plays of Shakespeare did. For example, in *The Country Wife* by William Wycherley, there are thirteen characters plus several extras. In addition to the main plot concerning Horner, who has an affair with Margery, the country wife of Mr. Pinchwife, there is a subplot dealing with a fop named Sparkish, who allows his fiancée to be stolen from under his eyes by a friend of Horner's. The scene shifts back and forth from Horner's house to Pinchwife's house, and there are two scenes in other locations. At the same time, there is an organic quality about the play usually associated with climactic drama. The action takes place in a relatively short period of time, and there is unity of action in the two plots.

The climactic and episodic forms have frequently been mixed successfully in the modern period. There are plays which fall primarily into one category but incorporate features of the other. *Cyrano de Bergerac*, by Edmond Rostand, has the traditional five acts of climactic drama; at the same time it has a multitude of characters—well over fifty—and between the fourth and fifth acts there is a gap of fifteen years. Chekhov, who generally wrote about one principal action and set his plays in one household, usually has more characters than is customary in climactic drama—fifteen in *The Cherry Orchard*, for instance. Frequently, too, Chekhov's plays cover a period of several months or years.

Arthur Miller, in *Death of a Salesman*, combined the two forms in still a different way. The main frame of the story is in climactic form and covers the last hours of Willie Loman's life. Events from the past, however, are not

Combining the climactic and the episodic.
The plays of Chekhov combine features of the climactic and episodic forms. The plays often occur in one place but range over a period of time and involve a number of characters. A good example is *The Sea Gull*. The scene here, showing several sets of characters, is from a production at the Circle Repertory Theater.

described in exposition, as is usually the case, but are presented as full-fledged scenes. Rather than hear about the past, we see it enacted in a series of flashback scenes. In this way Miller achieved the finality of the climactic play but opened his drama up in the fashion of an episodic drama.

DRAMATIC DEVICES USED WITH CLIMACTIC AND EPISODIC PLOTS

Before leaving climactic and episodic plots, we should look at two devices that frequently occur in conjunction with these structures.

A Chorus or Narrator

A technique used in many plays is a *dialectic* or *counterpoint* between a party outside the play and characters in the central action. (Counterpoint is

The narrator in *The Glass Menagerie*. A structural device sometimes used in either climactic or episodic plays is a narrator who speaks directly to the audience. In *The Glass Menagerie* by Tennessee Williams, Tom, played here by Bruce Davison, addresses the audience, explaining and commenting on the action.

a term from music denoting a second melody that accompanies or moves in contrast to the main melody.) Good examples of the device are the chorus in Greek drama and the narrator in a modern play.

In the modern play *Our Town,* author Thornton Wilder used the Stage Manager to comment on the action. Wilder set up a counterpoint between the episodes of the play—most of them mundane, everyday events—and the more general, universal observations of the Stage Manager. By setting one element next to the other, he gave broader meaning to specific episodes and, at the same time, a concrete down-to-earth reality to philosophical observations. As an example, at the opening of the play, Joe Crowell, Jr., while delivering the morning paper, sees Doc Gibbs, and talks to him about such things as the marriage of Joe's schoolteacher and his trick knee— perfectly ordinary topics of conversation. But later in the play, the Stage Manager gives a broader perspective to Joe's life when he tells us that after graduating from high school with honors, Joe won a scholarship to MIT, only to die shortly thereafter in France fighting in World War I. As the Stage Manager observes, "All that education for nothing."

Bertolt Brecht used a narrator, and sometimes singers, in more drastic fashion. He wanted to startle members of the audience by a sudden shift from the main story to a foreign element. In *The Caucasian Chalk Circle,* Grusha, the innocent, peace-loving peasant woman, steps out of character at one point to sing a song extolling the virtues of a general who loves war. Grusha, in other words, is asked to sing a song with a point of view opposite to her own. This wrenching of characters and attitudes is deliberate on Brecht's part: to make us think about war and the ravages of war. The pieces are meant to fit together, not in the play itself, but rather in the minds of the spectators.

Intellectual or Conceptual Conflict

A second device used in conjunction with traditional plot structure is the intellectual debate. This occurs particularly in the type of drama called the *play of ideas,* whose main conflict or problem is intellectual. It is worth pointing out that the purely intellectual approach to theater can be dangerous. When carried to extremes, it concentrates entirely on abstruse arguments, leaving behind flesh-and-blood characters. It ignores completely the foundation of theater, namely, the experience embodied in the actor-audience relationship. Occasionally writers present a discourse or debate in play form. But this is really a subterfuge. Such a play is a treatise in disguise, and no more related to the experience of theater than a description of the values of the heart would be to falling in love. Ideas, insight, and perception are essential to meaningful drama, but they must serve the play and not the other way around.

At times a playwright successfully gives theatrical form to an intellectual concept. A good example is *Six Characters in Search of an Author,* by the Italian playwright Luigi Pirandello (1867–1936). Pirandello establishes an opposition between actors rehearsing a play and a group of fictional characters who are not real people but creations like Hamlet or Hedda Gabler. The characters urge the actors to perform their story, which has never been presented in final form, and in the process of this confrontation Pirandello raises questions of appearance versus reality, and fiction versus fact.

In this chapter we have examined two basic forms of dramatic structure—climactic and episodic—together with combinations of the two. We have also looked at other elements used with these forms. In Chapter 9 we will look at other forms of dramatic structure—some new forms and variations of old forms.

SUMMARY

1 There are several basic types of dramatic structure. The form adopted by the Greeks and used frequently since then is the *climactic* form. Its characteristics are a plot beginning quite late in the story, a limited number of characters, a limited number of locations and scenes, little or no extraneous material, and tight construction, including a cause-and-effect chain of events.

2 The *episodic* form of dramatic structure involves a plot covering an extended span of time, numerous locations, a large cast of characters, diverse events (including the mixing of comic and serious episodes), and parallel plots or subplots. Shakespeare's plays are good examples of the episodic form.

3 The climactic and episodic forms can be combined, as they have been in the modern period in the works of Anton Chekhov, Arthur Miller, and others.

4 Devices sometimes used with traditional plot structures are a narrator or chorus and an intellectual debate.

9
DRAMATIC STRUCTURE: OTHER FORMS

9
DRAMATIC STRUCTURE: OTHER FORMS

Circular structure in *Waiting for Godot*.
Samuel Beckett's play does not unfold like the typical dramatic narrative. The two main characters, shown here, meet every day at a crossroads in the hope that the mysterious Godot will come and make their lives better; but Godot never comes. The second act goes through the same cycle as the first. Events occur and patterns are repeated; but unlike climactic or episodic drama, the action of the play does not move from the beginning of a story to its resolution. The actors here are Winston Ntshona and John Kani in a production at the Long Wharf Theater.

169

Though climactic or episodic structure—or some combination of the two—has frequently been dominant, other forms of dramatic structure have emerged in theater history. In this chapter we will look at several of these important types of structure.

THEATER OF THE ABSURD: NONSENSE AND NON SEQUITUR

Following World War II a new type of theater emerged in Europe and America. The critic Martin Esslin has called it the *theater of the absurd*. Although the dramatists whose work falls into this category do not write in identical styles and are not really a "school" of writers, they do share enough in common to be considered together. Esslin took the name for this form of theater from a quotation in *The Myth of Sisyphus* by the French writer, dramatist, and philosopher Albert Camus. Camus maintains that in the present age we have lost the comfort and security of being able to explain the world by reason and logic. As he puts it in *The Myth of Sisyphus*:

> A world that can be explained by reasoning, however faulty, is a familiar world. But in a universe that is suddenly deprived of illusions and light, man feels a stranger. His is an irremediable exile, because he is deprived of memories of a lost homeland as much as he lacks hope of a promised land to come. This divorce between man and his life, the actor and his setting, truly constitutes the feeling of Absurdity.[1]

Camus is saying that the modern world is absurd; it makes no sense. One cannot explain the injustices, the inconsistencies, and the malevolence of today's world in terms of the moral yardsticks of the past.

Plays falling into the absurdist category express the ideas articulated by Camus and others like him. In one way or another they convey a sense of alienation and of people's having lost their bearings in an illogical, unjust, and ridiculous world. Although serious, this viewpoint is generally depicted in plays with considerable humor; an ironic note runs through much of the theater of the absurd. For example, in Samuel Beckett's *Waiting for Godot,* the chief characters frequently say one thing and do just the opposite. One says to the other, "Well, shall we go?" and the other says, "Yes, let's go." But having said this, they don't move; they sit still, and the contrast between their words and deeds is funny.

Absurdist plays suggest the idea of absurdity both in what they say—their content—and in the way they say it—their form. Their structure, therefore, is a departure from dramatic structures of the past.

Nontraditional Structure

Traditional plot arrangements in drama proceed in a logical way from a beginning through the development of the plot to a conclusion. This in turn suggests an ordered universe. Even violent or disordered events, such as Macbeth's murder of Duncan or King Lear's madness, are presented in a rational framework. The same was true of writers in the 1920s and 1930s; many of their plays *described* absurdity, but the structure of their plays did not *demonstrate* absurdity. Some dramatists of the theater of the absurd—though certainly not all—set about correcting this discrepancy: their plays not only proclaim absurdity, they embody it.

An example is *The Bald Soprano,* by Eugène Ionesco. The very title of the play turns out to be nonsense; a bald soprano is mentioned once in the play, but with no explanation, and it is clear that the bald soprano has nothing whatever to do with the play as a whole. The absurdity of the piece is manifest the moment the curtain goes up. A typical English couple is sitting in a living room when the clock on the mantle strikes seventeen times; the wife's first words are, "There, it's nine o'clock." At one point a fire chief, dressed in full uniform, bursts into the living room. He claims to be looking for fires; but when he finds no fires, he stays to tell stories to the two couples present. It is obvious that there is no logical explanation for his being there. Other Ionesco plays have equally ridiculous elements—such as *Amedee,* in which a long-dead corpse continues to grow and finally crashes through the wall of the apartment on stage during the course of the play.

Edward Albee, an American playwright, has also written plays in the absurd form. *The American Dream,* a study of the banality and insensitivity of American family life, introduces a handsome young man of around twenty as the embodiment of the "American dream." The Mommy and Daddy of the play wish to adopt him because he seems perfect to them. We learn, however, that he is only half a person; he is all appearance, with no inner feelings. He is the other half of a child Mommy and Daddy mutilated and destroyed years before when it began to have feelings, wanting to touch things and expressing curiosity about the world. Obviously Mommy and Daddy care more for appearance than true human emotions. To further underscore the absurdity of Mommy and Daddy's world, Albee has them return from a search of their house to report that an entire room has disappeared. Plot, as well as other elements, becomes illogical.

It should be noted that not every play in the absurdist form abandons traditional plot structure altogether. At the same time that they contain elements of nonsense, a few absurdist plays adopt a conventional approach in developing the incidents of the play. The characters move through a series of episodes, which increase in tension, reach a climax, and then conclude. In Ionesco's *The Lesson,* a professor is teaching a student mathematics. As he moves to linguistics, he becomes increasingly agitated; he torments the student with growing menace until finally he stabs her to

Theater of the absurd.
Non sequitur, nonsense language, existential characters, ridiculous situations: these are the hallmarks of theater of the absurd. A good example is *The Bald Soprano* by Eugene Ionesco. The scene here is from a production at the North Carolina School of the Arts at Winston-Salem.

death in a climactic moment. In another Ionesco play, *The Chairs,* an old couple sets up chairs for a group of imaginary visitors, and the pace of the arrival of guests builds to the climax. Harold Pinter's plays, such as *The Birthday Party* and *The Homecoming,* also develop in the manner of more traditional plays. In absurdist plays in which the structure is familiar, the dislocation and disruption that we associate with the form occurs in the behavior of the characters, in unexpected incidents, and in language.

Verbal Nonsense

Events and characters are frequently illogical in the theater of the absurd, and so too is language. *Non sequitur* is a Latin term meaning "it does not follow"; it implies that one thing does not follow from what went before, and it perfectly describes the method of theater of the absurd, including the use of language. Sentences do not follow in sequence, and words do not mean what we expect them to mean. As Martin Esslin says, there is a tendency "toward a radical devaluation of language."

A passage from Ionesco's *The Bald Soprano* in which two couples are talking will illustrate the point.

MRS. SMITH: The car goes very fast, but the cook beats batter better.
MR. SMITH: Don't be turkeys; rather kiss the conspirator.
MRS. SMITH: I'm waiting for the aqueduct to come see me at my windmill.
MR. MARTIN: One can prove that social progress is definitely better with sugar.
MR. SMITH: To hell with polishing![2]

Most of the dialogue in the play is equally irrelevant and based on just such *non sequiturs*.

Another example of the irrationality or debasement of language is found in Samuel Beckett's *Waiting for Godot*. The character Lucky does not speak for most of his time on stage, but at the end of the first act he delivers a long speech of incoherent religious and legalistic jargon. The opening lines offer a small sample.

> Given the existence as uttered forth in the public works of Puncher and Wattmann of a personal God quaquaquaqua with white beard quaquaquaqua outside time without extension who from the heights of divine apathia divine athambia divine aphasia loves us dearly with some exceptions for reasons unknown but time will tell . . . [3]

Numerous examples of such language appear not only in the plays of Ionesco and Beckett but in those of many absurdist writers.

Existential Characters

A significant feature of the structure of absurdist plays lies in the handling of characters. Not only is there an element of the ridiculous in their actions, but they frequently exemplify an *existential* point of view toward human behavior. Most traditional philosophies hold that essence precedes existence—that is, that there is a quality for everything which is present even before it exists. There is a quality for apples, for instance, before an individual apple appears on a tree and, in personal terms, a *self* for each person preceding his or her existence. *Existentialism,* on the other hand, holds that existence precedes essence; a person creates himself or herself in the process of living. Beginning with nothing, the person develops a self—as essence—in taking action and making choices.

Waiting for Godot (1954)

SAMUEL BECKETT (1906–)

CHIEF CHARACTERS:

Estragon
Vladimir
Lucky
Pozzo
A boy

SETTING: A country road with a tree.

TIME: The present.

BACKGROUND: Estragon and Vladimir have been coming to this bleak spot every day for some time to wait for an unknown person called Godot. While they wait, they pass the time discussing the nature of humankind, religion, what they did yesterday, or whatever else happens to be on their minds.

ACT I: Estragon is attempting to pull off his boot when Vladimir enters. They discuss where Estragon spent the night and how he was beaten up again. Vladimir relates the tale of the two thieves who were crucified with Christ and describes how current religious scholars cannot agree on what happened to the thieves. As Estragon paces, the scene is punctuated by pauses which enhance the feeling of waiting. They occasionally talk of leaving and then decide that they cannot because they are waiting for Godot. They consider leaving each other; they argue; they make up. They discuss hanging themselves from the tree but decide that they can't do it because the limb might break.

At the point where they have decided not to do anything, Pozzo and Lucky enter. Lucky has a rope around his neck held by Pozzo. Pozzo jerks occasionally on the rope and barks commands to Lucky, who responds mechanically. Pozzo sits, eats, and smokes his pipe. Estragon asks why Lucky doesn't put down the bags and Pozzo explains that Lucky wants to impress him so Pozzo will keep him. Pozzo says that it would be best to kill Lucky, which makes Lucky cry. Estragon tries to comfort Lucky, and Lucky kicks him. As the sky changes from day to night, Pozzo tells Lucky to dance, which he does. Pozzo tells Lucky to think, and Lucky, who has been silent until this moment, goes into a long incoherent tirade which agitates the others. When they take Lucky's "talking hat" off, he stops talking and collapses in a heap. They say good-bye, but no one is able to leave. Pozzo finally gets up and exits with Lucky in the lead, with the rope around his neck as before.

A Boy enters to tell Vladimir and Estragon that Godot will not be coming today, but will surely come tomorrow. After he exits, the moon suddenly rises. Estragon says that he will bring some rope the next day so they can hang themselves. They talk about parting, but they don't, as the curtain falls.

ACT II: The next day at the same time, in the same place. The scene opens with Estragon's boots and Lucky's hat on stage. The tree that was bare now has four or five leaves. Vladimir enters in an agitated state, paces back and forth, and then begins to sing. Estragon enters and appears to be in a foul mood. They embrace and Estragon says that he was beaten again the night before. Also, Estragon can't remember what happened the day before. They talk about random things so that they will not have to think. They are amazed that leaves could appear on the tree overnight. They discover Estragon's boots, but they seem to be the wrong color: perhaps someone came along and exchanged boots. They discuss leaving but can't because they are waiting for Godot. Estragon takes a nap, and Vladimir sings a lullaby. Estragon wakes, as if from a nightmare; Vladimir comforts him. They discover Lucky's hat, and do a comic hat-switching routine. They hear a noise and think that finally Godot is coming. They are both afraid and rush around in an excited state, but nothing happens; no one comes. Once more, they insult each other and then make up.

Pozzo and Lucky enter, and Pozzo is now blind. Lucky stops short, falls, and brings Pozzo down with him. Pozzo calls for help, but Vladimir and Estragon think that finally Godot has arrived. They then discover that it is Pozzo and Lucky. Vladimir and Estragon try to help Pozzo up, but they fall also. They all finally get up. Estragon goes to Lucky and kicks him, and, by so doing, he hurts his foot. Lucky gets up, gathers his things together, and he and Pozzo exit as before.

Estragon tries in vain to take off his boots and then he falls asleep, as Vladimir philosophizes. The Boy enters and again tells Vladimir that Godot will not be coming that night, but that he will come the next night. The Boy exits. The sun sets and the moon rises quickly. Vladimir and Estragon discuss leaving, but they can't go far because they have to be back the next day to wait for Godot. They talk again of hanging themselves on the tree, but don't have any rope. They test the strength of Estragon's belt, but it breaks and his pants fall to the ground. Vladimir tells Estragon to pull up his trousers and he does. Vladimir says, "Well? Shall we go?" Estragon says, "Yes, let's go." But they do not move, and they remain on stage as the play ends.

When applied to theater, existentialism suggests that characters have no personal history before the play begins, no background and therefore no specific causes for their actions. This is contrary to the practice of most traditional drama. Take the case of Blanche DuBois in *A Streetcar Named Desire*. We learn in the play that Blanche has come from an aristocratic southern background, has had several unfortunate experiences with men, and has lost both money and prestige at home. These facts explain why she is so desperate when she arrives in New Orleans to stay with her sister and brother-in-law.

By contrast, the two main characters in Beckett's *Waiting for Godot* are devoid of biography and personal motivation. We are told nothing of their backgrounds or their family life or their occupations. As characters they exist; they are, but without explanation. They meet every day at a crossroads to wait for Godot, but how long they have been coming there, or what they do when they are not there, remains a mystery. They exist for the moment, in the here and now.

This lack of concern for background and motivation has an effect on structure—specifically, in the absence of exposition. In the theater of the absurd we see characters for whom little or no explanation is offered. We catch them in midair, or midstream, and this is what the dramatist wants. There is no preoccupation with the past, no solving of riddles, as in *Oedipus*. The structure leads us, not to seek solutions, but to confront a view of modern life, a view both existential and absurd.

RITUAL AND PATTERN AS DRAMATIC STRUCTURE

Thus far, we have looked at two forms of traditional structure—the climactic and the episodic—and one more contemporary form—absurdist theater. We turn now to two other forms of structure, which are used in combination with other forms or serve as the basis of structure by themselves—ritual and pattern.

Rituals

Like acting, ritual is a part of everyday life of which we are generally unaware. Basically, *ritual* is the repetition or reenactment of a proceeding or transaction which has acquired special meaning. It may be a simple ritual like singing the national anthem before a sports contest, or a deeply religious one such as the mass in the Roman Catholic Church or the kaddish for the dead in the Jewish faith. Every one of us in our personal or family life develops rituals: a certain meal we eat with the family once a week, or a routine we go through every time we take an examination in school.

Occasions like Thanksgiving, Christmas, and Passover become family

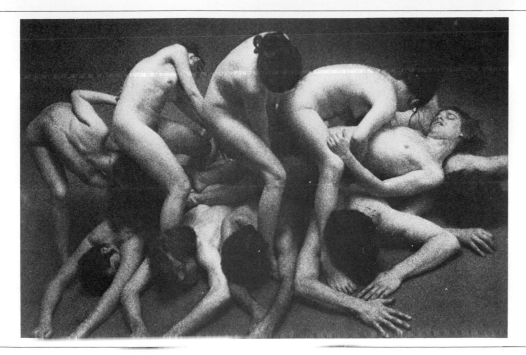

Ritual in modern theater.
The Performance Group incorporated an Asmat birth ritual from New Guinea in its production of *Dionysus in 69*. Through repetition and formalization, ritual gives significance to events for those who take part or observe.

rituals, with the same order of events each year, the same menu, and perhaps even the same conversation. Rituals give continuity, security, and comfort to human beings. Often, as in the case of primitive tribes, those performing a ritual assume that by carrying out a ceremony faithfully they will be blessed or their wishes granted. Conversely, they assume that a failure to follow the ritual to the letter will lead to punishment.

In the theater, ritual is an area where the old and new come together. Traditional plays are full of rituals: coronations, weddings, funerals, and other ceremonies. And in modern theater, ritual has been discovered and given new life. Martin Esslin states that the plays of the French dramatist Jean Genet can best be understood in terms of ritual. According to Esslin, "The concept of the ritual act, the magical repetition of an action deprived of reality, is the key to any understanding of Genet's theater."[6] Of Genet's play *The Balcony* Esslin says, "Essentially the play is a series of rituals, followed by their equally ritual debunking. . . ."[7]

The British playwright David Storey (1933–) incorporated a type of ritual in the structure of his plays *The Contractor* and *The Changing Room*. In each play a group of men go about a task or repeat a routine they have been through many times before. In *The Contractor* a crew of laborers erect a tent for the wedding of their employer's daughter. In the first act they set up the tent, in the second act they decorate it, and in the third act they take it down. Their individual jobs—putting in stakes, unfolding canvas, tying ropes—become ritualized through repetition. *The Changing Room* develops in a similar way. In the first act we see a semiprofessional English rugby team in the locker room preparing for a Saturday afternoon match. In the second act we see the team at halftime, and in the third, we see the exhausted players after the game. The symbolic values the men attach to small routines, and the sustenance they draw from them, are brought sharply into focus in both of these plays.

Ritual has structure. Actions are repeated in a set fashion; they have a beginning, middle, and end, and there is a natural progression of events. Storey has made the structure of ritual a part of the structure of his plays. The modern avant-garde movement has made a conscious attempt to develop new rituals or revive old ones. The Performance Group's *Dionysus in 69* included a birth ritual adopted from an Asmat New Guinea ritual. In *The Serpent,* the Open Theater created a ritualistic version of the assassination of President John F. Kennedy. The scene is the car in which the president and Mrs. Kennedy and Governor John Connally of Texas and his wife rode. There are twelve frozen scenes or tableaux representing various stages in the assassination, beginning with the actors waving to the crowds. We move from this to a still-life scene of the president being shot in the neck, then to the governor being shot, then to the president falling against his wife, and so forth. The actors assume the twelve poses as numbers from one to twelve are shouted out, and once the actors have gone through the sequence, they repeat it in reverse order. This "stop action" lets us concentrate on individual moments in the incident; it clothes the event in a ritual which can be repeated. At the same time, this method of presentation evokes images of single frames from a movie film, or "freeze frames" on television.

Patterns

Related to ritual is a pattern of events. In Samuel Beckett's *Waiting for Godot,* the characters have no personal history, and the play does not build to a climax in the ordinary way. But if Beckett has sacrificed traditional plot structure, he has replaced it with a repeated sequence of events containing its own order and logic. The play has two acts, and in each act a series of incidents is duplicated. Each act opens with the two chief characters coming together on a lonely crossroads after having been separated. Then in both acts a similar sequence of events occurs: they greet each other, they despair of Godot's ever coming, they attempt to entertain themselves. Two other men, Pozzo and Lucky, appear and, following a lengthy scene, disappear. The men are left alone once more. The two acts continue to follow the same sequence: a small boy comes to tell them that Godot will not come that day, the boy leaves, and the men remain together for another night. There are important differences between the two acts—differences which give the play meaning and resonance—but the identical sequence of events in each act achieves a pattern which takes on a ritualistic quality.

The Serpent, which contains within it such rituals as the assassination of Kennedy, also develops a pattern of action. It opens with a contemporary scene, then moves back in time to the garden of Eden in biblical times. It returns to the present, then moves once more to Adam and Eve, and so on—alternating between Old Testament times and the present. With their regularity and rhythm, such patterns provide us with a sense of structure which takes the place of plot development in a traditional play.

When ritual occurs in theater, we might ask: Where are the dynamics and tension? Does ritual not deteriorate into dull routine or hollow repetition? It can, of course; but ritual, though sometimes known by heart, is not static. Remember, it is a reenactment, or reliving, of an episode or occasion, and as such is active, not passive. Beyond that, ritual has special powers; it carries with it the magic or mystery of a meaningful, almost holy act. This can be its source of energy in theater, as it is in life.

EXPERIMENTAL AND AVANT-GARDE THEATER: SPECIAL STRUCTURES

During the 1960s and 1970s, a number of theater groups in Europe and the United States experimented with theatrical forms, including ritual. These included Polish Laboratory Theater headed by Jerzy Grotowski (1933–   ), and the Living Theater, the Open Theater, and the Performance Group in the United States. These groups were questioning long-held beliefs about theater. They had two things in mind. On one hand, they felt that the theater of the past was no longer relevant to the problems of the present and that new forms must be found to match the challenges and aspirations unique to the latter part of the twentieth century. On the other hand, they had an impulse to look back past the traditions of the last 2500 years to the beginning of theater, to scrape off the many layers of formality and convention accumulated through the centuries and rediscover the roots of theater.

In many cases these two impulses led to similar results; and from the experiments of this radical theater movement several significant departures from traditional theater practice were developed. Among them were the following: (1) emphasis on nonverbal theater, that is, theater where gestures, body movements, and sounds without words are stressed rather than logical or intelligible language; (2) reliance on improvisation or a scenario developed by performers and a director to tell the story, rather than a written text; (3) interest in ritual and ceremony; (4) stress on the importance of the physical environment of theater, including the spatial relationship of the performers to the audience.

The theater groups that developed these ideas are referred to as *avant-garde,* a French term that literally means the advance guard in a military formation. The term has come to mean an intellectual or artistic movement in any age that breaks with tradition and therefore seems ahead of its time.

Segments and Tableaux as Structure

The experimental theater pieces of the directors Robert Wilson (1944–   ) and Richard Foreman (1937–   ) (who were noted in Chapter 7), like other types of avant-garde theater, often stress nonverbal elements. At times they include *non sequitur* as well. In spite of this, their work does have structure. Often the various elements are united by a theme, or at least a pronounced point of view on the part of the director. Also, the material is organized into units analogous to the frames of film and television, or to the still-life tableaux of painting or the moving tableaux of dance.

In his experimental productions Richard Foreman sits at a table facing the performers and rings a bell to indicate that one section is over and a new one is beginning. The performers move through one segment—sometimes repeating actions, sometimes prolonging them—completing the activities assigned to them before proceeding to the next segment. Foreman also separates space in his theater. A series of horizontal strings are stretched across the theater, and the stage area is often divided by railings or levels. By separating the production into units—in both time and space—Foreman provides a form of organization for his theater piece.

Robert Wilson, in productions such as *A Letter to Queen Victoria* and *Einstein on the Beach,* begins a segment with a visual picture, like a large three-dimensional painting. The performers move from this static image into the activities of the segment. When one segment has concluded, another picture or tableau will be formed to initiate the next segment.

Frequently directors like Foreman and Wilson will employ rapid movements—as in silent films—or slow-motion movements. At times several activities will occur simultaneously. All of these, however, relate both to an image and to a tableau or frame.

Random Structures

Practitioners of some forms of experimental theater abandon logic in putting scenes together. Their argument is that life itself is unstructured and therefore art should be too. To this extent, the viewpoints of the absurdists and these experimental groups are related, but there are essential differences in focus and intent. The dramatists of the theater of the absurd wish to create an absurd world in their art, whereas the exponents of abandoning structure attempt to avoid art or creation altogether. With the latter the emphasis is more on the random, disconnected quality of life than its absurd, ridiculous quality. Rather than write a single play such as *The Bald Soprano* or *The American Dream,* they advocate stringing together a series of unrelated activities or events. Sometimes various arts, such as painting, film, and music, are combined.

Michael Kirby, an expert on this kind of theater, describes a typical sequence of events offered to an audience in this type of presentation.

> A piano is destroyed. The orchestra conductor walks on stage, bows to the audience, raises his baton, and the curtain falls. A formally dressed man appears with a french horn under his arm; when he bows, ball bearings pour forth from the bell of a horn in a noisy cascade. A person asks if La Monte Young is in the audience; when there is no answer, he leaves. A man sets a balloon on stage, carefully estimates the distance as he walks away from it, then does a backward flip, landing on the balloon and breaking it.[4]

John Cage (1912–   ), an avant-garde composer who was also active in creating events, describes the purpose behind a lack of structure in a theater presentation.

> The structure we should think about is that of each person in the audience. In other words, his consciousness is structuring the experience differently from anybody else's in the audience. So the less we structure the theatrical occasion and the more it is like unstructured daily life, the greater will be the stimulus to the structuring faculty of each person in the audience.[5]

Cage is saying that if the audience is given a series of unrelated events, or several events simultaneously, each member of the audience will put them together like a personal jigsaw puzzle. Perhaps, too, Cage is suggesting that the result will be more meaningful because it will belong to the individual audience member and to no one else.

Of course, making spectators more aware—raising their consciousness— is important, but the argument for a totally unstructured work of art is debatable. Just as there is a distinction between the roles of the performer and the spectator, so is there a distinction between the roles of the creators of theater—writers, directors, and designers, as well as actors and actresses —and the observer. We go to the theater to see a different vision of life from the one we carry with us every day. Reflecting life in an imaginative way—the job of the artist—is not the same thing as simply duplicating it. Besides, any attempt to demonstrate the random quality of life in a theatrical context always takes on a special aura because it is being "presented."

In fact, complete formlessness is an extreme even among the avant-garde. Most avant-garde pieces, like the major portion of the theater of the absurd, present an illogical structure, or a series of *non sequiturs,* with a definite artistic purpose in mind. There is sense to the nonsense. Such presentations, while not necessarily leading to logical conclusions, do create dramatic tension and lead us to ask why such puzzling material is being shown to us. For some dramatists this is enough—for us to ask questions. At the very least, this technique creates uncertainty and expectancy in wondering what will happen next or what it all means. At its best, however, it does much more than that—it brings us face to face with a view of the world which many feel accurately reflects the chaos and uncertainty of the modern world. When this is done with intelligence and inventiveness—and with humor, as it often is—this type of theater is fulfilling the ancient function of the art in providing us with a unique experience of ourselves and our world.

STRUCTURE IN MUSICAL THEATER

Musical theater ranges all the way from *grand opera*—in which nothing is spoken and everything is sung—to a play with a few songs. In between are such forms as *operetta, musical comedy,* and the *musical revue.*

Opera and operetta, though closely related to drama, are generally considered to be separate artistic genres. Opera, especially, is regarded as a branch of music. Even so, it is possible to see a clear structure in opera. The story is told in a series of musical numbers in which solos, duets, quartets, choral numbers, and ballets alternate with each other. Between musical numbers characters sing recitatives—sections of action or explanation. In operetta the recitatives are spoken.

In form, operetta can be very close to *musical comedy;* and when we come to musical comedy, by common consent, we enter the realm of theater. Actually, the term *musical theater* might be better than musical comedy because many musicals of the last thirty or forty years have been closer to drama than comedy. These include musicals like *Carousel, West Side Story,* and *Sweeney Todd.*

A Brief History of the Musical

The modern musical is considered to be largely an American achievement. In the late nineteenth and early twentieth centuries, Europe had operettas and Great Britain had *vaudeville* and *variety shows.* In vaudeville and variety, comic sketches alternated with musical numbers. The United States in the nineteenth century had its own brand of vaudeville as well as minstrel shows, the latter being variety shows featuring white performers in blackface.

From these influences the American musical slowly emerged. In the early part of the twentieth century, writers in the United States created European-influenced operettas, such as *Naughty Marietta, The Desert Song,* and *The Student Prince.* In the same period, George M. Cohan (1878–1942) and others wrote a form of musical that foreshadowed later work. In the 1920s and 1930s a truly American musical began to take shape. The plots were usually trivial and silly; but the songs—by composers like Irving Berlin (1888–   ), Jerome Kern (1885–1945), George Gershwin (1898–1937), Cole Porter (ca. 1892–1964), and Richard Rodgers—were often outstanding and are still popular today.

Along with the many simplistic musicals, efforts were made to achieve more serious work. In 1927, *Show Boat* appeared. In addition to a remarkable musical score, *Show Boat* could list other accomplishments. It dealt with relations between American blacks and whites and eliminated the chorus line of pretty girls most musicals had included before that time. The year 1935 saw another ambitious musical in George Gershwin's *Porgy and Bess,* about a crippled black man in Charleston, South Carolina, who loses his woman to a slick character named Sportin' Life.

In 1943, *Oklahoma!,*—by Richard Rodgers and Oscar Hammerstein II (1895–1960)—began what is sometimes considered the golden age of the American musical. For the next quarter-century, through the creation of *Fiddler on the Roof,* there was an outpouring of American musicals that achieved worldwide recognition and are revived regularly today. A few examples of these are *South Pacific; The King and I; Kiss Me, Kate; Guys and Dolls; My Fair Lady;* and *Annie Get Your Gun.* In addition to songs and choral numbers, dance and ballet became an important feature of these musicals.

Structure of the Musical

While each of the musicals noted above has its own shape, we can detect a structure that many of them follow. A good example is *My Fair Lady.* The *book* or *libretto* (the words and outline of the musical) is by Alan Jay Lerner (1918–   ) and is based on George Bernard Shaw's play *Pygmalion.* Lerner also wrote the lyrics, and Frederick Loewe (1904–   ) composed the music.

My Fair Lady concerns a speech teacher, Henry Higgins, who claims that the English judge people by how they speak. He bets his friend Colonel Pickering that he can take an ordinary cockney flower girl, Eliza Doolittle, and by teaching her correct diction, pass her off as a duchess. It was characteristic of musicals of this era to have a comic subplot, and *My Fair Lady* is no exception. The subplot deals with Eliza's father, Alfred P. Doolittle, a ne'er-do-well who doesn't want to achieve middle-class respectability because then he will have to marry the woman he lives with.

This form generally alternates musical numbers—solos, choruses, dances—with spoken
scenes. *Dreamgirls* tells in musical form the story of a black singing group that became
enormously successful. Along the way one member was dropped in an unpleasant way.
The original three are shown here, played by Vanessa Townsell, Loretta Devine, and
Sheryl Lee Ralph.

(Martha Swope)

The first song in the show is by Higgins—"Why Can't the English Learn to
Speak?" The next song shifts to Eliza and her dreams of luxury as she sings
"Wouldn't It Be Loverly?" She is joined in this number by a chorus. The
action now shifts to the subplot, and Alfred Doolittle is joined by two
buddies to sing of how he hopes to avoid working "With a Little Bit of
Luck." We then move back to a scene with Higgins, who is pushing Eliza
very hard to learn to speak properly. Higgins, who is anything but ordinary,
nevertheless protests in a song "I'm an Ordinary Man." Eliza vows revenge
on the harsh Higgins in her next song: "Just You Wait." After this Eliza
begins to improve her speech. She celebrates this in a song with Higgins and
Pickering called "The Rain in Spain." The scene then shifts to the Ascot
horse races, where Eliza is dressed as a lady. This is an ensemble number,
"The Ascot Gavotte."

The musical proceeds in this manner, moving from one character to another, from a solo number to a trio to an ensemble number. There is variety in these numbers—some are serious, some are comic, some explain the characters' feelings, some describe a situation. It is in the alternation—from one kind of song to another, from one scene to another, from one set of characters to another—that musical theater structure is built. Always, too, it must be remembered, spoken scenes are interspersed with musical numbers. Also, ballet or modern dance routines are generally interspersed with other numbers. The aim, as with other forms of theater, is to build excitement as the musical progresses.

In recent years there have been experiments with other types of musical structure. *A Chorus Line,* for instance, takes the form of an audition for dancers who want to be in the chorus line of a Broadway show. One by one the people who hope to be chosen are asked to tell about their lives and ambitions. These statements culminate in songs or dances. The audition scheme provides a framework that leads to a succession of songs, just as a plot leads to songs in a conventional musical.

(Martha Swope)

A musical based on Shakespeare.
West Side Story is a modern musical version of Shakespeare's classic love tragedy *Romeo and Juliet.* In addition to setting the play in a contemporary American city, the authors of the musical compressed scenes and transformed other scenes into singing or dancing numbers. This scene from a Broadway production shows one of the street gangs in the story.

DRAMATIC STRUCTURE: OTHER FORMS

The musical revue.
This popular form of musical entertainment includes songs, dance numbers, and dramatic sketches. There is no overall story, but rather a mixture of musical and dramatic numbers. Shown here is a scene from the *Ziegfeld Follies,* one of the best known and most lavish of all revues. A new one was produced almost every year from 1907 to 1931.

One other musical form to take note of is the *revue*—an anthology or collection of songs and dramatic skits. The revue will be discussed in the section below.

SERIAL STRUCTURE

A special kind of structure is a series of acts or episodes—individual theater events—offered as a single presentation. In this case, individual segments are strung together like beads on a necklace. Sometimes a central theme or common thread holds the parts together; sometimes there is little or no connection between the various parts.

The musical revue is a case in point. In the revue, short scenes, vignettes, skits, dance numbers, songs, and possibly even vaudeville routines are presented on a single program. There may be an overall theme, such as political satire or the celebration of a certain year from the past. Sometimes a master of ceremonies provides continuity for the various segments. In a revue in which there is no visible connection between the parts, the primary consideration is the pace and variety of the acts. A song is usually followed by a dramatic scene, a serious number by a comic one, and so forth. Another form of musical revue is one that contains only musical numbers. Two shows of the late 1970s, *Ain't Misbehavin'* and *Eubie*, celebrating the music of the famous black composers Fats Waller and Eubie Blake respectively, are examples of this form.

In today's theater we frequently see a program of short plays. Sometimes there will be a bill of one-act plays by the same author, but at other times two or three plays by different authors. Also, on some occasions an attempt is made to relate the separate plays to a central theme, but on others the plays are chosen simply to complete an evening's entertainment.

In Chapters 7, 8, and 9, we have been examining the responsibility of the playwright in developing the dramatic structure for a play. Whether the play is climactic or episodic, a ritual, pattern, or revue, it is the job of the dramatist to create some form of framework. In Chapter 10, we turn to another responsibility of the playwright: creating dramatic characters.

SUMMARY

1   Nonsense or *non sequitur*, a feature of the theater of the absurd, can be the basis of dramatic construction: events do not logically follow one another, suggesting the chaos and absurdity of the world in which we live.
2   Avant-garde theater sometimes arranges events in a random way to suggest the random or haphazard manner in which life unfolds in everyday situations.
3   Ritual or pattern is often used as the basis of dramatic structure. Words, gestures, and events are repeated; they have a symbolic meaning acquired both through repetition and through the significance invested in them from the past.
4   Some experimental groups of the 1960s and 1970s used radical forms, including nonverbal and improvisational structure.
5   Segments and tableaux have also been used as structure.
6   Musical theater builds by alternating scenes of spoken dialogue with musical numbers. The musical numbers vary from solos and duets to choral numbers and dance numbers.
7   In certain cases theater events are strung together to make a program. This could include a group of unrelated one-act plays and a group of skits and songs in a revue. In this case structure is within the individual units themselves; among the units the only structure might be the separate elements unfolding; or there can be a common theme uniting them.

10
DRAMATIC CHARACTERS

Medea: An exceptional character.
The heroes and heroines of traditional theater stand apart from ordinary people—in position and personality. They are often "larger than life," people who live at the outer edge of experience. A good example is Medea, the title character in the play by the Greek playwright Euripides. Medea, portrayed in this scene by Zoe Caldwell, arranged the death of the young woman whom her husband left her to marry. To add to her revenge on her husband, Medea later murdered her own children.

Though they often seem like real people when presented on stage, dramatic characters begin in the mind of the playwright. They are a construct. By carefully selecting certain features and emphasizing them, while eliminating others, the dramatist can show us in two hours the entire history of a person whom it could take us a lifetime to know in real life. In Tennessee Williams's *A Streetcar Named Desire,* for example, we come to know the leading character, Blanche DuBois, in all her emotional complexity better than we know people we see every day. The dramatist reveals to us not only Blanche's biography but her soul, and we become intimately acquainted with the inner workings of her mind.

Also, the playwright has wide latitude in what to emphasize and how to present the character. A stage character can be presented in different ways: (1) drawn with a few quick strokes, as a cartoonist sketches a political figure, (2) given the surface detail and reality of a photograph, or (3) fleshed out with the more interpretive and fully rounded quality of an oil portrait. Whatever the form, however, to achieve maximum impact as an image or symbol, a dramatic character must stand out. Traditionally, several major types of characters have proved effective in the theater.

EXTRAORDINARY CHARACTERS

The heroes and heroines of most important dramatic works of the past are extraordinary in some way. They stand apart from ordinary people and are "larger than life." Historically, major characters have been kings, queens, bishops, members of the nobility, or other figures clearly marked as holding a special place in society. Such characters are extraordinary in the first place by virtue of their position. A queen, for instance, is accorded respect because of her authority, power, and grandeur. In the same way, we respect Supreme Court justices because of the high place they occupy.

Dramatists go one step further, however, in depicting extraordinary characters. Not only do these characters fill prestigious roles, they generally represent men and women at their worst or best, at some extreme of human behavior. Lady Macbeth is not only a noblewoman, she is one of the most ambitious women ever depicted on the stage. In virtually every instance with extraordinary characters we see men and women at the breaking point, at the outer limits of human capability and endurance.

Antigone and Saint Joan, for example, are the epitome of the independent, courageous female, willing to stand up to male authority and suffer whatever consequences they are forced to endure. Prometheus, Oedipus, and the biblical figure Abraham are men willing to face the worst the gods can throw at them and meet it with strength and dignity. The Cid, hero of the play by Pierre Corneille, represents the warrior at his most noble and chivalrous. Thomas à Becket, archbishop of Canterbury under King Henry II of England—the subject of *Becket* by Jean Anouilh, and *Murder in the Cathedral* by T. S. Eliot (1885–1965)—was martyred for his defiance of a king.

Among those qualifying as men and women at their worst are Medea, who murdered her own children; and the brothers of the heroine of *The Duchess of Malfi* by John Webster, who forbade their sister to get married so that they could get her estate. When the brothers discovered that she had married, they had her and her children imprisoned, cruelly tortured, and eventually strangled.

Comic characters can also be extremes. The chief character in *Volpone* by Ben Jonson (1572–1637) is a greedy, avaricious miser who gets people to present him with expensive gifts because they think he will remember them in his will.

Many traditional characters fall between the poles of extreme virtue and extreme vice; but they nevertheless possess exceptional, sometimes strongly contradictory, qualities. Faustus, treated by Christopher Marlowe in *Doctor Faustus* and by Johann Wolfgang von Goethe in *Faust,* was a great scholar, but so bored with his existence and so ambitious that he made a compact with the devil, forfeiting his life in return for unlimited power. Cleopatra, an exceedingly vain, selfish woman, had, at the same time, "immortal longings." Electra's strong sense of family honor led her, on the one hand, to stand up for her murdered father, but, on the other, to arrange the murder of her own mother and stepfather. Queen Elizabeth I of England and Mary, Queen of Scots, rivals in real life, have made admirable dramatic characters, being women of both strong virtues and telling weaknesses.

In short, the heroes and heroines of traditional theater have been exceptional, not only by virtue of their station in life, but because they possess traits common to us all—ambition, generosity, malevolence, fear, and achievement—in such great abundance.

CHARACTERS IN MODERN THEATER

Kings and queens have continued to be treated in drama in the modern period—that is, in the last hundred years. But beginning in the eighteenth century, ordinary people took over from royalty and the nobility as the heroes and heroines of drama—a reflection of what was occurring in real life. The chief figures in drama, therefore, frequently became people without the symbolic significance of a titled or regal person.

Exceptional Characters

Even so, the leading figures of drama continued in many cases to be exceptional men and women at their best and worst.

Hedda Gabler:
A modern dramatic character.
The leading figures in contemporary drama
are usually not kings or queens, but they are
often exceptional in other ways. The leading
character in Ibsen's *Hedda Gabler*, here portrayed by Jane Alexander, will go to any
lengths to control the people around her.
When she loses that control, she shoots herself.

The heroine of August Strindberg's *Miss Julie* is a neurotic, obsessive
woman at the end of her rope. So, too, in her own way is Blanche DuBois in
A Streetcar Named Desire. In *Mother Courage* by Bertolt Brecht, we see the
portrait of a woman who will sacrifice almost anything to survive; she even
loses a son by haggling over the price of his release. *Emperor Jones,* by
Eugene O'Neill, shows the downfall of a powerful black man who has made
himself the ruler of a Caribbean island.

Among modern characters who stand for people at their worst are Joe
Keller of Arthur Miller's *All My Sons* and Regina of *The Little Foxes* by Lillian
Hellman. Keller, in his insatiable desire for profit, manufactures defective
airplane parts during World War II, leading to the death of several pilots.
Regina, a cunning, avaricious woman, stands by while her dying husband
has a heart attack, refusing to get the medicine which can save his life.

Ordinary or Typical Characters

When ordinary characters took over from kings and queens, a new type of leading character emerged alongside the extraordinary character, a character who is also fully rounded and three-dimensional. Rather than being exceptional as the worst, the best, or some other extreme, these characters are exceptional in the way they *embody* the characteristics of an entire group: not as a caricature, but as a complete picture of a person.

A good example of such a character from modern drama is Nora Helmer, the heroine of Henrik Ibsen's *A Doll's House*. A spoiled, flighty woman, she secretly forged a signature to get money for her husband when he was very ill and needed medical attention. All her life, first by her father, then by her husband, she has been treated like a doll or a plaything, not as a mature, responsible woman. In the last act of the play Nora rebels against this attitude; she makes a declaration of independence to her husband, slams

(Martha Swope)

Modern characters are often ordinary people.

The characters in modern drama are frequently people from the middle class or lower middle class who have everyday occupations. The two waiters in *Master Harold and the Boys*, by the South African playwright Athol Fugard, are a good example. The waiter in the center is played by James Earl Jones, the one at the right by Delroy Lindo. The actor at the left, Michael White, plays the son of the owner of the tea shop where they work.

the door on him, and walks out. It has been said that Nora's slamming of the door marked the beginning not only of modern drama but of the emancipation of modern women. Certainly Nora's defiance—her claim to be treated as an equal—has made her a prototype of all housewives who refuse to be regarded as house pets. She is an ordinary wife and mother in one sense, far from an Antigone or a Lady Macbeth, but she is exceptional in the way she sums up an entire group of women. *A Doll's House* was written in 1879; but today, 100 years later, Nora is still a symbol of modern woman. The play is revived year after year, and Nora's message does not lose its relevance.

In *Who's Afraid of Virginia Woolf?* by Edward Albee, the main characters are a husband and a wife, quite commonplace in a way. He is a somewhat ineffectual college professor; she is the college president's daughter. They argue and fight almost to the point of exhaustion. Another unhappily married couple? Yes. But again, they are quintessential; that is, they contain the essence of a certain type of married couple. To Albee, they represent an American type: a bitter, alienated couple, bored with themselves and each other. And to underline this point, he names them Martha and George, giving them the same first names as Martha and George Washington—America's "first couple."

Another example is the main character in the play *The Basic Training of Pavlo Hummel* by David Rabe (1940–   ). The background of the play is the Vietnamese war. Pavlo, a born loser, has difficulty in coping with the confusion, alienation, and corruption of modern life, and as a result he becomes both a victim and a person who victimizes others. He personifies a number of troubled young people who grew up in the difficult period of the 1960s and early 1970s.

Similarly, Willy Loman, in Arthur Miller's *Death of a Salesman,* sums up all salesmen, traveling in their territories on a "smile and a shoeshine." He has bought the false dream that by putting up a good front and being "well liked," he will be a great success and achieve material wealth.

Nora Helmer, Martha and George, Pavlo Hummel, and Willy Loman: all are examples of ordinary characters who stand apart from the crowd, not by standing above it, but by summing up in their personalities the essence of a certain type of person.

STOCK CHARACTERS

Many characters in drama are not as complete as the three-dimensional characters described above. Rather, they symbolize in bold relief some particular type of person or some outstanding characteristic of human behavior to the exclusion of virtually everything else. They appear particularly in comedy and melodrama, though they can be found in almost all kinds of drama.

The stock characters of commedia dell'arte.
Italian comedy of the Renaissance developed stereotyped characters who were always the same: each character was famous for a certain trait—greed, boastfulness, gullibility, etc.—and always wore a certain kind of costume. This etching by Jacques Callot shows two such characters. Notice the elaborate headdress and the half masks that were characteristic of commedia characters.

Traditional Examples

Among the *stock* characters, some of the most famous examples are those in *commedia dell'arte,* a form of popular comedy which flourished in Italy during the sixteenth and seventeenth centuries. In commedia dell'arte, there were no scripts, but rather scenarios which gave an outline of the story. The performers improvised or invented words and comic actions to fill out the play. The stock characters of commedia were either straight or exaggerated, and were divided into servants and members of the ruling class. In every case, however, one particular feature or trait was stressed. Wherever they appeared, these characters had the same propensities and wore the same costumes. The bragging soldier, called the *Capitano,* always boasted of his courage in a series of fictitious military victories. (A forebear of this character had appeared in Roman comedy centuries before.) The young lovers were fixtures as well. Older characters included *Pantalone,* an elderly merchant who spoke in clichés and chased young girls, and a

DRAMATIC CHARACTERS

pompous lawyer called *Dottore,* who spoke in Latin phrases and attempted to impress others with his learning. Among servants, *Harlequin* was the most popular; displaying both cunning and stupidity, he was at the heart of every plot complication. These are but a few of a full range of characters, each with his or her own peculiarities. As for other examples of stock characters in drama, we are all familiar with such figures as the lovely young heroine "pure as the driven snow," and the villain, lurking in the shadows, twirling his moustache.

Modern Examples

The familiar figures on weekly situation comedies on television are a good example of stock or stereotypical characters. The conceited high school boy, the prejudiced father, the harried mother, the dumb blond waitress, the efficient career woman, the tough private detective: these characters are stereotypes whom we see every day on television. As with all stereotypes, their attitudes and actions are always predictable.

Characters with a Dominant Trait

Closely related to stock characters are characters with a single trait or "humor." A theory that the body was governed by four humors, which must be kept in balance for a person to be healthy, was widely held during the Renaissance. In the sixteenth century it was extended to include psychological traits, and the playwright Ben Jonson followed this notion extensively in his plays. In *Every Man in His Humour* and *Every Man out of His Humour,* for instance, he portrayed characters in whom one humor came to dominate all others, making for an unbalanced, often comic, personality. Jonson often named his characters for their single trait or humor. In *The Alchemist* he includes Subtle, Face, Dapper, Surly, Wholesome, and Dame Pliant.

During the English Restoration and after, playwrights continued to give characters names indicating their personalities. In *The Way of the World,* by William Congreve, one character is called Fainall, meaning that he feigns all, or pretends everything. Other characters are named Petulant, Sir Wilful Witwoud, Waitwell, and Lady Wishfort, the last being a contraction of "wish for it." In another play from the English Restoration, *The Country Wife* by William Wycherley, there are Mr. Pinchwife (a man who hides his wife from other men), Sparkish (a man who thinks he sparkles with wit), Sir Jasper Fidget, and Mrs. Squeamish. Names of characters in other English plays of the seventeenth and eighteenth centuries include Lady Sneerwell, Careless, Snake, Sir Benjamin Backbite, Mrs. Candour, Scandal, Tattle, and Mrs. Frail. The French playwright Molière, while generally giving his characters regular names, frequently emphasized the dominant trait of the main character in the title: *The Miser, The Misanthrope, The Would-Be Gentleman,* and *The Imaginary Invalid.*

Characters with a dominant trait.
Related to stock characters are characters with one outstanding tendency or "humor."
Typical is the title character in Molière's *The Miser*, shown here on the right played by
Robert Symonds. Everything in the Miser's character is subordinated to his extreme
greed, which controls all his actions and leads to many comic excesses.

MINOR CHARACTERS

Stock characters or characters with a dominant trait are characters who play
an important role in a drama. Though these characters are one-sided, they
are not to be confused with *minor characters*. Minor characters are
those—in all types of plays—who play a small part in the overall action.
Generally they appear briefly and serve chiefly to further the story or to
support more important characters. Examples of minor characters are
servants, soldiers, and so forth. Even doctors, lawyers, or close friends of
leading characters are considered minor if they play only a small part in the
action. Since we see so little of these characters, they usually can show only
one facet of their personalities. This is a different case, however, from that of
a main character who is deliberately portrayed as one-sided or as a
stereotypical figure from beginning to end.

The Way of the World (1700)

WILLIAM CONGREVE (1670–1729)

CHIEF CHARACTERS:

Mirabell—in love with Mrs. Millamant
Mrs. Millamant—niece of Lady Wishfort
Lady Wishfort—enemy of Mirabell
Fainall—in love with Mrs. Marwood
Mrs. Fainall—wife of Fainall and daughter
  of Lady Wishfort
Mrs. Marwood—friend to Mr. Fainfall
Sir Wilfull Witwoud—nephew of Lady
  Wishfort
Witwound—follower of Mrs. Millamant
Petulant—follower of Mrs. Millamant
Waitwell—servant of Mirabell
Foible—maid of Lady Wishfort

BACKGROUND: The play takes place among
members of the upper class in London in the
late seventeenth century. The society it depicts
is highly artificial and values gossip, intrigue,
deception, seduction, and sparkling conversation above everything else.

ACT I: A chocolate shop. Mirabell complains
to Fainall that his attempt to win the love of
Millamant is not succeeding because Millamant's aunt and guardian, Lady Wishfort
has turned against him. Lady Wishfort is infatuated with Mirabell but she feels he has not
been attentive enough. Witwoud and Petulant,
followers of Millamant, join the conversation.

ACT II: In St. James Park, Mrs. Fainall and Mrs.

Marwood are talking when Fainall and Mirabell join them. (Mrs. Fainall is Mirabell's mistress, though he really loves Millamant.) When
Mirabell and Mrs. Fainall are alone, Mrs.
Fainall complains that she detests Fainall
whom Mirabell compelled her to marry.
Though disappointed in Mirabell, Mrs. Fainall's passion for him leads her to help him in
his next scheme, even though it involves her
mother, Lady Wishfort. Mirabell wants to
marry the beautiful and wealthy Millamant,
but her aunt is jealously withholding her consent. With Mrs. Fainall's connivance, Mirabell
arranges to have his servant, Waitwell, in the
guise of an uncle called Sir Rowland, pay
court to Lady Wishfort. Then, since Mirabell
already has accomplished a secret marriage
between Waitwell and Lady Wishfort's maid,
Foible, he declares his intention to expose the
scandal. He will remain silent only if he can
have Mrs. Millamant and her fortune.

ACT III: With the scheme perfected, the scene
shifts to Lady Wishfort's house. Foible tells
Lady Wishfort that a man known as Sir
Rowland has seen her picture and is infatuated
by her. A meeting is arranged, but their plot is
overheard by Mrs. Marwood, another of Mirabell's conquests and herself a crafty schemer.
Desiring Mirabell for herself, Mrs. Marwood
promptly influences Lady Wishfort to agree
that her rival Mrs. Millamant shall be married

to Sir Wilfull, a rich and amiable dunce. Then Mrs. Marwood, to make sure of success, enlists the help of Fainall who is infatuated with her and jealous of Mirabell. Fainall agrees to Mrs. Marwood's plan: she will write a letter to be delivered to Lady Wishfort when Waitwell, as Sir Rowland, is with her. The letter will expose the fraud and Mirabell will be ruined. Mrs. Marwood neglects to tell Fainall that she wants to save Mirabell for herself.

ACT IV: Lady Wishfort is atwitter as she awaits the bogus Sir Rowland. Meanwhile, Mirabell and Millamant discuss the kind of common-sense "contract" they believe a husband and wife should agree to for their marriage to succeed. The action then returns to Lady Wishfort and the arrival of Sir Rowland. He and Lady Wishfort get along famously; he begs for an early marriage, declaring that his nephew, Mirabell, will poison him for his money if he learns of the romance. The jealous Lady Wishfort promptly agrees, suggesting that Sir Rowland starve Mirabell "gradually, inch by inch." Then Mrs. Marwood's letter, denouncing Sir Rowland as Waitwell, arrives, but Sir Rowland deftly declares the letter to be the work of his nephew, and he leaves claiming he must fight a duel.

ACT V: Lady Wishfort learns of the deception that is being practiced on her and turns on Foible. The frightened Foible confesses that Mirabell conceived the whole plot, and Lady Wishfort is planning a dire revenge when more trouble comes: Fainall, her son-in-law, demands that his wife turn over her whole fortune to him, or else he and Mrs. Marwood will reveal to the world that Mrs. Fainall was Mirabell's mistress before her marriage and that she continues to be. Lady Wishfort is reflecting upon this new humiliation when Mirabell comes to her asking forgiveness.

The susceptible Lady Wishfort offers to forgive Mirabell if he will renounce his idea of marrying Mrs. Millamant. Mirabell offers a compromise: if she will permit her niece to marry him, he will contrive to save Mrs. Fainall's reputation and fortune. If he can do this, Lady Wishfort agrees, she will forgive all and consent to anything. Mirabell then tells her: "Well, then, as regards your daughter's reputation, she has nothing to fear from Fainall. For his own reputation is at stake. He and Mrs. Marwood—we have proof of it—have been and still are lovers. . . . And as regards your daughter's fortune, she need have no fear on that score, either: acting upon my advice, and relying upon my honesty, she has made me the trustee of her entire estate." Cries Fainall: "'Tis outrageous!" Says Mirabell: "'Tis the way of the world."

Performers play nonhuman parts.
Sometimes theatrical characters are nonhuman, though they usually have human characteristics. Many of the characters in *Alice in Wonderland* are examples. Seen here in a scene with Kate Burton as Alice is the character of Humpty-Dumpty.

NONHUMAN CHARACTERS

In Greece in the fifth century B.C., and in many primitive cultures, actors portrayed birds and animals; and the practice has continued to the present. Aristophanes, the Greek comic dramatist, used a chorus of actors to play the title parts in his plays *The Birds* and *The Frogs*. In the modern period, Eugène Ionesco has men turn into animals in *Rhinoceros;* and Edmond Rostand, a French playwright, wrote a poetic fable about a rooster called *Chantecler.* Karel Capek (1890–1938), a Czechoslovakian dramatist, collaborated with his brother, Josef, to write *The Insect Comedy,* a picture of insect life as seen in the delirium of a dying vagabond.

Occasionally performers are called on to play other nonhuman parts. Karel Capek also wrote a play entitled *R.U.R.,* in which people play robots. (The initials in the title stand for Rossum's Universal Robots, and it was from this play that the word *robot* derives.) In the medieval morality play *Everyman,* characters represent ideas or concepts, such as Fellowship, Good Deeds, Worldly Possession, Beauty.

In certain forms of avant-garde—particularly in *happenings,* a freeform improvisation that combines art and dance with theater—performers might be used as objects or automatons. In the words of Michael Kirby, a commentator on happenings, "Occasionally people are used somewhat as inanimate objects."[1] An example would be an actress performing a "task" such as climbing a stepladder over and over again, or an actor crouching on hands and knees to serve as a bench for another actor. In such cases there is some doubt that questions of "dramatic characters" or "acting" even enter the picture. Performers are serving another purpose, in the way that dancers sometimes use their bodies as moving shapes in abstract ballets.

Dramatic characters in the guise of animals or robots are the exception rather than the rule. When they do occur, more often than not it is the human quality of the animal or robot which is being emphasized, and sometimes the reverse: the animalistic or robotlike quality of the human being.

JUXTAPOSITION OF CHARACTERS

Since characters are symbols of people, the playwright can use them in combination with one another to bring out certain qualities.

Protagonist and Antagonist

From the Greek theater we have the terms *protagonist* and *antagonist.* The protagonist is the main character in the play—Othello, for instance—and the antagonist is the main character's chief opponent. In the case of *Othello,* the antagonist is Iago. It is through the contest of the two characters that their individual qualities are developed.

Contrasting Characters

There is another way in which dramatists combine characters: by contrasting them. Sophocles created two exceptionally strong-willed, independent female characters—Antigone and Electra—each one the title character in a play. Both are young women intent on defying an older person and willing to risk death to fight for a principle. But Sophocles was not content to present them as they were on their own. Unlike other dramatists who had told the same story, Sophocles gave them sisters whose characters contrasted sharply with theirs. To Antigone he gave Ismene, a docile, compliant sister who argued with Antigone that she should obey the law and give in to authority. To Electra, Sophocles gave a sister, Chrisothemis, a meek, frightened creature who protested that as women they were powerless to act. Sophocles strengthened and clarified both Antigone and Electra by providing them with contrasting characters to show off their determination and courage.

Frequently a dramatist will introduce secondary characters to act as foils or counterparts to the main characters. In *Hedda Gabler,* by Henrik Ibsen, the main character is a willful, destructive woman, bent on having her own way; Hedda wishes to possess men but is unable to love them. Mrs. Elvsted, another character in the play, is her opposite in almost every way: a trusting, warm, sincere woman, able to give of herself to others. This technique of setting parallel or contrasting characters beside one another is like putting one color next to another. A single color is sometimes difficult to judge; but the moment we put others beside it, we become aware of its relative brightness. A bright red, for instance, looks even brighter next to pink; a dark green looks much darker when it is seen next to pale green.

Major and Minor Characters

Earlier, minor characters were mentioned. The *major* characters in a play are the important figures, the ones about whom the play revolves. In *Hamlet* the major characters include Hamlet, Claudius, Gertrude, Polonius, Laertes, and Ophelia; the minor characters include Marcellus and Bernardo, who are standing watch when the ghost appears, and Reynaldo, a servant to Polonius. Sometimes characters fall halfway between major and minor; examples in *Hamlet* are Rosencrantz and Guildenstern, or the gravedigger. In these instances the characters, each of whom has a distinctive personality, play a small but quite important part in the play.

One function of minor characters is to stand in contrast to the important figures in a play. In the same way that a dramatist selects certain features of a person to emphasize and eliminates others, so the dramatist focuses on the main characters and places others in the background. Otherwise, the viewer would have no perspective and sense of proportion with regard to the various characters.

ORCHESTRATION OF CHARACTERS

Anton Chekhov, the Russian dramatist, is said to have "orchestrated" his characters. The reference is to a musical composition in which the theme is played first by one section of the orchestra, such as the violins, and then by another, such as the brass or woodwinds. Not only is the theme taken up by various sections, but it can be played in different ways, first in a major key and then in a minor. In his plays, Chekhov drew a series of characters with a

The orchestration of characters: A Chekhov grouping.
Characters in a play serve as contrasts, counterparts, or complements to each other. Sometimes one group of characters is set in opposition to another. Chekhov was a master at combining and contrasting characters. Here we see a scene from Chekhov's *The Three Sisters*, a play about a group of people who live lives of frustration.

common problem, and each of the characters represented some aspect of the central theme. In Chekhov's *Uncle Vanya,* for example, the theme of disillusionment and frustration with life is shared by virtually every character in the play; but each in his or her own way. Uncle Vanya has been working on an estate to help support a professor who he discovers is a fraud. In the midst of his disillusionment Vanya falls in love with the professor's young wife, but she does not return his love. A neighbor, Dr. Astrov, has made sacrifices to be a doctor in a small rural community and then has grown dissatisfied with his life. He too loves the professor's wife, but nothing can come of it. Vanya's niece, a plain woman who works hard for little reward, is in love with Dr. Astrov, but he cannot return her love. And so it goes; practically everyone embodies the theme. But it is subtly and carefully done. No one person stands alone; the theme is brought out through the overall effect in which gradations and shadings of meaning are interwoven like threads in a tapestry.

Chekhov was a master at orchestrating his characters, but he was not the only dramatist to employ the technique. In one way or another, most dramatists try to arrange their characters so that they produce a cumulative effect. It is not what one character does or says, but what all the characters do together, that creates the effect.

DRAMATIC CHARACTERS: IMAGES OF OURSELVES

Dramatic characters sometimes have an impact that seems more "real than real." In fact, Luigi Pirandello, an Italian dramatist, wrote a play, *Six Characters in Search of an Author,* in which he argued that dramatic characters are more permanent and less of an illusion than human beings. Speaking through the character of the Father, he says, "He who has had the luck to be born a character can laugh even at death. He cannot die. The man, the writer, the instrument of the creation will die, but his creation does not die." Arguing with a theater manager in the play, the Father points out that whereas human beings are always changing, and are different from one day to the next, characters remain the same. The Manager picks up the argument, with the character of the Father:

THE MANAGER: Then you'll be saying next that you . . . are truer and more real than I am.

THE FATHER: But of course; without doubt! . . .

THE MANAGER: More real than I?

THE FATHER: If your reality can change from one day to another . . .

THE MANAGER: But everyone knows it can change. It is always changing, the same as anyone else's.

THE FATHER:	No, sir, not ours! Look here! That is the very difference! Our reality doesn't change; it can't change! It can't be other than what it is, because it is already fixed forever.[2]

Their permanence, however, is not the only feature of the dramatic characters. When well drawn, they present us with a vivid, incisive picture of ourselves. We see individuals at their best and their worst; we see them perform acts of heroic courage, acts we like to feel we ourselves are capable of; and we see deeds of cowardice and violence—again, actions we fear we might commit in moments of weakness or anger. We see outrageous cases of human folly and pretension, which make us laugh uproariously. In short, we see ourselves in the revealing and illuminating mirror theater holds before us.

We have seen that the exchange between performer and spectator is the basic encounter of theater. But the dramatic characters impersonated by the performers are images of ourselves. In truth, therefore, the basic encounter of theater is with ourselves. Sometimes, watching a theater event, we see a part of ourselves on stage and realize for the first time some truth about our lives. This confrontation is at the heart of the theater experience.

The people who bring characters to life who afford us the opportunity to have a confrontation with ourselves—are the performers. In Part Four, we turn to a study of the performers and of the directors who guide them.

SUMMARY

1   Dramatic characters are symbols of people and fall into several categories; the chief characters of traditional theater are extraordinary characters, men and women at the outer limits of human behavior.
2   In modern serious theater we frequently find significant typical characters complete, fully rounded portraits of people who embody a whole group or type. An example is Willy Loman, the salesman in *Death of a Salesman*.
3   Some characters are stereotypes. Stock characters, for instance, are predictable, clearly defined types. Other characters feature one dominant trait which overshadows all other features.
4   Occasionally performers are asked to play nonhuman parts—animals, birds, etc.—but generally with a strong human flavor.
5   Characters are placed together by the playwright in certain combinations to obtain maximum effectiveness. A *protagonist* may be opposed by an *antagonist; minor* characters support *major* characters; and characters are orchestrated into a whole.
6   Dramatic characters are symbols of people; therefore, the basic confrontation in theater is with ourselves.

The audience meets the performers.

The essence of the theater experience is the exchange between performers and spectators—the "chemistry" or "electricity" that flows between them during a performance such as the one at the Oregon Shakespeare Festival shown on the opposite page.

The faces of tragedy.
In every play, the playwright establishes a point of view. In tragedy, it is a serious view of life, often expressed in the fate of the central character. Opposite page: top, the Greek heroine Antigone; bottom, Shakespeare's King Lear. This page, above, Othello; left, a modern trage-

Comedy through the ages.
Along with tragedy, comedy has been one of the staples of theater. The laughter of comedy is exemplified in Shakespeare's *The Comedy of Errors* (opposite page, top); Oliver Goldsmith's eighteenth-century play *She Stoops to Conquer* (opposite page, bottom); and *A Flea in Her Ear*, a nineteenth-century farce by George Feydeau (this page, above). On the left is a modern tragicomedy, Samuel Beckett's *Waiting for Godot*. This form combines serious and comic elements in a single play.

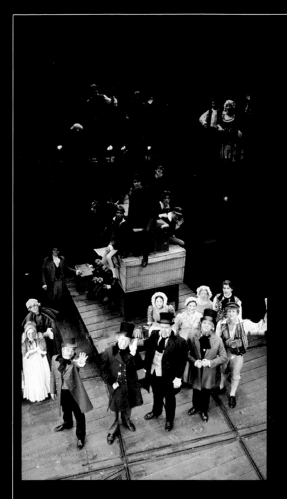

Acting: A combination of talent and skill.
Performers must learn many skills to meet diverse challenges: provide convincing portrayals of individual characters in Chekhov's *The Three Sisters* (opposite page), play in different styles and work as an ensemble in Dickens's *Nicholas Nickleby* (above, left); play classic roles and speak verse in Shakespeare's *All's Well That Ends Well* (above, right); develop special physical and vocal skills for musicals like *Forty-Second Street* (left).

The director coordinates the elements.
Opposite page, top: The director Michael Bennett on the night that *A Chorus Line* became the longest-running musical in Broadway history. Behind him are members of the creative team he supervised: writers, composers, designers, and performers. The scene at bottom opposite shows the end result of a director's work—in this case, the musical *Forty-Second Street*, directed by Gower Champion. Two people the director works with closely are the scene designer and the lighting designer, who supervise the visual elements of a production. This page: above, a setting for the musical *Nine*; left, a special stage environment for a production of *Hamlet*.

Scenery and lighting set the stage.
Designers must create an environment
that suits the style and subject of the
play. Opposite page: a festive scene
from a new version of Shakespeare's
As You Like It. This page: above, a
stage tableau from *Sunday in the Park
with George*, a musical that shows
how the painter George Seurat created
his most famous painting; left, an abstract set for Brecht's *The Good
Woman of Setzuan*.

Costumes reveal character.
Stage costumes indicate time and place and the style of the production, as well as the personality of the character. Far left above, an actress as Queen Elizabeth; to her right, an elaborate costume worn in the musical *Nine;* lower left, an actress in a pig mask in Ibsen's *Peer Gynt.* On the opposite page are two sets of show costumes: top, the singers in *Dreamgirls;* bottom, the men dressed as women in the chorus of *La Cage aux Folles.*

The diversity of modern theater.
Audiences today can enjoy a wide variety of theater experiences. Opposite page, top: Chekhov's tragicomedy *The Cherry Orchard*; bottom, an avant-garde play, *Dead End Kids*. On this page, Brecht's epic drama *Mother Courage* (above left); a look at the contemporary scene in Sam Shepard's *Fool for Love* (above right); and an old-fashioned vaudeville routine in *Sugar Babies* (left).

Overleaf: Two additional types of productions in today's theater—revivals of classics such as Shakespeare's *All's Well That Ends Well* (top), and fantasies like *Alice in Wonderland* (bottom).

PART 4

THE PERFORMERS AND THE DIRECTOR

Stage acting: The excitement and the demands.

Along with the rewards of being a stage performer, there are many requirements, including extensive training in a number of areas. A good example is *The Life and Adventures of Nicholas Nickleby* as performed by the Royal Shakespeare Company, shown in a drawing by Al Hirschfeld on the following pages. Except for Nicholas and his friend Smike at the center, all the performers had to play several roles in a variety of styles. The entire production was coordinated by the directors, Trevor Nunn and John Caird. Acting and directing are the subject of the three chapters of Part Four.

11

ACTING: OFFSTAGE AND ON

(Negro Ensemble Theater—Bert Andrews)

Playing a part—in theater and in life.
In life people play many roles—as parents, teachers, students, lawyers, etc. The theater often depicts these roles, a good example being the role of soldier. The characters in *A Soldier's Play* by Charles Fuller are shown here in a scene from the play. Charles Brown is on the left and Berkeley Harris on the right.

Performers bear a heavy responsibility in making the theater experience meaningful and enjoyable. By their presence they set theater apart from films, television, and the visual arts; but, more than that, they serve as the direct, immediate contact which members of the audience have with theater. They embody the heart and soul of theater. The words of the script, the characters created by the dramatist, and the scenery and costumes come to life only when an actor or actress steps on a stage.

Frequently, acting is looked on as glamorous—successful performers are interviewed on television or written up in newspapers or magazines; books are written about them. The publicity, however, is deceptive: it disguises the fact that acting is a difficult, disciplined profession. In addition to talent and ability, it requires years of arduous training. (In Chapter 12, we will look at some of this training.)

In order to gain a preliminary understanding of the process of acting, it might be helpful to examine certain activities with which everyone is familiar—types of "acting" in everyday life. Though markedly different from stage acting, they demonstrate some of the resources on which performers draw.

"ACTING" IN EVERYDAY LIFE

Two forms of "acting" in daily life are *imitation* and *role playing*. We will begin by looking at each of these and go on to look at some studies of everyday "acting."

Imitation

It may surprise some of us to realize to what degree "acting" is a part of our lives, beginning almost the day we are born. This takes several forms, one of the most common being imitation, where one person mimics or copies another's vocal patterns, gestures, facial expressions, posture, and the like. Children are among the best imitators in the world; and we are frequently amused at a child who imitates a parent or some other grownup: the 5-year-old girl, for instance, who puts on a long dress, makeup, and high heels.

For children, imitation is more than just a matter of show; it is also a way of learning: in other words, it is a matter of education and survival. The child watches a parent open a door or walk up stairs and learns by imitation how to complete the same maneuver. Speech patterns, too, are imitated by children.

Imitating role models.
Public figures like James Dean—as he appeared in the 1955 film *Rebel without a Cause*—become models whom people imitate in dress, mannerisms, etc. Such imitation is a form of acting in everyday life.

As we grow older, imitation continues to be a part of our experience: in every class in school, from elementary through college, there is usually one person—a clever mimic—who imitates the teacher or the principal with great humor, and sometimes cruelty. A familiar type of imitation is the attempt to follow the lifestyle of a hero—a singer, a film actor, or some other well-known personality. In the 1950s it was Elvis Presley or James Dean; in the 1960s, the Beatles; in the 1970s, Isaac Hayes, Mick Jagger, Carly Simon, James Taylor, or John Travolta; and in the 1980s, Michael Jackson. The imitator adopts the same wardrobe, the same stance, the same physical movements, the same hairstyles as the hero or heroine.

Role Playing

A second type of "acting" prevalent in our daily lives is role playing, about which much has been written in recent years. Broadly speaking, roles can be classified as *social* and *personal*.

Social roles   Social roles are general roles recognized by society: father, mother, child, police officer, store clerk, teacher, student, business executive, physician, and so on. Every culture expects definite types of behavior from people in these roles. For many years in western culture, for example, the roles of women as secretaries or housewives were considered subordinate to the roles of men. Even when women held similar positions to those of men in business and the professions, they frequently received smaller salaries for the same job. In recent years, women's liberation has challenged the notion of subservient roles of women. So entrenched was the idea, however, that it took an entire movement to call it into question. (*Consciousness-raising* was one aspect of the movement, making people aware of social attitudes to women.) Before changes could be made in the subordinate roles some women played, everyone had to understand that they *were* roles. The same challenge has been hurled at other roles. Positions of authority, for instance—such as those held by teachers, parents, priests, and rabbis, who for generations were treated with respect by society—have been questioned in recent years.

In role playing, anyone occupying a given position is expected to adopt a predetermined attitude: a store clerk, for instance, is expected to take care of customers with patience and courtesy, and not bring individual frustrations to the job. It is important to remember, too, that each of us fills not one but many social roles. A young woman in college, working part time, might have the following roles: student, employee, daughter, sister, and friend, not to mention female, young person, and citizen.

Personal roles   Aside from social roles, we develop personal roles with our family and friends. For example, some of us become braggarts, boasting of our feats and accomplishments (some of them imaginary), and we embellish the truth to appear more impressive than we are. Others become martyrs, constantly sacrificing for others, and letting the world know about it. A third type consists of conspirators, people who pull their friends aside to establish an air of secrecy whenever they talk. Frequently, two people fall into complementary roles, one dominant and the other submissive, one active and the other passive. In some cases this takes the form of a sadomasochistic relationship.

Role playing illustrated in drama   Interestingly enough, drama contains many illustrations of the kind of acting we do in our everyday lives. A good example is a scene from *Death of a Salesman* by Arthur Miller, in which Happy, the salesman's son, tries to be a "big shot" in a restaurant where he is scheduled to meet his father and his brother, Biff. Happy's father, the salesman, has just lost his job and is on the verge of losing his sanity as well. Happy should be thinking only of his father, but he cannot resist trying to impress a woman who enters the restaurant. (Biff, Happy's brother, enters in the middle of the scene. As the scene begins, Stanley, the waiter, speaks to Happy about the woman.)

Playing the big shot.

A scene from the Hartman Theatre Company production of Arthur Miller's *Death of a Salesman*, in which Happy tries to impress a woman with his importance. He overstates his accomplishments just as people in life sometimes do.

STANLEY:	I think that's for you, Mr. Loman.
HAPPY:	Look at that mouth. Oh, God, and the binoculars.
STANLEY:	Geez, you got a life, Mr. Loman.
HAPPY:	Wait on her.
STANLEY:	*[Going to the Girl's table]* Would you like a menu, ma'am?
GIRL:	I'm expecting someone, but I'd like a—
HAPPY:	Why don't you bring her—excuse me miss, do you mind? I sell champagne, and I'd like you to try my brand. Bring her a champagne, Stanley.
GIRL:	That's awfully nice of you.
HAPPY:	Don't mention it. It's all company money. *[He laughs]*
GIRL:	That's a charming product to be selling, isn't it?
HAPPY:	Oh, gets to be like everything else, selling is selling, y'know.
GIRL:	I suppose.

HAPPY:	You don't happen to sell, do you?
GIRL:	No, I don't sell.
HAPPY:	Would you object to a compliment from a stranger? You ought to be on a magazine cover.
GIRL:	[Looking at him a little archly] I have been. [Stanley comes in with a glass of champagne]
HAPPY:	What'd I say before, Stanley? You see? She's a cover girl.
STANLEY:	Oh, I could see, I could see.
HAPPY:	[To the Girl] What magazine?
GIRL:	Oh, a lot of them. [She takes the drink] Thank you.
HAPPY:	You know what they say in France don't you? "Champagne is the drink of the complexion"—Hiya, Biff! [Biff has entered and sits with Happy]
BIFF:	Hello, kid. Sorry I'm late.
HAPPY:	I just got here. Uh, Miss—?
GIRL:	Forsythe.
HAPPY:	Miss Forsythe, this is my brother.
BIFF:	Is Dad here?
HAPPY:	His name is Biff. You might've heard of him. Great football player.
GIRL:	Really? What team?
HAPPY:	Are you familiar with football?
GIRL:	No, I'm afraid not.
HAPPY:	Biff is quarterback with the New York Giants.
GIRL:	Well, that is nice, isn't it? [She drinks]
HAPPY:	Good health.
GIRL:	I'm happy to meet you.
HAPPY	That's my name. Hap. It's really Harold but at West Point they called me Happy.
GIRL:	[Now really impressed] Oh, I see. How do you do? [She turns her profile]
BIFF:	Isn't Dad coming?
HAPPY:	You want her?
BIFF:	Oh, I could never make that.
HAPPY:	I remember the time that idea would never come into your head. Where's the old confidence, Biff?
BIFF:	I just saw Oliver—
HAPPY:	Wait a minute. I've got to see that old confidence again. Do you want her? She's on call.
BIFF:	Oh, no. [He turns to look at the Girl]
HAPPY:	I'm telling you. Watch this. [Turning to the Girl] Honey? [She turns to him] Are you busy?
GIRL:	Well, I am . . . but I could make a phone call.

HAPPY:	Do that, will you, honey? And see if you can get a friend. We'll be here for a while. Biff is one of the greatest football players in the country.
GIRL:	*[Standing up]* Well, I'm certainly happy to meet you.
HAPPY:	Come back soon.
GIRL:	I'll try.
HAPPY:	Don't try, honey, try hard.[1]

In this scene, Happy is pretending to be something he is not. He is "playing the role" of the successful operator—the man with numerous accomplishments and abilities, which, of course, he does not actually possess. Like imitation and similar activities, this kind of "acting" is encountered frequently in daily life.

Studies of "Acting" in Daily Life

Erving Goffman states in his book *The Presentation of Self in Everyday Life,* "Life itself is a dramatically enacted thing. All the world is not, of course, a stage, but the crucial ways in which it isn't are not easy to specify."[2] Goffman is saying, in effect, that acting is so much a part of the real world that it is often difficult to identify it.

In an article about Jacqueline Kennedy Onassis, Nelson W. Aldrich used theatrical terms to describe certain qualities that have made Mrs. Onassis a celebrity.

> What marks Jacqueline Onassis off from her class, however, and what marked her for celebrity almost from the beginning, was the theatricality she brought to her performance . . . even as a girl she was a performer in the narrower sense as well, a trouper. She became an adept at occasional theater, the theater of social occasion.
>
> She was not, of course, an actress. She never wished to create the illusion that she was someone else. Her aim, the aim of all practitioners of good form is not to thrill the audience but to charm it. The actress depends for her effect on the audience's knowledge that she is acting; the upper-class performer is concerned that the audience not know she is acting, but, on the contrary, believe that what she is doing is, again, the result of "good breeding." Charming is like acting in that it's a form of disciplined playing, but it is also more ambitious, riskier, because it is so close to deceiving.[3]

Erving Goffman's work on "acting" in daily life was quoted above. Studies by others—scholars and popular writers alike—attest to the importance of various kinds of "acting" in real life. Among studies on this subject are *Games People Play,* a successful book of a few years ago concerned with role playing in interpersonal relationships; and *Body Language,* dealing with the gestures and movements we make to signal feelings, emotions, and responses to one another.

In a more scholarly vein, writers have argued that only in our various roles do we have any personality at all. Robert Ezra Park, in an important book, *Race and Culture,* noted a relationship between the words *person* and *mask*—the latter being closely associated with theater. He writes:

> It is probably no mere historical accident that the word person, in its first meaning, is a mask. It is rather a recognition of the fact that everyone is always, and everywhere, more or less consciously, playing a role. . . . It is in these roles that we know each other. It is in these roles that we know ourselves.[4]

ACTING ONSTAGE

Acting Onstage and Acting in Life: Similarities and Differences

The better we understand acting in daily life, the better we understand acting on the stage. There are similarities between the two: the processes and techniques which ordinary people employ to convey an image of themselves —words, gestures, "body language," tone of voice, subtle suggestions of intent—are the same tools actors use to create a stage character. Further, an actor or actress plays both a social and a personal role. An actress playing the part of a matronly woman dominating her household adopts the mannerisms and attitudes of a strong mother figure as understood in a given society.

For all the similarities between the two kinds of acting, however, the differences are crucial and reveal a great deal about the nature of stage acting. Some of the differences are obvious. For one thing, actors and actresses on stage are always being observed. In real life there may be observers, but their presence is not essential to the event. Bystanders on a street corner where an accident has occurred form a kind of audience, but their presence is incidental and unrelated to the accident itself. On stage, however, the performer is always on display and always in the spotlight.

Acting onstage, too, requires a performer to play roles he or she does not play in life. A scene between a father and his son arguing about money, or between a young husband and wife discussing whether they will have children or not, is one thing when it actually occurs, but something quite different on stage. Generally, the roles we play in life are genuine. A man with children, if he accepts his responsibilities toward his children, does not just *play* a father; he *is* a father. A woman who writes for a magazine does not just *play* a magazine writer; she *is* one. In real life, a lawyer knows the law; but on stage, an actor playing the role of a lawyer may not know the difference between jurisprudence and habeas corpus, and probably has

Performers play many different parts.
In the theater, unlike life, performers are often called on to play widely diverse roles. Frequently, too, these parts are people unlike themselves. An example is afforded by the many roles undertaken by character actor Robert Prosky. At the top, he plays the historical figure of Galileo, the scientist and inventor, in Brecht's play *Galileo*. By contrast, in the scene at the bottom he is seen (second from the right) as a modern gambler in the 1930s farce *Three Men on a Horse*.

Doubling: Playing two parts in one play.
Sometimes performers must play two or more roles in a single production. In the revue *Greater Tuna* Joe Sears and Jaston Williams each played a multitude of characters in a small town in Texas, including female characters. At the top they are two farmers. At the bottom, Mr. Williams, on the right, is a journalist interviewing a woman in the town, played by Mr. Sears. Such doubling requires versatility as well as technique.

THE PERFORMERS AND THE DIRECTOR

Playing several parts at one time.

At times, performers are called on to transform themselves without the benefit of costumes or makeup. The performers in *The Dining Room* by A.R. Gurney, Jr., play a range of roles—as many as five or six roles each. They do this by changing their voice and posture, but without elaborate alterations in costumes or makeup. Shown here is the original company (clockwise from the left): Remak Ramsay, Pippa Pear-Three, W.H. Macy, Lois de Manzie, John Shea, and Ann McDonough.

never been inside a law school. Playing widely divergent parts or parts outside their personal experience requires actors and actresses to stretch their imagination and ability. For example, a young actress at one time or another might be called on to play parts as dissimilar as the fiery, independent Antigone in Sophocles' play; the vulnerable, lovestruck Juliet in *Romeo and Juliet*; and the neurotic, obsessed heroine in Strindberg's *Miss Julie.*

At times performers even have to *double,* that is, play several parts in one play. In the Greek theater it was customary to have only three principal actors; each of them had to play several parts, putting on masks and different costumes to assume the various roles. Bertolt Brecht, a German dramatist, wrote many large-cast plays which call for doubling. His play *The Caucasian Chalk Circle* has forty-seven speaking parts, but it can be produced with no more than twenty-five performers. *The Screens,* a play by the French playwright Jean Genet, has ninety-eight characters; but—as Genet himself has written—"each actor will be required to play five or six roles."

Another important difference between acting onstage and in real life is that a theatrical performance is always conscious. There is an awareness by actors and audience that the presentation has been planned ahead of time. Paradoxically, this consciousness of a performance sometimes leads to a more truthful reenactment than we encounter in real life. The facade or false face people sometimes present can never occur in stage acting, because there is no attempt to deceive anyone in that way. As Theodore Shank explains it: "Acting is not pretense. An actor does not pretend to be Macbeth as an imposter pretends to be what he is not; instead he creates an appearance which is intended for perception as an illusion."[5]

Shank's statement that a performer "creates an appearance which is intended for perception as an illusion" underscores a significant difference between acting for the stage and "acting" in life, namely, that dramatic characters are not real people. In discussing symbol and metaphor earlier, we said that an actress standing onstage in the role of Joan of Arc was a metaphor for Joan. Any stage character—Joan of Arc, Antigone, Oedipus, Hamlet—is a symbol or an image of a person. Stage characters are fictions created by dramatists and performers to represent people. They remind us of people—in many cases they seem to *be* the people—but they are not. They have no corporeal reality as you and I do, but rather exist in our imaginations.

The Job of Acting

Unlike "acting" in daily life, performing on the stage is always observed, requires performers to play roles not part of their own training and experience, and is conscious and deliberate. Because of these factors, acting for the stage is hard work. Professional acting calls for a dedication of resources, a mental toughness, and a willingness to persist that is often camouflaged by the glamorous life and the financial rewards that are reported in the media. For all its glamour, it requires years of study and training—and weeks or months of preparation for a single role.

One objective of a performance is to make it look natural and easy—to suggest to the audience that playing the role is effortless, just as a juggler attempts to look as casual and carefree as possible. One reason for the attempt to make acting look effortless is to relax the audience and let it concentrate on believing in the character rather than focusing on the lengthy and arduous preparation required of the performer.

To achieve such ease and grace of performance calls for a dedication and discipline that few people outside competitive sports or the performing arts can understand. Rigorous training, long hours of dull repetition, bouncing back from discouragement: all this and more is called for if one is to make even a beginning in the profession. Just how one prepares for stage acting is the subject of Chapter 12.

SUMMARY

1   Acting is not as mysterious or removed from daily life as it is sometimes thought to be; all human beings engage in certain forms of acting.

2   Imitation and role playing are excellent examples of acting in everyday life.

3   Acting on the stage differs from acting in everyday life, in the first place, because the stage actor or actress is always being observed by an audience.

4   Acting for the stage involves playing roles for which the performer has no direct experience in life.

5   Stage performers must play roles which are symbolic and which make special demands on their skills and imagination.

6   Acting is a difficult, demanding profession. Despite its glamour, it calls for arduous training and preparation.

12

STAGE ACTING

The challenge of acting for the stage.
A performer must learn to develop both outward techniques and inner emotional resources to play a character convincingly. The actress Meryl Streep is seen here playing Flora in *27 Wagons Full of Cotton*, by Tennessee Williams. In this scene with the actor Roy Poole, the slovenly, childlike, sensuous Flora is totally different from other characters Ms. Streep has played on the stage and in films, such as the Polish refugee in the movie *Sophie's Choice*.

In general, it can be said that there are two main challenges to becoming a successful actress or actor: first, to learn how to make the characters portrayed believable; and, second, to acquire the many special skills—both physical and vocal—that stage performances demand. As if these two tasks were not enough, there is a third challenge, perhaps the most difficult of all: to integrate these two—special skills with credibility of the character.

In order to understand better these two aspects of acting, we will examine them separately, beginning with the believability of the character. We will then examine how they are combined.

MAKING DRAMATIC CHARACTERS BELIEVABLE

In order for the audience to believe the characters onstage, performers must be credible and convincing in their roles. Actors and actresses must study human behavior carefully so that they can present the outward appearance of the character accurately. They must also understand and transmit the inner feelings of the character they portray.

One enemy of credibility on the stage is exaggeration. The stage is a showplace: a performer stands on a platform in the spotlight—the focus of the audience's attentions. The natural temptation under these circumstances is to "show off"—to use broad, grandiose gestures; speak in a loud, rhetorical voice; or otherwise call attention to oneself. Some exaggeration is necessary in stage acting, and certain roles call for eloquent speech and the grand gesture, particularly in classical theater, but never to the point of overacting or doing too much. When the audience focuses on the performer's behavior, the character is forgotten; in its most extreme form overacting becomes laughable.

Historical Precedents of Naturalistic Acting

In view of this, it is not surprising that throughout the history of theater we find commentators cautioning performers against excessive, unnatural acting. In Shakespeare, Hamlet's advice to the players is an example.

> Speak the speech, I pray you, as I pronounced it to you, trippingly on the tongue: but if you mouth it, as many of your players do, I had as lief the town-crier spoke my lines. Nor do not saw the air too much with your hand, thus, but use all gently; for in the very torrent, tempest, and, as I may say, the whirlwind of your passion, you must acquire and beget a temperance that may give it smoothness. O, it offends me to the soul to hear a robustious periwig-pated fellow tear a passion to tatters, to very rags. . . . Be not too tame neither, but let your discretion be your tutor: suit the action to the word, the

word to the action; with this special observance, that you o'erstep not the modesty of nature: for anything so overdone is from the purpose of playing, whose end, both at the first and now, was and is, to hold, as't were, the mirror up to nature. . . .

Shakespeare himself was an actor, and no doubt he had seen performers "saw the air" with their hands and "tear a passion to tatters."

In France, in the seventeenth century, Molière spoke out for honest acting in his short play *The Impromptu of Versailles*. He mocked actors in a rival company who ended each phrase with a flourish in order to get applause. (The term *claptrap,* incidentally, comes from the habit of performers of that period of punctuating a speech or an action with some final inflection or gesture, thereby setting a "clap trap" and provoking applause.) Molière criticized actresses who preserved a silly smile even in a tragic scene; he pointed to the ridiculous practice of two performers in an intimate scene—two young lovers together or a king alone with his captain— declaiming as if they were addressing the multitudes.

In England, throughout the eighteenth and nineteenth centuries, acting alternated between exaggerated and natural styles. Most performers tended toward the former approach; but every generation or so, someone would come along to bring acting back to a more natural, down-to-earth style. A good example was the actor David Garrick (1717–1779), who in the eighteenth century gained fame for his reasonable approach to acting. A commentator described the contrast between Garrick and his predecessors in playing Richard III.

> Instead of declaiming the verse in a thunderous, measured chant, this actor [Garrick] *spoke* it with swift and "natural" changes of tone and emphasis. Instead of patrolling the boards with solemn pomp, treading heavily from pose to traditional pose, he moved quickly and gracefully. Instead of standing on his dignity and marbling his face into a tragedian's mask, his mobile features illustrated Richard's whole range of turbulent feelings. He seemed, indeed, to identify himself with the part. It was all so *real*.[1]

From the mid-seventeenth century on, serious attempts were being made to define the craft or technique of acting, the most noteworthy being those of Denis Diderot (1713–1784) in the eighteenth century and François Delsarte (1811–1871) in the nineteenth century. Diderot attempted to introduce more realism and believability into acting, endorsing, for example, the use of prose dialogue, but with only a minimum of success. Later, Delsarte devised a system of expression in which the performers' thoughts and emotions are reduced to a fixed and specific series of poses and attitudes accomplished through a selective use of body and voice. In time, Delsarte's system became overly mechanistic and unworkable.

Realistic acting.
In contrast to some of the classics—which call for full-blown acting—many modern plays require more natural performances, closer to what we see in daily life. A good example is *Crimes of the Heart* by Beth Henley. The sisters in the play come from a small town in the south and are everyday characters. In this scene we see the actresses in the Broadway production: Mary Beth Hurt, Lizbeth Mackay, and Mia Dillon.

Realistic Acting Techniques in the Modern Theater: The Stanislavski System

Creating a believable character is an important part of any acting where the characters resemble recognizable human beings. But a realistic approach became more important than ever at the close of the nineteenth century, when drama began to depict characters and situations close to everyday life. Not only the spirit of the part, but also the details, had to conform to what people saw of life around them. This placed great demands on actors and actresses to avoid any hint of fakery or superficiality.

Before the late 1900s, and people like Delsarte, no one had devised a method for achieving this kind of absolute believability. Individual actresses and actors through their talent and genius had achieved it, of course, in every age; but no one had devised a system whereby it could be taught to others and passed on to future generations. The person who did this most successfully was the Russian actor and director Constantin Stanislavski.

A cofounder of the Moscow Art Theater in Russia and the director of Chekhov's most important plays, Stanislavski was an actor as well as a director. He was involved in both traditional theater—using nonrealistic techniques—and the emergence of the modern realistic approach. It is the latter aspect of his work that we will look at.

By closely observing the performances of great actors of his day—such as Tommaso Salvini, Eleanora Duse, and Fyodor Chaliapin—and by drawing on his own acting experience, Stanislavski isolated and described what these gifted performers did naturally, intuitively. From his observations he compiled and then codified a series of principles and techniques which today are regarded as fundamental to the training and performance of the performer—in all facets of theater.

At first glance, it would seem to be the easiest thing in the world for performers to stand on stage and be themselves: to wear their own clothes and to speak normally. All we have to remember, however, is what it is like to stand up in front of a classroom to make a statement or give a report. Even if we only have to "say a few words," our mouth goes dry, our legs tremble, and the most difficult task in the world is to "be natural." You can multiply this feeling—*stage fright* it is sometimes called—many times over for actors and actresses who stand on stage, bright lights in their eyes, trying to remember lines and movements, knowing that hundreds of eyes are focused on them. Fine actresses and actors learn to deal with the feeling—and even turn it to advantage—but many will admit that they never completely lose the terror any human being feels when being observed and judged by others.

Stanislavski, keenly aware of this problem, wrote:

> All of our acts, even the simplest, which are so familiar to us in everyday life, become strained when we appear behind the footlights before a public of a thousand people. That is why it is necessary to correct ourselves and learn again how to walk, sit, or lie down. It is essential to re-educate ourselves to look and see, on the stage, to listen and to hear.[2]

Stanislavski went about the "reeducation" to get rid of mechanical, external acting and to put in its place naturalness and truth. In his words: "The actor must first of all believe in everything that takes place onstage, and most of all, he must believe what he himself is doing. And one can only believe in the truth."[3]

To give substance to his ideas, Stanislavski studied how people acted in everyday life and how they communicated feelings and emotions; and then he found ways to accomplish the same things on stage. He developed a series of exercises and techniques for the actor which had the following broad aims:

1   To make the outward activities of the performer—the gestures, the voice, the rhythm of movements—natural and convincing.
2   To have the actor or actress convey the inner truth of a part. Even if all the visible manifestations of a character are mastered, a performance will appear superficial and mechanical without a deep sense of conviction and belief.
3   To make the life of the character on stage not only dynamic but continuous. Some performers tend to emphasize only the high points of a part; in between, the life of the character stops. In real life people do not stop living, however.
4   To develop a strong sense of *ensemble* playing with other performers in a scene.

Let us now look in some detail at Stanislavski's techniques.

Relaxation   In his observation of the great actors and actresses of his day, Stanislavski noticed how fluid and life-like their movements were. They seemed to be in a complete state of freedom and relaxation, allowing the behavior of character to come through effortlessly. He concluded that unwanted tension has to be eliminated and that the performer must attain at all times a state of physical and vocal *relaxation*.

> As long as you have this physical tenseness you cannot even think about delicate shadings of feeling or the spiritual life of your part. Consequently, before you attempt to create anything it is necessary for you to get your muscles in proper condition, so they do not impede your actions.[4]

Concentration and observation   Along with relaxation, Stanislavski discovered that the gifted performer always appeared fully concentrated on some object, person or event while *onstage*. It is as if fully concentrated actors and actresses achieve "public solitude" because they appear oblivious of the audience. That is, while in the presence of the audience, their concentration separates them from the audience. The extent or range of concentration Stanislavski referred to as a *circle of attention*. When the performers have established a small circle of attention, they can then enlarge concentration outward from this point. In this way they will stop worrying about the audience and lose their self-consciousness.

To help actresses and actors develop powers of concentration on stage, Stanislavski encouraged them to observe and concentrate in real life. They had to learn to see, not superficially, but with penetration and depth, storing images for eventual use on stage. They were to seek out beauty, especially in nature, as well as familiarize themselves with "the darker side of life"; they had to be knowledgeable about human relationships.

> After you have learned how to observe life around you and draw on it for your work you will turn to the study of the most necessary, important, and living emotional material on which your main creativeness is based. I mean intercourse with other human beings. This material is difficult to obtain because in large part it is intangible, indefinable, and only inwardly perceivable.[5]

Importance of specifics   One of Stanislavski's techniques was an emphasis on concrete details. A performer should never try to act *in general*, that is, try to convey the idea of a feeling such as fear or love in some vague, amorphous way. In life, Stanislavski said, we express emotions in terms of specifics: an anxious woman twists a handkerchief, an angry young boy throws a rock at a trash can, a nervous businessman jangles his keys. Actors and actresses must find the same *concrete* activities. Stanislavski points out how Shakespeare has Lady Macbeth in her sleepwalking scene—at the height of her guilt and emotional upheaval—try to rub blood off her hands.

Many times playwrights provide such specifics for performers: King Lear wants his coat unbuttoned in his final moments; Laura, in *The Glass*

(Ken Howard)

Techniques of acting:
The importance of specifics.
In keeping with Constantin Stanislavski's notion that performers should concentrate on specifics, the playwright Tennessee Williams in *The Glass Menagerie* established Laura's small glass animals as concrete objects that the actress can concentrate on. At the same time, the glass animals are symbolic of her fragile condition. Shown here in the part of Laura is Amanda Plummer.

Menagerie by Tennessee Williams, has her glass animals. Bertolt Brecht in *Mother Courage* gives the characters many specific props to work with: for example, the wagon which Mother Courage and her children pull throughout the play and the drum which her mute daughter Kattrin beats to warn a nearby town of imminent danger.

When a script does not indicate such tangible actions, the actor or actress must find them. Michael Chekhov, nephew of the playwright and a follower of Stanislavski, coined the term *psychological gesture* for a typical, characteristic movement or activity which would sum up a character's motives and preoccupations. A man who is confused, or has trouble "seeing clearly," for example, might continually try to clean his glasses.

Inner truth   The most innovative aspect of Stanislavski's work is in the realm of *inner truth,* which deals with the inner or subjective world of characters—that is, their thoughts and emotions. Coincidental with Stanislavski's research was his work directing the major dramas of Chekhov. Plays like *The Cherry Orchard* have less to do with external action and what the characters say than with what the characters are feeling and thinking and often do not verbalize. It becomes apparent that the Stanislavski approach would be very beneficial in realizing the inner life—the values—of such characters.

We can better understand Stanislavski's achievements in the theater if we compare "inner truth" with the pioneering efforts of Sigmund Freud in psychology. Before Freud, little was understood about the function of the unconscious mind and its effects on emotional health. But Freud, by using such techniques as hypnosis and dream analysis, was able to reach the unconscious mind. Similarly, Stanislavski discovered that the unconscious, creative energies of the performer (which are inaccessible to his or her will) can be tapped through a conscious, controllable technique.

Inner truth is what we sense when a performer's conveying of an emotion or feeling—sorrow, anger, joy—is an accurate reflection of a character's feelings. Even when we are confronted with hypocrisy or insincerity, we can see beyond these to a truthful representation of the character's inner state.

Stanislavski had several ideas of how to achieve a sense of inner truth, one being the "magic if." *If* is a word which can transform our thoughts. Through it we can imagine ourselves in virtually any situation. "*If* I suddenly became rich . . ." "*If* I were in Europe . . ." "*If* I had great talent . . ." "*If* that person who insulted me comes near me again . . ." *If* is a powerful lever of the mind, which can lift us out of ourselves and give us a sense of absolute certainty about imaginary circumstances. In this sense, it is similar to the reality of dreams and fantasies discussed earlier.

To take an example: if we spend a night alone in a strange room—in a cabin in the woods or a house far from home—and we hear a noise in the night, such as a floorboard creaking or a door opening, we become frightened, particularly if there have been stories of burglaries or break-ins in the area. If the noise comes again, our anxiety increases. We lie absolutely still, our breath shortens and our heartbeat quickens. Finally, after a time, if nothing has happened, we find the courage to get out of bed and turn on a light. It turns out to be nothing—a rusty hinge on a door, or a tree limb brushing the side of the house—but before we discovered the truth, the power of the "magic if" has worked its magic: we were convinced we were in great danger.

Stanislavski urged actors and actresses to use this same power of fantasy and imagination as a tool to induce reality on the stage. A performer can never actually *be* a dramatic character, but the performer can use *if*. "If *I* were a frightened, crippled young woman, how would *I* feel about meeting a young man I once admired?" This is the question an actress playing Laura in *The Glass Menagerie* can ask herself. Through the power of imagination she can put herself in Laura's place.

Emotional recall A useful tool in achieving a sense of emotional truth onstage is what Stanislavski referred to as *emotional recall*, which is the remembering of a past experience in the performer's life that is similar to the one in the play. By recalling sensory impressions of an experience in the past (such as what a room looked like, any prevalent odors, any contact with objects), emotions—from that time—are aroused and can be used as the basis of feelings called for in the play.

A good example would be a scene of farewell, such as Emily saying good-bye to her family in Thornton Wilder's *Our Town*. Though dead, Emily is allowed to go back to earth for one day, after which she must leave forever. The actress playing Emily might recall a time in her own life when she had to say good-bye and was reluctant to do so—the first time she left home, perhaps, or the time she said good-bye to a young man she loved. Again, Stanislavski emphasizes details; the important thing for the actress to remember is where she was, what she wore, who she was with—not how she felt. From these concrete facts and images the feeling will follow. In Stanislavski's words:

> On the stage there cannot be under any circumstances, action which is directed immediately at the arousing of a feeling for its own sake. . . . All such feelings are the result of something that has gone on before. Of the thing that goes before, you should think as hard as you can. As for the result, it will produce itself.[6]

Action on stage: What? Why? How? Another important principle of Stanislavski's system is that all action onstage must have a purpose and be

Mother Courage and Her Children (1939)

BERTOLT BRECHT (1898–1956)

CHIEF CHARACTERS:

Mother Courage
Kattrin—her dumb daughter
Eilif—her elder son
Swiss Cheese—her younger son
Cook
Chaplain
Yvette Pottier—a prostitute

SETTING: Various army camps in Sweden, Poland, Bavaria, Germany.
TIME: 1624–1636.

BACKGROUND: Mother Courage is a canteen woman, Anna Fierling, who follows army camps with her wagon and sells her wares to soldiers. She has two sons and a daughter—all from different fathers—who help pull the wagon.

SCENE 1: Spring 1624, on a highway. A Swedish recruiting officer complains to a sergeant how difficult it is to get recruits. Mother Courage and her children enter, pulling the wagon from which Courage sells her goods. The sergeant distracts Courage while the recruiting officer persuades her son Eilif to join the army.

SCENE 2: The years 1625 and 1626; the setting is the kitchen of the Swedish commander where the Cook is arguing with Mother Courage. The Swedish commander enters and praises Eilif for his bravery. When Courage

hears Eilif singing "The Song of the Wise Woman and the Soldier," she recognizes his voice and joins in.

SCENE 3: Three years later. Mother Courage, her two children, and parts of a Finnish regiment are prisoners. Courage's friend, Yvette Pottier, a prostitute who feels sorry for herself because her first husband left her, sings "The Fraternization Song" about loving a soldier. When cannon noises herald a surprise attack by the Catholics, Courage lends the Chaplain a cloak to disguise the fact that he is a Protestant. Swiss Cheese hides the cash box in the wagon while Courage rubs ashes onto Kattrin's face to make her less attractive to the soldiers. Three days later, while Courage and the Chaplain are gone, Swiss Cheese leaves to hide the cash box, but two soldiers, who have been watching, capture him. The soldiers return with Swiss Cheese, but Courage who has come back also, denies knowing him, even though he is her own son. While the Chaplain sings "The Song of the Hours," about Christ's death, Courage finds that she can free her son if she bribes the sergeant—but she haggles too long and Swiss Cheese is executed.

SCENE 4: Outside an officer's tent. A young soldier enters, raging against the captain who took his reward money. Mother Courage sings "The Song of the Great Capitulation," which persuades them both that there is no use complaining.

SCENE 5: Two years later. The Chaplain tells Courage that he needs some linen to help the peasants wrap up their wounds, and when she refuses, he takes the linen by force. After Kattrin rescues a child, Courage tells her to give it back to the mother.

SCENE 6: Bavaria, 1632—the funeral of the fallen commander. The men are getting drunk instead of going to the funeral. When Kattrin gets wounded, Courage thinks it is lucky because it will make Kattrin less appealing to the soldiers.

SCENE 7: A highway, with the Chaplain, Mother Courage, and Kattrin pulling the supply wagon. Courage sings a song about war being a business proposition.

SCENE 8: A camp, 1632. Voices announce that peace is at hand. Courage is distraught because she has just purchased a lot of supplies, and will be ruined because no one will buy them. Yvette goes with Courage to try to sell the goods. Eilif is arrested for killing some peasants—now that peace has come, such killing is a crime. Courage rushes back in with the news that the war is on again. The Cook and Kattrin pull the wagon while Courage sings.

SCENE 9: In front of a half-ruined parsonage; 1634. The cook tells Courage that his mother has left him an inn that he wants to run with her, but without Kattrin. Kattrin overhears them and is about to leave when Courage stops her; Courage turns the Cook down, and she and Kattrin harness the wagon and march off.

SCENE 10. 1635. Courage and Kattrin pull the wagon up to a prosperous farmhouse and hear someone singing about warmth and comfort and safety, conditions that stand in sharp contrast to their own bleak situation.

SCENE 11: January 1636, and the wagon, in disrepair, stands outside a farmhouse. Soldiers gather up the peasants and pull Kattrin out of the wagon; they ask the way to the town. An old man climbs on the roof and sees the soldiers getting ready to launch a surprise attack on the sleeping town. Kattrin gets a drum out of the wagon, climbs up on the roof and beats a warning to save the people in the town. When the lieutenant tries to stop the noise, Kattrin goes on drumming, and the soldiers kill her. Cannon noises and alarm bells announce that Kattrin's warning was successful—the town is saved.

SCENE 12: Courage sits in front of the wagon by Kattrin's body, singing a lullaby. The peasants tell Courage that she must leave and they will bury Kattrin. Courage harnesses up and this time all alone, pulls the wagon behind a passing regiment.

joined. This means that the performer's attention must always be focused on the enactment of a series of physical actions that are linked together by the circumstances of the play. Stanislavski determined these actions by asking three essential questions: What? Why? How? An action (the *what*) is performed, such as opening a door. What prompts the opening of the door is that someone calls the character's name (the *why*). The door is opened slowly, hesitantly (the *how*) because it is two o'clock in the morning and no one is expected.

Operating along with physical actions and forming an indivisible bond is the psychological aspect of stage action. Concerning this, Stanislavski said:

> The bond between body and soul is indivisible. The life of the one gives life to the other. Every physical act . . . has an inner source of feeling. Consequently we have both an inner and outer plane in every role, interlaced. A common objective makes them akin to one another and strengthens their bonds.[7]

In other words, for every physical action there is an underlying reason that justifies and motivates it.

Through line of a role In order to develop continuity in a part, the actor or actress should find the *superobjective* of the character. What is it, above all else, that the character wants from life? What is the character's driving force? If a goal can be established toward which the character strives, it will give the performer an overall objective. From this objective can be developed a core, or *through line,* which can be grasped, as a skier on a ski lift grabs a towline and is carried to the top.

Harold Clurman, a well-known critic and director, refers to the through line as the *spine;* and when directing a play, he assigns a spine or superobjective to characters as a group and to each character individually. For Chekhov's *Uncle Vanya,* Clurman says that all the characters are dissatisfied with their lives and grumble a great deal; their spine, therefore, is "to make life better, find a way to be happy."[8] The title character, Vanya, hopes to escape from his dull, frustrating existence, but he fails. Other characters follow equally futile courses in pursuit of happiness—in their spine or superobjective in the play.

To help develop the through line, Stanislavski urged performers to divide scenes into units (sometimes called *beats*). In each unit there is an objective, and the intermediate objectives running through a play lead ultimately to the overall objective.

Ensemble playing Except in one-person shows, performers do not act alone; they interact with other people. Stanislavski was aware that the tendency for many performers is to "stop acting," or lose their concentration, when they are not the main characters in a scene or when someone

Playing together.

Good actors are aware of the importance of ensemble playing. Performers coordinate their work by listening carefully to each other, sensing the other performers' actions and moods, and responding alertly. Ensemble playing is especially important in plays with crucial character interaction, such as *The Cherry Orchard* by Anton Chekhov. In this scene from a production of the play at the Williamstown Theater Festival are George Morfogen, Colleen Dewhurst, and Maria Tucci.

else is talking. These performers make a great effort when they are speaking but not when they are listening. This tendency destroys a performer's through line and causes the person to move in and out of a role.

To overcome this problem, Stanislavski urged performers to include other people onstage in their "circle of attention"—to listen carefully to others and to maintain their sense of inner truth even when they are not speaking or are not the focus of attention in a scene. In short, he stressed what he called *communication*.

Just as in life, Stanislavski stressed that the performer should respond to the unceasing flow of stimuli by listening and *hearing,* by looking and *seeing,* by using all five senses to respond believably—not mechanically—to the impact of external and internal stimuli. In time, when a group of performers work closely together—listening attentively to each other, responding genuinely and spontaneously—they begin to work as an *ensemble,* that is, a close-knit unit that communicates a sense of truth as a group, not just as individual actresses and actors.

Voice and body   Stanislavski championed the development of a highly trained voice and body that could express the myriad thoughts and feelings of the performer's inner life. He emphasized that the inner life of performers is insufficient by itself to convey to the audience the many shadings of character; therefore, a sensitive body and vocal instrument are an indispensible part of the craft of acting. This view is borne out in Stanislavski's last two books, *Building a Character* and *Creating the Role,* in which he stressed the importance of an extremely well-developed and responsive instrument.

Misconceptions and confusion about the Stanislavski system   Stanislavski's views have been the cause of some controversy since his books were translated into English, almost fifty years ago; mostly, this is because there have been some misconceptions and confusion about his contribution to theater, specifically his "system." These stem largely from followers of Stanislavski who mistakenly emphasize only the inner or emotional side of his technique. Also, because of the emergence of realism as a significant theater movement, the Stanislavski system has been seen by many as having value *only* in realistic theater and acting. But his system is in fact the equivalent of scales and études for a musician or bar work and body exercises for a dancer. Therefore, it is *fundamental* to the craft of acting. Stanislavski's work, viewed as a whole, is *universal,* serving the performer not only in realism but in stylized and avant-garde acting techniques. There is no argument that Stanislavski laid the foundation for the study and performance of acting in the twentieth century.

SPECIAL SKILLS OF ACTING

It was noted at the beginning of this chapter that there are two aspects to actors' training and the art of stage performance. The first, making a character believable, we have just examined. The second is a wide range of special skills. They are the equivalent of the technical skills in the other arts—such as learning the movements of ballet and developing the physical agility to carry them out, or learning to play a musical instrument and perfecting the skills required to master the most difficult pieces and perform them successfully in public.

Modern realistic plays require some of these skills—all acting does, in fact—but some of the more classical traditions make special demands. Greek, French, Spanish, and Elizabethan theater require mastery of both the voice and the body. So, too, do the nonrealistic plays of the modern era. We can understand these skills more clearly if we look at them separately, beginning with the voice.

Vocal Projection

One of the primary requirements for an actor or actress is to be seen and heard by the audience. In a modern realistic play this requirement is made more difficult by the necessity of maintaining believability. The words of a man and a woman in an intimate love scene in real life would be barely audible even to people a few feet away. In the theater, however, every word must be heard by the entire audience; and to be heard throughout a theater seating a thousand people, a performer must *project,* that is, throw the voice into the audience so that it penetrates to the uttermost reaches of the theater. The performers must strike a balance, therefore, between credibility—in the case of a love scene this means confidential, quiet tones—and the necessity of projection. In order to develop projection, and to achieve the kind of balance just described, the performer must train and rehearse extensively.

In traditional theater—the theater from the fifth century B.C. in Greece to the middle of the nineteenth century—vocal demands on actors and actresses were even greater. The language of the plays was most often poetry, and this required intensive training in order for the performer to speak it distinctly. There were added problems of projection, too. Greek amphitheaters, while marvels of acoustics, seated fifteen thousand spectators in the open air, and to throw the voice to every corner of the theater without strain was no small task.

In the Elizabethan period in England, Christopher Marlowe, a contemporary of Shakespeare's, wrote superb blank verse which makes severe demands on a performer's vocal abilities. An example is a speech in Marlowe's *Doctor Faustus,* addressed by Faustus to Helen of Troy, who has been called back from the dead to be with Faustus. In the speech Faustus says to Helen:

> O' thou art fairer than the evening's air
> Clad in the beauty of a thousand stars;
> Brighter art thou than flaming Jupiter
> When he appear'd to hapless Semele;
> More lovely than the monarch of the sky
> In wanton Arethusa's azured arms;
> And none but thou shalt be my paramour!

These seven lines of verse are part of a single sentence and, when spoken properly, should be delivered as part of one overall unit with the meaning carried from one line to the next. How many of us could manage that? A fine classical actor can speak the entire section at one time, giving it the necessary resonance and inflection as well. Beyond that, he can stand on the stage for two or three hours delivering such lines.

With the use of microphones and sound amplification so widespread today, we have increasingly lost our appreciation of the power of the spoken word. In the past, public speakers from Cicero to Abraham Lincoln stirred men and women with their oratory. Throughout its history, the stage has provided a natural platform for stirring speeches. Beginning with the Greeks, and continuing through the Elizabethans, the French and Spanish theaters of the seventeenth century, and other European theaters at the close of the nineteenth century, playwrights wrote magnificent lines, lines which performers, having honed their vocal skills to a fine point, delivered with zest. Any performer today who intends to act in a revival of a traditional play must learn to speak and project stage verse, which requires a vocal power and breath control usually found only in opera singers.

Physical Movement on Stage

Performers are seen as well as heard. In the eighteenth and nineteenth centuries, when every stage was a proscenium or picture-frame stage, the actors and actresses were like figures in a tableau or picture. In a love scene, or any scene, they were very much on display. For that reason it became a rule that a performer must never turn his or her back to the audience but always face the front, even when speaking to another character. This formal approach has long since been abandoned, but there is still a necessity for a performer's physical movements to be clearly visible. A performer who remains permanently turned away from a large part of the audience, for instance, is derelict in his or her obligations. Because dramatic characters are symbols, every movement counts, and the performer's gestures and facial expressions must be communicated to the audience clearly and instantaneously.

As with the voice, traditional theater makes strong demands on the performer's body. In Shakespeare, for instance, characters are always running up and down steps or ramps, having prolonged death scenes, or meeting other characters in sword fights. Anyone who has seen a first-rate sword fight on stage knows how difficult and impressive it can be. A duel, in which the combatants strike quickly at one another—clashing swords frequently without hitting each other—resembles a ballet in its precision and grace.

Adeptness in physical movement is also required in realistic acting. For example, an equivalent activity in a modern play would be a headlong fall down a flight of stairs. Such a fall occurred in the 1972 Broadway play *That Championship Season*. The story concerns a basketball team at a reunion, trying to relive past glory with their coach, twenty years after winning a

Physical demands of the stage.
Performers frequently must perform difficult physical feats which require training, discipline, and expert timing. An example is this sword fight in a production of *Hamlet* at the Circle Repertory Theater.

Demands of the musical stage.
Acting of all kinds makes strong vocal and physical demands on performers. Particularly demanding in this regard is the musical. Seen here are dancers, led by Debbie Allen, leaping through the air in *West Side Story*. Such grace and agility require rigorous training.

STAGE ACTING

championship. One actor, playing an alcoholic, was required to tumble head over heels down a full flight of stairs at every performance. He had to master the art of appearing to lose all control and yet never injure himself.

There are other cases requiring special discipline or training. Obviously musical theater requires talent in singing and dancing. Coordination is important too: the members of a musical chorus must sing, dance, or move together, frequently in unison. Pantomime provides another demanding category of performance: without words or props an actor or actress must indicate everything by physical suggestion, lifting an imaginary box or walking against an imaginary wind in a convincing fashion.

Similar stylization and symbolism characterize the acting of the classical theaters of India, China, and Japan. To achieve the absolute control, the concentration, and the mastery of the body and nerves necessary to carry out the movements, the performers of the various classical Asian theaters train for years under the supervision of master teachers. Every movement of the performers is prescribed and carefully controlled, combining elements

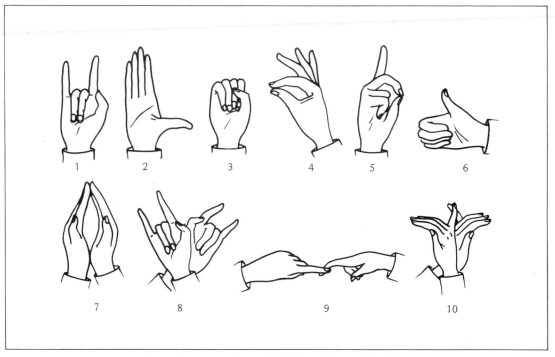

Finger language: A part of Indian acting and dancing.
The precise gestures of this Indian art—the graceful, symbolic movements—require extensive training and discipline to perfect. In the finger language shown here, the numbers indicate the following states or emotions: (1) separation or death, (2) meditation, (3) determination, (4) joy, (5) concentration, (6) rejection, (7) veneration, (8) proposal, (9) vexation, and (10) love. (*From Margaret Berthold*, A History of World Theater, *copyright © 1972 by Frederick Ungar Publishing Co., Inc.*)

The precise acting of Kabuki.
Most Asian acting requires careful, precise, formal gestures. Years of training are required to perform correctly in Japan's Kabuki theater as well as the more classic Noh theater. Shown here, with careful gestures of hand and head, is a scene from a Kabuki-style production of *Sleeping Beauty*.

of formal ballet, pantomime, and sign language. Each gesture tells a story and means something quite specific—a true symbolism of physical movement. Between the fourth and the ninth century, Sanskrit plays became the classical plays of India. For these Sanskrit dramas, the gestures of the performers were conventionalized and rigidly adhered to. These included thirteen movements of the head, thirty-six of the eyes, seven of the eyebrows, six of the nose, five of the chest, twenty-four of the hands, thirty-two of the feet, and so forth.

Acting Requirements of the Avant-Garde

Like the traditional theater of Europe and the United States, and the classical Asian theater, various forms of avant-garde theater of recent years require special techniques.

A good example is Eugène Ionesco's play *Rhinoceros*. During the course of the play, one of the two chief characters turns into a rhinoceros. The actor playing this part does not actually put on horns and an outfit with a leathery hide. Rather, he must physically transform himself by means of his posture,

A man becomes a rhinoceros. Without benefit of makeup or costume, the actor Zero Mostel transformed himself into an image of a rhinoceros in a play by Ionesco. Mostel used his voice, his facial expressions, and his body to create the change. Such effects require skill and practice.

voice, and general demeanor. The critic Walter Kerr described how actor Zero Mostel did this in the original Broadway production:

Now the rhinoceros beneath the skin begins to bulge a little at the eyes. The Kaiser Wilhelm mustache that has earlier adorned the supposed Mr. Mostel loses its spiky endpoints, droops, disintegrates into a tangle that makes it second cousin to a walrus. The voice starts to change. "I hate people—and I'll r-r-run them down!" comes out of a larynx that has stiffened, gone hollow as a 1915 gramophone record, and is ready to produce a trumpet-sound that would empty all of Africa. The shoulders lift, the head juts forward, one foot begins to beat the earth with such native majesty that dust—real dust—begins to rise like the afterveil that seems to accompany a safari. The transformation is on, the secret is out, evolution has reversed itself before your horrified, but nevertheless delighted, eyes.[9]

In another avant-garde play, Samuel Beckett's *Happy Days,* an actress is buried on stage in a mound of earth up to her waist in the first act, and up to her neck in the second. She must carry on her performance through the entire play while virtually immobile.

In some types of avant-garde theater, the performers become acrobats, make human pyramids, or are used like pieces of furniture. In the play *Suitcase* by the Japanese playwright Kobo Abe (1924–   ), the suitcase of the title is played by an actor who must move about as if he is being carried. In another play by Abe, *The Man Who Turned into a Stick,* an actor must play the part of a stick.

Groups such as the Open Theater and the Performance Group, who followed in the tradition of Jerzy Grotowski, also have made strong demands on the performer's voice and body. This type of theater stresses improvisation and ritual as well as the use of total person (mind, body, and emotions together). The voice becomes a means not only of communicating speech but of emitting sounds as well. As an example, rather than saying, "I am anguished" or expressing this feeling in a poetic phrase, such as, "How all occasions do inform against me," performers produce unintelligible but unmistakable cries from the soul: a "primal scream" on the stage. As with the voice, the body too becomes an instrument—like that of a dancer or acrobat—to perform feats or create aesthetic movement.

(George E. Joseph)

Special problems in acting.
Samuel Beckett's play *Happy Days* calls for the actress to play the first act buried in a mound up to her waist, and the second buried up to her neck. Shown here is the actress Irene Worth in a production at the New York Public Theater. Such limitations put severe pressure on the performer to convey all emotion, etc., by means of voice and facial expressions alone.

Acting demands of
the avant-garde theater.
In many instances avant-garde theater requires special training and techniques—acrobatics, tumbling, mime and special control of the voice, facial muscles, and body. The scene here is from *The Garden of Earthly Delights* by Martha Clarke with music by Richard Peaslee. The performers must fly (suspended from wires), act as serpents, and perform a number of feats that require skill in pantomime.

As a pioneer in the field, Jerzy Grotowski developed a training program for his performers, the purpose being not merely to condition the voice and the body, but chiefly to "discover the resistances and obstacles which hinder him in his creative task."[10] Of the voice Grotowski says, "special attention should be paid to the carrying power of the voice so the spectator not only hears the voice of the actor perfectly, but is also penetrated by it as if it were stereophonic." Further, he says, "the actor must exploit his voice in order to produce sounds and intonations that the spectator is incapable of reproducing or imitating."[11] Grotowski's training requires a series of rigorous vocal exercises, some more elaborate than any dreamed of by opera singers. As for physical exercises, Grotowski has one for every part of the body in every conceivable position: headstands, handstands, shoulder stands, back bends.

The theater of Robert Wilson, Richard Foreman, and Mabou Mines—a nonrealistic, avant-garde type of theater stressing visual images and arbitrary movement (see Chapter 9)—also makes special demands on performers. In Robert Wilson's work, performers are frequently called on either to move constantly or to remain perfectly still. In pieces such as his *A Letter to Queen Victoria,* two performers turn continuously in circles like dervishes for long periods of time, perhaps thirty or forty minutes. In works by Wilson and Richard Foreman, actresses and actors are also called on to remain frozen like statues. In other pieces, performers must move mechanically like robots or automatons.

The demands made on performers by experimental and avant-garde theaters are only the most recent example of the rigorous, intensive training which acting generally requires. In every age, performers must develop the sensitivity and insight to penetrate the secrets of the human soul and, at the same time, must train their voices and bodies to express their feelings in such a way that they are readily apparent to the audience.

COMBINING THE INNER AND OUTER SIDES OF ACTING

It was said earlier that the supreme challenge for a performer is to combine a realistic portrayal of a character with special vocal and physical skills. The two aspects of performing—the inner and the outer—must be integrated into a seamless whole and must reinforce and support one another.

In Chapter 2, on the imagination of the audience, we examined realistic and nonrealistic theater. It could be argued that realistic theater puts the primary emphasis on credibility and "inner truth," and that nonrealistic theater emphasizes vocal and physical techniques. There is some truth to this, but performing is almost never an either-or situation. Though the emphasis on making a character believable is paramount in a modern realistic play, control of the voice and body is still an essential part of the performer's training and technique. In a more classical piece—a Greek tragedy, or a farce from the Italian commedia dell'arte—vocal prowess and body movement come to the fore; even in the most far-out farce, however, employing pratfalls and perfect timing, a measure of belief in the characters is called for. In short, though the emphasis in various forms of theater may be on the inner or outer aspect of performing, both are essential in successful acting.

JUDGING PERFORMERS

As observers, we study the techniques and problems of acting so that we will be able to understand and judge the performances we see. If a performer is unconvincing in a part, we know that he or she has not mastered a technique leading to truthful acting, such as the one suggested by Stanislavski. We become watchful for exaggeration, overacting, and bombast. We recognize that if a performer moves awkwardly or cannot be heard clearly, the performer has not been properly trained in body movement or vocal projection. We learn, too, to notice how well performers play together: whether they listen to each other and respond properly. We also observe how well they establish and maintain contact with the audience.

Earlier we saw the necessity for projection of the performer's voice into the audience. In fact, the performer must project his or her total personality, because (as has frequently been noted) it is the contact between actor and audience which forms the basic encounter of theater. In many types of theater the performers appear to act as if the audience were not there; what of the actor-audience relationship in this situation? From the audience's standpoint, it is very intense, because audience members focus exclusively on the stage. The involvement is so intense that a cough or whisper, unnoticed in an ordinary room or on the street, is magnified a thousandfold. But the performers are conscious of the relationship too. They may concentrate on an object onstage, or on one another (as Stanislavski advised); but a part of them continually senses the audience.

In short, although performers are concentrating on one another, there is still great variation in the intensity and honesty with which they perform. If they are absorbed in a life-and-death struggle on stage, the audience will be absorbed too, like bystanders at a street fight. If they are listless and uninvolved with the play or each other, the audience will be turned off as well.

For the audience, the most immediate and powerful impact of a theater experience is the encounter with live performers: watching actors and actresses impersonate other human beings; admiring their imagination and skill; and, above all, feeling the strong link, the sense of communication, which develops between performers and spectators. The person who guides the performers in establishing this link is the director, whose work will be discussed in Chapter 13.

SUMMARY

1   Performers must make the characters they portray believable and convincing. One problem facing the performer is to avoid exaggerated gestures or speech. The tendency to "show off" destroys credibility.

2   Beginning with the end of the nineteenth century and continuing to the present, many plays have been written in a very realistic, lifelike style. The

characters in these plays resemble ordinary people in their dialogue, behavior, etc. The interpretation of the characters in these plays calls for truthful acting of a high order.

3 A Russian director, Constantin Stanislavski, developed a *system* or *method* of acting to enable performers to be truthful. His suggestions included relaxation and concentration; dealing with specific objects and feelings (a handkerchief, a glass of water, etc.); using the power of fantasy or imagination (the "magic if") to achieve a sense of inner truth in a role; developing a *spine* or *through line* which runs through a role from the beginning to the end of a play; playing together as an *ensemble;* and developing voice and body.

4 The stage makes demands aside from credibility in a role. Among these are the ability to project the voice, even in a quiet, intimate scene; the development of the voice in order to be able to speak verse and other declamatory speech; and the training of the body to fight duels, fall down stairs, and manage physical transformations (as in the play *Rhinoceros*).

5 The avant-garde theater makes additional demands on the performer in terms of voice and body training. The voice is sometimes used to emit odd sounds—screams, grunts, and the like. The body must perform feats of acrobatics and gymnastics.

6 Audience members should familiarize themselves with the problems and techniques of acting in order to judge performances properly.

13

THE
DIRECTOR

The director guides the performers.
The person who works most closely with the actors and actresses is the director. The director develops the production concept, explains it to the performers, helps performers with their roles, and shapes ensemble playing. A contemporary director responsible for many innovative stage productions is Peter Brook. For a production based on the opera *Carmen*, he reduced the size of the opera and eliminated the chorus, giving the piece more impact and immediacy. For the production he used five different actresses in the role of Carmen. The five are shown surrounding him in this photograph.

The person who works most closely with performers in the theater is the *director*. The director is also responsible for coordinating other aspects of the production, such as the ideas of the designers.

For the most part, spectators see theater as a unified experience, but many elements constitute that experience. As has been stated, theater is a complex art involving not one or two elements, but many simultaneously: script, performance, costumes, scenery, lighting, and point of view. These diverse elements—a mixture of the tangible and intangible—must be brought together into an organic whole, and that is the responsibility of the director.

Those working on a theater project have an obligation to create a single vision as they prepare a production. In Chapter 4, we saw that the playwright must incorporate a definite point of view in the script. The performers' interpretations of their roles must be consistent with the playwright's viewpoint; the costume designer must work closely with individual actors and actresses and with scene and lighting designers; and the scene designer must coordinate colors and shapes with the costume designer and understand the point of view of the script.

Though they work together, these artists must of necessity work on segments of the production rather than the entire enterprise. The performers, for instance, are much too busy working on their roles or their interactions with other performers to worry much about scenery. Also, a performer who appears only in the first act of a three-act play has no control over what happens in the second and third acts. The one person who does have an overall perspective is the director.

A HISTORICAL PERSPECTIVE

Certain theater historians are fond of saying that the director did not exist in the theater prior to 1874, when a German nobleman, George II, duke of Saxe-Meiningen, began supervising every element of his theatrical productions—rehearsals, scenic elements, and other aspects—coordinating them into an integrated whole. Beginning with Saxe-Meiningen, the director emerged as a full-fledged, indispensable member of the theatrical team, taking a place alongside the playwright, the performers, and the designers.

The title may have been new, but the *function* of the director had always been present in one way or another. We know, for example, that the Greek playwright Aeschylus directed his own plays and that the chorus for Greek plays rehearsed for many weeks under the supervision of a leader prior to a performance. At various points in theater history, the leading performer or playwright of a company served as a director, though without the name. Molière, for instance, was not only the playwright and the chief actor of his company but functioned as the director also. We know from Molière's short play *The Impromptu of Versailles* that he had definite ideas about the way actors and actresses should perform; no doubt the same advice he offered in that play was frequently given to his performers in rehearsal.

In England, from the seventeenth through the nineteenth century, there was a long line of actor-managers who gave strong leadership to individual theater companies and performed many of the functions of directors, although they were not called by that name. Among the most famous were Thomas Betterton (1635–1710), David Garrick, Charles Kemble (1775–1854), William Charles Macready (1793–1873), and Henry Irving (1838–1905).

Nevertheless, the term *director* did not come into common usage until the end of the nineteenth century. It is significant, perhaps, that the emergence of the director as a separate creative person coincides with important changes which began to take place in society during the nineteenth century. First, there was a breakdown in established social, religious, and political concepts which came with Freud, Darwin, and Marx. Second, there was a marked increase in communication. With the advent of the telegraph, the telephone, photography, motion pictures, and finally television, various cultures which had remained remote or unknown to one another were suddenly quite aware of each other. The effect of these two changes was to alter the monolithic, ordered view of the world which individual societies had maintained before.

Prior to these developments, consistency of style in theater was easier to achieve. Within a given society there was common ground among writers, performers, and spectators. For example, the comedies of the English writers William Wycherley and William Congreve, written during the Restoration period at the end of the seventeenth century, were aimed at a specific audience—the elite, upper class, which relished gossip, acid remarks, and well-turned phrases. The code of behavior of the society was well understood by performers and audience alike; and questions of style in a production hardly arose, because a common approach to style was already present in the fabric of society. The way a man took a pinch of snuff, a maid flirted with a nobleman, or a lady flung open her fan was so clearly delineated in daily behavior that actors and actresses had only to refine and perfect these actions for the stage. The director's task was not so much to impose a style on a production as to prevent the performers from overacting and to see that they spoke their lines properly and that the cast worked as a cohesive unit. Today, however, because style, unity, and a cohesive view of society are so elusive, the director's task is more important.

The director prepares the performance.
The director develops a "spine" for the play, shapes the acting of the performers, and also works closely with the designers to achieve a unified production. Here the director Arvin Brown, on the right, of the Long Wharf Theater in New Haven, discusses a scene from the play *Requiem for a Heavyweight* with the actors John Lithgow, David Proval, and Richard Dreyfus.

(Gerry Goodstein)

THE DIRECTOR'S TASK

The director's work on a production is one of the last elements of which the audience becomes aware. Performers, scenery, and costumes are on stage and are immediately visible to spectators, and the words of the playwright are heard throughout the performance; but the director's work consists of interpreting and blending these elements and takes place largely behind the scenes. It is therefore much less readily apparent to the audience. Except for the playwright, however, the director is the first person to become involved in the creative process of a production, and the choices he or she makes at every stage along the way largely determine whether the ultimate experience will be satisfactory for the spectators.

The Director and the Script

Frequently the director chooses the script to be produced. Generally it is a play which the director is attracted to or feels a special affinity for. If the director does not actually choose the script but is asked to direct it by a playwright or a producer, he or she must still have an understanding and appreciation of the material. The director's attraction to the script, and basic understanding of it, is an important step in launching a production. Once the script is chosen, the actual work on the production begins.

If the play is new and has never been tested in production, the director may see problems in the script which must be corrected before rehearsals begin. The director will have a series of meetings with the playwright to iron out the difficulties ahead of time. The director may feel, for example, that the leading character is not clearly defined or is underwritten, or that a clash of personalities between two characters never reaches a climax. If the playwright agrees with the director's assessment, steps will be taken to revise the manuscript. Generally there is considerable give-and-take between the director and playwright in these preliminary sessions, as well as during the rehearsal period. Ideally, there should be a spirit of cooperation, compromise, and mutual respect in this relationship.

The Directorial Concept

Once the script is selected, the director begins to prepare the production. One crucial task in this process is arriving at a *directorial concept*. Such a concept derives from a controlling idea, vision, or point of view which the director feels is appropriate to the play. The concept should also create a unified theatrical experience for the spectators.

Period To indicate what is involved for the director in developing a concept, let us begin with *period*. Consider Shakespeare's *Troilus and Cressida*. The play was written in the Elizabethan period but is set at the time of the Trojan war, when the ancient Greeks were fighting the Trojans. In presenting the play today, a director has several choices as to the period in which to set the production.

One director might choose to stick to the period indicated in the script and set the play in Troy, with both Trojans and Greeks wearing armor, tunics, and other appropriate garments. Another might set the play in the time when Shakespeare wrote it, and in this case the director and the designers would devise court and military costumes reflecting Shakespeare's day.

Another option for the director would be to modernize the play. There have been a number of modern productions of *Troilus and Cressida* in recent years. Shakespeare's words are retained; but since many of the play's antiwar sentiments and statements about the corruption of love in the face of war are quite relevant today, the play is transferred to the present by means of costumes, settings, and behavior. For example, in 1956 Tyrone Guthrie (1900–1971), a British director, presented a version which was set in the period just prior to 1914 in England, that is, just before World War I. The

The directorial concept.

For a production of Shakespeare's *All's Well That Ends Well*, the director Trevor Nunn developed a concept placing the play around 1900, in the late Edwardian era in England, rather than during the period when Shakespeare set it. All the lines, characters, and ideas of the play were retained, but the shift in time allowed the characters to wear elegant costumes and carry out activities such as serving tea in a way that illuminated the play.

play was shifted to English drawing rooms and other localities conveying the clear impression of England in the early twentieth century. The uniforms were those of English soldiers of the period, and the women wore dresses typical of that era. The set had grand pianos, the men drank cocktails, and the women used cigarette holders—all intended to portray a sophisticated urban environment.

This kind of transposition has been carried out frequently with Greek plays, Elizabethan plays, French plays of the seventeenth century, and other dramatic classics. The important consideration is that the director develop an overall *concept*. If a certain age or a certain nationality in the play is going to be stressed—if the scene is going to be shifted from France to the United States or the time shifted from the eighteenth century to the present—the director must make certain that this is done thoroughly and consistently. The total production—in details and overall mood—must reflect the chosen time and place.

Rather than place the play in a historical period, the director's concept might involve another approach. A director might decide, for instance, to develop a play around a controlling idea or image. To take an oversimplified example, a play with a narrator and episodic scenes might be conceived in circus terms, with the narrator serving as a ringmaster and scenes from the play taking place in circus rings. To carry this further, the performers might dress in clown outfits or other costumes of the circus.

A central image or metaphor   As suggested above, one way to implement a directorial concept is to find a *central image* or *metaphor* for a theatrical production. The circus image described in the previous paragraph would be one example. Another example would be a production of *Hamlet* that envisioned the play in terms of a vast net or spider web in which Hamlet is caught. The motif of a net or spider web could be carried out on several levels: in the design; in the ways in which the performers relate to one another; and in a host of details relating to the central image. There might be a huge rope net hanging over the entire stage, for instance, and certain characters could play string games with their fingers. In short, the metaphor of Hamlet's being caught in a net would be emphasized and reinforced on every level.

The concept should serve the play   The kinds of concepts described above—shifting the time period of the play or using a circus theme or a metaphor of a net—should be the exception rather than the rule. Nine times out of ten it is better to stick to the time and place indicated in the script, and to find the concept from the spine (which will be discussed below).

The best concept is one that remains true to the spirit and meaning of the script. If the director can translate that spirit and meaning into stage terms in an inspired way, he or she will have created an exciting theater experience, but if a director is too intent on displaying his or her own originality, the integrity of the script may be distorted or violated. The circus idea described above might appear to be theatrical and inventive, but it would be quite wrong for certain plays because it would distract the audience's attention from quieter moments or deeper meanings at the heart of the script. This would be the case, for example, with most realistic plays. A directorial concept which is flashy on the surface may very well call too much attention to itself and rob the spectators of the full, honest experience to which they are entitled.

In arriving at a concept, the director must keep these factors in balance. In most cases the best directorial concept is a straightforward one deriving from the play itself and not a scheme superimposed from the outside.

The "Spine" of the Play

One of the first steps for a director in preparing a production, and a helpful way to develop a concept (such as a central metaphor), is to discover the "spine" of the play. In his book *On Directing* Harold Clurman explains how the director should begin this process: "To begin active direction a formulation in the simplest terms must be found to state what general action motivates the play, of what fundamental drama or conflict the script's plot and people are the instruments."[1]

Clurman calls the formulation of the action or conflict the *spine* of the play. The spine could also be called the *main action*. It is a statement of the goal or purpose of the collective characters analogous to the spine of individual characters discussed in Chapter 12.

For example, Clurman says that the spine for the characters in Eugene O'Neill's *A Touch of the Poet* is "to make a place for themselves." In one way or another, Clurman feels, every character in the play is seeking this same goal. For O'Neill's *Long Day's Journey into Night* Clurman sees the spine as being "to probe within oneself for the lost 'something.' "[2]

By finding a spine for the play, the director has a key or springboard from which to develop the action. Different directors may find different spines for the same play. With *Hamlet,* for instance, several spines are possible: much will depend on the period in which the play is produced and the point of view of the individual director. Clurman says that such varied interpretations are to be expected and are acceptable as long as the spine chosen remains true to the spirit and action of the play.

Clurman warns of the dangers of not finding a main action or spine: "Where a director has not determined on a spine for his production, it will tend to be formless. Each scene follows the next without necessarily adding up to a total dramatic 'statement.' "[3]

The Style of the Production

Once the spine has been found, the second task for a director, according to Clurman, "is to find the manner in which the spine is to be articulated."[4] Clurman is speaking here of the *style* of the production.

Style in a theatrical production is a difficult concept to explain. It means the *way* in which a play is presented. In clothes, when we speak of a "casual style" or a "1920s style," we mean in the first case that the clothes are loose and informal, and in the second that the clothes have the look and feel of those worn in the 1920s.

In the theater one way to look at style is in terms of realistic or nonrealistic theater. In Chapter 2 the differences between these two types of theater were discussed, but they can be further subdivided.

Realism, for example, is of several types. At one extreme is *naturalism,* a kind of superrealism. (For a further discussion of naturalism and other forms, see Appendix 3.) The term *naturalism* was championed by several French writers in the nineteenth century. They wanted a theater that would show human beings—many of them in wretched circumstances—as products of heredity and environment. Aside from this special use, the term *naturalism* is used more broadly for attempts to put on stage as exact a copy of life as possible, down to the smallest detail. In a naturalistic stage set of a kitchen, for instance, a performer can actually cook a meal on the stove—the toaster makes toast, the water tap produces water, and the light in the refrigerator goes on when the door opens. Characters speak and act as if they had been caught unobserved by a camera and tape recorder. In this sense, naturalism is supposed to resemble an undoctored documentary film. Naturalism is sometimes called *slice-of-life* drama, as if a section has been taken from life and transferred to the stage.

At the other extreme of realism is *heightened realism*. Here the characters and their activities are intended to resemble life, but a certain license is allowed. The scenery, for example, might be skeletal—that is, incomplete and in outline—although the words and actions of the characters are realistic. Or perhaps a character is allowed a modern version of a soliloquy in an otherwise realistic play. All art calls for selectivity, and the idea that slice-of-life theater can fulfill the total artistic requirements of the theater by itself is impractical. Heightened realism recognizes the necessity for the artist to inject selectivity and creativity into the process.

Realism itself occupies the middle ground between naturalism and heightened realism but includes the extremes at each end.

Nonrealism can also be divided into types: two well-known types of nonrealism are allegory and expressionism.

Allegory is the representation of an abstract theme or subject through the symbolic use of characters, actions, or other elements of a production, such as scenery. Good examples are the medieval morality plays in which characters personify ideas in order to teach an intellectual or moral lesson. In *Everyman* actors play the parts of Good Deeds, Fellowship, Worldly Goods, and so on. In less direct forms of allegory, a relatively realistic story serves as a parable or lesson. Arthur Miller's play *The Crucible* is about the witch-hunts in Salem, Massachusetts, in the late seventeenth century; but it can also be regarded as dealing with specific investigations by the United States Congress in the early 1950s which Miller and others felt treated ordinary citizens unfairly, becoming modern "witch-hunts."

Although *expressionism* was at its height in art, literature, and the theater during the first quarter of the twentieth century, traces of it are still found today, and contemporary plays using its techniques are termed *expressionistic*. In simple terms, expressionism gives outward expression to inward feelings. In Elmer Rice's *The Adding Machine,* the feelings of Mr. Zero when he is fired from his job are conveyed by having the room spin around in a circle amid a cacophony of shrill sounds, such as loud sirens and whistles.

Another way to look at style is in terms of tragedy or comedy. Whether a play is serious or comic depends on the approach the playwright has taken to the material (see Chapters 4, 5, and 6). A serious or comic approach to material is a part of style and provides the director with an indication of how a play should be performed. *Farcical comedy,* for example, employs exaggeration. Performers often use extreme gestures and indulge in slapstick or pratfalls.

For the director, developing a style that is realistic, or expressionistic, or farcical involves giving a signature and an imprint to an entire production: the look of the scenery and lights; the way performers handle their costumes and props; the manner in which performers speak. It also involves the rhythm and pace at which the play moves, a subject to be taken up shortly.

When a director arrives at a style for a production, two things are essential: (1) the style should be appropriate for the play, and (2) it should be consistent throughout every aspect of the production.

Casting

Having picked the play and settled questions of concept and style, the director then casts the play.

Obviously derived from the phrase "casting a mold," the word *casting* in the theater means fitting actors and actresses into roles. Generally speaking, directors attempt to put performers in the role for which they are best suited insofar as their personalities and physical characteristics are concerned. A young woman will play Juliet in *Romeo and Juliet,* an elderly actor with a deep voice will play King Lear, and so on. When a performer closely resembles in real life the character to be enacted, this is known as *type casting.* There are times when a director will deliberately put someone in a role who is obviously wrong for the part. This is frequently done for comic or satiric purposes and is called *casting against type.* For example, a sinister-looking actor might be called on to play an angelic part.

In the modern theater, performers frequently *audition* for parts in a play, and the director casts from those performers who audition. In an audition, actors and actresses read scenes from a play or perform portions of the script to give the director an indication of how they talk and move and how they would interpret a part. From this the director determines whether a performer is right for a given part or not.

Historically, casting was rarely done by audition, because theatrical companies were more permanent. In Shakespeare's time, and in Molière's, certain people always played certain parts in a theatrical troupe: one person would play heroic parts, for example, while another always played the clown. Under these conditions, when a play was selected, it was a matter of assigning roles to the performers who were on hand; auditioning would occur only when a new member was chosen for the company.

From the audience's standpoint it is important to be aware of casting and the difference it can make in the effectiveness of a production. Perhaps the actor or actress is just right for the part he or she is playing. On the other hand, sometimes the wrong performer is chosen for a part: the voice may not be right, or the gestures or facial expressions may be inappropriate for the character being played. One way to test the correctness of casting is to imagine a different kind of actor or actress in a part while watching a performance.

Rehearsals

Once the play is cast, the director supervises all rehearsals. He or she listens to the performers as they go through their lines and begin to move about the stage. Different directors work in different ways in the early stages of rehearsal: some directors "block" the play in advance, giving precise instructions to the performers. (The term *blocking* means deciding where

(Martha Swope)

The director at work.
Trevor Nunn (in the center) and his choreographer Gillian Lynne (on the left) in a rehearsal with Terence V. Mann for the musical *Cats*. Working with choreographers and designers, as well as performers, the director must shape the entire work.

THE DIRECTOR

261

and when performers move and position themselves on the stage.) Other directors let the actors and actresses find their relationships, their movements, and their vocal interpretations on their own. And of course there are directors who do a bit of both. It is worth pointing out that in recent years directors have tended to move toward the less structured approach, directing far less in terms of specific instructions or commands than was the case throughout the whole of the nineteenth and the early part of the twentieth century. In former times it was customary for directors to give actors and actresses precise commands: "Move three paces to the right, and then turn to face the audience. Now speak the next line in a stage whisper." Today this approach is less common.

During the rehearsal period, the director must make certain that the actors and actresses are realizing the intention of the playwright—that they make sense of the script and bring out its meaning. Also, the director must ensure that the performers are working well together—that they are listening to each other and beginning to play as an ensemble. The director must be aware of performers' needs, knowing when to encourage them and when to challenge or criticize them. The director must understand their personal problems and help them overcome such obstacles as insecurity about a role or fear of failure.

Physical Production

At the same time that rehearsals with the performers are going forward, the director is also working with the designers on the physical production. At the outset—once the director's concept is established—the director confers with the costume, scene, and lighting designers to give shape and substance to the concept in visual terms. It is the responsibility of designers to provide images and impressions which will carry out the style and ideas of the production. (See Chapters 15, 16, and 17.)

During the preproduction and rehearsal period, the director meets with the designers to make certain that the work in their areas is on schedule and keeping pace with the rehearsals. Obviously the preparation of these elements must begin long before the actual performance, just as rehearsals must, so that everything will be ready before the performance itself takes place. Any number of problems can arise with the physical elements of a production: the appropriate props are not available, a costume does not allow an actor or actress enough freedom of movement, scene changes are too slow. Early planning will allow time to solve these problems.

The Audience's Eye

One could say that there are two people in theater who stand in for the audience, serving as surrogate or substitute spectators. One, the director, does his or her work before the event; the other, the critic, does his or her work after it.

The critic observes and then writes or talks about the play and the production, thereby giving the spectators additional information about the performance and a yardstick by which to measure their own reactions. The work of the critic has been discussed in Chapter 3.

Before the event, however, in the preparation of a theatrical production, the director acts as the eye of the audience. During rehearsals, the director is the only one who sees the production from the spectator's point of view. For this reason the director must assist the performers in showing the audience exactly what they intend to show. If one performer hides another at an important moment, if a crucial gesture is not visible, if an actor makes an awkward movement, if an actress cannot be heard when she delivers an emotional speech, the director points it out.

Also, the director underscores the meaning of specific scenes through *visual composition* and *stage pictures,* that is, through the physical arrange-

Using stage areas properly.
One responsibility of the director is to make appropriate use of stage areas. In the production of *Fanshen* at the Soho Rep, the director Michael Bloom had several areas to consider: the one nearest the audience with the characters on the floor; the platform where two sets of characters stand, and the upper level at the rear. The alternation of areas and the emphasis given to each become a part of the total effect.

The stage picture.

An important responsiblity of the director is blocking—the placement and movement of performers on stage. In this scene from a production of Shakespeare's *As You Like It* at the Arena Stage, the director Douglas C. Wager has balanced the two figures at the left with the kneeling figure at the right, and set between the two sides a pair of figures in the background.

ment of performers onstage. The spatial relationships of performers convey information about characters. As an example, important characters are frequently placed on a level above other characters: on a platform or step, for instance. Another spatial device is to place an important character alone in one area of the stage while grouping other characters in another area. This causes the eye to give special attention to the character standing alone. If two characters are opposed to each other, they should be placed in positions of physical confrontation on the stage.

Certain areas on the stage assume special significance: a fireplace, with its sense of warmth, can become an area to which a character returns for comfort and reassurance. A door opening on a garden can serve as a place where characters go when they want to renew their spirits or to escape from a hemmed-in feeling. By guiding performers to make the best use of stage space, the director assists them in communicating important visual images to the audience—images consistent with the overall meaning of the play.

Balance, Proportion, and Pace

The director gives shape and structure to a play in two spheres or dimensions: in *space,* in the way just described, and in *time.* Since a production occurs through time, it is important for the director to see that the *movement,* the *pace,* and the *rhythm* of the play are correct. If the play moves too quickly, if we miss words and do not understand what is going on, it is the director's fault. The director must determine whether there is too short or too long a time between speeches, or whether a performer moves too slowly across the stage. The director must attempt to control the pace and rhythm within a scene—the dynamics and the manner in which the actors and actresses move from moment to moment—and the rhythm between scenes.

One of the most common faults of directors is not to establish a clear rhythm in a production. An audience at a performance is impatient, almost unconsciously so, to see what is coming next; and if expectations are frustrated too long, the audience will become unhappy. The director must see to it that the movement from moment to moment and scene to scene has a thrust and a drive moving through the play, thus maintaining our interest. Variety is important too. If the play moves ahead at only one pace, whether slow or fast, the audience will be fatigued simply by the monotony of that pace.

The rhythm within scenes and between scenes becomes an important aspect of a production. This rhythm enters our psyche as we watch a performance and thus contributes to our overall response. Of course, it must be borne in mind that the responsibility for pace, proportion, and overall effect, while initially the director's, ultimately rests with the performers. Once the performance begins, the actors and actresses are onstage and the director is not. Unlike the cinema, in which the pace and rhythm can be determined in the editing room, in theater there is great elasticity and variety; so much depends on the mood of the performers. The director must instill and implant such a strong sense of inner rhythm in the performers in rehearsals that they have an internal clock which tells them how they should play. And, of course, audience reaction will vary from night to night and alter the pace as well. The director's work is done prior to the performance and behind the scenes. But if it is done well, the director will imbue the work with a rhythm that will shine through in the final performance.

Technical Rehearsal

Just prior to public performances a *technical rehearsal* is held. The actors and actresses are on stage in their costumes with the scenery and lighting for the first time, and there is a *run-through* of the show from beginning to end, with all props, costumes, and scene changes. The stagehands move scenery, the crew handles props, and the lighting technicians control the dimming and raising of lights. All of them must coordinate their work with that of the performers.

Let us say that one scene ends in a garden, and the next scene opens in a library. Once the performers leave the garden set, the lighting fades, the scenery is removed, and the garden furniture is taken off the stage. Following that, the scenery for the library must be "flown in" or brought in on wagons and adjusted by the stagehands; the books and other props are put in place. Then the performers for the new scene in the library take their places as the lighting comes up. Extensive rehearsals are required to ensure that the lighting comes up at just the moment when the scenery is prepared and the performers are in place. Any mishap on the part of the stage crew, lighting crew, prop crew, or performers would affect the illusion and destroy the aesthetic effect of the scene change. The importance of the technical rehearsals is therefore considerable.

Tryout or First Public Performance

Once the technical rehearsals are completed and the problems which occurred are solved, the next step arrives: a performance in front of an audience. We have stressed from the beginning the importance of actor-audience interaction and the fact that no play is complete until it is actually performed for an audience. It is crucial, therefore, for a production to be tried out before a group of spectators. What has gone before, in terms of script, rehearsals, and visual elements, must now meet the test of combining harmoniously in front of an audience. For this purpose there is a period of *tryouts*—also called *previews*—when the director and the performers discover which parts of the play are successful and which are not. Frequently, the director and performers find that one part of the play is moving too slowly; they know this because the audience becomes restless and begins to cough or stir. Sometimes, in a comedy, there is a great deal of laughter where little was expected, and the performers and the director must adjust to this.

The tryout is an important period, and these early audiences become genuine collaborators in the shaping of the play. (In the days when Broadway was the chief forum for new plays in the United States, tryouts were held in other cities—Philadelphia, New Haven, or Boston—before the play was exposed to critics in New York. When that opportunity was not available, a series of previews would be given.) After several performances in front of an audience, the director and the performers get the "feel" of the audience and know whether the play is ready or not.

For an idea of the director's full range of responsibilities, see the chart on the opposite page.

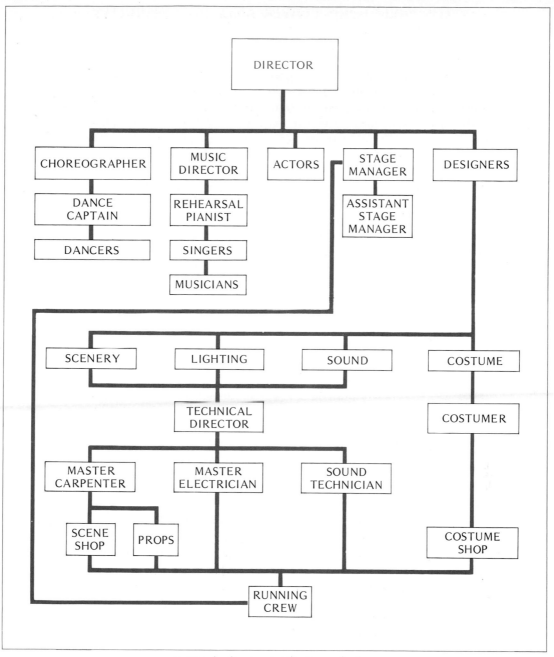

Duties of a director in a theater production.
Once a director has decided on a script (and worked with the playwright, if it is a new play), he or she must organize the entire artistic side of the production. This chart indicates the many people the director must work with and the many elements that must be coordinated. (Courtesy of Prof. Paul Antonie Distler.)

THE DIRECTOR'S POWER AND RESPONSIBILITY

Clearly, the director has great power, and one of the great dangers is that the director will use this power to overstress certain elements to the exclusion or detriment of other elements. A second danger lies in the possibility that the director will develop an inconsistent or incongruous scheme. As suggested previously, the director might go overboard with a production concept. For instance, a director might decide to make *Macbeth* into a cowboy play, with Duncan as a sheriff and Macbeth as a deputy who wishes to kill the sheriff in order to take the job himself. In this version, Lady Macbeth would be the deputy's wife, whom he had met in a western saloon. *Macbeth* could be done this way, but it would be ludicrous, carrying reinterpretation too far. It would be an attempt to rewrite the play and make the director's work more important than Shakespeare's.

Any artistic event must have a unity not encountered in real life. We expect the parts to be brought together so that the total effect will enlighten us, move us, or amuse us. All the parts must fit and be consistent with one another; there must be no jarring notes unless they are intentional. This is the director's responsibility. When the director has a strong point of view—one which is correct for the play—the experience for the audience is likely to be meaningful and exciting. By the same token, if the director gets too carried away with one idea or lets the scene designer create a design which overpowers the performers and buries the production in a mountain of scenic effects, then the experience will be neither satisfactory nor complete. The director must have a keen sense of proportion so that various elements work together rather than against one another. It is this juggling act, this weaving together of the tangible and the intangible, the spiritual and the physical, the symbolic and the literal, which must take place in the chemistry of theater, and it is the director who has the final responsibility to see that it occurs.

THE PRODUCER OR MANAGER

The director is responsible for bringing the artistic elements of a production together, but no production would ever be performed for the public without a technical and business component. Here, too, the coordination of elements is crucial, and the person chiefly responsible is the producer or manager.

The Commercial Producer

In a commercial theater venture, the producer has many responsibilities. (See the chart opposite.) In general, the producer oversees the entire business and publicity side of the production and has the following duties:

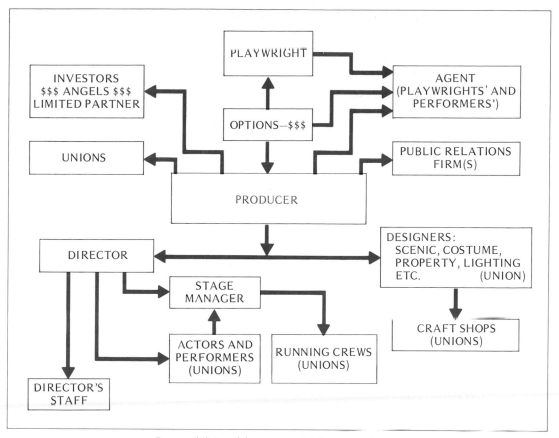

Responsibilities of the commercial theater producer.
When a commercial theater production is mounted, the person responsible for organizing the full range of nonartistic activities is the producer. This chart, which shows the producer at the center, indicates the people the producer must deal with and the numerous elements he or she must coordinate. *(Courtesy of Prof. Paul Antonie Distler.)*

1   Raise money to finance the production
2   Secure rights to the script
3   Deal with the agents for the playwright, director, and performers
4   Hire the director, the performers, the designers, and the stage crews
5   Deal with all theatrical unions
6   Rent the theater space
7   Supervise the work of those running the theater: in the box office, the auditorium, the business office
8   Supervise the advertising
9   Oversee the budget and the week-to-week financial management of the production

The producer must have the artistic sensibility to pick the right script and hire the right director if a production is to succeed. Aside from raising capital and having the final say in hiring and firing, the producer oversees all financial and business operations in a production. In a nonprofit theater the person having these same responsibilities is called the manager. In terms of day-to-day operations, the duties of the producer and manager are roughly equivalent.

Day-to-Day Duties of the Producer or Nonprofit Manager

Whether in a commercial production or the running of a nonprofit theater organization, the tasks of the person in charge are many and complex.

The producer or manager is responsible for the maintenance of the theater building, including the dressing rooms, the public facilities, and the lobby. The producer or manager is also responsible for the budget, making certain that the production stays within established limits. This includes salaries for the director, designers, performers, and stage crews, and expenditures for scenery, costumes, and music. Again, an artistic element enters the picture; important decisions as to whether a certain costume needs to be replaced or whether scenery needs to be altered affect costs. The producer or manager must find additional sources of money, or determine that changes are important enough artistically to take sums from another item in the budget. In other words, the producer or manager must work very closely with the director and the designers in balancing artistic and financial needs.

The producer or manager is also responsible for publicity. The audience would never get to the theater if it did not know when and where a play was being presented. The producer or manager must advertise the production and decide whether such advertisements should be placed in daily newspapers, on radio, on television, in student newspapers, in magazines, or elsewhere.

A host of other problems come under the supervision of the producer or manager: tickets must be ordered, the box office maintained, and plans made ahead of time for the way in which tickets are sold. The securing of ushers, the printing of programs, the maintenance of the auditorium— (usually called the *front* of the *house*)—are also the responsibility of the producer or manager.

Once again, plans must be made well in advance. In the case of many theater organizations, an entire season—the plays to be produced, the personnel who will be in charge, and requirements in terms of supplies—is planned a year ahead of time. It should be clear that coordination and cooperation are as important in this area as they are for the director and the production itself. (For the organization of a nonprofit company, see the chart on the opposite page.)

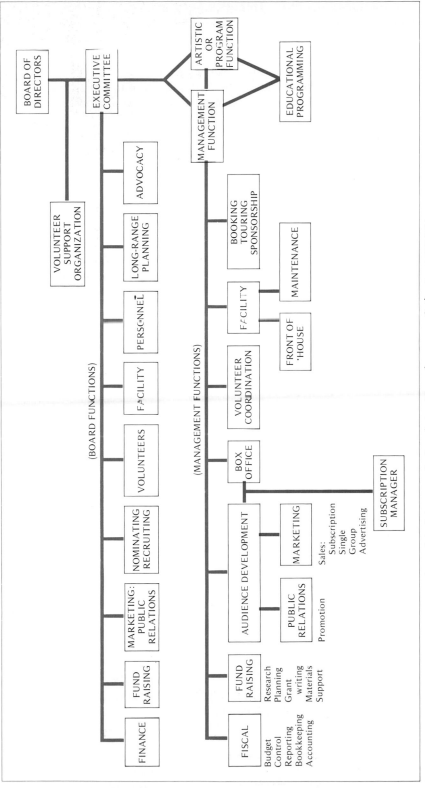

A model of the organizational structure of a nonprofit theater company.

A nonprofit theater is a complex institution with many facets. This chart shows the various activities that must be organized for the successful management of such a theater. (*Courtesy of Prof. Paul Antonie Distler.*)

COMPLETING THE PICTURE

A theater presentation can be compared to a mosaic consisting of many bright-colored pieces of stone fitting together to form a complete picture. The playwright puts the words and ideas together, the producer or manager puts the business side of a production together, and the director puts the artistic elements together. The separate pieces in the mosaic must be arranged into a pattern and become parts of an artistic whole, thereby providing a complete theater experience.

Important features of the mosaic are the physical environment in which a performance takes place and the visual elements—scenery, lighting, costumes—of the production. We turn to these elements in Part Five.

SUMMARY

1 The term *director* did not come into general use until the end of the nineteenth century. Certain functions of the director, however—organizing the production, instilling discipline in the performers, setting a tone for the production—have been carried out since the beginning of theater by someone in authority.

2 The director's duties became more crucial in the twentieth century. Because of the fragmentation of society and the many styles and cultures existing side by side, it became necessary for someone to impose a point of view and a single vision on individual productions.

3 The director has many responsibilities:

Selecting the script
Working with the writer on a new play
Finding the *spine,* or main action, of the play
Arriving at the style of the production
Evolving a *concept,* or an approach to the script
Holding auditions and casting roles
Conducting rehearsals
Ensuring that stage action communicates the meaning of the play
Working with the performers to develop their individual roles
Developing the visual side of the production with the designers
Supervising the technical and tryout rehearsals
Establishing proper pace and rhythm in the movement of the scenes
Establishing the dynamics of the production as a whole

4 Because the director has such wide-ranging power and responsibilities, he or she can distort a production and create an imbalance in elements or an improper emphasis. The director is responsible for a sense of proportion and order in the production.

5 The producer or manager of a production is responsible for the business aspects: maintaining the theater, arranging publicity, handling finances, and managing ticket sales, budgets, ushers, etc.

PART 5

THE DESIGNERS: ENVIRONMENT AND THE VISUAL ELEMENTS

The splash and color of costumes and scenery.
Visual elements play an important role in every theater production. They are particularly important to large musicals such as *La Cage aux Folles*, shown on the following pages in a drawing by Al Hirschfeld. The musical features elaborate scenery, elegant costumes, and sophisticated lighting. Stage environment and these visual elements—and also sound—are the subject of the four chapters of Part Five.

14

STAGE
SPACES

Delphi: A setting for Greek theater.

The physical environment for a theater production is an important part of the experience. Whether the theater space is indoors or outdoors, whether it is large or small, the shape of the stage and its relationship to the audience—all these help determine the nature of the theater experience. Ancient Greek drama was performed in an outdoor amphitheater carved into the side of the hill, like the one seen here in Delphi, where a production of *King Oedipus* is in progress. An audience in ancient Greece, such as the one here, surrounded a circular playing area that had a stage house at the rear. In the distance were the mountains near Delphi. The theaters of ancient Greece also held a large number of spectators—from 10,000 to 15,000—and theater was a communal affair.

For those who create theater, the experience begins long before the actual event. The dramatist spends weeks, months, or perhaps years writing the play; the director and designers plan the production well ahead of time; and the performers rehearse intensively for several weeks before the first public performance. For the spectator, too, the experience begins ahead of time, though not on the same scale. Members of the audience read or hear reports of the play; they anticipate seeing a particular actress or actor perform; they purchase tickets and make plans with friends to attend; and, at the time of the performance, they gather ahead of time outside the theater with other members of the audience.

CREATING THE ENVIRONMENT

Once spectators arrive at the theater for a performance, they immediately take in the environment in which the event will take place. The physical environment of a theater creates definite expectations about the event to come and conditions the experience once it gets under way. The atmosphere of the theater building itself has a great deal to do with the audience's mood in approaching a performance.

Spectators have one feeling if they come into a formal setting—a picture-frame stage surrounded by carved gold figures, with crystal chandeliers and red plush seats in the auditorium—and quite another if they come into an old warehouse converted into a theater, with bare brick walls, and a stage in the middle of the floor surrounded by folding chairs. If the environment of a theater is consistent with the kind of production to be presented, the total experience will be enhanced; if the environment runs counter to the production, it will be confusing and detract from the overall effect.

For many years people took the physical arrangement of a theater for granted. This was particularly true in the period when all houses were facsimiles of the Broadway theater, with its *proscenium* or picture-frame stage. In the recent past, though, not only have people been exposed to other types of theaters, they have become more aware of the importance of environment. Many experimental groups have deliberately made awareness of the environment a part of the experience.

An extreme example was a production in the early 1970s off-Broadway, *And They Put Handcuffs on the Flowers*—a radical political play by the Spanish dramatist Arrabal (1932–   ). In order to get into the theater, spectators had to enter a dark corridor one at a time. They were blindfolded, hit in the pit of the stomach, clutched by the throat, then hurled into the theater space. The idea was to give members of the audience a sense of what it was like to be treated as a prisoner.

A theater experience begins before the performance.
Here an audience gathers to enter a Broadway theater. When an audience arrives at a
theater, the physical environment sets up expectations of what is to come. A formal
space signals one kind of experience, an informal space another.

An avant-garde production of Euripides's *The Bacchae*, called *Dionysus in 69*, by the Performance Group in New York, was considerably less startling, but carried out the same idea of introducing the audience to the performance in a controlled manner. Spectators were not allowed in the theater when they arrived, but were made to line up on the street outside. The procedure is outlined in a book describing the production.

The audience begins to assemble at around 7:45 P.M. They line up on Wooster Street below Greenwich Village. Sometimes the line goes up the block almost to the corner of Broome. On rainy nights, or during the coldest parts of the winter, the audience waits upstairs over the theater. The theater is a large space, some 50 by 40 and 20 feet high. At 8:15 the performance begins for the audience when the stage manager, Vickie May Strang, makes the following announcement. Inside the performers begin warming up their voices and bodies at 7:45.

VICKIE: Ladies and gentlemen! May I have your attention, please. We are going to start letting you in now. You will be admitted to the theater one at a time, and

STAGE SPACES

279

if you're with someone you may be split up. But you can find each other again once you're inside. Take your time to explore the environment. It's a very interesting space, and there are all different kinds of places you can sit. We recommend going up high on the towers and platforms, or down underneath them. The password is "Go high or take cover." There is no smoking inside and no cameras. Thank you.

In an interview in the book, Strang gave her own view of this procedure.

We let the public in one at a time. People on the queue outside the theater ask me why. I explain that this is a rite of initiation, a chance for each person to confront the environment alone, without comparing notes with friends. People are skeptical. Some few are angry. Many think it's a put-on. I must confess to a perverse pleasure in teasing people on a line. Many will come up and ask anxiously, "Has it already begun?" "Well," I say, "it begins before we let anybody in, but it begins when everybody is in, and really it begins when you go in." True.[1]

By making spectators enter the theater in an unconventional way, and by rearranging the theater space itself, certain contemporary groups deliberately make the spectators conscious of the theater environment. But the feeling we have about the atmosphere of a theater building as we enter it has always been an important element in the experience. In the past, spectators may not have been conscious of it, but they were affected by it nevertheless. Today, with the many varieties of theater experience available to us, the first thing we should become aware of is the environment in which the event takes place. Whether it is large or small, indoors or outdoors, formal or informal, familiar or unfamiliar, will inevitably play a part in our response to the performance.

FOUR BASIC STAGE SPACES

A consideration of environment leads directly to an examination of the various forms and styles of theater buildings, including the basic arrangements of audience seating. Throughout theater history, there have been four basic types of stages, each with its own advantages and disadvantages, each suited to certain types of plays and certain types of productions, and each providing the audience with a somewhat different viewing experience. The four are (1) the proscenium or picture-frame stage, (2) the arena or circle stage, (3) the thrust stage with three-quarters seating, and (4) created and found stage space.[2]

Proscenium Stage

Perhaps the most familiar type of stage is the proscenium or picture-frame stage. Broadway theaters, which (as has been noted) were models for

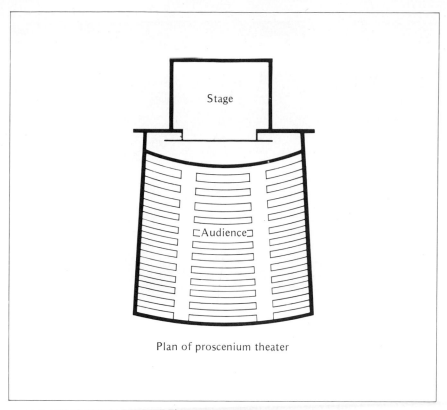

Plan of proscenium theater

The proscenium theater.
The audience faces in one direction, toward an enclosed stage encased by a picture-frame opening. Scene changes and performers' entrances and exits are made behind the proscenium opening, out of sight of the audience.

theaters throughout the country, have proscenium stages. The name *proscenium* comes from the open wall which separates the audience from the stage—in the past it was called an arch, but it is usually a rectangle—and which forms an outline for the stage itself. It resembles a large picture frame through which the audience looks at the stage. Prior to the 1950s there was invariably a curtain just behind the proscenium opening; when the curtain rose, it revealed the picture. Another term for this type of stage is *fourth wall,* from the idea that the proscenium opening is an invisible glass wall through which the audience looks at the other three walls of a room.

Because the action takes place largely behind the proscenium opening or frame, the seats in the auditorium all face in the same direction—toward the stage, just as seats in a movie theater face the screen. The auditorium itself is slanted downward from the back of the auditorium—or *house,* as it is called—to the stage. (In theater usage, the slant of an auditorium or stage

A formal proscenium theater.

The interior of the Covent Garden Theater in London in the nineteenth century was typical of proscenium theaters found throughout Europe and America. It featured elegant decor, tiers of boxes around the sides and rear of the auditorium, a large main floor, and a picture-frame stage.

floor is called a *rake*.) The stage itself is raised several feet above the auditorium floor to aid visibility. There is usually a balcony (sometimes there are two balconies) protruding about halfway over the main floor. The main floor, incidentally, is called the *orchestra*. In certain theaters, as well as concert halls and opera houses which have the proscenium arrangement, there are horseshoe-shaped tiers or *boxes,* which ring the auditorium for several floors above the orchestra floor.

The popularity of the proscenium stage on Broadway and throughout the United States in the nineteenth and early twentieth centuries was partly due to its wide acceptance throughout Europe. Beginning in the late seventeenth century, the proscenium theater was adopted in every European country. Examples of theaters in this style in the eighteenth century included the Drury Lane and Covent Garden in London; the Royal Theater in Turin, Italy; and Hôtel de Bourgogne in Paris; the Bolshoi in St. Petersburg, Russia; and the Drottningholm near Stockholm, Sweden (a theater still preserved in its original state). And in the nineteenth century they included the Teatro Español in Madrid; the Haymarket in London; the Park Theater and Burton's Chambers Street in New York; the Burgtheater in Vienna, Austria; and the Teatro alla Scala, Milan, Italy.

The stage area of these theaters was usually deep, allowing for elaborate scenery, including scene shifts, with a tall *fly loft* above the stage to hold scenery. The loft had to be more than twice as high as the proscenium opening so that scenery could be concealed when it was raised or flown. (The term *to fly* comes from the notion that when pieces of scenery are raised out of sight, they "fly.") Scenery was usually hung by rope or cable on a series of parallel pipes running from side to side across the stage. By hanging the pieces straight across, one behind the other, a great deal of scenery could be employed.

Several mechanisms for raising and lowering scenery were developed during the period when the proscenium stage itself was being adopted. An Italian, Giacomo Torelli (1608–1678), created a counterweight system in which weights hung on a series of ropes and pulleys balanced the scenery, allowing heavy scenery to be moved easily by a few stagehands. Torelli's system also allowed side pieces, known as *wings*, to move in and out of the stage picture. By attaching both the hanging pieces and the side pieces to a central drum below the stage, Torelli made it possible for a complete stage set to be changed at one time. Those seeing this effect when it was first developed must have thought it was magic; and indeed, Torelli was called *il gran stregone,* "the great wizard."

Shortly after Torelli, a dynasty of scenic artists emerged who carried scene painting to a degree of perfection rarely equaled before or since. Their family name was Bibiena, and for over a century, beginning with Ferdinando (1657–1743) and continuing through several generations to Carlo (1728–1787), they dominated the art of scene painting. Their sets usually consisted of vast halls, palaces, or gardens. Towering columns and arches framed spacious corridors or hallways which disappeared in an endless series of vistas as far as the eye could see.

Throughout this period, audiences, as well as scene designers and technicians, became so carried away with spectacle that it began to be emphasized to the exclusion of everything else, including the script and the acting. In Paris, the very name of the theater called *Salle des Machines*— "Hall of the Machines"—indicated that visual effects were the chief attraction. At times there was nothing on stage but visual display: cloud machines brought angels or deities from on high; rocks opened to reveal wood nymphs; the stage rotated on a turntable to change from a banquet hall to a forest; smoke, fire, twinkling lights, and every imaginable effect appeared as if by magic. Because the machinery and the workings of the scene changes can be concealed, the proscenium is the perfect arrangement for spectacle.

(From Guiseppi Calli Bibiena, Architectural and Perspective Design, Dover Publications, 1964)

An elaborate design for the proscenium stage.
During the eighteenth century, the Bibiena family from Italy created scene designs on a grand scale for theaters throughout Europe. The Bibienas painted backdrops with vistas which seemed to disappear into the infinite distance. This scene is by Giuseppe di Bibiena (1696–1757).

The days of such heavy concentration on spectacle have long since passed, but our fascination with it has not. We still find ingenious displays of visual effects in proscenium theaters. This is especially true of musicals.

A good example is *Dreamgirls,* a musical based on the story of a female singing group, the Supremes. During the course of *Dreamgirls,* one of the original singers, who is not chic or svelte enough, is dropped from the group. As the play chronicles the triumphs and personal problems of the singers we see a series of backstage and onstage performances. Sometimes the scene shifts, almost like a film, from behind the scenes to out front. To get the kaleidoscopic visual effects of the scenery, the designer Robin Wagner (1933–   ) created towers made of metal pipes in which spotlights were placed. These towers can move in any direction on the stage—frontwards, backwards, sideways—and can twist and turn. In addition to the flashy towers, there are curtains of sparkling beads and other curtains of shimmering lights. The result is a series of spectacular visual effects made possible by the proscenium frame.

In addition to providing the opportunity for spectacle, there are other advantages to the proscenium stage. Realistic scenery as well—a living room, an office, or a kitchen—looks good behind the proscenium frame. Also, the strong central focus provided by the frame rivets the attention of the audience. There are times, too, when members of the audience want the detachment, the distancing, which a proscenium provides.

There are disadvantages, however. Besides the temptation to use visual pyrotechnics, the drawbacks of the proscenium stage include its tendency to be remote and formal. In extreme cases proscenium theaters are decorated in gold and red plush, looking more like temples of art than theaters. In short, as with any theater environment, the proscenium theater offers clear advantages, together with attendant disadvantages.

(Martha Swope)

A beautiful stage picture.

Because the backstage area is hidden from the audience and the stage is enclosed in a frame, elaborate, magical visions are possible in a proscenium theater. In this setting by Lawrence Miller for the musical *Nine*, notice the elaborate vista seen through the portals in the background.

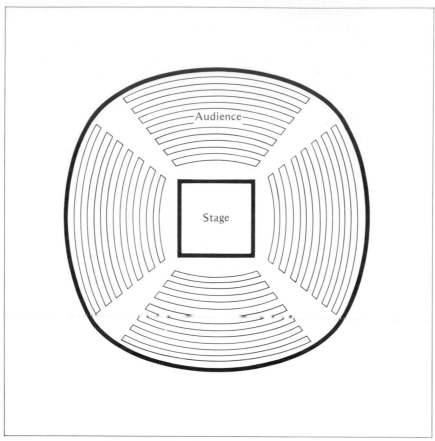

Plan of an arena stage.
The audience sits on four sides or in a circle surrounding the stage. Entrances and exits are made through the aisles or through tunnels underneath the aisles. A feeling of intimacy is achieved because the audience is close to the action and encloses it.

Arena Stage

In the period just after World War II, many people in theater wanted to break away from the formality which proscenium theaters tend to create. There was a desire to bring theater closer to everyday life: in acting styles, in the subject matter of the plays, in the manner of presentation, and in the shape of the theater space. This last had to do both with the atmosphere of the building and with the audience-actor relationship. One result of this reaction was to return to the *arena stage*.

The arena stage (also called *circle theater* or *theater-in-the-round*) has a playing space in the center of a square or circle, with seats for spectators around the circle or on the four sides. The arrangement is similar to that in sports arenas which feature boxing or basketball. The stage may be a raised area a few feet off the main floor, with seats rising from the floor, or it may be on the floor itself, with seats raised on levels around it. When seating is close to the stage, there is usually some kind of demarcation indicating the boundaries of the playing area. In the late 1940s and early 1950s arena theaters appeared in cities all over the United States: Houston, Seattle, Nashville, and Washington, D.C., to list a few.

There is no question that these theaters offer more intimacy than the ordinary proscenium. With the performers in the center, even in a larger theater, the audience can be closer to them. As an example, if the same number of people attend an arena and a proscenium event, at least half those at the arena will be nearer the action: someone who would have been

(Arena Stage, Washington, D.C.)

A performance in an arena theater.
At the Arena Stage in Washington, D.C., the audience surrounds the action. Lighting instruments are visible above, and scenery is minimal; but a strong sense of place is suggested, and everyone is close to the action.

STAGE SPACES

in the twelfth row in a proscenium theater will be in the sixth row in an arena theater. Besides the proximity to the stage, there is no frame or barrier to separate the performers from the audience.

Beyond these considerations, in the arrangement of arena seating there is the unconscious communion which comes from people in a circle. This seems basic to human beings, from the embrace of two people, to a circle for children's games, to a larger gathering where people form a human enclosure around a fire or an altar. It is no accident that virtually all primitive forms of theater were "in the round." An unusual event will automatically draw people into a circle to watch. At a street fight, notice how the onlookers form a circle—to get a close look without getting so near that they would become involved.

There is a more practical reason why there was such a proliferation of arena theaters in the United States a few years ago—economy. All you need for this kind of theater is a large room. You designate a playing space, arrange rows of seats around the sides, hang lights on pipes above, and you have a theater. Elaborate scenery is impossible because it would block the view of large parts of the audience. A few pieces of furniture, with perhaps a lamp or sign hung from the ceiling, are all you need to indicate where the scene takes place. Many low-budget groups found they could build a workable and even attractive theater-in-the-round when a proscenium theater would have been out of the question.

These two factors—intimacy and economy—no doubt explain why arena theater is one of the oldest stage forms. From as far back as we have records, we know that tribal ceremonies and rituals, in all parts of the world, have been held in some form of circle theater. The war dance of the Apache Indians is a good example, as are two ancient ceremonies which still survive today: the festival plays of Tibet, which portray the struggle of Buddhism to replace an earlier religion; and the Otomi ritual in Mexican villages, in which men fling themselves on a rope from a 70-foot tower pole and "fly" through the air in a wide arc until they touch the ground.

The Greek theater evolved from an arena form. Tribes beat down a circle in a field of thrashed grain; an altar was placed in the center, and ceremonies were performed around it, while members of the tribe stood on the edge of the circle. This arrangement was later made more permanent as the ceremonies and festivals and Dionysian revels—forerunners of the Greek theater—were held in such theaters.

The arena form has emerged at other times in history. Several of the cycle plays of the medieval period were performed in the round: in Lincolnshire and Cornwall in England, and in Touraine in France, for example. In Cornwall, the earthen embankments still survive that surrounded the circular playing area where the spectators stood. A plan survives, too, of an arena theater set up in a riverbed in Kyoto, Japan, in 1464, for three days of performances before the shogun, or ruler. The shogun sat at one end of the circle, and the actors entered at the other, while the audience sat in two semicircles around the playing area, encircling the actors.[3]

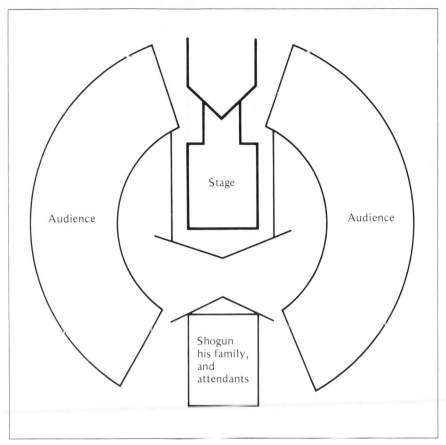

An Asian arena theater.

At Kyoto, Japan, in 1464, a theater was set up in a riverbed where an acting troupe performed for three days. The Shōgun and his family and attendants sat at one end. Other members of the audience surrounded the stage on two sides. (*From a drawing in* The Nō Plays of Japan *by Arthur Waley, published by Grove Press, Inc., New York.*)

In spite of its long history and its resurgence in recent years, the arena stage has often been eclipsed by other forms. One reason is that its design, while allowing for intimacy, also dictates a certain austerity. It is impossible to have elaborate scenery or much in the way of visual effects. On top of this, the performers must make all their entrances and exits along aisles that run through the audience, and they can sometimes be seen before and after they are supposed to be on stage. The arena's lack of adaptability in this respect may explain why some of the circle theaters which opened twenty or thirty years ago have since closed. A number survive, however, and continue to do well. One of the best known is the Arena Stage in Washington, D.C. In addition, throughout this country there are a number of musical *tent theaters* in the arena form where musical revivals and concerts are given.

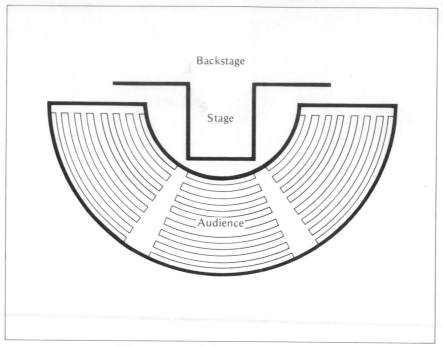

Thrust stage with three-quarter seating.
The stage is surrounded on three sides by the audience. Sometimes seating is a semicircle. Entrances and exits are made from the sides and backstage. Spectators surround the action, but there is still the possibility of scene changes and other stage effects.

Thrust Stage

Falling between the proscenium and the arena is a third type of theater: the *thrust stage* with three-quarter seating. In one form or another it has been the most widely used stage of all. The basic arrangement for this type of theater has the audience sitting on three sides, or in a semicircle, enclosing a stage which protrudes into the center. At the back of the playing area is some form of stage house providing for the entrances and exits of the actors as well as scene changes. The thrust stage combines some of the best features of the other two: the sense of intimacy for the audience, the "wraparound" feeling of the arena, and a focused stage set against a single background of the proscenium.

The thrust stage was developed by the Greeks for their great tragedies and comedies. They took the circle, called the *orchestra,* of the tribal rituals, and placed it at the base of a curving hillside. The slope of the hill formed a natural viewing area for the spectators, and the level circle at the foot formed the stage. At the back of the circle, opposite the hillside, they placed

A modern thrust stage.
The stage of the ACT Theater in Seattle, Washington, shows the seating surrounding the playing area on three sides. This stage provides intimacy for the spectators but also allows for a scenic background for the performers.

a stage house, or *skene*. The skene had formal doors through which characters made their entrances and exits and which formed a background for the action. It also provided a place for the actors to change their costumes.

During the time of the Greek playwright Aeschylus, in the first half of the fifth century B.C., the skene may have been a temporary structure, erected each year for the festivals. In the next two or three centuries, however, the skene was refined to the point where it became a permanent stone building, two or three stories in height, with a platform stage in front. At the same time, the wooden benches on the hillsides for the spectators were replaced by stone seats. The largest Greek theaters seated 15,000 or more spectators, and the design was duplicated all over Greece, particularly in the years following the conquests of Alexander the Great (356–323 B.C.). Remnants of these theaters remain throughout that part of the world, in such places as Epidaurus, Priene, Ephesus, Delphi, and Corinth, to name a few.

The Romans took the Greek form and simply built it as a complete structure. Instead of using the natural amphitheater of a hillside, they constructed a free-standing stone building, joining the stage house to the seating area, and making the orchestra a semicircle. In front of the stage house, decorated with arches and statues, they erected a long platform stage. The overall size and the basic arrangement, however, were similar to the Greek model. Counting the Greek and Roman period together, this form of theater was in use for over eight centuries. After they fell into disuse, there was a lapse of several centuries in formal theatrical presentations.

Around A.D. 1200, performances of religious plays, which had been held inside churches and cathedrals, were moved outdoors. One popular stage for these outdoor performances was the *platform stage*. A simple platform was set on trestles (it was sometimes called a *trestle stage*), with a curtain at the back which the actors used for entrances and costume changes. The area underneath the stage was closed off and provided, among other things, a space from which devils and other characters could appear, sometimes in a cloud of smoke. In some places the platform was on wheels (a *wagon stage*) and moved from place to place through a town. The audience stood on three sides of the platform, making it an improvised thrust stage. This type of stage was widely used between the thirteenth and fifteenth centuries in England and various parts of Europe.

The next step was a thrust stage which appeared in England in the sixteenth century, just before Shakespeare began writing for the theater. A platform stage would be set up at one end of the open courtyard of an inn. The inns of this period were three or four stories high, and the rooms facing the inner courtyard served as boxes from which spectators could watch the performance. On ground level, spectators stood on three sides of the stage, while the fourth side of the courtyard, behind the platform, served as the stage house.

Interestingly enough, an almost identical theater took shape in Spain at the same time. The inns in Spain were called *corrales,* the same name given to the theaters which developed there. In addition to the similarity of theaters in England and Spain, a further coincidence lies in the fact that a talented and prolific dramatist, Lope de Vega, was born within two years of Shakespeare's birth and emerged as his Spanish counterpart.

In England, the formal theaters of Shakespeare's day, such as the Globe and the Fortune, were similar to the inn theaters: the audience stood in an open area around a platform stage, and three levels of spectators sat in closed galleries at the back and sides. A roof covered part of the stage, and at the back, some form of raised area served for balcony scenes (as in *Romeo and Juliet*). At the rear of the stage, also, scenes could be concealed and then "discovered." On each side at the rear was a door used for entrances and exits.

These theaters were fascinating combinations of diverse elements: they were both indoors and outdoors; some spectators stood while others sat; and the audience was composed of almost all levels of society. The physical

An Elizabethan playhouse.
This drawing, based on a sketch from the period, shows the kind of stage on which the plays of Shakespeare and his contemporaries were first presented. A platform stage juts into an open courtyard, with spectators standing on three sides. Three levels of enclosed seats rise above the courtyard. There are doors at the rear of the stage for entrances and exits and an upper level for balcony scenes. (*Drawing from C. Walter Hodges,* The Globe Restored, *by permission of W. W. Norton and Co., Inc.*)

environment must have been a stimulating one: performers standing at the front of the thrust stage were in the center of a hemisphere of spectators, ranging on three sides around them as well as above and below. While these theaters held 2000 to 3000 spectators, no person was more than 60 feet or so from the stage, and most were much closer. Being in the midst of so many people, enclosed on all sides but with an open sky above, must have instilled a feeling of great communion among the members of the audience and the performers.

Shortly after Shakespeare's day, in the latter part of the seventeenth century, two things occurred in England and Spain, as well as throughout Europe: (1) the theater moved completely indoors; and (2) the stage began a

Performance on an outdoor thrust stage. A large audience surrounds the action at the New York Shakespeare Festival theater in Central Park. Though not seen in the photograph, the audience stretches around the stage on both the left and the right. This gives the performance a certain intimacy even though the theater is large and is set outdoors.

slow but steady retreat behind the proscenium, partly because of being indoors, but more because the style of theater changed. For over two centuries the thrust stage was in eclipse, not to reappear until about 1900, when a few theaters in England began using a version of the thrust stage to produce Shakespeare.

The return to the thrust stage resulted from a growing realization that Elizabethan plays could be done best on a stage similar to the one for which they had been written. In the United States and Canada, it was not until after World War II that the thrust stage came to the fore again. Since then a number of fine theaters of this type have been built, including the Tyrone Guthrie in Minneapolis; the Shakespeare Theater at Stratford, Ontario; the Mark Taper Forum in Los Angeles; and the Long Wharf in New Haven.

The basic stage of traditional Chinese and Japanese drama (including the Noh theater of Japan) is a form of thrust stage: a raised, open platform, frequently covered by a roof, with the audience sitting on two or three sides around the platform stage. Entrances and exits are made from doors or ramps at the rear of the stage.

Japanese version of a thrust stage.
The Japanese Noh theater has a thrust stage with the audience seated in front and at the left side. Musicians sit at the rear, in view of the audience and over the stage area supported by columns.

The obvious advantages of the thrust stage—the intimacy of the three-quarter seating and the close audience-actor relationship, together with the fact that so many of the world's great dramatic works were written for it—give it a permanent place alongside the other major forms.

Created or Found Space

Jerzy Grotowski and others in recent years who have challenged traditional concepts in theater have already been mentioned (see Chapters 9 and 12). They wished to reform theater at every level; and since the various elements of theater are inextricably bound together, their search for a more basic kind of theater included a close look at the physical arrangement of the playing area and its relationship to the audience.

The Performance Group, which led spectators one at a time into the production of *Dionysus in 69* (as described earlier in this chapter) is typical in this regard. It presented its productions in a large garage converted into an open theater space. At various places in the garage, scaffolding and ledges were built for audience seating.

The Performance Group, like other modern avant-garde companies, owed a great debt to a Frenchman, Antonin Artaud (1896–1948), one of the first theater people to examine in depth the questions raised by the avant-garde. An actor and director who wrote a series of articles and essays about the theater, Artaud was inconsistent but brilliant. (He spent several periods of his life in mental institutions.) Many of his ideas were to prove prophetic: notions he put forward in the 1920s and 1930s, considered mad or impossible at the time, have since become common practice among experimental theater groups. Among his proposals was one on the physical theater.

> We abolish the stage and auditorium and replace them by a single site, without partition or barrier of any kind, which will become the theater of the action. A direct communication will be reestablished between the spectator and the spectacle, between the actor and the spectator, from the fact that the spectator, placed in the middle of the action, is engulfed and physically affected by it. This envelopment results, in part, from the very configuration of the room itself.
>
> Thus, abandoning the architecture of present-day theaters, we shall take some hangar or barn which we shall have reconstructed according to processes which have culminated in the architecture of certain churches or holy places, and of certain temples in Tibet.
>
> In the interior of this construction special proportions of height and depth will prevail. The hall will be enclosed by four walls, without any kind of ornament, and the public will be seated in the middle of the room, on the ground floor, on mobile chairs which will allow them to follow the spectacle which will take place all around them. In effect, the absence of a stage in the usual sense of the word will provide for the deployment of the action in the four corners of the room. Particular positions will be reserved for actors and action at the four cardinal points of the room. . . . However, a central position will be reserved which, without serving, properly speaking, as a stage, will permit the bulk of the action to be concentrated and brought to a climax whenever necessary.[4]

Some of Artaud's ideas were put into practice later, when the movement to explore new concepts became widespread. In the generation after Artaud, Jerzy Grotowski included the physical arrangements of stage space in his experiments. Not only Grotowski, but others in the avant-garde movement, developed theater space in a variety of ways. We now look at some of these.

Use of nontheater buildings Artaud mentioned a barn or hangar for performances. In recent years virtually every kind of structure has been used: lofts, warehouses, fire stations, basements, churches, breweries, and gymnasiums. We should not confuse this practice with the conversion of unusual spaces to full-scale theaters; this has numerous precedents in the past. Historically, indoor tennis courts, palace ballrooms, and monastery

Created theater space.

For a production of *Candide* at Arena Stage in Washington, D.C., the designer Zack Brown created a series of spaces for playing areas. One of the trends in contemporary experimental theater is to create playing spaces not only in theaters but in warehouses, gymnasiums, lofts, and church buildings.

dining halls have been converted into theaters. We are speaking here of using unusual structures as they are, with their original architectural elements intact. Special areas are carved out for acting and viewing, as with the garage of the Performance Group, but they are not to be mistaken for traditional theater buildings.

Adaptation of space to fit individual productions   One practice frequently adopted was the use of space to fit the play, rather than making the play fit the space, as is normally the case. Grotowski, in particular, pursued the notion of a different configuration for each production, one which seemed appropriate to the play being done. In Grotowski's production of the Dr. Faustus story, Faustus gives a banquet. The theater was filled with two long tables at which spectators sat as if they were guests at a dinner party. The action took place at the heads of the tables and even on the tabletops.

For Grotowski's production of *The Constant Prince,* a fence was built around the playing area, and the audience sat behind it, looking over the fence, like spectators at a bullfight. In his version of *Kordian* the theater was transformed to resemble the ward of a mental institution, with viewers interspersed among the beds and patients. In the last quarter-century there have been similar attempts to deal with theater space throughout Europe and the United States.

Outdoor settings One development—which was actually a return to the practices in classical Greece and medieval Europe—was theater held out-of-doors. In 1971, the English director Peter Brook (1925–   ) created a theater piece called *Orghast* in the ruins of the ancient palace of Darius the Great at Persepolis in the mountains of Persia, known today as Iran. Spectators had to hike up the mountain to reach the site, where they saw performances at night with moonlight and blazing torches for illumination. No doubt it was a ghostly, awe-inspiring setting.

Not long ago, a new town called Nova Jerusalem was built in the wilderness of northeastern Brazil. It is a modern replica of ancient Jerusalem in the Holy Land and includes the temple, Pilate's forum, Herod's palace, and Calvary. In effect, the entire city is a stage set—in this case a very real one. Each year during Holy Week over 500 villagers and professional performers reenact the passion of Christ. And some 5000 spectators participate in the drama as well, moving to the scene of action, and walking each night with the actors and actresses along the road to Calvary.

Street theater Generally, street theater is of three types: (1) plays from the standard repertoire presented in the streets, (2) *neighborhood theater* in which an original play deals with the problems and aspirations of a specific area of a city—Puerto Rican, black, Italian, etc.—and (3) *guerilla theater,* aggressive, politically oriented theater produced by an activist group in the streets in an attempt to persuade audiences to become more politically involved. Whatever the form, the important point for our purposes is that these productions take place in the streets, not in a theater building.

In the recent past, theater has been presented not only in the streets, but in fields, parks, and bus stations—in fact, in almost every imaginable locale. At national political conventions, beginning with Chicago in 1968 and Miami in 1972, drama by protest groups has become commonplace. In New York City, plays have been presented outside jails and hospitals and in subway stations.

In these productions theater is brought to people who might not see it otherwise. Also, those watching theater in such unusual settings are challenged to rethink what theater is all about. On the other hand, there are inherent disadvantages to impromptu productions in the streets or other "found space": the audience must be caught on the run, and there is rarely time for more than a sketch or vignette. Nor are there facilities to present a fully developed work—but then, that is often not the purpose of these undertakings in the first place. Some street theater groups, realizing the limitations of the totally informal offering, have begun to acquire more sophisticated equipment and more permanent stage arrangements.

Multifocus environments An approach that sometimes accompanies these unusual arrangements is *multifocus theater.* In simple terms, this means not only that there is more than one playing area, such as the four corners of the room suggested by Artaud, but also that something is going on in several of them simultaneously. This is somewhat like a three-ring circus, where the spectator sees an activity in each ring and must concentrate on one.

There are several theories behind the idea of multifocus theater, most of them debatable. One is that a multifocus event is more like everyday life; if you stand on a street corner, there is activity all around you—in the four directions of the streets, in the buildings above—not just in one spot. You select which area you will observe, or perhaps you watch several at one time. The argument is that you should have the same choice in the theater.

In multifocus productions no single space or activity is supposed to be more important than any other. The spectator either takes in several impressions at once and synthesizes them in his or her own mind or selects one item as most arresting and concentrates on that. There is no such thing as the "best seat in the house"; all seats are equally good because the activity in all parts of the theater is equally important. Sometimes multifocus theater is joined with *multimedia theater*—presentations in which some combination of acting, films, dance, music, slides, and light shows is offered.

One problem with multifocus theater is that we seek in art precisely the selectivity and focus we do not find in everyday life. Besides, even those presentations which claim to be multifocus ultimately have a central point of interest—a three-ring circus, after all, has a center ring. It is difficult for a spectator to maintain interest in a multifocus event for very long. For some types of theater, a multifocus event is interesting, as well as appropriate; but by and large members of the audience want to concentrate their attention on one space and one group of characters at a time.

Taken all in all, whether single-focus or multifocus, indoors or outdoors, the recent innovations in theater milieu have added a further alternative, rich in possibilities, to the settings for theatrical productions. They have also called attention to the importance of environment in the total theater experience.

Historical precedents for found space   Because created or found space by definition is not permanent, there is not the same tradition of theater buildings for this arrangement as there is for arena, thrust, or proscenium theaters. But there are many historical precedents for performing in outdoor or impromptu settings. No doubt when theater first begins in any culture, the playing area and the audience arrangements are improvised. As mentioned before, the first Greek theater is thought to have been an open field, trampled down in the center to provide a playing area around which spectators stood. The medieval theater frequently took place on platforms or wagon stages in the streets. Also, the miracle plays of the medieval theater were sometimes presented in town squares, like the passion play at Nova Jerusalem described above. When we say, therefore, that street theater and other found environments are new, we mean new to our day, not that they have never appeared before.

VARIETY IN THEATER ENVIRONMENTS

Simply assigning a theater to a category does not adequately describe the environment. We must take into account a number of other variables in theater architecture as well. Two theaters may be of the same type and still be quite different in size, atmosphere, and setting. The small Sullivan Street Theater in New York, where the off-Broadway musical *The Fantasticks* has set records for its long run, seats fewer than 200 people. The theater experience in the Sullivan Street will be far different from that in another thrust theater several times larger, such as the Tyrone Guthrie in Minneapolis. Also, one theater may be indoors and another outdoors. Rather than having one type of theater building with only one form of stage, theater audiences today are fortunate in having a full range of environments in which to experience theater.

We have examined environmental factors influencing our experience at a theatrical event, including the location of the theater building, its size, its setting, its atmosphere, and its layout. In addition to a general environment in a theater building, there is a specific environment for the performer. Within the limits of the stage, or whatever has been designated as a playing area, a visual world is created for the actors and actresses to inhabit. Once a performance begins, the audience is always aware, even if unconsciously, of the scenery and lighting effects on stage. In Chapter 15 we will turn to a study of scenery.

SUMMARY

1   The atmosphere and environment of theater space play a large part in setting the tone of the event.
2   Experimental theater groups in recent years have deliberately made spectators aware of the environment.
3   Throughout theater history there have been four basic stage and auditorium arrangements.
4   The proscenium theater features the picture-frame stage, in which the audience faces directly toward the stage and looks through the proscenium opening at the "picture." This type of stage has the potential for elaborate scene shifts and visual displays because it generally has a large backstage area and a fly loft. It also creates a distancing effect which works to the advantage of certain types of drama. At the same time the proscenium frame sets up a barrier between the performers and the audience.
5   The arena or circle stage places the playing area in the center with the audience ranged in a circle or square around the outside. It offers an

economical way to produce theater and an opportunity for great intimacy between performers and spectators. It cannot offer full visual displays in terms of scenery and scene changes.

6 The thrust stage with three-quarter seating has a platform stage with seating on three sides. Entrances and exits are made at the rear, and there is an opportunity for a certain amount of scenery. It combines some of the scenic features of the proscenium theater with the intimacy of the arena stage.

7 Created or found space takes several forms: use of nontheater buildings, adaptation of a given space to fit individual productions, use of outdoor settings, street theater, and multifocus environments.

8 The size and the location (indoors or outdoors, etc.), along with the shape and character of the theater building, affect the environment.

15
SCENERY

(Martha Swope)

Scenery provides a convincing setting for performers. In his design for the play *K-2*, Ming Cho Lee created a wall of ice and snow. The play concerns two mountain climbers who are trapped on an icy ledge near the top of one of the world's tallest mountains. The setting looked incredibly real and provided an atmosphere of subzero temperatures; it also conveyed a sense of great danger as the men tried to maneuver on a snow-covered mountainside. The scenic designer is responsible for creating the physical and visual environment in which the actors and actresses perform.

The theater experience does not occur in a visual vacuum. Spectators sit in the theater, their eyes open, watching what unfolds before them. Naturally, they focus most keenly on the performers as they speak and move about the stage; but always present are the visual images of scenery, lighting, and costumes—transformations of color and shape which add a significant ingredient to the total mixture of theater. The creation of these effects is the responsibility of designers. A *designer* is a person who creates and organizes one of the visual aspects of a theater production.

The *scene designer* is responsible for the stage set, which can run the gamut from a bare stage with stools or orange crates to the most elaborate large-scale production. No matter how simple, however, every set has a design. Even the absence of scenery constitutes a stage set and can benefit from the ideas of a designer: in the way the furniture is arranged, for example.

Stage lighting, quite simply, includes all forms of illumination on the stage. The *lighting designer* makes decisions in every area of lighting: the color of the lights, the mixture of colors, the number of lights, the intensity and brightness of the lights, the angles at which the lights strike performers, and the length of time required for the lights to come up or fade out.

The *costume designer* is responsible for selecting, and in many cases creating, the outfits and accessories worn by the performers.

A fourth designer might be referred to as the *aural designer:* the person who arranges the sound system.

Designers must deal with practical as well as aesthetic considerations. A scene designer must know in which direction a door should open on stage and how high each tread should be on a flight of stairs. A lighting designer must know exactly how many feet above a performer's head a particular light should be placed, and whether it requires a 500-watt or a 750-watt bulb. A costume designer must know how much material it takes to make a certain kind of dress, and how to "build" clothes so that performers can wear them with confidence and have freedom of movement. A sound designer must know about acoustics and be familiar with echoes and electronic sound systems.

As in other elements of theater, symbols play a large role in design. A single item on stage can suggest an entire room: a bookcase, for instance, suggests a professor's office or a library; a stained-glass window suspended in midair suggests a church or synagogue. A stage filled with a bright yellow-orange glow suggests a cheerful sunny day, whereas a single shaft of pale blue light suggests moonlight or an eerie churchyard at night. The ways in which designers deal with the aesthetic and practical requirements of the stage will be clearer when we examine the subject in detail, beginning with scene design in this chapter and going on to lighting and sound (in Chapter 16) and costumes (in Chapter 17).

"STAGE SETS" IN EVERYDAY LIFE

As with other areas of theater, there is an analogue or parallel between scene design and our experiences in everyday life. Every building and room we go into can be regarded as a form of stage set. Interior decorating—the creation of a special atmosphere in a home or a public building—is scene designing for everyday life. A good example is the trend in recent years for restaurants to have a foreign motif—French, Italian, Spanish, Olde English. These restaurants have a form of setting or "scenery" to give the feeling that you are in a different world when, in fact, you have just stepped off the street. A church decorated for a wedding is a form of stage set; so is the posh lobby of a hotel, or an apartment with flowers, candlelight, and soft music.

In every case the "designer," the person who has arranged the setting, has selected elements which signal an impression to the viewer. The combination of colors, fabrics, furniture, and styles tells the person entering the space exactly where he or she is. These things are often calculated with great care, and a premium is set on an appropriate environment and atmosphere. When we see a library with leather-bound books, attractive wood paneling, comfortable leather chairs, and a beautiful carved wooden desk, we get a sense of stability, tradition, and comfort. A totally different kind of feeling would come from a modern room with everything white and black, with glass-top tables, furniture of chrome and stainless steel, and indirect lighting. From this spare, functional look, we get a "modern" feeling. Interior decorators know that appearance is important, that the visual elements of a room can communicate an overall impression to which an observer responds with a series of feelings, attitudes, and assumptions.

SCENERY FOR THE STAGE

We are accustomed to "stage settings" in everyday life; but, as with other elements in theater, there is an important difference between interior decorations in real life and set designs for the stage. Robert Edmond Jones (1887–1954), considered by many to be the most outstanding American scene designer of the first half of this century, put it in these terms:

> A good scene should be, not a picture, but an image. Scene-designing is not what most people imagine it is—a branch of interior decorating. There is no more reason for a room on a stage to be a reproduction of an actual room than for an actor who plays the part of Napoleon to be Napoleon or for an actor who plays Death in the old morality play to be dead. Everything that is actual must

undergo a strange metamorphosis, a kind of sea-change, before it can become truth in the theater.[1]

While a stage set signals an atmosphere to the viewer, in the same way as rooms in real life, the scene designer must go a step further. As has been pointed out many times, the theater is not life: it resembles life. It has both the opportunity and the obligation to be more than mere reproduction, as Jones suggests.

The special nature of scenery for the theater will be clearer when we examine the functions and objectives of scene design.

OBJECTIVES OF SCENE DESIGN

The scene designer has the following objectives:

1 Create an environment for the performers
2 Help set the tone and style of the production
3 Help distinguish realistic from nonrealistic theater
4 Establish the locale and period in which the play takes place
5 Develop a design concept
6 Where appropriate, provide a central image or metaphor for the production
7 Assure that the scenery is coordinated with other production elements
8 Solve practical design problems

Objectives 1 through 7 encompass the aesthetic aspects of stage design. Objective 8 encompasses several practical aspects. We now turn to a consideration of each of these elements.

AESTHETIC ASPECTS OF STAGE DESIGN

Creating the Scenic Environment

There have been times in the history of theater when scene design was looked on as the painting of a large picture. In the discussion of the proscenium stage, I noted the temptation to use the proscenium arch as a frame and put behind it a gigantic picture. The tradition of fine scene painting, begun in Italy in the late seventeenth century, continued throughout Europe in the eighteenth and nineteenth centuries. It was still flourishing in Europe and the United States in the early part of this century, when many famous painters—including Pablo Picasso, Salvador Dalí, and Marc Chagall —attempted scene design. Painters, accustomed to seeing their work stand on its own, are of course interested in the effect of the picture, the visual image itself, aside from the activity on the stage. But the static picture, in

An environment for performers.
A good stage design is not just a picture but provides a three-dimensional world for the performers to inhabit. In John Conklin's design for a production of *Romeo and Juliet* at the American Shakespeare Theater, the walls, the platform area, and the house at the right create a visual "universe" in which the play can unfold.

which the purely visual impression is more important than the environment, presents serious problems in the theater.

The distinction between scenery as painting and scenery as part of a total stage production can hardly be overemphasized. Frequently in the theater— particularly in an elaborate production—the audience breaks into applause when the visual image of the set is revealed as the curtain rises. There is nothing wrong with admiring the beauty or excitement of a stage picture. Taken to extremes, however, the emphasis on illustration or a "pretty picture" runs counter to the purpose of scene design. If members of the audience spend their time admiring the beauty of the scenery, they may miss the words of the playwright and the actions of the performers, and as a result they may not grasp the meaning of the play. This suggests how important it is to have a stage setting in tune with the total production.

In scene design, one element that must never be forgotten—just as it must never be forgotten when we read a play in book form—is the presence of the performer. Scene design creates an environment—a place for actors and actresses to move and have their being. Robert Edmond Jones spoke forcefully on this point when he said: "Players act in a setting, not against it."[2] He went on to explain:

> A stage setting holds a curious kind of suspense. Go, for instance, into an ordinary empty drawing-room as it exists normally. There is no particular suspense about this room. It is just—empty. Now imagine the same drawing-room arranged and decorated for a particular function—a Christmas party for children, let us say. It is not completed as a room, not until the children are in it. And if we wish to visualize for ourselves how important a part the sense of expectancy plays in such a room, let us imagine that there is a storm and the children cannot come. A scene on the stage is filled with the same expectancy. It is like a mixture of chemical elements held in solution. The actor adds the one element that releases the hidden energy of the whole. Meanwhile, wanting the actor, the various elements which go to make up the setting remain suspended, as it were, in an indefinable tension. To create this suspense, this tension, is the essence of the problem of stage designing.[3]

Jones is saying that a stage set, rather than being a complete picture in and of itself, is an environment with one element missing—the performer. Empty, it has a sense of incompleteness. A stage set is like a giant piece of mobile sculpture, motionless until set in motion by the performers. This, of course, fits with our notion that theater is an experience, an unfolding encounter which moves through time. If the stage picture were complete when we first entered the theater, or when the curtain went up, where would the experience lie? The job of the scene designer is to create not a beautiful shadowbox or three-dimensional painting but a world on stage which is practical as well as artistic.

Scene design should be neither so beautiful nor so "busy"—that is, so cluttered with detail—that it distracts the spectator's eye from the action on stage. Following Robert Edmond Jones's advice, the scene designer must see to it that the set does not call attention to itself. Otherwise, we have an inversion of the values of theater, for the performers and the play must be paramount. Scene design is at its best when it underlines and emphasizes the primary values of the play—not competing with the play or overpowering it, but enhancing and supporting it.

Setting Tone and Style

A stage setting can help establish the mood, style, and meaning of the play. A farce calls for comic, exaggerated scenery, in the manner of a cartoon, perhaps with outrageous colors. A satire calls for a comment in the design, like the twist in the lines of a caricature in a political drawing. A serious play calls for sober, straightforward scenery, even in a nonrealistic piece.

As examples of what is called for in scene design, let us consider two plays by the Spanish playwright Federico García Lorca (1899–1936). His *Blood Wedding* is the story of a young bride-to-be who runs away with a former lover on the day she is to be married. The two young lovers flee to a forest; and in the forest the play becomes expressionistic: allegorical figures of the Moon and a Beggar Woman, representing Death, appear in the forest to echo the fierce emotional struggle taking place within the characters. It would be quite inappropriate to design a realistic, earthbound set for *Blood Wedding,* particularly for the forest portion of the play. The setting must have the same sense of mystery, of the unreal, which rules the passions of the characters. We must see this visually in the images of the forest as well as in the figures of the Moon and the Beggar Woman.

Another play of Lorca's, *The House of Bernarda Alba,* tells of a woman and her five daughters. The woman has grown to hate and distrust men, and so she locks up her house, like a convent, preventing her daughters from going out. From a design point of view it is important to convey the closed-in, cloistered feeling of the house in which the women are held as virtual prisoners. The sense of entrapment must be omnipresent.

Occasionally, scenery runs deliberately counter to the play—as a comment on it. Ionesco's *The Bald Soprano,* a zany theater of the absurd piece (described in Chapter 9), might be set in a realistic family living room as an ironic contrast to the content of the play. This, however, is the exception rather than the rule.

Realistic versus Nonrealistic Scenery

The stage designer's role is of special importance in distinguishing between realism and nonrealism. In *realistic theater,* a setting is called for which looks very much like the same thing in real life. A kitchen resembles a kitchen, a dining room a dining room, and so on. One exponent of realism, David Belasco, a producer-director of the early twentieth century, sometimes reproduced an actual kitchen or a room from a house, including wallpaper and light fixtures, on stage.

A complete reproduction is an extreme, however, for even in realistic theater the stage designer selects items to go on stage, and his or her talent and imagination play an important role. The point is to make the room resemble, but not duplicate, its counterpart in real life. In the same way that a playwright does not simply take a tape recorder into the streets and record conversations, the scene designer does not reproduce each detail of a room. A set calls for selectivity and editing. In a realistic setting, it is up to the designer to pick and choose those items, or symbols, that will give the proper feeling and impression. The significance of these items must be

A realistic stage setting.

Stage design is particularly important in establishing the style of a production. This set, designed by John Kasorda for a production of *The Front Page* at the Williamstown Theater Festival, lets the audience know that this is a realistic play set in the 1920s. The press room in which the play takes place is complete with authentic desks, chairs, telephones, and hanging light fixtures.

highlighted by eliminating everything irrelevant or distracting. The result should convey to us not only the lifestyle but the individual characteristics of the persons in the play.

At times the designer may provide only partial settings for realistic plays. We will see a portion of a room—a cutout with only door frames and windows, but no walls, or walls suggested by an outline. The remaining elements will be realistic, but the total set will be fragmentary. In any case, it is through selectivity and emphasis that the designer provides an appropriate setting.

In *nonrealistic theater,* the designer can give full rein to imagination, and the use of symbol is of special importance. Chinese theater affords a graphic example of the possibilities of symbol in stage design. Chinese theater, during its long history, has developed an elaborate set of conventions in which a single prop or item represents a complete locale or action. An embroidered curtain on a pole stands for a general's tent, an official seal signifies an office, and an incense tripod stands for a palace. A plain table may represent a judge's bench; but when two chairs are placed at each end of the table, it can become a bridge. When performers climb on the table, it can be a mountain; when they jump over it, a wall. A banner with fish on it represents the sea, a man with a riding whip is riding a horse, and two banners with wheels are a chariot. Clearly, the Chinese have developed the art of scenic symbolism to a high level, and interestingly enough the symbols are thoroughly convincing even to westerners.

Productions in the United States also provide examples of imaginative nonrealistic scenery. In Chapters 2 and 13 the expressionistic play *The Adding Machine* was mentioned. In designing the original production of this play, Lee Simonson (1888–1967) used abstract settings, with vertical lines set at odd angles. Like the angle of vision in the play itself, the set was tilted, creating a sense of imbalance and unreality. For the revival of Sophocles's *Electra,* Ming Cho Lee (1930–   ), suspended large stone formations on three sides of the stage. This design suggested the three doors of the ancient Greek

A world off balance.

The odd angles in Lee Simonson's expressionistic set for the original Broadway production of *The Adding Machine* symbolize the off-center world of the main character, Mr. Zero. In this courtroom scene his life appears to be falling apart; the scenery is an outward manifestation of his inner feelings.

SCENERY

Imaginative design for Sophocles's *Electra*.
The designer Ming Cho Lee, basing his concept on the three doors of ancient Greek theater buildings, created a piece of stage sculpture as a setting for Sophocles's play. Simple yet forceful, with a beauty all its own, it is an ideal setting for this ancient tale of revenge and honor reclaimed. Shown is the designer's model of the set.

theater; but more important, it conveyed the solidity, dignity, and rough-hewn quality of the play. In contrast, Boris Aronson (1900–1980), for the musical *Company,* designed a sharp, sleek set of chrome and Lucite, with straight lines. Actors and actresses moved from one area to another in modern, open elevators, symbolic of the chic, antiseptic world of the characters. The set was the epitome of sophisticated urban living.

Establishing Locale and Period

Whether realistic or nonrealistic, the stage set should tell the audience where and when the play takes place. Is the locale a saloon? A bedroom? A courtroom? Perhaps it is a palace or an ominous forest. The set should also indicate the time period. A kitchen with old-fashioned utensils and no electric appliances sets the play in the past. An old radio and an icebox might tell us it is the 1920s. A spaceship or the landscape of a faraway planet would suggest a futuristic period.

In addition to indicating time and place, the setting can also tell us the kinds of characters in the play. The characters may be neat and formal, or lazy and sloppy. They may be kings and queens, or an ordinary suburban family. The scene design should tell us these things immediately.

A Design Concept

In order to convey information, the scene designer frequently develops a *design concept* similar to the directorial concept discussed in Chapter 13. It is a unifying idea carried out visually. Examples of such a concept would be the claustrophobic setting for Lorca's *Blood Wedding* and Ming Cho Lee's Greek-influenced setting for *Electra,* described above.

A strong design concept is particularly important when the time and place of a play are shifted. Modern stage designs for two plays by Shakespeare will illustrate the point. Shakespeare's *A Midsummer Night's Dream* is traditionally played in palace rooms and a forest, as suggested by the script. For Peter Brook's production of the early 1970s, however, designer Sally Jacobs (1932–) fashioned three white, bare walls—like the sides of a

An original design concept.
For a production of one-act plays by Anton Chekhov, the designer Harry Lines and the director Mira Felner developed a concept of treating the plays like circus acts. Mr. Lines designed a single-ring Russian circus in which the plays were performed. This gave a unity to the bill of plays and also created an atmosphere of fun in which the plays were performed.

white gymnasium. Trapezes were lowered onto the stage at various times for the performers and in some scenes they actually played their parts while suspended in midair. The clean, spare look of Jacob's setting was nontraditional, to say the least.

The concept developed by a scene designer for a stage setting is closely related to the idea of a central image or metaphor, discussed next.

Central Image or Metaphor

Stage design not only must be consistent with the play; it should have its own integrity. The elements of the design—the lines, the shapes, the colors—should add up to a whole. In many cases, a designer tries to develop a central image or metaphor.

For the original production of *The Royal Hunt of the Sun,* a play about Pizarro and the conquest of Peru, Michael Annals (1938–) set a huge sunburst, resembling a gold medallion, in midair at the back of the stage. Twelve feet in diameter and symbolizing both gold and the sun, the sunburst dominated the stage, providing a vivid focal point for the production.

In *Death of a Salesman,* Jo Mielziner (1901–1976) created a set combining various elements inherent in the play. On the one hand, there was the real home of Willy Loman: the kitchen with a refrigerator, table, and chairs. At the same time, surrounding the house was a skyline consisting of apartment houses closing in on Willy's world. When Willy moved from the present to his memory of the past, the lights would shift so that the audience could see through transparent walls of his house to the world around him. From the real world, Willy moved as if by magic through the walls of his home into the past, figuratively and literally. The hope and promise of Willy's youth, when his world was full of fresh, growing things, was symbolized by projections of green leaves thrown over the entire set. Once again, the set provided a central metaphor for the play, with the past and the present appearing simultaneously.

Coordination of the Whole

Because scenic elements have such strong symbolic values and are so important to the overall effect of a production, the designer has an obligation to provide scenery consistent with the intent of the play and the director's concept.

If the script and acting are highly stylized, the setting should not be mundane and drab. If the script and acting are realistic, the setting should not overpower the other elements in the production. It is a question, once again, of how the various parts of a production should contribute to an overall effect.

THE SCENE DESIGNER

In meeting the objectives described above, how does the scene designer proceed?

Although every designer has his or her particular method, usually a general pattern is followed. The director reads the script and develops ideas about the scenery. Depending on the director, ideas about the scenery may vary considerably. The ideas may be few and vague or they may include an exact picture of what the scenery should look like. Frequently they are somewhere between these two extremes. Meanwhile, the designer has developed his or her ideas.

The director and the designer meet at a preliminary conference. Both have read the script, and they exchange ideas about the design. During these discussions the director and designer will develop and discuss questions of style, a visual concept for the production, the needs of the performers, and so on. Following this the designer develops rough sketches, called *thumbnail sketches*, and rough plans to provide the basis for further discussions.

As the designer proceeds, he or she attempts to fill out the visual concept. In this work the designer makes use of the following elements:

1   Line, the outline or silhouette of elements on stage: for example, predominantly curved lines versus sharply angular ones
2   Mass and composition, the balance and arrangement of elements: for example, a series of high, heavy platforms or fortress walls versus a bare stage or a stage with one tree on it
3   Texture, the "feel" projected by surfaces and fabrics: the slickness of chrome or glass versus the roughness of brick or burlap
4   Color, the shadings and contrasts of color combinations

The designer will use these elements to produce effects on the audience in conjunction with the action and other aspects of the production.

Sometimes the designer will bring the director rough sketches showing several possible ideas, each emphasizing different elements to achieve different results.

When the director and the designer have decided on an idea and a rough design they like, the designer will make a more complete sketch, usually in color, called a *rendering*. If the director approves of this, the designer will make a three-dimensional, small-scale *model* which the director can use to help stage the show. There are two types of models. One only shows the location of the platform and walls, with perhaps some light detail drawn on, and it is usually white in color. The other is a complete finished model: everything is duplicated as fully as possible, including color and perhaps

Death of a Salesman (1949)

ARTHUR MILLER (1915–   )

CHIEF CHARACTERS:

Willy Loman
Linda—his wife
Biff—his older son
Happy—his younger son
Bernard—Biff's friend
The Woman—Willy's mistress
Charley—next-door neighbor, Bernard's father
Uncle Ben—Willy's brother

SETTING: Willy Loman's house in New York and various other locations in New York and Boston.

TIME: The present and flashbacks to the past.

BACKGROUND: Willy is an older traveling salesman who can't produce much business any more. Many of Willy's friends and business contacts are dead and he has a tendency to daydream, drifting off into a time when things were better. His sons are not the successes that Willy expected them to be—Biff, for example, had been a football star, but was not a good student and did not graduate from high school. Linda is a good wife and mother, trying desperately to keep the family, and Willy, from falling apart.

ACT I: Willy arrives home unexpectedly, having cut short a sales trip. He tells Linda that he

kept driving off the road. Linda tells Willy that he should persuade the company to let him work in New York and not on the road. Willy expresses disappointment about his son Biff, who has just returned home after being a drifter in the west. Meanwhile, in their upstairs bedroom, Biff and Happy discuss their concern about their father. Biff is frustrated because of his inability to find a career, and they discuss an old dream of starting their own business. Downstairs, Willy moves into a scene from the past in which he brags to young Biff about what a great salesman he is and the important people he knows. Bernard, the studious neighbor, idolizes the athletic Biff and wants to help Biff study so that he can pass his exams. Willy puts down Bernard as the "studious type" and tells Biff that personality will get him further than studying.

Willy, in a different flashback, is shown in Boston with the Woman, with whom he is having an affair. Back in the present, Willy and his neighbor Charley have a minor confrontation during which Willy speaks out loud to his brother Ben's ghost. In Willy's fantasy, Ben was a successful self-made man. Years ago, when Ben offered Willy the chance to go with him, Willy refused. Linda defends Willy to the boys and asks Biff to try to get along better with Willy. Linda confesses to the boys that she thinks Willy is trying to kill himself. Willy confronts Biff about Biff's career and is rude to

Linda while Biff stands up for her. Before they retire to bed, they make amends. Later, Biff finds the rubber tubing that Willy had hidden in order to kill himself.

ACT II: The next morning. Willy seems optimistic about the future: Biff represents Willy's final chance to prove that he has not been a total failure. He believes that Biff's former boss will give Biff a job. Also, Linda thinks that Willy has taken the rubber hose away and is no longer contemplating suicide, but later she finds out that it was Biff who removed it.

The scene shifts to Willy's office where Willy meets with his boss, Howard Wagner. Willy is aggressive, but becomes desperate when Howard refuses to give him a New York job and then fires him. Willy leaves in despair and vents his frustration on Ben's ghost.

The scene shifts to Charley's office where Willy and Charley's son, Bernard, now a successful lawyer, discuss the time when Biff failed mathematics. Willy blames Biff's failures on that one incident. Bernard says that he always wondered why Biff didn't go to summer school after he had failed, as he had planned. Willy is evasive. Willy asks Charley for a loan; but when Charley offers him a job, as he has in the past, Willy turns it down out of pride.

Biff and Happy are in a restaurant waiting for Willy. Happy is flirting with a young woman in the restaurant. Biff arrives and tells Happy that he had an unsuccessful meeting with his ex-boss; but when Willy comes in, he won't let Biff tell the real story—Willy only wants to hear the dream story. Willy admits to the boys that he was fired and recalls the time when Biff failed math.

The scene shifts to the past and the hotel room in Boston where Willy is with the Woman; the young Biff shows up unannounced and finds Willy with the Woman. He feels that everything Willy stands for is false and he returns home a beaten person. Back in the present, Happy and Biff leave Willy alone in the restaurant, distraught and fantasizing.

At home, a bitter Linda accuses the sons of deserting Willy in his hour of need. Willy, still caught up in fantasies, has returned home to plant a garden at night. He tells an imaginary Ben about his insurance policy—the $20,000 would help Biff get on his feet. Back in the present, Willy accuses Biff of blaming him for his own failure, though Biff denies it. Biff tells Willy that he has finally come to realize the truth about himself and Biff desperately tries to make Willy see the truth about his own failures. Though Willy cannot, there is a momentary reconciliation between him and Biff. Linda is still afraid for Willy and wants him to come to bed. Alone, he gets into his car, drives off, and kills himself in an automobile accident. At his funeral, Linda expresses her sorrow and confusion.

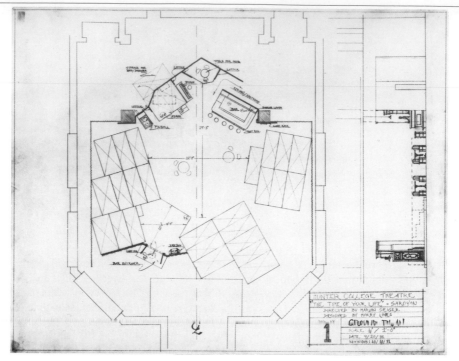

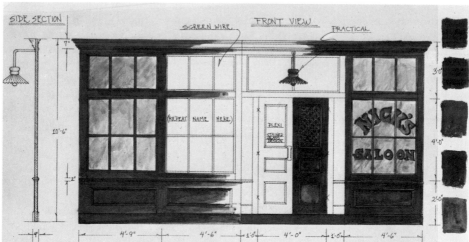

The designer prepares a production.

In moving from original sketches to final set construction the designer prepares a number of blueprints and other drawings. For a production of Saroyan's *The Time of Your Life*, directed by Marvin Seiger at Hunter College, the scene designer Harry Lines first made sketches of what the setting would look like. Then he drew a ground plan, shown at the top above, indicating where the walls, doors, furniture and so forth would be. Following that, he made painter's elevations, shown immediately above, that indicated how separate parts of the set should be painted. After the set was assembled and painted, the final result looked as it appears on the opposite page.

(Harry Lines)

318

moldings and texture. In developing his or her designs, the scene designer is attempting to fulfill the objectives discussed previously, both aesthetic and practical.

Once a rendering or model is complete and has been approved, it is turned over to the technical director of the production. The technical director is also given the necessary ground plans and blueprints. Together with the building and paint crews, the technical director then sees that the scenery is built, painted, and installed on stage.

PRACTICAL ASPECTS OF STAGE DESIGN

We have been examining aesthetic considerations of scenery and the process of design; but, as with everything in theater, there is a practical side to scenery as well.

Requirements of the Physical Layout

The playing area must fit into a certain stage space; and, more important, it must accommodate actors and actresses. In terms of space, a designer cannot plan a gigantic stage setting for a theater where the proscenium opening is only 20 feet wide and the depth of the stage is no more than 15 feet. By the same token, to design a small room in the midst of a 40-foot

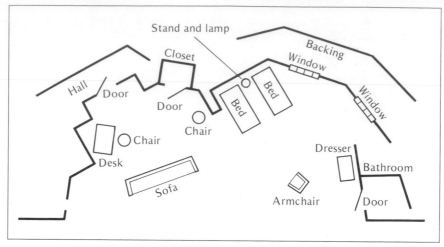

Ground plan.

In order to aid the director, performers, and stage technicians, the designer draws a ground plan, or blueprint, of the stage, showing the exact locations of furniture, walls, windows, doors, and other scenic elements.

stage would be ludicrous. As for the requirements of the play, the designer must take into account the physical layout of the stage space. If a performer must leave by a door on the right side of the stage, and a few moments later return by a door on the left, the designer must obviously make allowance for crossing behind the scenery. If performers need to change costumes quickly offstage, the scene designer must make certain that there is room offstage for changing. If there is to be a sword fight, the actors must have space in which to make their turns, to advance and retreat.

Any type of physical movement requires a certain amount of space, and the scene designer must allow for this in his or her *ground plan*. The ground plan is the blueprint, or floor plan, outlining the various levels on the stage and indicating the placement of all scenery, furniture, doors, windows, and so on. Working in conjunction with the director, the designer is chiefly responsible for a practical ground plan.

The way doors open and close, the way a sofa is set, the angle at which steps lead to a second floor—all are the responsibility of the designer and are important to both the cast and the play. Actresses and actors must be able to execute steps easily and to sit in such a way that the audience can see them clearly, and they must have the space to interact with other performers naturally and convincingly. If a performer opens a door on stage and is immediately blocked from the view of the audience, this is obviously an error on the part of the scene designer.

To designate areas of the stage, the scene designer uses terminology peculiar to the theater. *Stage right* and *stage left* mean the right and left side of the stage, respectively, as seen from the performer's position facing the

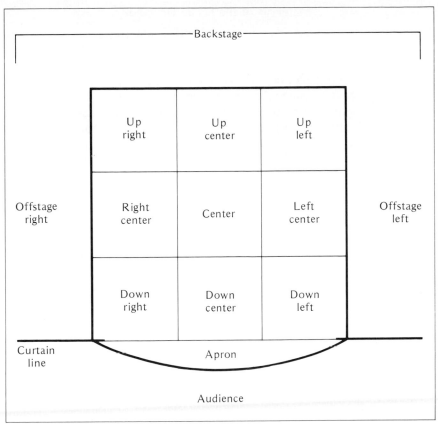

Stage areas.

Various parts of the stage are given specific designations. Near the audience is *downstage*; away from the audience is *upstage*. *Right* and *left* are from the performers' point of view, not the audience's. Everything out of sight of the audience is *offstage*. Using this scheme, everyone working in the theater can carefully pinpoint stage areas.

audience. In other words, when the audience looks at the stage, the side to *its* left is stage right, the side to its right is stage left. Also, the area of the stage nearest the audience is known as *downstage,* and the area farthest away from the audience is *upstage*. These designations, downstage and upstage, come from the time in the eighteenth and nineteenth centuries when the stage was raked (that is, the stage sloped downward from back to front). As a result of this downward slope, the performer farthest away from the audience was higher, or "up," and could be seen better. This is the origin of the expression "to upstage someone." The term has come to mean that one performer grabs the spotlight from everyone else and calls attention to himself or herself by any means whatever. At first, however, it meant that one performer was in a better position than the others because he or she was standing farther back on the raked stage and hence was higher.

Materials of the Scene Designer

In creating a stage set, the designer begins with the stage floor itself. Sometimes the stage floor is a turntable; that is, a circle is set into the floor which can turn mechanically to bring one set into view as another disappears. At times trapdoors are set in the floor through which performers can enter or leave the stage. For some productions, tracks or slots are set in the stage floor and set pieces or *wagons* are brought on stage in the tracks and stopped at the proper point. A wagon in this case is a low platform set on wheels. Wagon stages are brought on stage mechanically or by stagehands hidden behind them. This type of scene change is frequently used in musical comedy.

Instead of scenery coming from the sides, it can be dropped from the fly loft—*to fly,* it will be recalled, is the term used when scenery is raised into the fly loft out of the view of the audience.

From floor level, ramps and platforms can be built to any height desired. To create walls or divisions of other kinds, the most common element is the *flat,* so named because it is a single flat unit. It is usually about 4 feet wide by 8 feet high and consists of canvas stretched on wood. The side facing the audience can be painted to look like a solid wall. Used in conjunction with other flats, it can be made to look like a complete room. The scene designer's art comes into play at this point, creating the illusion—with flats and other units—of virtually any type of room or architecture required. Other vertical units are *cutouts*—small pieces made like canvas flats or cut out of plywood. Again, they can be painted to create the illusion of a solid piece of architecture.

A very special type of scenery is a *scrim.* The scrim is a gauze or cloth screen which can be painted like a regular flat. The wide mesh of the cloth, however, allows light to pass through. When light shines on a scrim from in front—that is, from the audience's point of view—it is reflected off the painted surface and the scrim appears to be a solid wall. When light comes from behind, however, the scrim becomes transparent and the spectators can see performers and scenery behind the scrim.

The flat: A basic unit of scene construction.
Opposite page: The designer Harry Lines has drawn these illustrations to show how the stage flat is built and used. In (a), we see the back side of a flat. It is made of a wooden frame with cross pieces and corner braces. On the reverse side of the flat a piece of canvas is stretched on which the walls of a room or other scenic effects can be painted. The flat is held upright on the stage floor by a stage brace (shown at the left) and is lashed to other flats by the rope at the right. In (b), we see the back view of two flats lashed together. In one flat a door is placed. Windows, doors, and other architectural features can be placed in flats. In (c), the two flats shown in (b) are reversed. This is how they will look from the audience's point of view. With wallpaper painted on the flats and molding on the walls and door, they form the corner of a room.

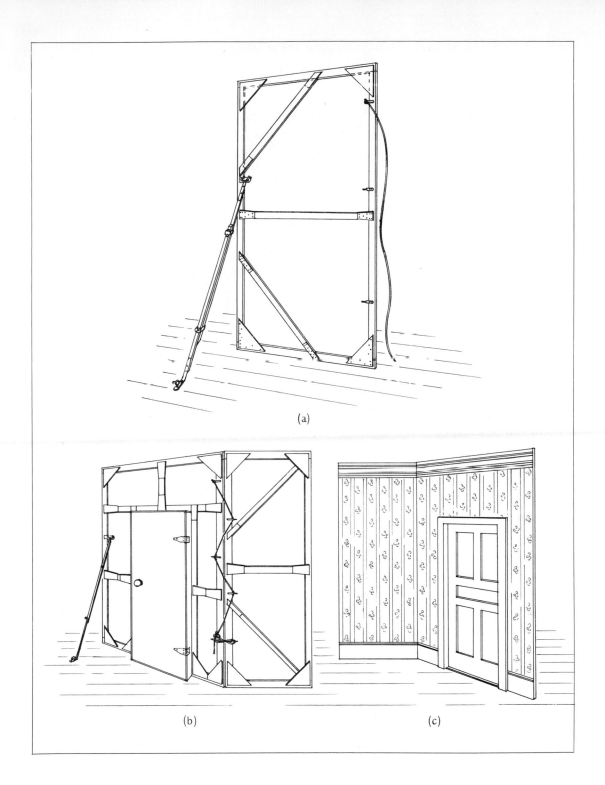

(a)

(b)

(c)

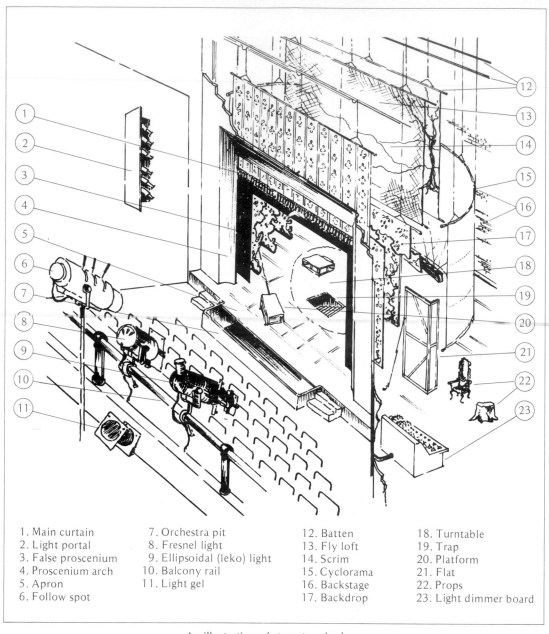

1. Main curtain	7. Orchestra pit	12. Batten	18. Turntable
2. Light portal	8. Fresnel light	13. Fly loft	19. Trap
3. False proscenium	9. Ellipsoidal (leko) light	14. Scrim	20. Platform
4. Proscenium arch	10. Balcony rail	15. Cyclorama	21. Flat
5. Apron	11. Light gel	16. Backstage	22. Props
6. Follow spot		17. Backdrop	23. Light dimmer board

An illustration of stage terminology.
This drawing by the designer Harry Lines shows some important elements on and around the stage.

The scrim is particularly effective in scenes where ghosts are called for or when an eerie effect is desired. Scrims are likewise useful in memory plays or plays with flashbacks: the spectators see the scene in the present in front of the scrim, and then, as lights in the front fade and those behind come up, they see through this gauzelike scrim a scene with a cloudy, translucent quality, indicating a memory or a scene in the past.

A development which has taken hold with great force in recent years is *screen projection*. A picture or drawing is projected on a screen either from in front—as in an ordinary movie house—or from behind the screen. The advantage of the latter is that because the actors and actresses will not be in the beam of the light, there will be no shadows or silhouettes. Obviously there are many advantages to projections: pictures can change with the rapidity of the cinema, and there is an opportunity to present vast scenes on stage in a way which would hardly be possible except with tremendously elaborate scene painting.

Projections: An effective scenic device.
Supplementing regular scenery are projections on a screen, or perhaps over most of the stage area, allowing for rapid changes of locale, panoramic views, or unusual abstract designs. In this scene from a production of Wedekind's *Lulu*, Fred Neumann as LeBow and Kathy Slade as LuLu perform in the foreground while an image of them is projected on a screen behind them.

SCENERY

Special Effects

The discussion of scrims and projections introduces the subject of *special effects*. These are the effects of scenery, lighting, sound, and props that seem miraculous or unusual. (The term *prop* comes from the word *property*. It is the name given to any object in the theater that is not a permanent part of the scenery or costumes. Props include such things as lamps, ashtrays, glasses, typewriters, walking sticks, umbrellas, fans, and the like.)

Special effects include fog, knives or swords that appear to stab victims, ghosts, walls that fall apart, and so on. In the modern era, films and television—because of their technical possibilities—have brought extreme realism to special effects. Examples include buildings on fire or blown-up cars. Special effects on stage, however, are almost as old as the theater itself. From the Greeks on, theater has tried to suspend natural laws and create the illusion of miraculous or extraordinary effects.

The see-through scrim and projections (mentioned above) are used to create a number of effects, such as dream sequences. Fog can be created by putting dry ice into water and then blowing the vapor on stage with fans.

In a production of *Something's Afoot* at Pennsylvania State University, the designers created a stage set with elements capable of murdering the entire cast of the play. These included an exploding staircase, a telephone that sent out poison gas, a hidden spear that sneaked up behind a woman and "strangled" her, a chandelier that dropped, and a large porcelain vase that swallowed another woman.

In the area of lighting there are several special effects that can be used to create interesting visual pictures. A simple one is positioning the source of light near the stage floor and shining the light on the performers from below. This creates shadows under their eyes and chins and gives them a ghostly or horrifying quality.

Another common special effect is the use of ultraviolet light. This is a very dark blue light that causes phosphorus to glow. When the stage is very dark, even black, costumes or scenery that have been painted with a special phosphorus paint will "light up" in the dark.

The effect of slow motion or silent movies, where actors seem to be moving in jerks, is created by the use of a strobe light. A strobe light is a very powerful and bright gas discharge light which flashes at rapid intervals to create the effect.

In the area of sound there are also a number of special effects. Sometimes speakers are placed completely around the audience and the sound can move around from side to side. Computerized noises and electronic music can be used to create special sounds for various situations, and tape loops can repeat the same sound over and over for a long period of time. Echoes can be created by means of a machine that causes reverberations in the sound waves.

It is clear from the foregoing that the scene designer has many resources and many responsibilities. Sometimes the designer goes beyond designing the scenery and special effects and designs the entire theater space.

Designing a Total Environment

In contemporary theater productions, where found space and overall environment are of paramount importance, the scene designer frequently decides where and how the audience will be placed as well as where the playing areas will be. This goes beyond deciding what will be placed on the

The total environment.
The scenic designer brings together all the physical and visual elements in creating a setting for a production. This design for Chekhov's *The Three Sisters* at the American Shakespeare Theater has a background of trees and the outdoors and, in front of that, the silhouette of a room with doorways, appropriate furniture, and clearly designated playing areas. Providing and coordinating these elements is the responsibility of the designer.

stage. For instance, in an open space such as a gym or a warehouse, a designer will build an entire theater, including the seats or stands for the audience and the designated acting areas. In this case, the designer considers the size and shape of the space, the texture and nature of the building materials, the atmosphere of the space, and the needs of the play itself. These conditions apply in the case of multifocus theater as well.

In this chapter we have examined the work of the scene designer. Next, in Chapter 16, we turn to someone whose work is closely related: the lighting designer. Chapter 16 also examines sound.

SUMMARY

1   We encounter forms of scene design in everyday life: in the carefully planned decor of a restaurant or hotel lobby, for instance.
2   Scene design for the stage differs from interior decorating in that it creates an environment and an atmosphere which are not filled until occupied by performers.
3   In addition to creating an environment, the scene designer has the following objectives: set tone and style, distinguish realism from non-realism, establish time and place, develop a design concept, provide a central design metaphor, coordinate with other elements, deal with practical considerations.
4   In practical terms the scene designer must deal with the limits of the stage space and the offstage area. For example, ramps must not be inclined too steeply and platforms must provide adequate playing area for the performers. In short, the stage designer must know the practical considerations of stage usage and stage carpentry, as well as the materials available, in order to achieve desired effects.
5   Special effects are those elements of scenery, lighting, costumes, props, or sound that appear miraculous or highly unusual. They require technical expertise to develop properly.
6   In dealing with created or found space, the designer must plan the entire environment: the audience area as well as the stage area.
7   The scene designer works closely with the director and other designers and creates a series of drawings (sketches and renderings) and models of what the final stage picture will look like.

16
LIGHTING
AND
SOUND

16

LIGHTING AND SOUND

The powerful effects of stage lighting.
Lighting is one of the most versatile and potent of the visual resources in the theater. It can be used to create special effects, such as the one shown here from a production of *Kid Twist* by Len Jenkin. The light surrounds the head of the character on the right, creating a frightening and eerie effect. Light is also used to isolate the face of the character on the left. The primary purpose of light in the theater is to illuminate performers and stage areas; but light can also create mood, indicate time of day, and help shift the action from one part of the stage to another.

Like scenery and other elements of theater, stage lighting and sound have counterparts in everyday life. For example, the basic function of lighting is illumination—to allow people to see at night and indoors. But there are many theatrical uses of light in daily life. Advertising signs feature neon lights or brightly colored bulbs. Restaurants feature soft lights and candles. In homes, people put spotlights on special parts of the room—on a portrait or the dining room table. Also, in homes people frequently put lights on a rheostat so that they can dim the lights to create a mood.

STAGE LIGHTING

A Brief History of Stage Lighting

Before looking at theater lighting today, it will be helpful to take a brief look at the history of stage lighting.

Lighting, the last design element incorporated in theater production from a historical point of view, is the most advanced in terms of equipment and technique. For the first 2000 years of its recorded history, theater was held mostly outdoors during the day—a primary reason being, no doubt, the need for illumination. Sunlight, after all, is an excellent source of illumination.

Since sophisticated lighting was unavailable, playwrights used imagination—the handiest tool available—to suggest nighttime or shifts in lighting. Performers brought on torches, or a candle, as Lady Macbeth does, to indicate night. Playwrights also used language. When Shakespeare has Lorenzo in *The Merchant of Venice* say, "How sweet the moonlight sleeps upon this bank," it is not just a pretty line of poetry: it also serves to remind us that it is nighttime. The same is true of the eloquent passage when Romeo tells Juliet he must leave because dawn is breaking.

Look, love, what envious streaks
Do lace the severing clouds in yonder East:
Night's candles are burnt out, and jocund day
Stands tiptoe on the misty mountain tops.

Around A.D. 1600, theater began to move indoors. Candles and oil lamps were used for illumination until 1803, when a theater in London installed gas lights. Though lighting became more manageable during the eighteenth and nineteenth centuries, it was always limited in its effectiveness. In addition, the open flames of the lighting systems posed a constant threat of fire. Through the years there were several tragic and costly fires in theaters, both in Europe and in the United States.

In 1879 Thomas Edison invented the incandescent lamp (the electric light bulb) and the era of imaginative lighting for the theater began. Not only are incandescent lamps safe, but they can be controlled. The brightness or intensity can be increased or decreased: the same lighting instrument will produce the bright light of noonday or the dim light of dusk. Also, by putting a colored film over the light, color can be controlled. The resulting flexibility is a remarkable tool in achieving stage effects.

Aesthetic Functions of Light

Adolphe Appia (1862–1928), a Swiss scene designer, was one of the first to see the vast aesthetic or artistic possibilities of light in the theater. He wrote: "Light is to the production what music is to the score: the expressive element in opposition to the literal signs; and, like music, light can express only what belongs to the inner essence of all vision's vision.'" Norman Bel

(Gerry Goodstein)

Light establishes mood and creates a stage composition.
In this scene from a CSC Repertory Company production of *Peer Gynt*, the shafts of light isolate characters on the stage. Separate groupings surround the one figure in the center. The lighting illuminates some characters and silhouettes others. A mood of theatricality and unreality is created by the downward thrust of light beams.

LIGHTING AND SOUND

333

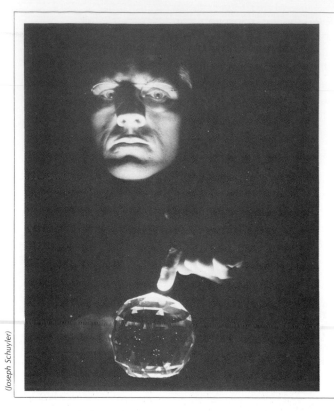

Lighting produces unusual effects.
Lighting is particularly effective in creating mysterious or otherworldly effects. In this scene from the Soho Repertory production of *Dark Ride* by Len Jenkin, light isolates the crystal ball and is thrust upward on the face of the character to give him a ghostly, unnatural appearance.

Geddes (1893–1958), an imaginative American designer and follower of Appia, put it in these words: "Good lighting adds space, depth, mood, mystery, parody, contrast, change of emotion, intimacy, fear."

Gordon Craig (1872–1966), an innovative British designer, spoke of "painting with light." The lighting designer can indeed paint with light, but far more can be done; on the deepest sensual and symbolic level, the lighting designer can convey something of the feeling, and even the substance, of the play.

Objectives of Lighting Design

The following are the functions and objectives of stage lighting:

1 Provide visibility
2 Help establish time and place
3 Assist in creating mood
4 Reinforce the style of the production
5 Provide focus on stage and create visual compositions
6 Establish a rhythm of visual movement
7 Reinforce a central visual image

THE DESIGNERS: ENVIRONMENT AND THE VISUAL ELEMENTS

Visibility   On the practical side, the chief function of lighting is illumination or visibility. We must be able, first and foremost, to see the performers' faces and their actions on stage. Occasionally, lighting designers, carried away with the atmospheric possibilities of light, will make a scene so dark that we can hardly see what is happening on stage. Mood is important, of course, but obviously seeing the performers is even more so. At times the script calls for the lights to dim—in a suspense play, for instance, when the lights in a haunted house go out. But these are exceptions. Ordinarily, unless you can see the actors and actresses, the lighting designer has not carried out his or her assignment.

Time and place   By its color, shade, and intensity, lighting can suggest the time of day, giving us the pale light of dawn, the bright light of midday, the vivid colors of sunset, or the muted light of evening. Lighting can also

(Gerry Goodstein)

Lighting creates sunshine and shadow.
In this scene from the Circle Repertory Company production of *Angels Fall* by Lanford Wilson, we see sunlight created by the lighting designer. The play is set in the southwestern United States, and the light streaming in the window suggests a bright, hot sun. It also throws a warm glow on the face of the actor Bernard Hughes, playing a priest.

LIGHTING AND SOUND

indicate the season of the year, with winter or summer lights; and it can suggest place, by showing indoor or outdoor light.

Mood Light, together with scenery and costumes, can help performers create a certain mood. Rarely can lighting alone create mood. For example, if the stage is filled with blue light, it might be moonlight—bright and romantic—but it could also be a cold, dark, evil situation. The action, scenery, and words, together with light, tell exactly what the mood is. A happy, carefree play calls for bright, warm colors: yellows, oranges, and pinks. A more somber piece will lean toward blues, blue-greens, and muted tones.

Style Lighting can indicate whether a play is realistic or nonrealistic in style. In a realistic play, the lighting will simulate the effect of ordinary sources—table lamps and outside sunlight. In a nonrealistic production, the designer can be more imaginative: shafts of light can cut through the dark, sculpturing performers on stage; a glowing red light can envelop a scene of damnation; a ghostly green light can cast a spell over a nightmare scene. By its tone and texture, lighting can indicate immediately the style of a production.

(*Theater Collection, Museum of the City of New York*)

Painting with light.
In this sketch for *Machinal*, the designer Robert Edmond Jones demonstrates the sculptural effect of light. A sharp beam of light cuts through the darkness and pinpoints the three figures at the lower left.

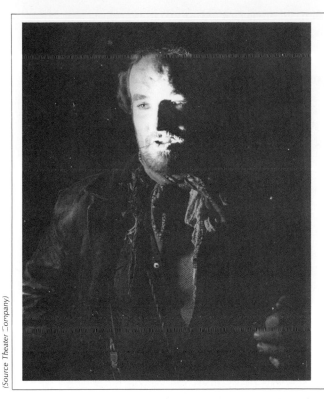

The sculptural quality of light.
Shown here is the actor Bart Whiteman, appearing in a production of Saroyan's *The Time of Your Life* at the Source Theater in Washington, D.C. Note the stark contrast between the left and right sides of his face. Because all light comes from one side, that side is illuminated—almost like a piece of sculpture—and the other side is completely in darkness.

Focus and composition   Focus in lighting directs our attention to one part of the stage—generally where the important action is occurring—and away from other areas. Lights should illuminate the playing area, not the scenery or some area offstage. Most stage scenery is not painted to withstand the harsh glare of direct light and will not be effective when too brightly lit. Also, if scenery is lit to the exclusion of everything else, spectators will focus on it rather than the performers. Therefore, the first object of focus is to aim the light in the right place. In this regard, designers must be careful to avoid *spill,* that is, allowing light from one area to fall into an adjacent area.

As an example of a positive benefit of focus: on a *split stage,* with half the action on one side of the stage and half on the other, the lights can direct our attention from side to side, as they go down in one area and come up in another.

By means of focus, light can create a series of visual compositions on stage. These can vary from turning the stage into one large area to creating small, isolated areas.

Rhythm   Since changes in light occur on a time continuum, they establish a rhythm running through the production. Abrupt, staccato changes with stark blackouts will convey one rhythm, whereas languid, slow fades and gradual cross-fades will convey another. Lighting changes are coordinated with scene changes for timing. The importance of this is recognized by directors and designers, who take great care to ensure the proper changes— "choreographing" shifts in light and scenery like dancers' movements.

Reinforcement of a central image Lighting, like scenery, costume, and all other elements, must be consistent with the overall style and mood of the production. The wrong lighting can distort, or even destroy, the total effect of a play. At the same time, because it is both the least obtrusive of the visual elements of theater and also the most flexible, lighting can aid enormously in creating the theater experience.

The Lighting Designer

The lighting designer must have a background in both the technical and mechanical aspects of lighting as well as a broad, creative visual imagination. The ability to translate words and actions and feelings into color, direction, and intensity comes only after much training and experience. The following is an example of the process a designer uses to light a show.

First, the lighting designer reads the script and begins to form some rough ideas and feelings about the play. He or she meets with the director and the scene designer to discuss visual concepts for the show. The lighting designer next receives copies of all the scenery plans from the set designer and usually consults with the costume designer to learn the shape and color of the costumes.

The lighting designer then makes a careful and complete script analysis to determine most of the lighting requirements. The designer will see one or perhaps several rehearsals to get the feel of the production, to see the exact location of various pieces of furniture and stage business, and to consult with the director about possible effects. Following this, the lighting designer draws a plan of lighting called a *light plot*. This includes the location and color of each lighting instrument. Also indicated is the kind of instrument called for and the area of the stage toward which it is focused.

When lighting instruments are moved into the theater and *hung* (that is, placed on pipes and other supports), the designer supervises the focusing. During technical rehearsals, the lighting designer works with the director to establish light *cues,* that is, when lights go on and off. The designer also sets the length of time for light changes and the levels of intensity on the dimmers.

The Qualities of Stage Lighting

When working on the lighting design for a production, the lighting designer knows what qualities of light will achieve the objectives discussed above.

The first quality light has is brightness, or *intensity*. Intensity can be controlled by devices called *dimmers,* which make the lights brighter and darker. A dimmer is an electric or electronic device that can vary the amount of power going to the lights. This makes it possible for a scene at night to take place in very little light and a daylight scene to take place in bright light.

The second quality that light has is *color*. Color is a very powerful part of lighting, and theater lights can very easily be changed to one of several hundred colors by putting a colored material similar to colored cellophane (usually called a *gel*—short for gelatin) in slots at the front of the lighting instruments. Color is mixed so that the strong tones of one shade do not dominate, giving an unnatural appearance. The lights beamed from one side are *warm* (amber, straw, gold) and from the other side, *cool* (blue, blue-green, lavender). Warms and cools together produce depth and texture, as well as naturalness. The exception to mixing angles and colors of light would be a scene calling for special effects; we expect stark shadows and strange colors, for example, when Hamlet confronts the ghost of his father.

The third quality that the lighting designer can use is *direction*, that is, the way the light is placed on or near the stage so that the light comes from a particular direction. In earlier days, *footlights*—a row of lights across the front of the stage—were popular. Because the light source was below the actors and actresses, however, footlights had the disadvantage of casting ghostly shadows on their faces. Footlights also created a kind of barrier between performers and audience. With the development of more power- ful, versatile lights, footlights were eliminated. Today, most lighting hits the stage from above, coming from instruments in front of the stage and from the sides. The vertical angle of light beams is close to 45 degrees, to approximate the average angle of sunlight. Generally, too, light on an area of the stage comes from several sources: from at least two lights above a proscenium stage, and from at least four above an arena stage. The lights converge from different sides to avoid the harsh shadows on the face which result when light hits only one side of the face. Once performers are properly illuminated by lights from the front and above, other lighting is added: *down lighting* from directly overhead, and *back lighting* from behind, to give further dimension and depth to the figures on stage.

The fourth quality is the *form* in which the light comes, whether as a shaft of light or as a diffuse light.

The last quality of light the designer can work with is *movement*. With various types of dimmers, the light can shift focus from location to location and from color to color. Also, time of day, sunsets, and so on, can help provide information for the audience.

For an example of how these qualities function, consider the lighting for a production of *Hamlet*. To emphasize the eerie, tragic quality of *Hamlet,* with its murders and graveyard scene, the lighting would be generally cool

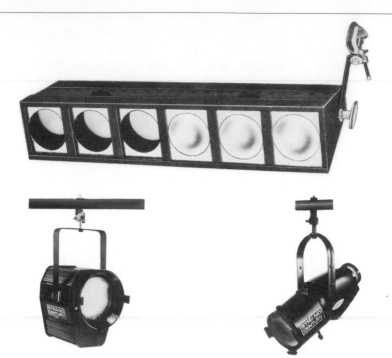

Different lighting instruments for different purposes.

Shown here are three instruments used to light the stage. Most stage lights have three key elements: a lamp that is the source of light, a reflector, and a lens through which the beams pass.

The instrument at the top is a *borderlight*. A row of borderlights is hung above the stage on a pipe, or *batten*, to provide general illumination to the stage or scenery. It can blend light in acting areas or "tone" the settings or costumes.

Below the top and to the left is a small spotlight known as a *fresnel* (pronounced freh-NEL). Spotlights illuminate restricted or limited areas of the stage with a concentrated beam of light. They can carefully define the area that is to be lighted and leave other areas in darkness. The fresnel spotlight has a spherical reflector and a special lens that is flat on one side and has ridges of concentric circles on the other. This arrangement allows the lens to be thinner and lighter than other lenses and softens the edges of the beam. The fresnel spotlight is generally used in positions near the stage—behind the proscenium opening or on arena or thrust stages mounted close to the action.

The other spotlight hanging from a U-shaped brace (to the right) is a larger, more powerful spotlight, known as an *ellipsoidal reflector spotlight*. It is a more efficient instrument and therefore can throw a stronger light farther than the fresnel. It differs from the fresnel by having an ellipsoidal-shaped reflector that partially surrounds the lamp and sends a strong beam through two plano-convex lenses. It is used when the distance between the instrument and the stage area is greatest—for example, from positions outside the proscenium opening in the auditorium. It might be mounted on the balcony rail, in a beam position above the audience, or on vertical booms along the side walls of the auditorium.

rather than warm. As for angles, if the production took place on a proscenium stage, there would be down lighting and back lighting to give a sculptured, occasionally unreal quality to the characters. In terms of movement, the lights would change each time there was a shift in locale. This would give a rhythm of movement through the play and also focus the audience's attention on particular areas of the stage.

Resources of Stage Lighting

Among the resources of the lighting designer are various kinds of lighting instruments and other kinds of technical and electronic equipment.

Types of stage lights   Basically, lights are of three types:

1   *Spotlights,* which throw a sharp, concentrated beam. (A mobile spotlight, with which an operator can follow a performer across the stage, is called a *follow spot.*)
2   *Area lights,* or *floodlights,* which cover a small area with general light.
3   *Strip* or *border lights,* a row of lights which bathe a section of stage or scenery in light.

Lighting controls   We have already considered some of the advances in lighting. In technical terms, lighting is easily the most highly developed aspect of theater. Lighting instruments can be hung all over the theater and beamed at every part of the stage; and these many instruments can be controlled by one person sitting at an electronic panel, or switchboard.

Lighting changes—or *cues,* as they are called—can be arranged ahead of time. Sometimes, in a complicated production (a musical, say, or a Shakespearean play) there will be from 75 to 150 light cues. A cue can range from a *blackout* (where all the lights are shut off at once), to a *fade* (the lights dim slowly, from brighter to darker), to a *cross-fade* (one set of lights comes down while another comes up). Moreover, with today's modern equipment, the changes can be timed automatically so that a cross-fade in lights will take exactly the number of seconds called for; guesswork is eliminated.

Cues can be prearranged by computer and stored on cards or in a memory bank on a magnetic tape. During a performance, the operator at the console pushes a button, and the entire change occurs automatically. As an illustration, Strindberg's *A Dream Play* has innumerable scene changes—after the manner of a dream—in which one scene fades into another before our eyes. At one point in the play, a young woman, called the Daughter, sits at an organ in a church. In Strindberg's words, "The stage darkens as the Daughter rises and approaches the Lawyer. By means of lighting the organ is changed to the wall of a grotto. The sea seeps in between basalt pillars with a harmony of waves and wind." At the light cue for this change, a button is pushed, and all the lights creating the majesty of the church fade as the lights creating the grotto come up.

SOUND IN THE THEATER

Though not one of the visual elements, a technical aspect of theater that must be coordinated with light and scenery is sound.

Sound has become an increasingly important element in theater productions. It may be said to include all sound effects, recordings, and electrical enhancements used in the theater—all sounds, that is, except spoken words and music which have no amplification. Audiences have become increasingly aware of sounds because of concerts by musical groups in which microphones are attached to musical instruments as well as used by performers and in which huge banks of speakers project the sound to the audience.

Sound effects can be defined as any sound produced by mechanical or human means to create for the audience a noise or sound associated with the play being produced. Aside from electronic amplification, various devices have been developed through the years to create these sounds. A wind noise, for example, can be produced by a wooden drum made from slats. The drum is usually 2 or 3 feet in diameter and covered with a muslin cloth. When the drum is turned, by means of a handle, it makes a noise like howling wind. For door slams a miniature door or even a full door in a frame can be placed just offstage and opened and shut. Two pieces of wood slammed shut can also simulate the sound of a closing door. In some cases this effect can sound like a gunshot. A gunshot can also be created by firing a gun using blank cartridges (real guns should never be used on stage; in some states there are laws forbidding the purchase of blank guns). The sound of thunder can be simulated by hanging a large, thick metal sheet backstage and gently shaking it.

In the area of electronic sound, there are two means of sound reproduction: records and tape recorders. In professional productions, all of the nonlive sound effects are recorded on magnetic tape and played back on tape recorders. These tapes are created in professional sound studios by sound engineers. Some shows require two or more tape recorders. The refinement of the home tape recorder has allowed many small theater groups, especially at schools, to take advantage of the new electronic techniques. Small groups (as well as large ones) often can get excellent sound effects on records that are either bought singly or found in a sound cue library.

The process of assembling sound tapes is similar for the professional and the nonprofessional. First, a list is made of all nonmusical sound effects required for the show. This list may come from the director or the stage

Sound: A complex art in today's theater. Sound amplification has become an integral part of productions in large theaters, especially musicals. Stage microphones and "body mikes" attached to performers pick up sound which is fed into a console, such as the one shown here, where the sound is "mixed" and put out through speakers. The complicated console in this picture, operated by the sound technician Otts Munderloh, is used for the Broadway show *Dreamgirls*.

manager. On shows with a great deal of sound or music, there may be a separate sound designer and music consultant. Once the list is decided upon, a master tape is made and the sounds are arranged in the order that they appear in the script. This process is called editing. When the production moves into the theater, there is a technical rehearsal without performers, during which each sound cue is listened to and the volume level is set. When the rehearsal starts with the actors in the theater, more changes will be made. Depending on the action and the timing of scenes, some cues will be too loud and others too soft, some will have to be made shorter and others made longer.

In the area of speech reinforcement—using a microphone to pick up dialogue and songs—several types of microphones are used. A *shotgun mike* is highly directional and is aimed from a distance at a specific area. A *general mike* picks up sounds in the general area toward which it is aimed. A *body mike* is a wireless microphone attached to a small radio transmitter fastened to the performer's clothing. All types of microphones must be hooked to an amplifier that increases the electronic energy in the sound and sends it through speakers.

Microphones are placed in various locations. One position is alongside the downstage edge of the stage where the footlights used to be located. Another position is hanging in the air near the lights. In the case of the body mike, the placement is on the performers themselves.

Placing microphones and speakers in a theater and on the stage is a complicated process. The goal is to get clear and unobtrusive sound. When electronic sound is not properly modulated, it can become an artificial barrier between the performers and the audience and can seriously interfere with the actor-audience relationship.

It should be noted that lighting and sound, like scenery, are means to an end: they implement the artistic and aesthetic aspects of a production. The colors, shapes, and lines of lighting effects and the qualities of sound interact with other elements of theater and contribute to the overall experience.

In Chapter 17 we look at costumes, another important visual element.

SUMMARY

1 Stage lighting, like other elements of theater, has an equivalent in the planning of lighting in homes, department stores, restaurants, etc.

2 Lighting—historically the last of the stage elements to be fully developed —is today the most mechanically sophisticated of all. Once the incandescent electric lamp was introduced, it was possible to achieve almost total control of the color, intensity, and timing of lights.

3 Lighting design is intended to provide illumination on stage, to establish time and place, to help set the mood and style of the production, to focus the action, and to establish a rhythm of visual movement.

4 Lighting should be consistent with all other elements.

5 The lighting designer uses a variety of instruments, colored gels, and control dimmers and panels to achieve his or her effects.

6 Related to visual effects is sound in the theater. Sound effects are created by mechanical means—pieces of wood slapped together for a door closing—or on tape. Microphones are used to enhance speaking or singing.

17
COSTUMES

17
COSTUMES

The transforming power of costumes.
By means of costumes, wigs, and makeup, performers become birds, animals, and other exotic creatures. Many tribal ceremonies and rituals include masks and costumes to change people into animals. A modern version of this practice is found in the musical *Cats*. By means of whiskers, fur, feathers, and makeup, human performers become the feline creatures who act out the characters in T. S. Eliot's poems about cats.

347

O f the various visual elements in theater, the most personal are costumes—along with makeup, hairstyles, and masks—because they are worn by the performers themselves. Visually, the performer and the costume are perceived as one; they merge into a single image on stage. At the same time, costumes have value in their own right, adding color, shape, texture, and symbolism to the overall effect.

COSTUMES IN EVERYDAY LIFE

Aside from theater, most people think of costumes in terms of a pageant with historical figures, such as Queen Elizabeth or George Washington, or a masquerade ball with bizarre outfits. As with other aspects of theater, however, costumes play a significant role in daily life. People wear clothes not only for comfort but for the information they wish to give others about themselves. If we look around us, we are surrounded by the costumes of daily life: the formal, subdued uniform of a police officer; the sparkling outfits of a marching band at a football game; sports gear such as hockey and baseball uniforms; the cap and gown for graduation; a priest's cassock; and brightly colored bathing suits at a swimming pool.

In Chapter 2, we examined the power of symbols. Nowhere is this power more manifest than in clothes and personal adornments. Primitive people put on animal skins to give themselves the characteristics of an animal—ferocity or courage, for instance. Feathers and elaborate headdresses were worn to accentuate height; bracelets and belts with charms were worn as sources of power.

Today we still wear clothes to symbolize different qualities in society. A young person might wear informal clothes as a statement of independence from his or her parents. Parents, on the other hand, might wear conventional clothes in order not to stand out in a crowd or be criticized by friends. How one appears to one's peers or to those in an outside group is a paramount issue with many people, and this is especially noticeable in styles of dress.

Frequently we judge others by their appearance, particularly when we first meet them. If we see a man in a dark blue pinstripe suit with a tie and vest, we assume that he is middle- or upper-middle class; we judge him to be conservative, and probably a banker or a lawyer. Beyond that, we make assumptions about his politics, his family life, his social attitudes, and in fact his whole psychological profile.

A good example of a symbolic outfit is a judge's robe. The black color of the robe suggests seriousness and dignity; also, the robe is draped from the shoulders straight to the ground, covering the whole person, thereby wrapping the person in the importance and presumed impartiality of the office. In our minds, the robe of a judge invests the wearer with authority and wisdom; and when we see someone in the judicial robe, we automatically accept that image. Though individual judges may be foolish or corrupt, it is considered important in our society for the *institution* of the judiciary to be just and incorrupt, and a judge's robe is an important factor in reinforcing that concept.

Clothes have always signaled a number of things regarding the wearer, including the following:

Position and status

Sex

Occupation

Relative flamboyance or modesty

Degree of independence or regimentation

Whether one is dressed for work, leisure, or a routine or a special occasion

The moment we see the clothes people are wearing, we receive a great many messages and impressions about them; we instantaneously relate those messages to past experience and to our preconceptions; and we form judgments, including value judgments. Even if we have never before laid eyes on someone, we feel we know a great deal when we first see the clothes that a person wears.

COSTUMES FOR THE STAGE

In the theater, clothes send us signals similar to those in everyday life; but, as with other elements of theater, there are significant differences between the costumes of everyday life and those in the theater. Stage costumes communicate the same information as ordinary clothes with regard to sex, position, and occupation; but on stage this information is magnified because every element in theater is in the spotlight. Also, on stage, costumes must meet other requirements not normally expected in everyday life. These requirements will be clearer after we look at the objectives of costume design.

Objectives of Costume Design

Stage costumes should meet the following seven requirements:

1   Help establish the tone and style of a production
2   Indicate the historical period of a play and the locale in which it occurs
3   Indicate the nature of individual characters or groups in a play: their stations in life; their occupations; their personalities

4 Show the relationships among characters: separating major characters from minor ones; contrasting one group with another

5 Where appropriate, symbolically convey the significance of individual characters or the theme of the play

6 Meet the needs of individual performers, making it possible for an actor or actress to move freely in a costume or (when required) to change quickly from one costume to another

7 Be consistent with the production as a whole, especially other visual elements

Indicating tone and style   Along with scenery and lighting, costumes should inform the audience about the style of a play. For a production taking place in outer space, for instance, the costumes would be futuristic. For a Restoration comedy, the costumes would be quite elegant, with lace at the men's collars and cuffs, and elaborate gowns for the women. For a tragedy, the clothes would be somber and dignified; seeing them, the audience would know immediately that the play itself was somber and its tone likely to be serious.

(Great Lakes Shakespeare Festival—Mark C. Schwartz)

Costumes convey style.
For a production of Shakespeare's *The Merry Wives of Windsor*, characters wore the imaginative costumes called for in one section. The fantastic nature of the costumes shows that we are in a world from the past—a magical, unreal world.

For the Broadway musical *Pippin,* the costume designer Patricia Zipprodt combined elements of medieval costumes—such as armor breastplates—with clown outfits, burlesque costumes, and commedia dell'arte costumes, including the traditional half masks. The play is a vaudeville version of a medieval story, filled with magic and theatricality, and Zipprodt's costumes made a forceful visual statement of that concept. She pulled the various elements of the musical together into a single pictorial image. The costumes were individually exciting, but they also suggested the period of the story and the style of the presentation. They announced to the spectators what kind of theater experience they were likely to have.

Indicating historical period and locale   Costumes indicate the period and location of a play: whether it is historical or modern, set in a foreign country or the United States, and so on. A play might take place in ancient Egypt, in Spain in the seventeenth century, or in modern Africa. Costumes should tell us when and where the action occurs.

Sometimes—as we have already seen—the costume designer and the director decide to shift the period of a play. For example, *Hamlet* might be

Costumes identify the period of the play and the status of the characters. *Tartuffe*, by Molière, is set in France in the seventeenth century. The costumes in this production tell us immediately that the play is set in a historical period. They also indicate the importance of the woman on the sofa, the youth of the woman in front of the window, and the fact that the woman at the far right is a maid.

COSTUMES

performed in modern dress; there have been productions in which Hamlet was in a tuxedo and Gertrude in a long evening dress. Obviously such a shift comes as a shock to the audience, and it is up to the costume designer to assist the audience in adjusting to it.

For most historical plays, the director and the costume designer have a range of choices, depending on the directorial concept. For a production of Shakespeare's *Julius Caesar,* for instance, the costumes could indicate the ancient Roman period when Caesar actually lived; in this case the costumes would include togas and Roman soldiers' helmets. Or the costumes for *Julius Caesar* could feature Elizabethan dress; we know that in Shakespeare's day costumes were heightened versions of the English clothes of the time, regardless of the period in which the play was set. As a third choice, the designer could create costumes for an entirely different period, including the modern. Whatever the choice, the historical period should be clearly indicated in the costumes.

Identifying status and personality   As clothes do in everyday life, costumes can tell us whether people are from the aristocracy or the working class, whether they are blue-collar workers or professionals. But in the theater, these signals must be clear and unmistakable. For example, a woman in a long white coat could be a doctor, a laboratory technician, or a beauty parlor operator. The costume on stage must indicate the exact occupation—by giving the doctor a stethoscope, for instance.

Costumes also tell us about the personalities of characters: a flamboyant person will be dressed in flashy colors; a shy, retiring person will wear subdued clothes.

Separating characters through costumes   Individuals and characters can be set apart by the way they are costumed. Major characters, for example, will be dressed differently from minor characters. Frequently the costume designer will point to the major characters in a play by dressing them in distinctive colors—in sharp contrast to other characters. Consider, for example, Shaw's *Saint Joan,* a play about Joan of Arc. Obviously, Joan should stand out from the soldiers surrounding her. Therefore, her costume might be bright blue while theirs are steel gray. Her costume signals her importance. In another play of Shaw's, *Caesar and Cleopatra,* Cleopatra should stand out from her servants and soldiers. Though dressed like them in an Egyptian costume, she should be in brighter colors and wear a more elegant outfit.

Costumes underline important group divisions. In *Romeo and Juliet,* the Montagues wear costumes of one color, and the Capulets, another. In a modern counterpart of *Romeo and Juliet,* the musical *West Side Story,* the two gangs of young men are dressed in contrasting colors: the Jets might be

Costumes indicate station in life.
In a production of Schiller's *Mary Stuart*, the figures of Mary, Queen of Scots (on the right), and Queen Elizabeth are clothed in gowns that indicate their noble birth and also their relationship to each other. Note that Queen Elizabeth is wearing the more elaborate outfit.

in various shades of pink, purple, and lavender, and the Sharks in shades of green, yellow, and lemon.

Costumes also indicate age. This is particularly helpful when an older actor is playing a young person, or vice versa. The young person can wear padding or a beard, for example.

Creating symbolic or nonhuman characters   In many plays, special costumes, denoting abstract ideas or giving shape to fantastic creatures, are called for. Here the costume designer must develop an outfit which carries with it the imaginative and symbolic qualities required. How does one clothe the witches in *Macbeth* or the ghost of Banquo, for instance? A way must be found to symbolize the qualities they represent. To illustrate how costumes can suggest ideas or characteristics, a costume of animal skins can symbolize bestiality, and a costume of feathers can indicate a birdlike quality, while a costume made of a metallic material can suggest a hard and mechanical quality.

In *Peer Gynt* by Ibsen, the main character, Peer, meets a supernatural being in the mountains. It is called the Boyg and is a symbolic presence urging Peer to compromise in life and go "roundabout." A costume designer might fashion for the Boyg a soft, round outfit with no sharp outlines or edges—a large blob like a sack of potatoes—to indicate its indecisive, amorphous quality.

A modern play which calls for exaggerated as well as symbolic costumes is *The Balcony,* by the French playwright Genet. The play is set in a house of prostitution where ordinary men act out their fantasies: one pretends to be a general, another a bishop, and a third a judge. They dress in exaggerated costumes, looking almost like caricatures of the originals, with platform shoes, shoulder pads wider than their own shoulders, and high headpieces.

(Design by Patricia Zipprodt—Martha Swope)

Exaggerated costumes.
In Genet's *The Balcony*, ordinary men pretend to be mighty figures. To emphasize their assumed importance, they wear oversized costumes with large shoulder pads and platform shoes. In this scene we see a man impersonating a high official and a prostitute dressed as a pony.

THE DESIGNERS: ENVIRONMENT AND THE VISUAL ELEMENTS

The woman who serve them also dress fantastically. The women serving the general is dressed as a horse, and the costume designer has the task of making a costume for her which will bring out her attractiveness as a person but still give her a horse's tail and mane.

Meeting the needs of individual performers   Virtually every aspect of theater has practical as well as aesthetic requirements, and costume design is no exception. No matter how attractive or how symbolic, stage costumes must work for the performers. A long, flowing gown may look beautiful; but if it is too long and the actress wearing it trips every time she walks down a flight of steps, the designer has overlooked an important practical consideration. If actors are required to duel or engage in hand-to-hand combat, their costumes must stand up to this wear and tear, and their arms and legs must have freedom of movement and not be bound by the costume. If performers are to dance, they must be able to turn, leap, and move freely.

Quick costume changes are frequently called for in the theater. In the Broadway musical *Gypsy,* when an emerging young star sang "Let Me Entertain You," she was required to go offstage between choruses and reappear a few seconds later in another costume. The actress went through three or four dazzling costume changes in seconds, to the astonishment of the audience. The costumes had to be made so that the actress, with the help of dressers offstage, would rapidly get out of one outfit and into another. Tearaway seams and special fasteners were used so that one costume could be ripped off and another quickly put on.

Unlike scenery, which stays in place until it is moved, a costume is constantly in motion; it moves as the performer moves. This provides an opportunity for the designer to develop grace and rhythm in the way a costume looks as it moves across the stage, but with that goes a great responsibility to make the costume workable and appropriate.

At times it is important for the costume designer to work closely with individual performers. Actresses and actors must know how to use the accessories and costumes provided for them. As an example, the character of Sparkish in the Restoration comedy *The Country Wife* by Wycherley is an outrageous fop. Sparkish wears a fancy wig, a hat, and petticoat breeches. He uses a handkerchief, a snuff box, and other hand accessories. In creating a costume for Sparkish, the designer must provide an outfit that not only is correct for the style of the production but suits the physique and appearance of the individual actor. If the actor has never worn a wig or breeches of this kind and has never worked with a handkerchief—which he keeps in the cuff of his jacket—or with a snuff box, he must learn to use these items, working closely with both the director and the costume designer.

Maintaining consistency   Finally, costumes must be consistent with the entire production—especially with the various other visual elements.

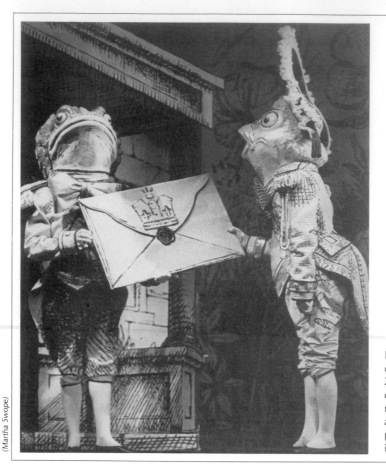

Costumes create
a world of make-believe.
For a production of *Alice in Won-derland*, the designer Patricia Zipprodt fashioned costumes that depict the characters from the famous book. Performers are dressed as animals, fish (as seen here), playing cards, kings, queens, and imaginary creatures.

The Costume Designer

The costume designer's responsibilities   The person putting into effect the ideas we have been discussing is the costume designer. Every production requires someone who takes responsibility for the costumes. When costumes are rented, the designer chooses the style, the period, the color, and the design of the rented costumes. When costumes are "built"—that is, cut and sewn from scratch—the costume designer sketches the way the costumes will look. Obviously, this requires both training and talent.

The costume designer should begin with a thorough knowledge of the play: its subject matter, period, style, and point of view. The costume designer must also have an intimate knowledge of the individual characters in the play. The designer must know each character's personality, idiosyncrasies, relative importance to the play, relationship to other characters, and symbolic value. The designer must be aware, too, of the physical demands of each role: what is called for in terms of sitting, moving from level to level, dancing, falling down, fighting, and so on. Finally, the designer must become thoroughly acquainted with the characteristics of the performers themselves in order to create costumes accommodating their physiques and movement patterns.

Resources of the costume designer Among the elements a costume designer works with are: (1) line, shape, and silhouette; (2) color; (3) fabric; and (4) accessories.

Of prime importance is the cut or *line* of the clothes. Do the lines of an outfit flow, or are they sharp and jagged? Do the clothes follow the lines of the body, or is there some element of exaggeration, such as shoulder pads for men or a bustle at the back of a woman's dress? The outline or silhouette of a costume has always been significant. There is a strong visual contrast, for instance, between the line of an Egyptian female garment, flowing smoothly from shoulder to the floor, and the empire gowns of the early nineteenth century in France, which featured a horizontal line high above the waist, just below the breasts, with a line flowing from below the bosom to the feet. The silhouettes of these two styles stand in marked contrast to a third design: the female dress in the United States of the early 1930s, a short outfit with a prominent belt or sash cutting horizontally across the hips.

The importance of line in costume. These three outfits suggest the variety of effects achieved by altering the outline or silhouette of a costume. The Egyptian dress has no horizontal lines but falls straight from the shoulders to the floor. The Empire style—popular in Europe in the early nineteenth century—is broken by a strong horizontal line just below the bosom, and the flapper dress from the 1920s has a much lower horizontal line across the hips. Not only various outlines but different fabrics and colors determine the appearance of costumes.

THE BRUTE - CHEKHOV

MRS. POPOU   SMIRNOU   LUKA

(Harry Lines)

harry lines

A designer's sketch.

Most costume designers make sketches to show the director and the performers, as well as the person making the costume, what the finished product should look like. In these sketches, we see the designer Harry Lines's ideas for the outfits of three characters in a one-act play by Chekhov presented at Hunter College. From the sketch, the people who sew and make the costumes know how to construct them. Along with the sketch, which indicates the colors and lines of the costumes, the designer specifies the fabrics to be used.

Undergarments are an aspect of costume design often overlooked by audience members. For women's costumes these may consist of hoop skirts that make ball gowns stand out from the body, bustles that exaggerate the lines in the rear, and corsets. Corsets can make a tremendous difference in the posture and appearance of women. In some cases they cause women to stand very straight. In the first decade of the twentieth century, women in society often bent forward. This was due to a curved corset that forced them to thrust their shoulders and upper body forward. A costume designer will be aware of the importance of undergarments and will use them to create the proper silhouette, not only in the costume itself but in the bearing and movement of performers.

A second important resource for costume designers is *color*. Earlier we saw that the leading characters can be dressed in a color which contrasts with the colors worn by other characters and that the characters from one family can be dressed in a different color from those in a rival family. Color also suggests mood: bright, warm colors for a happy mood, and dark, somber colors for a more serious mood. Beyond these applications, however, color can indicate changes in character and changes in mood. Near the beginning of Eugene O'Neill's *Mourning Becomes Electra,* General Manon, who has recently returned from the Civil War, dies, and his wife and daughter wear dark mourning clothes. Lavinia, the daughter, knows that her mother had something to do with her father's death, and she and her brother conspire to murder the mother. Once they have done so, Lavinia feels a great sense of release. She adopts characteristics of her mother, and as an important symbol of this transformation she puts on brightly colored clothes in the same colors her mother had worn before.

Fabric is a third tool of the costume designer. Burlap or other roughly textured cloth suggests people of the earth or of modest means. Silks and satins, on the other hand, suggest elegance, refinement, and perhaps even royalty.

Ornamentation and accessories can be utilized, too. Fringe, lace, ruffles, feathers, bolts, beads—these can add to the attractiveness and individuality of a costume. Also, walking sticks, parasols, purses, and other items carried or worn by people can give distinction and definition to an outfit.

Using the combined resources of line, color, fabric, and accessories, the costume designer arrives at individual outfits which tell us a great deal about the characters who wear them and convey important visual signals about the style and meaning of the play as a whole.

MAKEUP AND HAIRSTYLES IN THE THEATER

Makeup

Related to costume is *makeup*—the application of cosmetics (paints, powders, and rouges) to the face and body. Makeup used to be more popular in the theater than it is today. In a modern small theater, actors and actresses playing realistic parts will simply go without makeup of any consequence. But makeup has a long and important history in the theater. Sometimes it is a necessity, a good example being makeup to highlight facial features which would not otherwise be visible in a large theater. Even in a smaller theater, bright lights tend to wash out cheekbones, eyebrows, and so on.

Use of makeup is often essential because the age of a character differs from that of the performer. Suppose that a 19-year-old performer is playing the part of a 60-year-old character. Through the use of makeup—putting a little gray in the hair or simulating wrinkles—the appropriate age can be suggested. Another situation calling for makeup to indicate age is a play in which the characters grow older during the course of the action. In the musical *I Do, I Do,* based on the play *The Fourposter,* a husband and wife are shown in scenes covering many years in their married life, from the time when they are first married until they are quite old. In order to convey the passing years and their advancing ages, the actress and actor playing the wife and husband must use makeup extensively. For fantastic or other nonrealistic creatures makeup is a necessity too.

Asian theater frequently relies on heavy makeup. For instance, the Japanese *Kabuki,* a highly stylized type of theater, employs completely nonrealistic makeup. The main characters must apply a base of white covering the entire face, over which bold patterns of red, blue, black, and brown are painted. The colors and patterns are symbolic of the character. In Chinese theater, too, the colors of makeup are symbolic: all white means treachery; black means tough integrity; red means loyalty; green indicates demons; yellow stands for hidden cunning; and so forth.

(Tadashi Kimura, Japan Foundation)

Makeup: To change the face or create a new one.
Makeup is frequently used to restore facial features that would be washed out by bright lights, or to change the appearance of a performer—to make the person look older, for example. At other times, makeup is used to create a kind of mask on the face. This is true of the Kabuki theater of Japan, where the colors and lines on the face have symbolic significance. In this picture we see a Kabuki actor applying his elaborate makeup.

THE DESIGNERS: ENVIRONMENT AND THE VISUAL ELEMENTS

Whiteface in a black play.
In Douglas Turner Ward's *Day of Absence*, the black performers wore white makeup. In this case the makeup provides a strong satirical comment on society and underlines the theme of the play.

Douglas Turner Ward (1930–), a black playwright, wrote *Day of Absence* to be performed by black actors playing in whiteface. The implications of this effect are many, not the least being the reversal of the old minstrel performances in which white actors wore blackface. Ward is not the first to put black actors in white face; Genet had part of the cast of his play *The Blacks* wear white masks.

When makeup is used, the face becomes almost like a canvas for a painting. The features of the face may be heightened or exaggerated; or symbolic aspects of the human face may be emphasized. In either case, makeup serves as an additional tool for the performer in creating an image of the character.

Hairstyles and Wigs

Closely related to makeup are *hairstyles*. In certain periods men have worn wigs: the time of the American Revolution is a good example. In England, judges wear wigs to this day.

For women, hairstyles can denote period and social class. In the middle of the nineteenth century, for example, women often wore ringlets in the manner of Scarlett O'Hara in the film *Gone with the Wind*. A few decades

COSTUMES

Wigs and hairstyles.
The way the hair is worn indicates to the audience the social status and other facts about a character. Hairstyles also provide information about the time period when the play takes place. Here we see a wig worn by the actor Allen Nouce in the part of Bob Acres, in an Oregon Shakespeare Festival production of *The Rivals* by Sheridan. Set in England in the late eighteenth century, the play deals with upper-class life at a time when men of that class wore such wigs.

later, in the late 1800s, women wore their hair piled on top of their heads in a pompadour. This was referred to as the *Gibson Girl look.* In the 1920s, women wore their hair marcelled in waves, sometimes slicked down close to the head. In the modern period, women wear their hair in more natural styles; but again there is a tremendous variety. Some women wear short hair; others wear long hair down to their waist.

MASKS

Masks seem to be as old as theater, having been used in ancient Greek theater and in the drama developed by primitive tribes. In one sense, the mask is an extension of the performer—a face on top of a face. There are several ways to look at masks: they remind us, first of all, that we are in the theater, that the act going on before our eyes is not real in a literal sense, but is rather a symbolic or an artistic presentation. For another thing, masks allow the face to be frozen in one expression: a look of horror, perhaps, which we see throughout a production. Masks can also make the face larger than life, and they can create stereotypes, similar to stock characters (see Chapter 10) in which one particular feature—e.g., cunning, haughtiness—is emphasized to the exclusion of everything else.

THE DESIGNERS: ENVIRONMENT AND THE VISUAL ELEMENTS

Masks. An ancient theatrical device.
Masks have been used in theater almost from the beginning. They can change the appearance of a performer, make the face and head larger than life, and freeze the face into a fixed expression. The highly unusual mask worn by the character in the center is from a modern drama, *Puppetplay*, produced by the Negro Ensemble Theater. The character represented a fantasy or nightmare figure in the lives of the two women shown on each side. The mask conveyed the unreal quality of the character.

There are other symbolic possibilities with the use of masks. In his play *The Great God Brown*, Eugene O'Neill calls for the actors to hold masks in front of their faces. When the masks are in place, the characters present a facade to the public, withholding their true characters. When the masks are down, the characters reveal how they feel inside. In *Motel,* a short play and part of a trilogy called *America Hurrah!* by Jean-Claude van Itallie, the actors—a man, a woman, and a woman motel keeper—wear enlarged papier-mâché heads and arms, giving the appearance of huge, somewhat grotesque dolls. The play deals with violence and loss of humanity in American life; and these impersonal, masklike figures underline the theme.

COORDINATION OF THE WHOLE

Costumes, makeup, hairstyles, and masks must be integrated with other aspects of a production. First, they have a close relationship with the performers and the parts they play. Each is highly personal in nature, being literally attached to a performer and moving when the performer moves.

They are so much a part of the performers that we sometimes lose sight of them as separate entities. Actors and actresses, however, would have great difficulty in creating a part without the proper costume, and in some cases without makeup and a mask as well. They help the performer define his or her role.

On another level, costumes, makeup, and masks are essential in carrying out a point of view in a production. Masks, for instance, are clearly nonrealistic and signal to the audience that the character wearing the mask and the play itself are likely to be nonrealistic too. Costumes suggest whether a play is a comedy or a serious play, a wild farce or a stark tragedy.

To be effective in this respect, costumes must be coordinated with scenery and lighting. The wrong kind of lighting can wash out or discolor costumes and makeup. It would be self-defeating, too, if scenery were in one mood or style and the costumes in a different one. Ideally, these elements should support and reinforce one another, and spectators should be aware of how essential it is for them to work together. Visually, if something looks out of place in a production, lack of coordination among these elements might be the reason.

In Part Five we have examined the physical environment and the visual elements of theater, exploring the contributions they make to the total theater experience. In Part Six we will examine the total experience, bringing all the elements together.

SUMMARY

1   The clothes we wear in daily life are a form of costume. They indicate station in life, occupation, and a sense of formality or informality.

2   On the stage, costumes similarly convey information about the people wearing them; more than that, they are consciously chosen and are designed to provide the audience with important information.

3   The objectives of costume design are to set tone and style, indicate time and place, characterize individuals and groups, underline personal relationships, create symbolic outfits when appropriate, meet practical needs of performers, and coordinate with the total production.

4   The designer works with the following elements: line and shape, color, fabric, and accessories.

5   Makeup and hairstyles are also important to the appearance of the performers and are part of the designer's concern.

6   Where called for, masks, too, are under the direction of the costume designer.

PART 6

THE
TOTAL
EXPERIENCE

The elements combine in a finished production.

For a stage production, many elements are brought together to create the performance seen by the audience. The creative forces—playwright, director, performers, designers, producer—combine their efforts to develop a production. Ultimately, what appears on stage is brought together by the perception of each audience member. A good example is the original stage version of *A Streetcar Named Desire* by Tennessee Williams. On the following pages is a drawing by Al Hirschfeld of this production, which starred Jessica Tandy as Blanche DuBois and Marlon Brando as Stanley Kowalski.

18

BRINGING THE ELEMENTS TOGETHER

(New York Public Library Theatre Collection: Astor, Lenox, and Tilden Foundations)

The elements come together in *A Streetcar Named Desire.*

The talents of many people come together to create a stage production. This is especially true when a new script is presented for the first time. A memorable collaboration occurred for the premiere production of *A Streetcar Named Desire* by Tennessee Williams. The heroine of the play is Blanche DuBois, a faded southern belle who is trying to cling to poetry and beauty in the oppressive surroundings of her sister and brother-in-law's apartment in New Orleans. Creating the role of Blanche in the first production was Jessica Tandy, shown here in a scene from the play.

Theater is a remarkable convergence of human and artistic endeavors. This is underscored by the many elements that must come together to produce a theater event: the writing of a play and the planning of a production, which may take weeks, months, perhaps even years; the rehearsal period; the designing and building of scenery and costumes; the technical coordination of light changes, scene shifts, and performers' activities: the adjustments made to the responses of preview audiences. All these contribute to the moment when members of the audience see the performance itself.

The excitement which comes to a group of performers working together or to a crew working backstage on scenery or lights is difficult to describe adequately, as is any human endeavor in which a group joins forces to achieve a goal. An athletic team for example which has trained for weeks has its moment of triumph on the playing field. Any group which works for a common purpose—to win an election, to accomplish some scientific breakthrough, or to organize a neighborhood to make it better—has the same sense of group achievement. Each member knows that he or she could not have achieved the task alone.

Theater is a supreme example of this phenomenon, because, with the possible exception of opera, it is the most complex of the arts. It passes through many hands, and the contribution of each person is essential to its success. When the people creating a theater event work effectively together, they share with one another the deep satisfaction of having collaborated on a difficult but eminently rewarding task. And when the work is performed on stage, the audience senses this achievement, and joins in the collaboration with its response to the work.

PRODUCING *A STREETCAR NAMED DESIRE*

It will be easier to understand this process if we examine how a single production was brought together—in this case, the original Broadway production *A Streetcar Named Desire* by Tennessee Williams.

The Playwright

The play began with the playwright. In his autobiography, Williams writes that in 1946 he was working on his play *Summer and Smoke*.[1] When he read a draft of that play to a friend, however, the reaction was negative; and so he returned to work on *A Streetcar Named Desire,* which at that point he called *The Poker Night.* The play is set in New Orleans, where Williams was living at the time. It concerns a southern woman, Blanche, who is forced to move from her family home in Mississippi to the apartment of her sister Stella and Stella's husband, Stanley, in New Orleans. Stanley's regular poker game figures prominently in the play—hence the original title.

Williams read the play to two friends, one a woman who ran a theater in Houston, Texas. "I think they were shocked by it," Williams writes, "and so was I. Blanche seemed too far out."[2] Nevertheless, Williams continued to work on the play. At the time, his grandfather was living with him; and he drove with his grandfather to Key West, Florida, where they took rooms in a hotel. "It was there," Williams says, "that I really began to get *Streetcar* in shape."[3]

Williams wrote every day until he had finished the play. The form he chose is a modified climactic structure: the play has one central action and only a few characters, and it takes place in one setting. The time period, however, extends over several weeks in a series of scenes.

As for purpose and point of view, Williams emphasized the characters in his play—their motivation, their aspirations, their conflicts, their frustrations. He also emphasized language—especially the lyricism of Blanche's speeches. Seen from Blanche's point of view, *Streetcar* is a modern tragedy; though she fights hard to maintain her sense of self, in the end she is crushed by Stanley.

The Producer

When Williams finished the play, he mailed it to Audrey Wood, his agent in New York. She in turn showed it to the producer Irene Selznick. Wood and Selznick asked Williams to meet them at a hotel in Charleston, South Carolina; and there Selznick told him she wanted to produce the play. A new phase of the collaborative process had begun.

The Director

One of Selznick's first tasks was to select a director who would audition, cast, rehearse, and stage the play. She sought a director who could bring out vividly not only the explosive, external action of the play, but the complex, inner life of the characters—what Stanislavski called the *subtext*.

Her choice was Elia Kazan, who had distinguished himself as the director of Arthur Miller's *All My Sons*, the New York Drama Critics' Circle Award winner of 1946. Four years earlier, Kazan had achieved great success directing Thornton Wilder's *The Skin of Our Teeth*, also a Drama Circle Award winner. Kazan's other important credits included being a cofounder of the Actors Studio and a former member of the heralded Group Theatre Company. The Group Theater Company was known for its excellent work in *psychological realism*.

A Streetcar Named Desire (1947)

TENNESSEE WILLIAMS (1911–1983)

CHIEF CHARACTERS:

Blanche DuBois—30 years old
Stella Kowalski—her sister, 25 years old
Stanley Kowalski—Stella's husband, 28 years old
Harold Mitchell (Mitch)—Stanley's friend
Eunice Hubbell—upstairs neighbor

SETTING: A two-story apartment building on a street named Elysian Fields in New Orleans. The section is poor but has a raffish charm.

SCENE 1: Blanche DuBois arrives from Mississippi at Stella and Stanley's New Orleans apartment. Blanche, who is homeless, destitute, and in an anxious state, expresses disapproval of Stella's "earthy" living conditions.

SCENE 2: The next evening. Stanley's friends are coming over for a poker game; Stella takes Blanche out for dinner because her "sensibilities" will be upset by the men's crudeness. Later, Stanley accuses Blanche of swindling them by selling Belle Reve, the family estate, without giving Stella her share.

SCENE 3: The Poker Night. The women come home late; Blanche flirts with Mitch, and Stella dances to music on the radio. Stanley, who is very drunk, throws the radio out the window and attacks Stella. The men subdue him while Blanche takes Stella, who is pregnant, to Eunice's apartment upstairs. Stanley yells for Stella to come home, and she obeys; Mitch sits with the distraught Blanche on the front steps.

SCENE 4: The next morning. Blanche is upset and harried, but Stella is happy. Blanche talks to Stella about leaving Stanley, whom she calls an "ape," but Stella tells her that she loves him. Stanley overhears Blanche saying that he is "common" and "bestial." He sneaks out and reenters loudly, pretending that he hasn't heard.

SCENE 5: Blanche, highly nervous, begins drinking. Stanley asks her if she ever knew a man from a disreputable hotel in Laurel, Mississippi. She denies it, but her reaction makes it obvious that she did know the man. She finds relief in the idea of her forthcoming date with Mitch and admits to Stella that she is attracted to him.

SCENE 6: 2 A.M. that night. Mitch and Blanche come home from their date, go inside, have a drink, and chat awkwardly. Mitch has spoken to his sick mother, whom he lives with, about a possible future with Blanche, who confides to him that her first husband was a homosexual who killed himself.

SCENE 7: A late afternoon in mid-September. While Stella is preparing for Blanche's birthday party, Stanley tells Stella he has heard bad stories about Blanche's former life. Stanley admits that Mitch won't be coming to the party because he now knows the stories. When Blanche comes out of the bathroom, she realizes that something is wrong.

SCENE 8: Forty-five minutes later. Mitch has not appeared at the dismal birthday party, and Blanche is miserable. Stanley belligerently presents Blanche with his "present"—a one-way bus ticket back to Laurel, Mississippi. Blanche gets hysterical and runs into the bathroom; Stella gets so agitated while confronting Stanley that she goes into labor and is rushed to the hospital.

SCENE 9: Later that evening. Blanche is home alone when Mitch arrives drunk. Mitch says he's never seen her in full light; he rips the paper lantern off the light bulb and turns it on. When he looks at her, she cries out and covers her face. He makes a play for Blanche, but she breaks away and he runs out.

SCENE 10: A few hours later. Blanche, who has been drinking, is alone. Stanley returns from the hospital; he has been drinking too. She tells him a millionaire has invited her to go away. She also makes up a story about Mitch coming to beg her forgiveness. Stanley knows it is a lie. He puts on silk pajamas that he "wore on his wedding night." The two of them struggle, and he brutally carries her to bed offstage, where he rapes her.

SCENE 11: Several weeks later. Stella is packing Blanche's things while the men play poker: they are sending Blanche to a mental hospital. Blanche told Stella what Stanley did to her, but Stella won't believe it. When the doctor and matron arrive, Blanche thinks it is her millionaire; when she sees it is not, she runs into the bedroom. The doctor comes in and gently leads Blanche out. Eunice hands Stella's baby to her, as she stands crying, and Stanley comforts her.

The producer, director, and playwright get together.
Three key people who collaborated to create the original production of *A Streetcar Named Desire* are shown here conferring during rehearsals: the producer, Irene Selznick; the director, Elia Kazan; and the playwright, Tennessee Williams.

Selecting the Designers

Following the signing of Kazan as director, Selznick's next task was to select the scenic, lighting, and costume designers. After consulting with Kazan, who made recommendations, Selznick chose Jo Mielziner for scenery and lighting, and Lucinda Ballard for costumes—both established professionals in their respective fields. A determining factor in selecting Mielziner was his unusual and imaginative approach to traditional set design. Mielziner believed that the new, innovative staging introduced in the American musical of the 1930s and 1940s made possible a freer, more imaginative set and light design, permitting a departure from the limits of the traditional box set—a view shared by Kazan.

Working on the Script

Meanwhile, Kazan familiarized himself with the script, determining "what the play is about." Kazan saw the play basically as a clash between two lifestyles: the fragile, poetic values of an obsolescent southern culture of manners, refinement, and gentility, set against a harsh, brutal, post-World War II subculture in the French quarter of New Orleans.

Kazan's next step was to decide on the theme of the play. In his notebook on *Streetcar*, published in *Directors on Directing*, Kazan states: "Theme— this a message from the dark interior. This little twisted, pathetic confused bit of light and culture puts out a cry. It is snuffed out by the crude forces of violence, insensibility and vulgarity which exist in our South—this is the cry of the play."[4]

In addition Kazan conceived the style that he felt would express the theme, a style that evolves primarily from Blanche's character. In his notebook Kazan explained his selection and the reasons for it:

> Style—one reason a "style," a stylized production is necessary is that a subjective factor—Blanche's memories, inner life, emotions, are a real factor. We cannot really understand her behavior unless we see the effect of her past on her present behavior. This play is a poetic tragedy. We are shown the final dissolution of a person of worth, who once had great potential, and who, even as she goes down, has worth exceeding that of the "healthy," coarse-grained figures who kill her.[5]

The Designers Begin Work

Now that Kazan had defined his directorial concept, he met with his scenic and light designer, and his costume designer, to share his viewpoint of the play. They were asked to prepare sketches which would incorporate and express his concept. Mielziner as scenic and light designer had to wed the aesthetic ideas—the style, the mood, the locale—to practical questions such as playing areas for the performers. He also had to consider the aesthetic and practical aspects of lighting. To do this he made drawings of both the set and the light plot.

In considering the concept of *Streetcar,* Mielziner had to satisfy several demands. He needed a cramped apartment for Stanley and Stella, because the close quarters contribute to the trapped feeling Blanche has. He also needed the surrounding area—the sensual, loose atmosphere of New Orleans. He solved the problem by placing the small, crowded apartment in a larger setting and by using scrims (these are described later).

Ballard, as costume designer, set to work to find the proper clothes to suit not only the place and period of the play, but the personality of each character. For Blanche, for instance, she wanted clothes that were fragile

Costume designs for *Streetcar*.
The designer Lucinda Ballard made the sketches shown here of costumes for characters in *Streetcar*. The figure of Blanche is in the center, with Stella on the left and Stanley on the right. All elements of the production—including costumes, scenery and lighting—had to be coordinated to create the end result.

and faded—dresses that had once been elegant but were now out of style, like Blanche herself. Moreover, she would later measure each performer carefully to see that the costumes fit well and could be changed easily when necessary.

"Spine" of the Characters

Kazan's next concern was casting the parts. In preparation for this, he prepared a careful analysis of the play's characters, including the application of Stanislavski's technique of defining each character's "spine," especially the four principals: Blanche, Stanley, Stella, and Mitch.

In describing the spine of Blanche, Kazan wrote the following:

Spine—find Protection: the tradition of the old South says that it must be through another person. Her problem has to do with her tradition. Her notion of what a woman should be. She is stuck with this "ideal." . . . It serves the demands of her notion of herself, to make her *special* and different, out of the tradition of the romantic ladies of the past. . . . Because this image of herself cannot be accomplished in reality, certainly not in the South of our day and time, it is her effort and practice to accomplish it in fantasy.[6]

Kazan went on to write a thorough analysis of Blanche's character and included ideas of the way she would behave, the props she would use, and so forth.

He developed similar analyses of the other main characters. Of Stanley, for example, he wrote that his spine is to "keep things his way (Blanche the antagonist). The hedonist, objects, props, etc. Sucks on a cigar all day because he can't suck a teat. Fruit, food, etc. He's got it all figured out, what fits, what doesn't. The pleasure scheme."[7]

Kazan wrote of Stella that her main purpose was to "hold onto Stanley (Blanche the antagonist). . . . (Stella) has an unconscious hostility toward Blanche. Blanche is so patronizing, demanding and superior toward her . . . makes her so useless, old-fashioned and helpless . . . everything that Stanley has got her out of. Stanley has made a woman out of her."[8]

Finally, Kazan made notes on Mitch—his spine, he said, was to "get away from his mother (Blanche the lever). He wants the perfection his mother gave him. . . . Naturally no girl, today, no sensible, decent girl will give him this. But the tradition will."[9]

Auditions; Casting; Stage Manager

Having a clear conception of play and character, Kazan was now ready to hold auditions in order to cast *Streetcar*. By now a stage manager had been hired, who had, as one of his first duties, to organize and help conduct the auditions for the director. In some instances the director knows, without the benefit of an audition, the performer he or she would like to cast in a given role. That was the case with the role of Stanley Kowalski. Kazan offered the part to a highly successful motion picture actor, and a former colleague from the Group Theatre, John Garfield; but Garfield declined, because he felt that the role was secondary to the part of Blanche. Following a careful period of auditioning, Kazan cast a relatively unknown actor, Marlon Brando, who had studied with the famous acting teacher Stella Adler. His choice for Blanche was a well-known, accomplished actress, Jessica Tandy. He then cast Kim Hunter in the role of Stella and Karl Malden as Mitch, and cast all the secondary roles.

Production; Rehearsal Schedules

About the time rehearsals were scheduled to begin, production and rehearsal meetings were held, at which Kazan approved the final sketches of sets and costumes, and lighting plot. One of the main purposes of these meetings was to prepare detailed production and rehearsal schedules. The production schedule reflects when sets will be built, costumes sewn, furniture and props built or gathered, lights hung and focused, and the like. The rehearsal schedule informs the actors when, where, of what type, and how long rehearsals will be. The rehearsal period covered six weeks, from the early readings through the final dress rehearsal.

The dramatist on the set. Tennessee Williams, author of *A Streetcar Named Desire*, sits on the set of the original Broadway production. The final product began with his script but ended with performances before an audience. In between came many hours of planning, rehearsal, and coordination of the elements.

Rehearsals

During the first few weeks, rehearsals were held in a rehearsal hall—not in the theater itself. As in the case of auditions, it was the responsibility of the stage manager to set up or prepare the rehearsal space with whatever was needed to rehearse. At the beginning, the stage manager arranged for a large table and chairs, around which Kazan held initial readings of the play with the actors. The play was read, discussed, and reread a number of times. Shortly, with Kazan's encouragement, the actors began to move about, once they got a "feel" of the characters. They moved freely, a technique which Kazan believes helps performers to "discover" their characters.

Meanwhile, the stage manager, using the set designer's ground plan as a guide, designated an area as the acting area. It was the equivalent in size and shape to the actual performing area of the theater. Using masking tape, the stage manager taped the floor, specifying where the set units and furniture were to be located. The rehearsals now moved to this "floor map" area; and articles of furniture, such as table and chairs, were used in place of the actual ones to be used in performance. This was also true of props, which were facsimiles of the actual ones.

In the early stages on the taped floor, Kazan, as he had done around the large table, encouraged the actors to move spontaneously, as "the spirit moved them." He made suggestions from time to time; but for the most part he wanted the movement patterns to evolve naturally, through the meaning of the play. As they became more familiar with the characters, the actors were asked by Kazan to improvise various scenes in order to explore deeper, more hidden values. Because Kazan believed that Williams had much to offer in the way of suggestions and explanations, he welcomed the playwright's attendance of rehearsals. Kazan regarded Williams as a *play constructionist,* capable of making valuable recommendations about staging and about the behavior of the characters.

All the while, the performers were working on their individual roles. They had been discovering the "spine" in their own way, memorizing lines, learning the blocking or stage movements, and adjusting to the other performers.

The Producer at Work

Both before and during rehearsals, the producer, Selznick, has been occupied with the business and administrative side of the production. First, she raised the capitalization to pay all expenses: sets, costumes, advertising, theater rental, and salaries for both artistic and technical personnel. Then she set about lining up other aspects. She rented the Ethel Barrymore Theater. She hired a general manager who arranged for tickets, ushers, and so forth. She hired a press agent who would contact the press and radio, including the critics. She hired an advertising agency which arranged for newspaper ads. Finally, she coordinated these activities with the budgetary requests of Kazan, Mielziner, and Ballard.

The Set Is Built

By creating a set that combined realistic and nonrealistic elements, Mielziner had succeeded in realizing Kazan's concept of *Streetcar* as a poetic tragedy. Through the use of scrim and lights, Mielziner used a single set for both exterior and interior scenes. When the lights struck the scrim from in front, the scrim appeared as an exterior wall or the outside of the two-story building. When the lights were brought up from behind the scrim, the interior of the apartment was revealed. Also, behind the structure was a large backdrop or *cyclorama* on which lights could be projected with many variations of color and intensity, producing an ever-changing atmosphere and mood. At times the house appeared as "a form that is transparent in space, an illusion of infinity—or the skeleton of a house of terror." By the third or fourth week of rehearsal, most of the set has been built, except for some of the more detailed elements.

Set design for *Streetcar*.

Above: The scene designer Jo Mielziner made sketches such as the one shown here for the set of the original *Streetcar*. He conceived of the Kowalski apartment, with steps to the street and the surroundings of New Orleans showing through a scrim on occasion. As scene designer, he also had to provide a number of technical drawings such as a ground plan and painter's elevations.

The finished set.

Below: Based on the designs of Jo Mielziner, the set was completed. A portion of the finished set is shown here, as Stella and Stanley embrace on the outside stairs at the left while the men play poker inside. Compare the completed set with the sketch.

THE TOTAL EXPERIENCE

Rehearsals in the Theater

Now the actors rehearsed in the actual theater and playing area of performance. Kazan began to *set* or fix the staging. That is, he set permanent patterns of movement to be used in performance. Meanwhile, the stage manager had been assuming another important responsibility: the preparation of the production or *prompt book*. In it he recorded all facets of staging, including all changes made from rehearsal to rehearsal. He also recorded any *stage business* done by the actors—for example, Stanley's throwing a package of meat around like a football. Eventually, the prompt book was used in performance by the stage manager to give acting, set, light and sound cues.

Technical and Dress Rehearsals

As rehearsals drew near to performance time, Kazan began *run-throughs* for the purpose of attaining the continuity and flow of the show—as well as establishing the play's rhythm and tempo. At these rehearsals the actors were wearing parts of or all of their costumes and using the actual furniture and props to be used in performance. They were also working on the completed set. During the final week of rehearsals, all the technical elements set, lights, sound, props, costumes, makeup—were being coordinated at "tech" rehearsals, which were followed by dress rehearsals to coordinate all technical and artistic (acting) elements in the production. Following minor changes at the final dress, at which Kazan gave notes to the actors and technical people, *Streetcar* was ready for performance.

It opened on Broadway December 3, 1947, to great popular and critical acclaim.

ASPECTS OF THE TOTAL EXPERIENCE

The Creators: Risks and Opportunities

As we have seen in this description of the first production of *A Streetcar Named Desire,* a great many people must work closely together to create a stage production. The danger in theater is that the number of people involved increases the chance of failure. Any one link in the creative chain can affect the outcome. The opportunity for a mistake is much greater, for example, than it is with a painting on which one artist works with a canvas and paints. A stagehand can destroy an entire scene by a miscue; so can a lighting technician. A performer can forget his or her lines, negating much of the work that has gone into a special moment. Any one person can interrupt or short-circuit the final effect.

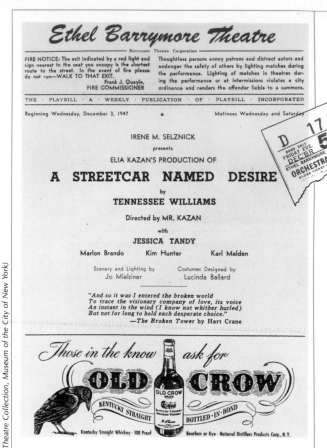

Ethel Barrymore Theatre

Barrymore Theatre Corporation

FIRE NOTICE: The exit indicated by a red light and sign nearest to the seat you occupy is the shortest route to the street. In the event of fire please do not run—WALK TO THAT EXIT.
Frank J. Quayle,
FIRE COMMISSIONER

Thoughtless persons annoy patrons and distract actors and endanger the safety of others by lighting matches during the performance. Lighting of matches in theatres during the performance or at intermissions violates a city ordinance and renders the offender liable to a summons.

THE · PLAYBILL · A · WEEKLY · PUBLICATION · OF · PLAYBILL · INCORPORATED

Beginning Wednesday, December 3, 1947   •   Matinees Wednesday and Saturday

IRENE M. SELZNICK
presents

ELIA KAZAN'S PRODUCTION OF

A STREETCAR NAMED DESIRE

by

TENNESSEE WILLIAMS

Directed by MR. KAZAN

with

JESSICA TANDY

Marlon Brando   Kim Hunter   Karl Malden

Scenery and Lighting by   Costumes Designed by
Jo Mielziner   Lucinda Ballard

"And so it was I entered the broken world
To trace the visionary company of love, its voice
An instant in the wind (I know not whither hurled)
But not for long to hold each desperate choice."
—*The Broken Tower* by Hart Crane

Those in the know   ask for

OLD CROW

KENTUCKY STRAIGHT   BOTTLED·IN·BOND

Kentucky Straight Whiskey · 100 Proof   Bourbon or Rye · National Distillers Products Corp., N.Y.

The play opens.

When the production of *A Streetcar Named Desire* opened in December 1947, at the Ethel Barrymore Theater in New York, the audience had an opportunity for the first time to see the efforts of the many people who worked on it. The audience completed the circle of the production. As a prelude to the performance—the beginning of the total experience—the audience purchased tickets (a copy of a ticket is shown here) and read the opening-night program (also shown).

Furthermore, because so many creative people are involved, there is always the possibility that divergent points of view will be at war with one another. The director and the playwright may not see eye to eye on the interpretation of the script. A creative actor or actress is yet another vital force who may be at odds with either the playwright or the director, or both. When we add the ideas of the scene designer, the lighting designer, and the costume designer, and perhaps others involved—a music composer, for example—we can see the possibilities for conflicts. The risk we run when we go to the theater is that the inconsistencies arising from these conflicts will mar the outcome; namely, that the level of the performances will not be up to the grandeur of the text or that the play will not measure up to the performances.

Generally, however, everyone working on a production is doing his or her best to make it successful. The great opportunity in theater is that many people working together can produce results that no one person working alone ever could. The teamwork of theater can produce extraordinary moments of magic and insight. The audience, too, has a chance to share in this unique collaborative effort.

Fortunately, we do not need to encounter the ideal each time we go to the theater for the experience to be meaningful. A production can fall short of perfection and still be exciting. In a production of *Streetcar,* for example, if the performance of the actor playing Mitch is not quite as strong as that of the other performers, it need not destroy the overall effect. And if a member of the audience does not understand every subtlety and nuance in the text, it will not lessen the basic impact of the production. As long as those who create a theater event present the audience with a reasonably clear and cohesive vision on stage, they will have provided the basis for a genuine theater experience. The rest is up to the audience.

The Audience: Integrating the Elements

Observation and assimilation   The ultimate integration of a theater event takes place in each spectator's mind. No matter how closely the people who produce a theater event work together, and no matter how well the director coordinates the various elements, individual audience members must eventually bring the parts together. So many elements make up a theater production that we might wonder how a spectator can combine them. The answer lies in our ability to handle many kinds of information and bring this information together to form a complete picture. Our everyday activities suggest that human beings have a great capacity to absorb data and stimuli and to integrate them into a single experience.

A good example is what happens when someone drives an automobile. The person at the wheel is aware, first of all, of the parts of the car itself: the steering wheel, the accelerator, the brakes. He or she concentrates on the road, anticipating turns in the highway or stoplights ahead. There are also other cars and pedestrians to consider; the driver is aware of automobiles to the left and right, and glances in the rear-view mirror to see what is behind. In addition, the driver might be listening to the radio or to the conversation of other passengers in the car. While dealing with these mechanical or personal details, the driver might also be daydreaming—thinking of some past event or imagining a future one.

This same ability to absorb and deal simultaneously with an abundance of activities and thoughts can be brought to bear on every kind of undertaking; it applies to emotional and intellectual as well as physical tasks. Without it we would not be able to survive.

Our powers of assimilation make it possible to form a cohesive whole out of the fragments we see before us on stage: we watch individual performers in action and tune in to their personalities; we observe the costumes, scenery, and lighting effects; we note the progress of the action as characters confront one another; we hear the words of the playwright; and we associate ideas and emotions in the play with our own experiences.

Along the way we relate each present moment with the past. Two kinds of memories contribute to this process. First, we have a lifetime of personal memories—experiences which an event on stage might trigger in our mind—linking our individual past with what is happening on stage. Second, we have the memory of what has just occurred in the play itself. When we attend the theater our attention is sharply focused on the stage; we have come for the express purpose of seeing one event, and everything centers our attention on that event. The lights converge on the playing area, and the audience becomes abnormally quiet in order to hear what is being said. The ability of spectators to pick up clues is heightened as they become keenly aware of what every character does or says. If the audience sees someone hide a gun in a desk drawer in the first act, and a character goes to the drawer in the third act, the audience knows that the gun is about to be used.

Not only do we connect the past with what is happening at each moment in a performance; we also anticipate the future. People have immense curiosity about what lies ahead; they are fascinated by prophecies and predictions of future events, in everything from religion to horse racing. Again, this is a human activity which comes into play in the theater. We ask ourselves: How will Electra react when she finds that the brother she thought was dead is actually alive? What will Blanche DuBois do when Stanley Kowalski shows her the bus ticket that will send her out of town to oblivion? We constantly speculate on the fate of characters and look forward—with both fear and excitement—to their encounters with one another.

Each moment in the theater forms a miniexperience of its own, resulting from a series of collisions or intersections on many levels: the past meets the present, the present meets the future, performers interact with their roles, ideas combine with emotions, sights fuse with sounds, and so forth. If the playwright, director, performers, and designers have worked together to present a single vision, these impressions and collisions do not result in a fragmented experience; rather, because of the audience's ability to integrate a number of stimuli, they can be pulled together to form a rich, multilayered experience. In order for spectators to get the most out of this experience, however, they must do two things: (1) be aware of the separate elements in a production, knowing what each contributes to the whole, and (2) combine and integrate the elements into a full, complete picture.

Observing individual elements as parts of a whole In different sections of this book we have seen how separate elements contribute to the overall theater experience. By using the extraordinary powers of perception described above, spectators can focus on specific areas in a production

The elements come together for the audience.
The climax of all theater preparation is the performance. The audience brings all the elements together as it watches—scenery, costumes, lighting, text, and especially the performances. Shown here are the three principals from the original production of *A Streetcar Named Desire*: Marlon Brando as Stanley, Jessica Tandy as Blanche, and Kim Hunter as Stella.

without losing sight of the total effect. They can also relate individual elements to one another. If members of the audience learn to use these powers to the fullest, their enjoyment and understanding of theater events will be enhanced.

We can concentrate for a time on acting, for instance, and ask ourselves whether a particular performer is giving the proper interpretation to the role. Perhaps an actor is being too realistic in a nonrealistic role, or an actress is calling attention to herself and overplaying her part, thereby destroying the character's credibility. We can ask, too, how well the performers are playing with one another. Do they look at each other when they speak, and do they listen to the other actors and actresses and respond?

As we watch a play unfold, we can also take a moment to observe the visual elements. Do the costumes suit the play? Does the scenery make a statement of its own consistent with the theme and concept? Is the setting symbolic, and if so, what does it symbolize? Do the colors in the scenery convey a particular mood or feeling?

Though the elements of structure and viewpoint are not as visible as the acting or scenery, it is possible to pause during a performance and consider them as well. As events occur on stage, we can determine what structure is being developed and whether it is maintained. If the play is climactic in structure, we can ask if the events in the play are plausible and follow one another logically. If the play is absurdist, we can judge whether the actions, though illogical and seemingly crazy, nevertheless present a pattern which makes us aware of a method in the madness or of an underlying theme.

In looking at separate elements of theater in this fashion, we need not fear that we will lose sight of the whole. If we set our minds to it, our power to absorb and integrate data can pull the experience together for us. The more we become aware of distinct elements, the more we can fit them into the overall picture. In watching a nonrealistic comedy, for instance, we can observe how the acting underlines and points up the humor of the script; we can note how the costumes assist the performers in creating comic characters—perhaps with an exaggeration of style—and, at the same time, observe how the costumes present a visual image of their own, appropriately bright and lighthearted; we can observe, too, how lighting reinforces the comic spirit of the costumes and the performers. In short, we can see how the various aspects fuse and combine, how they heighten, underscore, and collaborate with one another to create the final experience.

The Overall Effect: What Does Theater "Mean"?

The overall effect of a play raises the question of what a play "means." In a discussion of a play we might hear someone ask: "But what does it mean?" The reply frequently is a catchphrase or a brief summary: "The meaning of this play is that love conquers all," or "he who hesitates is lost," or "all's well that ends well." Someone might say, for instance, that the meaning of Shakespeare's *Othello* is that people should not be too hasty to believe gossip and should trust those they love. Certainly one can conclude that *Othello* contains ideas which could be interpreted this way. But is this really what *Othello* means? Isn't this a simplistic and perhaps even erroneous idea of what *Othello* is about? Can we ever summarize the meaning of a play in one sentence?

There are two ways to look at meaning when we are discussing drama. Some plays specifically underscore a meaning in the text. They seem almost to have been written to point toward a moral or to teach a lesson. The title of Lillian Hellman's *The Little Foxes* comes from the Song of Solomon in the Bible; the verse reads, "Take us the foxes, the little foxes, that spoil the vines: for our vines have tender grapes." The idea of the quotation is that the foxes are evil because they spoil the vines and ravage and destroy the grapes. The title, therefore, introduces a theme of plunder and exploitation, and this theme is carried out in the action. At the close of the play the theme is summed up by a young woman, Alexandra, who has come to realize what has been happening in her family. Recognizing that her mother is one of the greediest and most cunning of the foxes, she confronts her with this newfound knowledge. Alexandra says to her mother: "Addie said there were people who ate the earth and other people who stood around and watched them do it. And just now Uncle Ben said the same thing. . . . Well, tell him for me, Mama, I'm not going to stand around and watch you do it. Tell him I'll be fighting as hard as he'll be fighting some place where people don't just stand around and watch."

In a case like *The Little Foxes* the author has invited us to find a "meaning" in the play which can be put in a few straightforward sentences. Most plays, however, (such as *A Streetcar Named Desire*) do not contain such direct statements of their meaning. Their substance resides, rather, in their total effect on the spectator. Even the relatively few plays like *The Little Foxes* which have clean-cut themes are far more complex than a few sentences suggest.

In the final analysis, a theater event does not mean; it *is*—its existence is its meaning. The writer Gertrude Stein (1879–1946) once said, "Rose is a rose is a rose is a rose." On the face of it, this seems to be a simple, repetitive statement; a reiteration of the obvious. As far as art is concerned, though, there is a great truth hidden in Stein's words. She is telling us that a rose is itself, not something else. In any other form it ceases to have its own existence and thus loses its unique quality. A poetic description, an oil painting, or a color photograph of a rose might have a certain beauty and give us a notion of a rose, but none of these can take the place of the real thing. A picture or a description can never duplicate the experience of seeing a real rose in a garden or in a vase of flowers. Only in its presence can we see the texture of the petals and smell the fragrance of the rose. If our direct experience of a rose is irreplaceable, how much more irreplaceable is our experience of a complex art like theater. The theater experience is the sum total of all the impressions we receive from a production.

The Modern Theater: Different Purposes, Different Experiences

Each theater event has its own meaning and impact, but in today's theater these vary widely from one event to another. The elements we have examined in the various sections of this book can be combined in so many different ways that the results offer a variety of experiences. The same play might be performed in one instance in an outdoor theater with realistic acting and in another instance in a small, indoor theater with nonrealistic acting. Conversely, the same space might serve two quite different productions: a bare stage with no scenery can be the setting for a stark tragedy or an intimate musical comedy. The combination of the play itself with the way it is presented will determine the final outcome.

As we have seen, in a given historical period or within a given society, the kinds of plays presented and the ways in which they were produced were frequently limited. During the past hundred years, however, there have been marked changes in society and in the theater, with an acceleration of these changes in the past quarter-century. In the post-World War II period, we began to see a rapid shift in moral and social mores. Long-held beliefs and customs—in dress and in attitudes toward women, minority groups, and the family—were challenged and changed.

This breakdown of traditional attitudes and customs, along with the introduction of new ideas, was reflected in the theater. No longer was the proscenium stage the chief architectural form for presentations. There was a proliferation of arena and thrust stages, and the use of found space was introduced. No longer, either, were the episodic and climactic forms of structure the only ones considered by playwrights and directors; the absurdist form emerged, as did multifocus, unstructured forms.

The result of these changes was a multiplicity of theater offerings. It is probably safe to say that never in any culture, at any time in history, has there been such a diversity of theater events available to the public as is available today to audiences in metropolitan centers throughout the western world. This same diversity also reaches into areas outside the major cities. The variety of theater productions makes it incumbent on spectators to be keenly aware of the separate elements we have discussed—audiences, performers, dramatic characters, structure, point of view, environment, and visual elements—and to understand what each contributes to the whole and how these elements work together.

Not only do conditions vary widely in today's theater, but the intentions of writers, directors, and producers vary too. Audience members should keep in mind when they attend the theater that different productions are presented for different purposes, as discussed in Chapter 4. Some plays— farces like *Charley's Aunt* or comedies like *The Odd Couple*—are intended to entertain us and make us laugh. The intention of serious dramas, on the other hand, like *King Oedipus* or *Long Day's Journey into Night,* is to make us feel deeply about the human condition and identify with the people who are suffering. Some plays are presented for the express purpose of giving us information about a person or an event; others are little concerned with facts—their purpose is to have us lose ourselves in the experience and let sounds and images wash over us without regard for literal truth. Some plays show us horror and violence, not to celebrate or exploit horror and violence, but to make us hate them so much that we will rebel against them and do everything in our power to prevent them in the future. This kind of theater hopes to shock us into recognition and awareness. Other types of

Plays serve different purposes.
Plays are intended for various purposes. Some are out-and-out farces, intended merely to entertain. Family dramas remind us of our own families or families we know. Tragedy, like *King Lear*, from which a scene is shown here, makes us feel deeply about the human condition and makes us think about the nature of people and identify with them.

theater—such as melodrama—show us horror and violence mainly for the thrill of it. Still other plays attempt to inspire us or raise our spirits.

Then, too, there are productions with combined aims: plays which entertain us but also raise serious questions or plays which make us laugh and weep at the same time—a phenomenon we encountered in examining tragicomedy.

In the end, we come to the fact that while there are common denominators in theater—the actor-audience encounter being chief among them—each theater experience is unique. It has its own combination of elements and its own particular aim or intention. In turn, audience members have their individual responses to each event. With so much variety in contemporary theater, we cannot expect every production to be equally satisfying to every spectator. What we can look forward to are many kinds of experiences in the theater, some of which bring us a sense of fun and some of which arouse in us thoughts and emotions we never knew were there.

BRINGING THE ELEMENTS TOGETHER

The Future: What Lies Ahead?

What of the future? Given the many facets of theater, what can we expect in the years ahead? For one thing, we can expect the variety to continue, with plays of all kinds presented under different conditions. But we might also find a consolidation of the forces that have been let loose in the theater in the past few decades. The joining of the old with the new, of free-form techniques with more traditional ones, can give the theater new strength. The vitality and energy unleashed in the breaking down of restrictive attitudes and forms, if integrated with time-honored truths about the human condition, can add further to the rich mixture already available in the contemporary theater.

When we go to the theater, we become part of a group with a common bond: an audience sharing an experience. In the exchange between performers and audience, we take part in a direct, human encounter. And from the stage, we hear the dark cry of the soul, we listen to the joyous laughter of the human spirit, and we witness the tragedies and triumphs of the human heart. As long as people wish to join together in a communion of the spirit or share with one another their anguish and suffering, the theater experience provides them with a unique way to do it.

SUMMARY

1 Ultimately, the goal in theater is to bring all the elements together to create one, integrated whole.

2 The way this process occurs can be illustrated by looking at the way a production has taken place, such as the original Broadway production of *A Streetcar Named Desire*.

3 The development of *A Streetcar Named Desire* began with the script by Tennessee Williams. A producer, Irene Selznick, agreed to mount a production. She chose Elia Kazan to direct the play, and he in turn selected the performers for the various roles. Designers were also chosen; designs were completed; rehearsals were held; and all production elements were brought together for the end result.

4 Theater is a gamble. The many steps leading to a production, and the great number of people involved in bringing it about, increase the chances for error along the way. Fortunately, we do not need perfection in a theater event for it to be meaningful; a small miscalculation or mistake will not necessarily mar the overall effect.

5 Human beings have an enormous capacity to absorb and integrate data. In the theater this allows us to take the images and stimuli we receive and merge them into a single experience. The ultimate integration of a theater event takes place in each spectator's mind.

6   While watching a theater event, we should be aware of the separate elements of a production and what each contributes to the whole. We must also note how they relate to one another and synthesize them in our minds.

7   "Meaning" in the theater is sometimes understood to consist of the ideas expressed in the text. Some plays stress this aspect of meaning by emphasizing lines which present the author's position; but in the final analysis, meaning is the sum total of the theater experience. It includes the emotional and sensory data as well as the intellectual content. Any attempt to summarize the meaning of a play in a few words, or to reduce it to a formula, robs it of its full meaning.

8   Each theater event forms a complete experience; but in today's theater, experiences can vary widely. Different kinds of theater buildings and environments, many performance styles, and variety in the plays themselves ensure a diversity of theater productions.

9   Because of its complexity, and because it is so people-centered, theater affords audience members a particularly rare experience—especially when the elements of a production come together successfully.

APPENDIXES

1
THEORIES OF TRAGEDY AND COMEDY

Hedda Gabler: A modern tragedy.
The following appendix gives a historical overview of the theories of tragedy and comedy. The discussion of tragedy begins with Aristotle's ideas about Greek tragedy. Ibsen's play, shown at the left, is the type of play described in the discussion as a "tragedy of the common man," or in this case, "the common woman." Theories of comedy are discussed in the second part of the appendix.

THEORIES OF TRAGEDY

From classical Greece to the present day, there has been a search for a definition of tragedy. One of the earliest and most influential definitions is found in Aristotle's *Poetics* (ca. 335 B.C.):

> Tragedy, then, is an imitation of an action that is serious, complete, and of certain magnitude; in language embellished with each kind of artistic ornament, the several kinds being found in separate parts of the play; in the form of action, not of narrative; through pity and fear effecting the proper purgation of these emotions.[1]

While there is no scholarly consensus on the meaning of Aristotle's definition, his description of classical Greek tragedy provides insight into the genre. Aristotle defined the tragic hero or heroine as one of noble birth, who is neither all good nor all bad, but who suffers a major reversal in fortune *(peripeteia)* because of a tragic flaw in character *(hamartia)*. The hero or heroine must learn from this downfall. Aristotle pointed out that the classical tragedies focused on one main action. He was later misinterpreted as requiring the unities of time, place, and action; but he had merely observed that classical tragedy "endeavors, as far as possible, to confine itself to a single revolution of the sun, or but to slightly exceed this limit" and had a single action. He never mentioned the unity of place.

Horace, whose *Art of Poetry* (24–20 B.C.) is the only complete piece of dramatic theory from the Roman period, prescribed rules for tragedy. He stressed consistency in character and the exclusion of comic relief. For Horace, the function of tragedy was to teach. He also dictated a five-act structure.

The Italian Renaissance critics devised rigid criteria for tragedy that were debated for centuries. Among these critics were Julius Caesar Scaliger (1484–1558) and Lodovico Castelvetro (1505–1571). For these men, tragedy dealt with individuals of high birth. Mixture of genres was forbidden. The unities of time (twenty-four hours), place, and action were inviolable. The tragic playwright, they indicated, should strive for an illusion of reality (verisimilitude). Tragedies were to be didactic.

In Elizabethan England, Sir Philip Sidney (1554–1586) in *The Defense of Poesy* (1583), supported the Italian neoclassical ideals. In Spain, Lope de Vega defended his breaking of the neoclassical rules for tragedy in his essay *The New Art of Writing Plays* (1609).

During the eighteenth century, there was a movement away from strict adherence to the Italian ideals. Dr. Samuel Johnson's *Preface to Shakespeare* (1765) is a defense of Shakespeare's tragic style. Gotthold Ephraim Lessing, in *Hamburg Dramaturgy,* suggested that the neoclassical critics had misinterpreted Aristotle. He also called for critical acceptance of domestic tragedy, which dealt with lower social classes. In the late eighteenth and nineteenth centuries, the German romantics, among whom were Johann Wolfgang von Goethe and Friedrich von Schiller, began writing tragedies that followed Shakespeare rather than the Greeks.

Throughout the nineteenth century, philosophers attempted to determine the relationship of tragedy to contemporary life. Samuel Taylor Coleridge, like most of the romantics, emphasized the need for tragedy to transcend mundane existence. Later, the naturalists, such as Emile Zola (1840–1902) suggested that tragedy should mirror daily life. Friedrich Nietzsche's essay *The Birth of Tragedy* (1871) was probably the most important theoretical essay of the century. For Nietzsche, a German philosopher, tragedy was born out of the fusion of the Dionysiac and the Apollonian, the primitive and the rational.

During the twentieth century, writers have incorporated discoveries about ritual and other past theatrical practices into theories of Greek and Elizabethan tragedy. Recent notions of the tragic universe suggest more comprehensive causes for the disorder reflected in these plays than a single factor such as the *tragic flaw.*

As for tragedy in the present day, the twentieth century has seen the breakdown of generic definitions and differentiations. Arthur Miller, in his essay "Tragedy and the Common Man," argues that "the common man is as apt a subject for tragedy in its highest sense as Kings were" because "the tragic feeling is evoked . . . when we are in the presence of a character who is ready to lay down his life . . . to secure . . . his sense of personal dignity."[2] Francis Ferguson, in *The Idea of a Theatre* (1949), argued that in tragedy the hero is committed to a *purpose,* that is, a goal which may lead to his or her destruction; that the purpose is carried out with *passion;* and that the quest results in a *perception* of the tragic actions. The critical disillusionment with definitions of genre is reflected in Georg Steiner's title *The Death of Tragedy* (1961). Similarly, the Swiss playwright Friedrich Duerrenmatt (*The Visit,* 1956) has suggested that tragedy may no longer be possible in the "Punch and Judy show of our century."

THEORIES OF COMEDY

If tragedy has proven to be difficult to define, comedy seems to have been even more problematic for theorists. In the seventeenth century, Dr. Samuel Johnson's bewilderment led him to exclaim that "comedy has been particularly impropitious to definers."

Aristotle's *Poetics* (ca. 335 B.C.) contains very few references to the lighter genre. According to the Greek philosopher, "comedy is an artistic imitation of men of an inferior moral bent; faulty, however, not in every way, but only insofar as their shortcomings are ludicrous." In comedy, he noted, these shortcomings cause no real pain or harm.

The Renaissance critics took a very rigid and academic approach in their attempts to define comedy. For these critics, comedy dealt with trifling matters. But, more important, they suggested that the comic genre dealt with characters of the lower social strata. Thus, class became a key factor in defining the genre. The use of class to define comedy was probably derived from the character types who roamed through Greek "new comedy" as well as from Horace's insistence that each genre observe consistency in character. The Roman critic stressed that the tragic character must be noble and the comic character foolish. (For a description of Greek and Roman "new comedy," see the entry *Comedy* in Appendix 3.)

Comedy of characters, developing out of the Renaissance commedia dell'arte, and comedy of manners flourished in the seventeenth and eighteenth centuries. The French playwright Molière believed that his audiences could learn from dramatizations of ridiculous universal types. The English Restoration playwrights focused primarily on comic sexuality and social pretensions; hence John Dryden emphasized that comedy should portray the eccentricity of character; William Congreve, the author of *The Way of the World* (1700), also subscribed to this theory of comedy.

In the nineteenth century, the social functions of comedy intrigued theorists. The English critic George Meredith, in *An Essay on Comedy* (1877), pointed to the corrective function of comedy. Comedy, he suggested, is "the fountain of sound sense" and the "ultimate civilizer." The French critic Henri Bergson, in *Laughter* (1900), viewed the basis of comedy as "something mechanical inlaid on the living."

In our century, some theorists have continued to search for definitions and explanations of the comic, among them the psychoanalyst Sigmund Freud who proposed that comedy is "the last laughter of childhood" and a means of releasing tensions. Most, however, seem to be in agreement with the Swiss playwright Friedrich Duerrenmatt's disregard for differentiation between the types. Tragicomedy and the theater of the absurd have proven how blurred the distinctions between genres have become. The absurdist playwright Eugene Ionesco went so far as to say: "I never have been able to understand the distinction between the comic and the tragic."

2
TECHNICAL TERMS

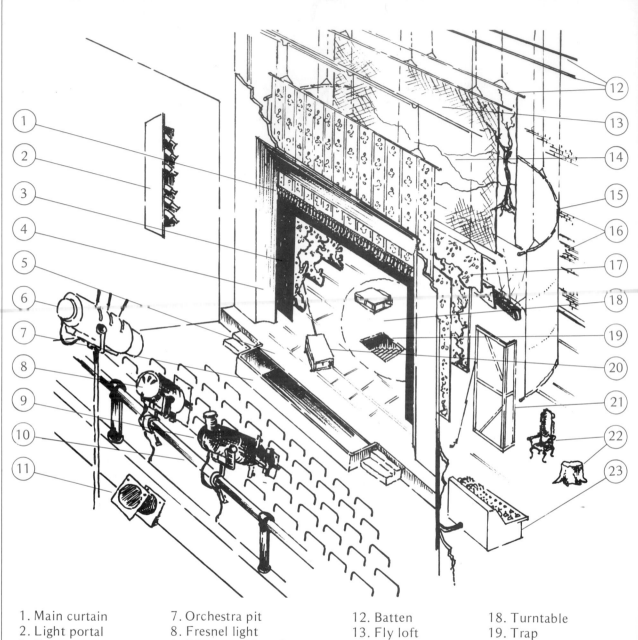

1. Main curtain
2. Light portal
3. False proscenium
4. Proscenium arch
5. Apron
6. Follow spot

7. Orchestra pit
8. Fresnel light
9. Ellipsoidal (leko) light
10. Balcony rail
11. Light gel

12. Batten
13. Fly loft
14. Scrim
15. Cyclorama
16. Backstage
17. Backdrop

18. Turntable
19. Trap
20. Platform
21. Flat
22. Props
23. Light dimmer board

2
TECHNICAL TERMS

Explaining theater terminology.
This drawing by the designer Harry Lines illustrates some of the specialized quipment and other stage elements used in theater production. A wide range of theater terms are described or defined in the appendix that follows.

Above   Upstage or away from the audience. A performer crossing *above* a table keeps it between himself or herself and the front of the stage.

Acting area   One of several areas into which the stage space is divided in order to facilitate blocking and the planning of stage movement.

Ad lib   To improvise lines of a speech, especially in response to an emergency, such as a performer's forgetting his or her lines.

Aesthetic distance   Physical or psychological separation or detachment of the audience from the dramatic action, regarded as necessary to maintain the artistic illusion in most kinds of theater.

Amphitheater   A large oval, circular, or semicircular outdoor theater with rising tiers of seats around an open playing area; an exceptionally large indoor auditorium.

Antagonist   The chief opponent of the protagonist in a drama. In some cases there may be several antagonists.

Apron   The stage space in front of the curtain line or proscenium; also called the *forestage*.

Arena   A type of stage which is surrounded by the audience on all four sides; also known as *theater-in-the-round*.

At rise   An expression used when describing what is happening onstage at the moment the curtain first rises or the lights come up at the beginning of the play.

Backdrop   A large drapery or painted canvas which provides the rear or upstage masking of a set.

Backstage   The stage area behind the front curtain; also, the areas beyond the setting, including wings and dressing rooms.

Basic situation   The specific problem or maladjustment from which the play arises; for example, Romeo and Juliet come from families with a strong mutual rivalry and antipathy.

Batten   A pipe or long pole suspended horizontally above the stage, upon which scenery, drapery, or lights may be hung.

Beam projector   A lighting instrument without a lens which uses a parabolic reflector to project a narrow, nonadjustable beam of light.

Below   Opposite of *above*; toward the front of the stage.

Blackout   To plunge the stage into total darkness by switching off the lights; also the condition produced by this operation.

Blocking   The arrangement of the actors' movements on stage with respect to each other and the stage space.

Book   (1) The spoken (as opposed to sung) portion of the text of a musical play. (2) To schedule engagements for artists or productions.

Border   A strip of drapery or painted canvas hung from a batten to mask the area above the stage; also, a row of lights hung from a batten.

Box set   An interior setting using flats to form the back and side walls and often the ceiling of a room.

Business   Obvious and detailed physical movement of actors to reveal character, aid action, or establish mood (e.g., pouring drinks at a bar, opening a gun case).

Catharsis   A Greek word, usually translated as "purgation," which Aristotle used in his definition of tragedy. It refers to the vicarious cleansing of certain emotions in the members of the audience through their representation on stage.

Catwalk   A narrow metal platform suspended above the stage to permit ready access to lights and scenery hung from the grid.

Center stage A stage position in the middle acting area of the stage or the middle section extended upstage and downstage.

Chorus In ancient Greek drama, a group of performers who sang and danced, sometimes participating in the action but usually simply commenting on it. Also, performers in a musical play who sing and dance as a group rather than individually.

Complication The introduction in a play of a new force which creates a new balance of power and makes a delay in reaching the climax necessary and progressive. It is one way of creating conflict and precipitating a crisis.

Conflict Tension between two or more characters that leads to crisis or a climax. The basic conflict is the fundamental struggle or imbalance underlying the play as a whole. May also be a conflict of ideologies, actions, etc.

Counterweight A device for balancing the weight of scenery in a system which allows scenery to be raised above the stage by means of ropes and pulleys.

Crew The backstage team assisting in mounting a production.

Cross A movement by a performer across the stage in a given direction.

Cue Any prearranged signal, such as the last words in a speech, a piece of business, or any action or lighting change that indicates to an actor or stage manager that it is time to proceed to the next line or action.

Cue sheet A prompt book marked with cues, or a list of cues for the use of technicians, especially the stage manager.

Curtain (1) The rise or fall of the physical curtain, which separates a play into structural parts. (2) The last bit of action preceding the fall of the curtain.

Cyclorama A large curved drop used to mask the rear and sides of the stage, painted a neutral color or blue to represent sky or open space. It may also be a permanent stage fixture made of plaster or similar durable material.

Denouement The moment when final suspense is satisfied and "the knot is untied." The term is from the French and was used to refer to the working out of the resolution in a well-made play.

Deus ex machina Literally "the god from the machine," a resolution device in classic Greek drama. A term used to indicate the intervention of supernatural forces—usually at the last moment—to save the action from its logical conclusion. Denotes in modern drama an arbitrary and coincidental solution.

Dimmer A device which permits lighting intensities to be changed smoothly and at varying rates.

Dim out To turn out the lights with a dimmer, the process usually being cued to a predetermined number of seconds or counts.

Director In American usage, the person who is responsible for the overall unity of the production of coordinating the efforts of the contributing artists. The director is in charge of rehearsals and supervises the performers in the preparation of their parts. The American director is the equivalent of the British producer and the French *metteur-en-scène*.

Downstage The front of the stage toward the audience.

Drop A large piece of fabric, generally painted canvas, hung from a batten to the stage floor, usually to serve as backing.

Ensemble playing Acting which stresses the total artistic unity of the performance rather than the individual performances of specific actors and actresses.

Entrance The manner and effectiveness with which a performer comes into a scene as well as the actual coming onstage; also, the way it is prepared for by the playwright.

Epilogue A speech addressed to the audience after the conclusion of the play and spoken by one of the performers.

Exit A performer's leaving the stage, as well as the preparation for his or her leaving.

Exposition The imparting of information necessary for an understanding of the story but not covered by the action on stage. Events or knowledge from the past, or occurring outside the play, which must be introduced for the audience to understand the characters or plot. Exposition is always a problem in drama because relating or conveying information is static. The dramatist must find ways to make expositional scenes dynamic.

Flat A single piece of scenery, usually of standard size and made of canvas stretched over a wooden frame, used with other similar units to create a set.

Flood A lighting instrument without lenses which is used for general or large-area lighting.

Fly loft or flies The space above the stage where scenery may be lifted out of sight by means of ropes and pulleys when it is not needed.

Follow spot A large, powerful spotlight with a sharp focus and narrow beam which is used to follow principal performers as they move about the stage.

Footlights A row of lights in the floor along the edge of the stage or apron; once a principal source of stage light, but now only rarely used.

Forestage See *Apron.*

Freeze To remain motionless on stage; especially for laughs.

Fresnel (fruh-NEL) A type of spotlight used over relatively short distances with a soft beam edge which allows the light to blend easily with light from other sources; also, the type of lenses used in such spotlights.

Front of the house The portion of the theater reserved for the audience, as opposed to the stage and backstage areas; sometimes simply referred to as the *house.*

Gauze See *Scrim.*

Gel A thin, flexible color medium used in lighting instruments to give color to a light beam. Properly speaking, the word applies only to such material made of gelatin, but it is often applied to similar sheets made of plastic.

Grid A metal framework above the stage from which lights and scenery are suspended.

Hand props Small props carried on or offstage by actors during the performance. See *Props.*

Inner stage An area at the rear of the stage which can be cut off from the rest by means of curtains or scenery and revealed for special scenes.

Irony A condition the reverse of what we have expected or an expression whose intended implication is the opposite of its literal sense. A device particularly suited to theater and found in virtually all drama.

Kill To eliminate or suppress, as to remove unwanted light or to ruin an effect through improper execution (e.g., to kill a laugh).

Left stage The left side of the stage from the point of view of a performer facing the audience.

Mask (1) To cut off from the view of the audience by means of scenery the backstage areas or technical equipment, as to mask a row of lighting instruments. (2) A face covering in the image of the character portrayed, sometimes covering the entire head.

Masking   Scenery or drapes used to hide or cover.

Mise-en-scène   The arrangement of all the elements in the stage picture, either at a given moment or dynamically throughout the performance.

Multiple setting   A form of stage setting, common in the Middle Ages, in which several locations are represented at the same time; also called *simultaneous setting*. Used also in various forms of contemporary theater.

Objective   Stanislavski's term for that which is urgently desired and sought by a character, the desired goal which propels a character to action.

Obstacle   That which delays or prevents the achieving of a goal by a character. An obstacle creates complication and conflict.

Offstage   The areas of the stage, usually in the wings or backstage, which are not in view of the audience.

Onstage   The area of the stage which is in view of the audience.

Open   To turn or face more toward the audience.

Orchestra   The ground-floor seating in an auditorium.

Pace   The rate at which a performance is played; also, to play a scene or an entire play in order to determine its proper speed.

Period   A term describing any representation on stage of a former age, as *period costume, period play.*

Platform   A raised surface on the stage floor serving as an elevation for parts of the stage action and allowing for a multiplicity of stage levels.

Platform stage   An elevated stage which does not make use of a proscenium.

Plot   As distinct from story, the patterned arrangements of events and characters for a drama. The incidents are selected and arranged for maximum dramatic impact. The plot may begin long after the beginning of the story (and refer to information regarding the past in flashbacks or exposition).

Point of attack   The moment in the story when the play actually begins. The dramatist chooses a point in time along the continuum of events which he or she judges will best start the action and propel it forward.

Preparation   The previous arranging of circumstances, pointing of character, and placing of properties in a production so that the ensuing actions will seem reasonable; also, the actions taken by a performer getting ready for a performance.

Producer   The person responsible for the business side of a production, including raising the necessary money. In British usage, a producer is the equivalent of an American director.

Prologue   An introductory speech delivered to the audience by one of the actors or actresses before the play begins.

Prompt   To furnish a performer with missed or forgotten lines or cues during a performance.

Prompt book   The script of a play indicating performers' movements, light cues, sound cues, etc.

Props   Properties; objects used by performers onstage or necessary to complete the set.

Proscenium   The arch or frame surrounding the stage opening in a box or picture stage.

Protagonist   The principle character in a play, the one whom the drama is about.

Rake   To position scenery on a slant or angle other than parallel or perpendicular to the curtain line; also, an upward slope of the stage floor away from the audience.

Raked stage   The stage which slopes upward away from the audience toward the back of the set.

Regional theater   (1) Theater whose subject matter is specific to a particular geographic region. (2) Theaters situated outside major theatrical centers.

Rehearsal   The preparation by the cast for the performance of a play through repetition and practice.

Repertory or repertoire   A kind of acting company which at any given time has a number of plays which it can perform alternately; also, a collection of plays.

Reversal   A sudden switch or reversal of circumstances or knowledge which leads to a result contrary to expectations. Called *peripeteia* or *peripety* in Greek drama.

Revolving stage   A large turntable on which scenery is placed in such a way that, as it moves, one set is brought into view while another one turns out of sight.

Right stage   The right side of the stage from the point of view of a performer facing the audience.

Scene   (1) A stage setting. (2) The structural units into which the plays or acts of the play are divided. (3) The location of the play's action.

Scrim   A thin, open-weave fabric which is nearly transparent when lit from behind and opaque when lit from the front.

Script   The written or printed text, consisting of dialogue, stage directions, character descriptions, and the like, of a play or other theatrical representation.

Set   The scenery, taken as whole, for a scene or an entire production.

Set piece   A piece of scenery which stands independently in the scene.

Slapstick   A type of comedy or comic business which relies on ridiculous physical activity—often violent in nature—for its humor.

Spill   Light from stage-lighting instruments which falls outside of the areas for which it is intended, such as light that falls on the audience.

Spine   In the Stanislavski method, the dominant desire or motivation of a character which underlies his or her action in the play; usually thought of as an action and expressed as a verb.

SRO   Standing room only. A notice that all seats for performance have been sold and only standees can be accommodated.

Stage door   An outside entrance to the dressing rooms and stage areas which is used by performers and technicians.

Stage convention   An understanding established through custom or usage that certain devices will be accepted or assigned specific meaning or significance on an arbitrary basis, that is, without requiring that they be natural or realistic.

Stage house   The stage floor and all the space above it up to the grid.

Stanislavski method   A set of techniques and theories about the problems of acting which promotes a naturalistic style stressing "inner truth" as opposed to conventional theatricality.

Strike   To remove pieces of scenery or props from onstage or to take down the entire set after the final performance.

Subtext   A term referring to the meaning and movement of the play below the surface; that which is implied and never stated. Often more important than surface activity.

Summer stock   Theater companies which operate outside of major theatrical centers during the summer months (usually June through August) and have an intensive production schedule, often doing a different play every week.

Teaser   A short horizontal curtain just beyond the proscenium used to mask the fly loft and effectively lowering the height of the proscenium.

Technical   A term referring to functions necessary to the production of a play other than those of the cast and the director, such as functions of the stage crew, carpenters, and lighting crew.

Theme   The central thought of the play. The idea or ideas with which the play deals and which it expounds.

Tragic flaw   The factor which is a character's chief weakness and which makes him or her most vulnerable; often intensifies in time of stress. An abused and often incorrectly applied theory from Greek drama.

Trap   An opening in the stage floor, normally covered, which can be used for special effects, such as having scenery or performers rise from below, or which permits the construction of a staircase which ostensibly leads to a lower floor or cellar.

Unities   A term referring to the preference that a play occur within one day (unity of time), in one place (unity of place), and with no action irrelevant to the plot (unity of action). *Note:* contrary to accepted opinion, Aristotle insisted only upon unity of action. Certain neoclassic critics of the Renaissance insisted on all three.

Unity   A requirement of art; an element often setting art apart from life. In drama, refers to unity of action achieved in a play's structure and story; the integrity and wholeness of a production which combine plot, character, and dialogue within a frame of time and space to present a congruous, complete picture.

Upstage   At or toward the back of the stage, away from the front edge of the stage. (The word dates from the time when the stage sloped upward from the footlights.)

Wagon stage   A low platform mounted on wheels or casters by means of which scenery is moved on and offstage.

Wings   Left and right offstage areas; also, narrow standing pieces of scenery, or "legs," more or less parallel to the proscenium, which form the sides of a setting.

Work lights   Lights arranged for the convenience of stage technicians, situated either in backstage areas and shaded or over the stage area for use while the curtain is down.

3

MAJOR THEATRICAL FORMS AND MOVEMENTS

(New York Public Library at Lincoln Center; Astor, Lenox and Tilden Foundations. Vandamm)

Expressionism in the theater.
One of the many forms and movements in theater described in this appendix is expressionism. An illustration of scenery used in an expressionist play is Lee Simonson's design, shown here, for *The Adding Machine* by Elmer Rice. Note that the windows, the judge's stand, and the rails are built at an angle, indicating a world off balance.

Absurdism See *Theater of the absurd.*

Allegory The representation of an abstract theme or themes through the symbolic use of character, action, and other concrete elements of a play. In its most direct form—as, for example, the medieval morality play—allegory uses the device of personification to present characters representing abstract qualities, such as virtues and vices, in an action which spells out a moral or intellectual lesson. Less direct forms of allegory may use a relatively realistic story as a guise for a hidden theme. For example, Arthur Miller's *The Crucible* can be regarded as an allegory of the McCarthy congressional investigation in the United States after World War II.

Avant-garde A French term that literally means the "advance guard" in a military formation. It has come to stand for an intellectual, literary, or artistic movement in any age that breaks with tradition and appears to be ahead of its time. Avant-garde works are usually experimental and unorthodox. In twentieth-century theater, such movements as expressionism, surrealism, absurdism, and the theories of Antonin Artaud and Jerzy Grotowski have been considered avant-garde.

Burlesque A ludicrous imitation of a dramatic form or a specific play. Closely related to satire, it usually lacks the moral or intellectual purposes of reform typical of the latter, being content to mock the excesses of other works. Famous examples of burlesque include Beaumont's *The Knight of the Burning Pestle* and, more recently, such burlesques of the movies as *Dames at Sea*. In the United States the term has come to be associated with a form of variety show which stresses sex.

Comedy As one of the oldest enduring categories of Western drama, comedy has gathered under its heading a large number of different subclassifications. Although the range of comedy is broad, generally it can be said to be a play that is light in tone, is concerned with issues tending not to be serious, has a happy ending, and is designed to amuse and provoke laughter. Historically, comedy has gone through many changes. Aristophanic or Greek "old comedy" was farcical, satiric, and nonrealistic. Greek and Roman "new comedy," based on domestic situations, was more influential in the development of comedy during the Renaissance. Ben Jonson built his "comedies of humors" on Roman models. In Jonson's plays, ridicule is directed at characters who are dominated to the point of obsession by a single trait, or humor. The comedy of manners became popular in the late seventeenth century with the advent of Molière and the writers of the English Restoration. It tends to favor a cultivated or sophisticated milieu, witty dialogue, and characters whose concern with social polish is charming, ludicrous, or both. The twentieth century has seen an expansion in the territory covered by comedy as well as a blurring of its boundaries. In the final decades of the nineteenth century, George Bernard Shaw used it for the serious discussion of ideas, while Chekhov wrote plays variously interpreted as sentimental and tragicomic. Since then the horizon of the comic has been expanded by playwrights such as Pirandello and Ionesco, whose comic vision is more serious, thoughtful, and disturbing than that found in most traditional comedies.

Commedia dell'arte A form of comic theater which originated in Italy in the sixteenth century, in which dialogue was improvised around a loose scenario calling for a set of stock characters, each with a distinctive costume and traditional name. The best known of these characters are probably the *zannis*, buffoons who usually took the roles of servants and who had at their disposal a large number of slapstick routines, called *lazzis*, which ranged from simple grimaces to acrobatic stunts.

Documentary See *Theater of fact.*

Domestic drama Also known as *bourgeois drama,* domestic drama deals with problems of members of the middle and lower classes, particularly problems of the family and home. Conflicts with society, struggles within a family, dashed hopes and renewed determination are frequently characteristics of domestic drama. It attempts to depict on stage the lifestyle of ordinary people—in language, in dress, in behavior. Domestic drama first came to the fore during the eighteenth century in Europe and Great Britain when the merchant and working classes were emerging. Because general audiences could so readily identify with the people and problems of domestic drama, it continued to gain in popularity during the nineteenth and twentieth centuries and remains a major form today.

Environmental theater A term used by Richard Schechner and others to refer to a branch of the avant-garde theater. Among its aims are the elimination of the distinction between audience space and acting space, a more flexible approach to the interactions between performers and audience, and the substitution of a multiple focus for the traditional single focus.

Epic theater A form of presentation which has come to be associated with the name of Bertolt Brecht, its chief advocate and theorist. It is aimed at the intellect rather than the emotions, seeking to present evidence regarding social questions in such a way that they may be objectively considered and an intelligent conclusion reached. Brecht felt that emotional involvement by the audience defeated this aim, and he used various devices designed to produce an emotional "alienation" of the audience from the action on stage. His plays are episodic, with narrative songs separating the segments and large posters or signs announcing the various scenes.

Existentialism A set of philosophical ideas whose principal modern advocate is Jean-Paul Sartre. The term *existentialist* is applied to plays by Sartre and others which illustrate these views. Sartre's central thesis is that there are no longer any fixed standards or values by which one can live and that each individual must create his or her own code of conduct regardless of the conventions imposed by society. Only in this way can one truly "exist" as a responsible, creative human being; otherwise one is merely a robot or automaton. Sartre's plays typically involve people who are faced with decisions forcing them into an awareness of the choice between living on their own terms and ceasing to exist as individuals.

Expressionism A movement which developed and flourished in Germany during the period immediately preceding and following World War I. Expressionism in the drama was characterized by the attempt to dramatize subjective states through the use of distortion, striking and often grotesque images, and lyric, unrealistic dialogue. It was revolutionary in content as well as in form, portraying the institutions of society, particularly the bourgeois family, as grotesque, oppressive, and materialistic. The expressionist hero or heroine was usually a rebel against this mechanistic vision of society. Dramatic conflict tended to be replaced by the development of themes by means of visual images. The movement had great influence because it forcefully demonstrated that dramatic imagination need not be limited to either theatrical conventions or the faithful reproduction of reality. In the United States, expressionism influenced Elmer Rice's *The Adding Machine* and many of O'Neill's early plays. The basic aim of expressionism was to give external expression to inner feelings and ideas; theatrical techniques which adopt this method are frequently referred to as *expressionistic.*

Farce One of the major genres of drama, sometimes regarded as a subclassification of comedy. Farce has few, if any, intellectual pretensions. It aims to entertain, to provoke laughter. Its humor is the result primarily of physical activity and visual effects, and it relies less on language and wit than do so-called higher forms of comedy. Violence, rapid movement, and accelerating pace are characteristic of farce. In bedroom farce it is the institution of marriage that is the object of the fun, but medicine, law, and business also provide material for farce.

Happenings A form of theatrical event which was developed out of the experimentation of certain American abstract artists in the 1960s. Happenings are nonliterary, replacing the script with a scenario which provides for chance occurrences. They are performed (often only once) in such places as parks and street corners, with little attempt being made to segregate the action from the audience. Emphasizing the free association of sound and movement, they avoid logical action and rational meaning.

Heroic drama A form of serious drama, written in verse or elevated prose, which features noble or heroic characters caught in extreme situations or undertaking unusual adventures. In spite of the hardships to which its leading figures are subjected, heroic drama—unlike tragedy—assumes a basically optimistic world view. It either has a happy ending or, in cases where the hero or heroine dies, a triumphant one in which the death is not regarded tragically. Plays from all periods, and from Asia as well as the west, fall in this category. During the late seventeenth century in England, plays of this type were referred to specifically as *heroic tragedies.*

History play In the broadest sense, a play set in a historical milieu which deals with historical personages, but the term is usually applied only to plays which deal with vital issues of public welfare and are nationalistic in tone. The form originated in Elizabethan England, which produced more history plays than any comparable place and time. Based on a religious concept of history, they were influenced by the structure of the morality play. Shakespeare was the major writer of Elizabethan history plays. His style has influenced many later history plays, notably those by the Swedish playwright Strindberg.

Impressionism A style of painting developed in the late nineteenth century which stressed the immediate impressions created by objects—particularly those resulting from the effects of light—and which tended to ignore details. As such its influence on the theater was primarily in the area of scenic design, but the term *impressionistic* is sometimes applied to plays like Chekhov's, which rely on a series of impressions and use indirect techniques.

Kabuki The most eclectic and theatrical of the major forms of Japanese theater. It is a more popular form than the aristocratic Noh drama and uses live actors, unlike the puppet theater, or Bunraku. Nevertheless, it has borrowed freely from both of these forms, particularly the Bunraku. Roles of both sexes are performed by men in a highly theatrical, nonrealistic style. Kabuki combines music, dance, and dramatic scenes with an emphasis on color and movement. The plays are long and episodic, composed of a series of loosely connected dramatic scenes which are often performed separately.

Masque A lavish and spectacular form of private theatrical entertainment which developed in Renaissance Italy and spread rapidly to the courts of France and England. Usually intended for a single performance, the masque combined poetry, music, elaborate costumes, and spectacular effects of stage machinery. It was a social event which had members of the court acting as both spectators and performers. Loosely constructed, masques were usually written around allegorical or mythological themes.

Medieval drama   There is only meager evidence of theatrical activity in Europe between the sixth and tenth centuries, but by the end of the fifteenth century a number of different types of drama had developed. The first of these, known as *liturgical drama,* was sung or chanted in Latin as part of a church service. Plays on religious themes were also written in the vernacular and performed outside of the church. The *mystery plays* (also called *cycle plays*) were based on events taken from the Old and New Testaments. Many such plays were organized into historical cycles which told the story of humanity from the creation to doomsday. The entire performance was quite long, sometimes requiring as much as five days. The plays were produced as a community effort, with different craft guilds usually being responsible for individual segments. Other forms of religious drama were the *miracle play*—which dealt with events in the life of a saint—and the *morality play.* The morality play was a didactic and allegorical treatment of moral and religious questions, the most famous example being *Everyman.* The medieval period also produced several types of secular plays. Other than the *folk plays,* which dealt with legendary heroes like Robin Hood, most were farcical and fairly short.

Melodrama   Historically, a distinct form of drama popular throughout the nineteenth century which emphasized action and spectacular effects and employed music to heighten the dramatic mood. Melodrama employed stock characters and clearly defined villains and heroes. More generally, the term is applied to any dramatic play which presents an unambiguous confrontation between good and evil. Characterization is often shallow and stereotypical, and because the moral conflict is externalized, action and violence are prominent in melodrama, usually culminating in a happy ending meant to demonstrate the eventual triumph of good.

Mime   A performance in which the action or story is conveyed through the use of movements and gestures without words. It depends on the performer's ability to suggest or create his or her surroundings through physical reactions to them and the expressiveness of the entire body.

Musical theater   A broad category which includes opera, operetta, musical comedy, and other musical plays (the term *lyric theater* is sometimes used to distinguish it from pure dance). It includes any dramatic entertainment in which music and lyrics (and sometimes dance) form an integral and necessary part. The various types of musical theater often overlap and are best distinguished in terms of their separate historical origins, the quality of the music, and the range and type of skills demanded of the performance. Opera is usually defined as a work in which all parts are sung to musical accompaniment. Such works are part of a separate and much older tradition than the modern musical, which is of relatively recent American origin. The term *musical comedy* is no longer adequate to describe all the musical dramas commonly seen on and off Broadway, but they clearly belong together as part of a tradition that can easily be distinguished from both opera and operetta.

Naturalism   A special form of realism. The theory of naturalism came to prominence in France and other parts of Europe in the latter half of the nineteenth century. The French playwright Emile Zola advocated a theater that would follow the scientific principles of the age, especially those discovered by Charles Darwin.

Zola was also impressed by the work of Auguste Comte (1778–1857) and a physician named Claude Bernard (1813–1878). According to Zola's theory of naturalism, drama should look for the causes of disease in society the way a doctor looks for disease in a patient. Theater should therefore expose social infection in all its ugliness. Following Darwin, theater should show human beings as products of heredity and environment. The result would be a drama often depicting the ugly underside of life and expressing a pessimistic point of view. Also, drama was not to be carefully plotted or constructed but was to present a "slice of life": an attempt to look at life as it is. Very few successful plays fulfilled Zola's demands. Some of the works of Strindberg, Gorki, and others came closest to meeting the requirements of naturalism. In the contemporary period the term *naturalism* is generally applied to dramas that are superrealistic, that is, those that conform to observable reality in precise detail. Naturalism attempts to achieve the verisimilitude of a documentary film, to convey the impression that everything about the play—the setting, the way the characters dress, speak, and act—is exactly like everyday life.

New theater   Sometimes used interchangeably with the term *new stagecraft* in the first half of this century. Both expressions referred to a movement, primarily affecting the visual aspects of theater, which was pioneered largely by Gordon Craig and included such adherents as Robert Edmond Jones, Norman Bel Geddes, and Lee Simonson. The emphasis was on the creative and evocative use of light, color, and form rather than strict realistic representation. Many of their innovations have become standard practice in the theater today. (See also *Avant-garde*.)

Noh   (also spelled Nō) A rigidly traditional form of Japanese drama which in its present form dates back to the fourteenth century. Noh plays are short dramas combining music, dance, and lyric with a highly stylized and ritualistic presentation. Virtually every aspect of the production—including costumes, masks, and a highly symbolic setting—is prescribed by tradition.

Pantomime   Originally a Roman entertainment in which a narrative was sung by a chorus while the story was acted out by dancers. Now used loosely to cover any form of presentation which relies on dance, gesture, and physical movement. (See *Mime*.)

Play of ideas   A play whose principal focus is on the serious treatment of social, moral, or philosophical ideas. The term *problem play* is used to designate those dramas, best exemplified in the work of Ibsen and Shaw, in which several sides of a question are both dramatized and discussed. It is sometimes distinguished from the *pièce à thèse,* or thesis play, which makes a more one-sided presentation and employs a character who sums up the "lesson" of the play and serves as the author's voice.

Poor theater   A term coined by Jerzy Grotowski to describe his ideal of theater stripped to its barest essentials. The lavish sets, lights, and costumes usually associated with the theater, he feels, merely reflect base materialistic values and must be eliminated. If theater is to become rich spiritually and aesthetically, it must first be "poor" in everything that can detract from the performer's relationship with the audience.

Realism   Broadly speaking, realism is the attempt to present on stage people and events corresponding to those observable in everyday life. Examples of realism can be found in western drama—especially in comedies—in the Greek, Roman, medieval, and Renaissance periods. Sections of plays from these periods show people speaking, dressing, and acting in the manner of ordinary people of time. Certain landmark plays are considered forerunners of modern realism. These include *Arden of Feversham* (ca. 1590), an English play about greed and lust in a middle-class family; *The London Merchant* (1731), about a young apprentice led astray by a prostitute; *Miss Sara Sampson* (1755), a German version of *The London Merchant;* and *The Inspector General* (1836), exposing corruption in a provincial Russian town. It was in the latter part of the nineteenth century, however, that realism took hold as a major form of theater. As the middle class came more and more to dominate life in Europe and the United States, and as scientific and psychological discoveries challenged the heroic or romantic viewpoint, drama began to center on the affairs of ordinary people in their natural surroundings. The plays of Ibsen, Strindberg, and Chekhov showed that powerful, effective drama could be written about such people. The degree of realism varies in drama, ranging from *slice-of-life naturalism* to *heightened realism*. In the latter, nonrealistic and symbolic elements are introduced into a basically realistic format. Despite frequent challenges from other forms during the past hundred years, realism remains a major form of contemporary theater. (See also *Naturalism*.)

Restoration drama   English drama after the restoration of the monarchy, from 1660 to 1700. Presented for an audience of aristocrats who gathered about the court of Charles II, drama of this period consisted largely of heroic tragedies in the neoclassical style and comedies of manners which reflected a cynical view of human nature.

Romanticism   A literary and dramatic movement of the nineteenth century which developed as a reaction to the confining strictures of neoclassicism. Imitating the loose, episodic structure of Shakespeare's plays, the romantics sought to free the writer from all rules and looked to the unfettered inspiration of artistic genius as the source of all creativity. They laid more stress on mood and atmosphere than on content, but one of their favorite themes was the gulf between human beings' spiritual aspirations and their physical limitations.

Satire   Dramatic satire uses the techniques of comedy, such as wit, irony, and exaggeration, to attack and expose folly and vice. Satire can attack specific public figures, as does the political satire *Macbird,* or it can point its barbs at more general traits which can be found in many of us. Thus Molière's *Tartuffe* ridicules religious hypocrisy, Shaw's *Arms and the Man* exposes the romantic glorification of war, and Wilde's *The Importance of Being Earnest* attacks the English upper classes.

Street theater   A generic term which includes a number of groups that perform in the open and attempt to relate to the needs of a specific community or neighborhood. Many such groups sprang up in the 1960s, partly as a response to social unrest and partly because there was a need for a theater which could express the specific concerns of minority and ethnic neighborhoods.

Surrealism   A movement attacking formalism in the arts which developed in Europe after World War I. Seeking a deeper and more profound reality than that presented to the rational, conscious mind, the surrealists replaced realistic action with the strange logic of the dream and cultivated such techniques as automatic writing and free association of ideas. Although few plays written by the surrealists are highly regarded, the movement had a great influence on later avant-garde theater—notably the theater of the absurd and the theater of cruelty.

Symbolism   Closely linked to symbolist poetry, symbolist drama was a movement of the late nineteenth and early twentieth centuries which sought to replace realistic representation of life with the expression of an inner truth. Hoping to restore the religious and spiritual significance of theater, symbolism used myth, legend, and symbols in an attempt to reach beyond everyday reality. The plays of Maurice Maeterlinck (1862–1949) are among the best-known symbolist dramas.

Theater of cruelty Anton Artaud's visionary concept of a theater based on magic and ritual which would liberate deep, violent, and erotic impulses. He wished to reveal the cruelty which he saw as existing beneath all human action—the pervasiveness of evil and violent sexuality. To do this, he advocated radical changes in the use of theatrical space, the integration of audience and actors, and the full utilization of the affective power of light, color, movement, and language. Although Artaud had little success implementing his theories himself, he had considerable influence on other writers and directors, particularly Peter Brook, Jean-Louis Barrault, and Jerzy Grotowski.

Theater of fact A term which encompasses a number of different types of documentary drama which have developed during the twentieth century. Methods of presentation differ. The Living Newspaper drama of the 1930s used signs and slide projections to deal with broad social problems; other documentary dramas use a more realistic approach. Contemporary theater of fact, as represented by such plays as *The Deputy* and *The Investigation,* tries to portray actual events with an appearance of authenticity.

Theater of the absurd A phrase first used by Martin Esslin to describe certain playwrights of the 1950s and 1960s who expressed a similar point of view regarding the absurdity of the human condition. Their plays are dramatizations of the dramatist's inner sense of the absurdity and futility of existence. Rational language is debased and replaced by clichés and trite or irrelevant remarks. Repetitious or meaningless activity is substituted for logical action. Realistic psychological motivation is replaced by automatic behavior which is often absurdly inappropriate to the situation. Although the subject matter is serious, the tone of these plays is usually comic and ironic. Among the best-known absurdists are Beckett, Ionesco, and Albee.

Theatricalism A style of production and playwriting which emphasizes theatricality for its own sake. Less a coherent movement than a quality found in the work of many artists rebelling against realism, it frankly admits the artifice of the stage and borrows freely from the circus, the music hall, and similar entertainments.

Tragedy One of the most fundamental dramatic forms in the western tradition, tragedy involves a serious action of universal significance and has important moral and philosophical implications. Following Aristotle, most critics agree that the tragic hero or heroine should be an essentially admirable person whose downfall elicits our sympathy while leaving us with a feeling that there has in some way been a triumph of the moral and cosmic order which transcends the fate of any individual. The disastrous outcome of a tragedy should be seen as the inevitable result of the character and his or her situation, including forces beyond the character's control. Traditionally tragedy was about the lives and fortunes of kings and nobles, and there has been a great deal of debate about whether it is possible to have a modern tragedy—a tragedy about ordinary people. The answers to this question are as varied as the critics who address themselves to it; but most seem to agree that though such plays may be tragedies, they are of a somewhat different order.

Tragicomedy   During the Renaissance the word was used for plays that had tragic themes and noble characters yet ended happily. Modern tragicomedy combines serious and comic elements. Tragicomedy is, in fact, increasingly the form chosen by "serious" playwrights. Sometimes comic behavior and situations have serious or tragic consequences—as in Duerrenmatt's *The Visit*. At times the ending is indeterminate or ambivalent—as in Beckett's *Waiting for Godot*. In most cases a quality of despair or hopelessness is introduced because human beings are seen as incapable of rising above their circumstances or their own nature; the fact that the situation is also ridiculous serves to make their plight that much more horrible.

Well-made play   A type of play popular in the nineteenth and early twentieth centuries which combined apparent plausibility of incident and surface realism with a tightly constructed and contrived plot. Well-made plays typically revolved about the question of social respectability, and the plot often hinged on the manipulation of a piece of incriminating evidence which threatened to destroy the facade of respectability. Although the well-made play is less popular now, many of its techniques continue to be used by modern playwrights.

4

HISTORICAL OUTLINE

An eighteenth-century comedy.
In the following appendix the history of theater is traced in a clear, concise time line, with theater events in one column and events in politics, science, and related arts in another column. For example, the comedy shown here, Oliver Goldsmith's *She Stoops to Conquer*, was written in 1773; and in the time line we see that at the same period the English painter Thomas Gainsborough was active and the American Revolution was about to take place.

(Illinois State University)

THE ANCIENT WORLD

THEATER		SOCIETY, POLITICS, CULTURE
EGYPT		
	ca. 3100 B.C.	Old Kingdom (ca. 3100–2185 B.C.)
Ritual drama	ca. 2750 B.C.	
Abydos Passion Play (ca. 2500–550 B.C.)	ca. 2500 B.C.	
	2133 B.C.	Middle Kingdom (2133–1786 B.C.)
	1580 B.C.	New Kingdom (ca. 1580–1085 B.C.)
GREECE		
	ca. 800 B.C.	Homer
	ca. 585 B.C.	Thales of Miletus begins natural philosophy (physics)
Play contests begun in Athens	534 B.C.	
Thespis "first actor" fl.	ca. 530 B.C.	
	ca. 520 B.C.	Pythagoras fl.
	510 B.C.	Democracy in Athens
	499 B.C.	Persian wars (499–478 B.C.)
	490 B.C.	Battle of Marathon
Comedy introduced to City Dionysia	487 B.C.	
Aeschylus introduces second actor	ca. 471 B.C.	
Sophocles introduces third actor	ca. 468 B.C	
	ca. 460 B.C.	Periclean Athens—"golden age" (ca. 460–429 B.C.)
Oresteia, Aeschylus (525–456 B.C.)	458 B.C.	Socrates (469–399 B.C.)
Prizes for tragic acting awarded	449 B.C.	
	447 B.C.	Beginning of Parthenon; Herodotus flourishes
Oedipus the King, Sophocles (496–406 B.C.)	ca. 430 B.C.	Peloponnesian War (431–404 B.C.)
The Trojan Women, Euripides (480–406 B.C.)	415 B.C.	Plato (429–348 B.C.)

Note ca. means "circa," or approximately the date at which the event took place; fl. means "flourished" at the time; r. means "reigned."

THEATER			SOCIETY, POLITICS, CULTURE
Lysistrata, Aristophanes (448–380 B.C.)		411 B.C.	
		399 B.C.	Trial and execution of Socrates
		384 B.C.	Aristotle born
		371 B.C.	Theban hegemony (371–362 B.C.)
Poetics (ca. 335–323 B.C.), Aristotle (384–322 B.C.)		335 B.C.	Alexander the Great (356–323 B.C.) occupies Greece
Theater of Dionysus completed	ca.	325 B.C.	
Greek theaters built throughout Mediterranean area (ca. 320–ca. 100 B.C.)	ca.	320 B.C.	Hellenistic culture spreads throughout eastern Mediterranean
Menander (343–291 B.C.) writer of *new comedy*			
Menander's *Dyskolos*		316 B.C.	
Artists of Dionysus recognized		277 B.C.	

		ROME	
		753 B.C.	Traditional date for the founding of Rome
		264 B.C.	First Punic War (264–241 B.C.) Greek influence on Roman culture
Roman farce comedy begins			
Regular comedy and tragedy added to Ludi Romani		240 B.C.	
		218 B.C.	Second Punic War (218–201 B.C.)
Menaechmi (ca. 205–184 B.C.) Plautus (ca. 254–184 B.C.)		205 B.C.	
Phormio, Terence (ca. 190–159 B.C.)		161 B.C.	
		147 B.C.	Rome annexes Macedonia
		144 B.C.	First high level aqueduct in Rome
Vitruvius' *De Architectura*		90 B.C.	
First permanent theater in Rome		55 B.C.	Golden age of Roman literature: Catullus, Cicero, Vergil, Ovid (83 B.C.–A.D. 14)
		44 B.C.	Assassination of Julius Caesar
Horace's *Art of Poetry*		24 B.C.	
Seneca (ca. 4 B.C.–65 A.D.) writes tragedies		27 B.C.	Emperor Augustus Caesar begins reign; rules until A.D. 14

THEATER		SOCIETY, POLITICS, CULTURE
Roman theater and amphitheaters built in first and second centuries	ca. A.D. 30	Crucifixion of Jesus
	A.D. 161	Marcus Aurelius rules until A.D. 180
Theater from first through fourth century is mostly mime, pantomime, and spectacle	A.D. 250	Persecution of Christians builds for next fifty years
	324	Emperor Constantine rules until 337
Strong church opposition to theater		St. Augustine (354–430) St. Jerome (ca. 340–420)
Council of Carthage decrees excommunication for those who attend theater rather than church on holy days, actors forbidden sacraments	398	
	410	Sack of Rome
	476	Collapse of Western Roman Empire

Note For almost a thousand years—from the first through the tenth century—there was little formal theater in western civilization. We must skip from Rome at the beginning of the Christian era to the Middle Ages to find significant information concerning theater.

MIDDLE AGES

THEATER		SOCIETY, POLITICS, CULTURE
Traveling performers (500–925)	500	
	527	Justinian becomes Byzantine emperor
	570	Mohammed born
	800	Charlemagne crowned emperor of Holy Roman Empire
Quem Quaeritis trope (introduction of choral dialogue into church service)	ca. 925	
Hrosvitha, a nun, writes Christian comedies based on Terence	ca. 970	
(Liturgical drama in Latin, tenth century and later)	1066	Normans conquer England
	1095	First Crusade (until 1096)
Play of Adam, oldest known scriptural drama in the vernacular	ca. 1140	(earliest manufacture of paper in Europe)
(Drama moves out of the church)	1215	Magna Carta
Festival of Corpus Christi established	1264	Roger Bacon (1214–1294) Thomas Aquinas (d. 1274)

THEATER		SOCIETY, POLITICS, CULTURE
The Play of the Bower, beginning of secular drama in France	ca. 1276	Giotto (ca. 1266–1337), Italian painter
	ca. 1310	*The Divine Comedy,* Dante Alighieri (1265–1321)
	1338	Hundred Years' War between England and France (until 1456)
		Petrarch (1304–1374)
Vernacular religious drama flourishes; Peak of medieval theater (1350–1550)	1350	
	1353	*Decameron,* Giovanni Boccaccio (1313–1375)
Second Shepherds Play, one of a series of *cycle* plays based on Bible	ca. 1375	Geoffrey Chaucer (ca. 1342–1400)
	1378	Urban VI in Rome; Clement VII at Avignon
The Castle of Perseverence	ca. 1425	
	1431	Joan of Arc burned at the stake
	ca. 1450	Guttenberg, invention of movable type
	1453	Constantinople falls to the Turks

RENAISSANCE TO 1700

THEATER		SOCIETY, POLITICS, CULTURE
	1396	Manuel Chrysoloras opens Greek classes in Florence; beginning of revival of Greek literature in Italy
Twelve of Plautus' lost plays rediscovered	1429	
	1434	Cosimo de Medici rules Florence
	1440	Founding of Platonic Academy in Florence
	1452	Leonardo da Vinci born
	1455	Wars of the Roses in England (until 1485)
Pierre Pathelin, one of many popular farces in France	ca. 1464	
	1469	Spain united under Isabella and Ferdinand
(Plays in Latin, modeled on Roman drama, written in the academies of Italy)	1478	Lorenzo de Medici controls Florence (until 1492)
		Inquisition established in Spain

THEATER		SOCIETY, POLITICS, CULTURE
(First professional acting companies in Spain; beginnings of secular drama)	ca. 1480	
	1484	*Birth of Venus,* by Sandro Botticelli (1446–1510), Italy
Vitruvius' *De Architectura* published	1486	
	1492	Expulsion of the Jews from Spain; Columbus discovers America; conquest of Granada
(Growth of professional acting troupes)		
	1494	The Italian wars weaken Italy politically but spread its cultural influence
Plays by Aristophanes published by Aldine Press in Venice	1498	
Everyman, morality play	1500	
	1504	*David,* Michelangelo (1474–1564), Italy
	1505	*Mona Lisa,* Leonardo da Vinci (1452–1519), Italy
I Suppositi, Lodovico Ariosto (1474–1533), Italian vernacular comedy based on Plautus and Terence	1509	Henry VIII of England (r. 1509–1547)
(Interest in classical drama in schools and universities in England)		
Mandragola, Niccolò Machiavelli (1469–1527), Italy	ca. 1512	Sistine Chapel ceiling, Michelangelo (1508–1512)
Sofonisba, Giangiorgio Trissino (1478–1550), Italian tragedy based on classic models	1513	*The Prince,* Machiavelli, Italy
	1515	Francis I of France (r. 1515–1547)
	1516	*Utopia,* Thomas More (1428–1535), England
	1517	Martin Luther (1483–1546) posts theses, Germany
Confrérie de la Passion given theatrical monopoly in Paris	1518	
	1519	Hernán Cortés (1485–1547) conquers Aztecs for Spain
	1530	Francisco Pizarro (ca. 1475–1541) takes Peru

THEATER		SOCIETY, POLITICS, CULTURE
	1532	*Pantagruel,* François Rabelais (1494–1553), France
	1534	Act of Supremacy begins English Reformation
Ralph Roister Doister, English, "school drama"	1540	
Serlio's *Architettura* describes scene design and stage effects	1545	
Lope de Rueda (ca. 1510–1565), first important popular dramatist in Spain		
Religious plays prohibited in France; Hôtel de Bourgogne opens; perspective scenery used for first time at Lyon for performance celebrating marriage of Henri II and Catherine de Medicis	1548	
Peak of Commedia dell'arte (1550–1650)	1550	
Grammer Gurton's Needle, English, "school drama"	ca. 1552	
	1556	Philip II of Spain (r. 1556–1598)
	1558	Elizabeth I of England (r. 1558–1603)
	1560	Uffizi Museum at Florence founded
Gorboduc, Sackville and Norton, first English tragedy; drama at the Inns of Court	1561	
	1564	St. Peter's Cathedral in Rome (begun 1546)
	1567	Netherlands revolts against Spain
Castelvetro requires unities	1570	
	1572	St. Bartholomew's Day Massacre in France, Protestants murdered
The Theater and the Blackfriars, first permanent theaters in England	1576	
Coral de la Cruz, first permanent theater in Spain	1579	El Greco (1541–1614), Spain
	1580	*Essays,* Michel Eyquem de Montaigne (1533–1592), France
Corral del Principe built in Madrid	1583	

THEATER		SOCIETY, POLITICS, CULTURE
Teatro Olimpico, first permanent theater in Italy	1584	(Italy divided politically and largely under foreign rule)
(Commedia dell' arte, improvised popular theater in Italy)		
The Spanish Tragedy, Thomas Kyd (1558–1594), England	ca. 1587	
	1588	Defeat of the Spanish Armada
Alexandre Hardy (ca. 1572–1632) first French professional playwright		
Doctor Faustus, Christopher Marlowe (1564–1593), England	1589	Henry IV (r. 1589–1610) unites France
	1593	The Faerie Queene, Edmund Spenser (ca. 1552–1599), England
Alleyn's Lord Admiral's Men and Burbage's Lord Chamberlain's Men the major companies in London	1594	
	1598	Edict of Nantes ends religious wars in France; Phillip II of Spain (rules to 1621)
The Globe Theater built in England	1599	
Hamlet, William Shakespeare (1564–1616), England	ca. 1600	
Lord Chamberlain's men become the King's men	1603	James I of England (r. 1603–1625)
	1605	Cervantes Don Quixote, Part I, Spain
Volpone, Ben Jonson (1572–1637), England; Aleotti uses flat wing (ca.) England	1606	
	1607	Jamestown, Virginia, founded
	1610	Henri IV of France assassinated; Louis XII (rules to 1643)
	1611	King James Bible, England
The Duchess of Malfi, John Webster (ca. 1580–1630), England	1613	
The Sheep Well, Lope de Vega (1562–1635), Spain	ca. 1614	
The Cave of Salamanca, Miguel de Cervantes (1547–1616), Spain		
	1616	Don Quixote, Cervantes, Spain
Teatro Farnese in Italy, first surviving proscenium arch theater	1618	

THEATER		SOCIETY, POLITICS, CULTURE
Inigo Jones (1573–1652), court masques in England, Jacobean playwrights: Beaumont, Fletcher, Webster, Shirley, and Ford	1620	*Novum Organum*, Francis Bacon (1561–1626), England
	1621	Philip IV of Spain (rules to 1665)
(Italian commedia popular in France)	1624	Administration of Richelieu consolidates power of the king in France (until 1642)
	1625	Charles I of England (r. 1625–1649)
	1629	Charles I dissolves English Parliament
'Tis Pity She's a Whore, John Ford (1586–1639), England	ca. 1633	
The Cid, Pierre Corneille (1606–1684), France	1636	
Life Is a Dream, Calderón de la Barca (1600–1681), Spain		
	1637	French Academy founded; *Discourse on Method,* René Descartes (1596–1650)
The Opinions of the French Academy on The Cid establish the rule of neoclassicism in France	1638	Galileo Galilei (1564–1642), Italy
Theaters in England closed by Parliament; theatrical performances banned (until 1660)	1642	English Civil War (until (1646) Rule of Cardinal Mazarin in France (until 1661)
	1643	Death of Louis XIII; Louis XIV of France (rules to 1715)
New Marais Theatre in Paris with proscenium arch	1644	
Torelli brings Italian scenery to France	1645	
Invention of chariot-and-pole system of scene shifting permits rapid change of scenes		
	1649	Charles I of England beheaded; the Commonwealth (until 1660)
	1651	*Leviathan,* Thomas Hobbes (1588–1678), England
Italian scene designers (Sabbatini, Torelli, Parigi) famous throughout Europe		
	1659	Peace of the Pyrenees; decline of Spanish power

THEATER		SOCIETY, POLITICS, CULTURE
English theaters reopened; royal patents establish theatrical monopolies	1660	Restoration of the English monarchy; Charles II (r. 1660–1685)
	1661	Louis XIV, the "Sun King," absolute ruler of France (r. 1661–1715)
Thomas Betterton (ca. 1635–1710), foremost English actor	1662	Royal Society founded in England, dedicated to science
Molière's troupe given Palais Royal; *The Misanthrope,* Molière (1622–1673), France	1666	
	1667	*Paradise Lost,* John Milton (1608–1674), England
	1669	*Pensées,* Blaise Pascal (1623–1662), France
Drury Lane Theater, England	1674	
The Country Wife, William Wycherley (1640–1715), England	1675	
All for Love, John Dryden (1631–1700), England; *Phaedra,* Jean Racine (1639–1699), France	1677	
Comédie Française, first national theater company in France	1680	
	1687	Isaac Newton (1642–1727) formulates laws of universal gravitation
Comédie Française gets new theater, to be used until 1770	1689	Glorious Revolution in England of William and Mary (r. 1689–1702)
	1690	*Essay Concerning Human Understanding,* John Locke (1632–1704), England
Jeremy Collier publishes attack on the immorality of the English stage	1698	
The Way of the World, William Congreve (1670–1729), England	1700	

EIGHTEENTH CENTURY

THEATER		SOCIETY, POLITICS, CULTURE
(Bibiena family dominates scene design throughout century—"baroque," lavish, and ornate)	1701	War of the Spanish Succession in France (until 1714)

THEATER		SOCIETY, POLITICS, CULTURE
		Peter the Great (r. 1682–1725) begins westernization of Russia
(French and Italian influence in the court theaters of Germany, Scandinavia, and Russia)	1702	Queen Anne of England (r. 1702–1714)
Ferdinando Bibiena introduces angle perspective	ca. 1703	
	1711	*The Spectator* begun by Addison and Steele in England
	1714	George I of England (r. 1714–1727), House of Hanover; Baroque music: Johann Sebastian Bach (1685–1750) and George Frederick Handel (1685–1759)
	1715	Louis XIV of France dies
	1719	Daniel Defoe's *Robinson Crusoe*
	1721	Robert Walpole, first English prime minister (1721–1742)
Jeppe of the Hill, Ludvig Holberg (1684–1754), beginning of Danish drama	1722	
(Johann Gottsched (1700–1766) and Caroline Neuber (1697–1760) begin reforms of German theater)		
	ca. 1724	Baroque music flourishes (Bach and Handel)
The Conscious Lovers, Richard Steele (1672–1729), rise of sentimental comedy in England		
	1726	*Gulliver's Travels,* Jonathan Swift (1667–1745), England
The Beggar's Opera, John Gay (1685–1732), England	1728	
The London Merchant, George Lillo (1693–1732), English bourgeois drama	1731	
Zaire, Voltaire (1694–1788), French neoclassical tragedy	1732	(Italy remains divided throughout century)
Licensing Act imposes severe censorship on theater in England	1737	(French painters Jean Antoine Watteau, François Boucher, and Jean Honoré Fragonard stress rococo sensuality in painting)
(First permanent theaters in Germany)	1740	Frederick the Great of Prussia (r. 1740–1786), "enlightened despotism"

HISTORICAL OUTLINE

THEATER		SOCIETY, POLITICS, CULTURE
Charles Macklin's Shylock—an attempt at costume reform		
David Garrick (1717–1779) becomes actor-manager at Drury Lane	1747	
Garrick, innovations in English acting	1748	*Clarissa,* Samuel Richardson (1689–1761), England
Encyclopedia (1748–1772) in France, edited by Denis Diderot (1713–1784), advocates more realistic drama and staging		
P.J. DeLoutherbourg (1740–1812), realism and "local color" in English scene design	1749	*Tom Jones,* Henry Fielding (1707–1754), England
Hallam acting troupe in Virginia	1752	
The Mistress of the Inn, Carlo Goldoni (1707–1793), Italy	1753	
Voltaire's *Orphan of China*	1755	*Dictionary,* Samuel Johnson (1709–1784), England
	1756	Seven Years' War (until 1763); loss to France of much of colonial empire
The Father of a Family, Diderot, bourgeois drama, France	1758	
		Joshua Reynolds (1723–1792), English painter
Spectators banished from French stage	ca. 1759	Voltaire's *Candide*
("Boulevard" theaters 1762 built in Paris; growth of popular drama); Gozzi's *Turandot*	1762	*Social Contract* and *Emile,* Jean-Jacques Rousseau (1712–1778), France
		Catherine the Great (r. 1762–1796) expands Russian power
	1765	Watt's steam engine, England
Drottningholm in Sweden completed Southwark theater in Philadelphia	1766	
Hamburg National Theater (to 1769)	1767	
"Storm and stress" movement (to 1787)		
Minna von Barnhelm, Gotthold Lessing (1729–1781), Germany		
Hamburg Dramaturgy, Lessing; first major German dramatic criticism		

THEATER		SOCIETY, POLITICS, CULTURE
She Stoops to Conquer, Oliver Goldsmith (1730–1774), England	1773	Thomas Gainsborough (1734–1802), English painter
	1775	American Revolution (until 1783)
("Storm and Stress" playwrights in Germany. Friedrich Schröder (1744–1818), major German actor)		
	1776	Declaration of Independence (American Revolution 1775–1781)
		Wealth of Nations, Adam Smith (1723–1790), England
The School for Scandal, Richard Brinsley Sheridan (1751–1816), England	1777	(Rise of English colonial power; industrial revolution)
	1781	*Critique of Pure Reason,* Immanuel Kant (1724–1804), Germany
The Marriage of Figaro, Pierre-Augustin Caron de Beaumarchais (1732–1799), France	1783	
(Impulse toward national theater and drama grows in Europe. Beginnings of German romanticism)	1787	*Don Giovanni,* Wolfgang Amadeus Mozart (1756–1791), Germany
	1789	French Revolution (until 1797)
(Attempts made at greater realism in costumes and scenery)	1793	Painting, *Death of Marat,* Jacques Louis David (1748–1825), France
	1799	Consulate of Napoleon
Johann Wolfgang von Goethe (1749–1832) "directs" Weimar Court Theater; Friedrich Schiller (1759–1805) assists	1798	
Mary Stuart, Schiller, Germany	1800	

NINETEENTH CENTURY

THEATER		SOCIETY, POLITICS, CULTURE
	1803	The Louisiana Purchase
Francois-Joseph Talma (1763–1823), foremost French actor	1804	Napoleon I becomes Emperor of France
	1807	*Fifth Symphony* of Ludwig van Beethoven (1770–1827), Germany
Faust, Part I, Goethe, Germany	1808	

THEATER		SOCIETY, POLITICS, CULTURE
René C.G. de Pixérécourt (1773–1844), rise of French melodrama	1810	Mme. de Staël (1766–1817); German romanticism brought to France
The Broken Jug, Heinrich von Kleist (1777–1811), Germany	1811	Beethoven's 5th Symphony
	1815	Battle of Waterloo; the "Metternich system" imposes strict censorship and impedes growth of liberalism in Germany
Chestnut Street Theater in Philadelphia becomes first totally gas-lit theater	1816	
The Cenci, Percy Bysshe Shelley (1792–1822), England	1819	
	1822	Eugène Delacroix (1798–1863), painter, France
Charles Kemble's (1775–1854) production of *King John* in England; historical accuracy in costumes and sets	1823	The Monroe Doctrine
Boris Godunov, Alexander Pushkin (1799–1837), Russia	1825	Decembrist Rising in Russia
	1829	Andrew Jackson, president of United States (until 1837)
Edmund Kean (1787–1833), romantic acting in England		
Hernani, Victor Hugo (1802–1885); "romantic" rebellion against neoclassicism in France	1830	In France, Revolution establishes "July Monarchy" of Louis Philippe (r. 1830–1848); *The Red and the Black,* Stendhal (1783–1842); Auguste Comte founds positivism
	1832	Upper-middle class enfranchised in England
Lorenzaccio, Alfred de Musset (1810–1857), France	1834	
The Inspector General, Nikolai Gogol (1809–1852), Russia; *Woyzeck,* Georg Büchner (1813–1837), Germany	1836	
	1837	Victoria of England (r. 1837–1901)
William Charles Macready (1793–1873), reforms in English acting and staging		

THEATER		SOCIETY, POLITICS, CULTURE
	1838	*Oliver Twist,* Charles Dickens (1813–1870), England
	1839	Chartist agitation in England to improve condition of working classes
The Glass of Water, Eugène Scribe (1791–1861); well-made plays, France	1840	
Theater Regulation Act abolishes monopoly of patent theaters in London	1843	
Maria Magdalena, Friedrich Hebbel (1813–1863), Germany	1844	
	1848	Italian War of Independence in France (until 1849)
		Revolution in Germany and Austria (until 1849)
Astor Place Theater riot in New York	1849	
A Month in the Country, Ivan Turgenev (1818–1883), Russia	1850	
	1851	*Moby Dick,* Herman Melville (1819–1891), United States
		Rigoletto, Giuseppe Verdi (1813–1901), Italy
Camille, Alexandre Dumas fils (1824–1895); "thesis" plays, France	1852	The Second French Empire, Napoleon III (r. 1852–1870)
First production of *Uncle Tom's Cabin,* most popular American play of century; use of touring companies		
	1853	Crimean War (until 1856)
	1857	*Les Fleurs du Mal,* Charles Baudelaire (1821–1867); *Madame Bovary,* Gustave Flaubert (1821–1880), France
The Thunderstorm, Alexander Ostrovsky (1823–1886), Russia	1859	*Tristan und Isolde,* Richard Wagner (1813–1883), Germany
		Origin of Species, Charles Darwin (1809–1882); *Idylls of the King* (1st vol.), Alfred, Lord Tennyson (1809–1892); first oil well
M. Perrichon's Journey, Eugène Labiche (1815–1888), France	1860	

THEATER		SOCIETY, POLITICS, CULTURE
Victorien Sardou (1831–1908), *A Scrap of Paper*		
	1861	American Civil War (until 1865)
		Liberation of the serfs in Russia
	1862	Bismarck becomes minister-president of Prussia
Edwin Booth (1833–1893) plays Hamlet for 100 nights in London; long "runs" become common	1864	
Georg II, Duke of Saxe-Meiningen (1826–1914) begins reforms in staging; beginning of modern director, Germany	1866	*Crime and Punishment,* Fyodor Dostoevsky (1821–1881), Russia
	1867	*Das Kapital,* Karl Marx (1818–1883), Germany
Booth's Theater in New York	1869	*War and Peace,* Leo Tolstoy (1828–1910), Russia
	1870	Franco-Prussian War (1870–1871); Paris Commune; Third Republic established; unification of Italy complete
	1871	German Empire founded
Thérèse Raquin, Émile Zola (1840–1902); naturalism in drama, France	1873	
Paris Opera built, epitome of nineteenth-century theater architecture	1874	French impressionist painters
Wagner's Bayreuth theater, innovations in theater architecture, Germany	1876	*Tom Sawyer,* Mark Twain (1835–1910); telephone patented
H.M.S. Pinafore, W. S. Gilbert (1836–1911) and Arthur Sullivan (1842–1900), England	1877	
A Doll's House, Henrik Ibsen (1828–1906), Norway	1879	Invention of the incandescent lamp
Savoy Theater employs electricity in London	1881	
The Vultures, Henry Becque (1837–1899), France	1885	
Henry Irving (1838–1905), first English actor to be knighted, established role of the director in commercial theater		

THEATER		SOCIETY, POLITICS, CULTURE
The Power of Darkness, Leo Tolstoy, Russia	1886	
French actress Sarah Bernhardt (1845–1923), most famous "star" of the century		
Antoine's Théâtre Libre founded in Paris; electricity replaces gas in theater lighting	1887	
The Father, August Strindberg (1849–1912), Sweden	1888	William II (r. 1888–1918), Emperor of Germany
Freie Bühne Theater, formed in Germany	1889	
Independent Theater of London	1891	
The Second Mrs. Tanqueray, Arthur Wing Pinero (1855–1934), England	1893	
Shaw's *Arms and the Man*	1894	Dreyfus affair in France (until 1906)
The Importance of Being Earnest, Oscar Wilde (1856–1900), England	1895	
The Sea Gull, Anton Chekhov (1860–1904), Russia	1896	
Ubu Roi, Alfred Jarry (1873–1907), precursor of absurdism, France		
Moscow Art Theater founded	1898	

TWENTIETH CENTURY

THEATER		SOCIETY, POLITICS, CULTURE
	1900	Freud's *Interpretation of Dreams,* Austria
Riders to the Sea, John Millington Synge (1871–1909), Ireland	1901	Theodore Roosevelt (until 1909), Open Door policy
	1903	Wright brothers make successful airplane flight
The Art of the Theater, Gordon Craig (1872–1966); *Major Barbara,* George Bernard Shaw (1856–1950), England	1905	Einstein's theory of relativity; insurrection in Russia
		Separation of church and state in France

THEATER		SOCIETY, POLITICS, CULTURE
	1907	*Les Demoiselles d' Avignon,* Pablo Picasso (1881–1973), cubist painting
Adolphe Appia (1862–1928), pioneer in nonillusionistic scene design		Marcel Proust (1871–1922)
Justice, by John Galsworthy (1867–1933), England	1910	
Théâtre du Vieux Columbier (1879–1949), France	1913	*Le Sacré du Printemps,* Igor Stravinsky (1882–1971), Russia, United States
	1914	World War I (until 1918)
Provincetown Players organized, United States	1915	
	1916	Easter Rebellion in Ireland
	1917	United States enters war; Bolshevik Revolution in Russia
Theatre Guild founded, United States	1918	Spengler's *Decline of the West* predicts fall of western civilization, Germany
	1919	Eighteenth Amendment begins prohibition (until 1933), United States
	1920	Nineteenth Amendment extends suffrage to women, United States
Man and the Masses, Ernst Toller (1893–1939), German expressionism	1921	Irish Free State founded
Six Characters in Search of an Author, Luigi Pirandello (1867–1936), Italy		
The Circle, Somerset Maugham (1874–1965), England		
	1922	*Ulysses,* James Joyce (1882–1941); Mussolini's fascists take power in Italy
Yevgeny Vakhtangov (1883–1922), Oleg Yevreinov (1879–1853), Alexander Taïrov (1885–1950), Vsevelod Meyerhold (1874–1942): period of postrevolutionary creativity and innovation in Russia (until 1972)		
	1923	Hitler's "Beer-Hall putsch" in Munich

THEATER		SOCIETY, POLITICS, CULTURE
My Life in Art, Constantin Stanislavski (1863–1938), revolution in acting, Russia	1924	*The Trial,* Franz Kafka (1003–1924), Czechoslovakia; death of Lenin, Russia
First Surrealist Manifesto, André Breton (1896–1966), France		
Desire Under the Elms, Eugene O'Neill (1888–1953), United States; *Juno and the Paycock,* Sean O'Casey (1884–1964), Ireland		
	1925	*The Dehumanization of Art,* José Ortega y Gasset (1883–1955), Spain
		The Magic Mountain, Thomas Mann (1875–1955), Germany
Meyerhold's production of *The Inspector General,* "constructivist" staging, Russia	1926	Arnold Schoenberg (1874–1951), "twelve-tone" music, Austria
The Three-Penny Opera, Bertolt Brecht (1898–1956), "epic theater," Germany	1928	
	1929	*Look Homeward Angel,* Thomas Wolfe (1900–1938); *The Sound and the Fury,* William Faulkner (1897–1962); stock market crash
Max Reinhardt (1873–1943), foremost director in Europe		
Private Lives, Noël Coward (1899–1973), England	1930	
Group Theater (until 1941); brought Stanislavski methods to the United States	1931	Collapse of Spanish monarchy
	1933	New Deal legislation begins; Nazis take power in Germany
Brecht and other writers and artists leave Germany		
"Socialist realism" declared official Soviet style	1934	
The Infernal Machine, Jean Cocteau (1892–1963), France		
Brecht and other German artists emigrate; Gielgud's *Hamlet*		
Tiger at the Gates, Jean Giraudoux (1882–1944), France; *House of Bernarda Alba,* Federico García Lorca (1899–1936), Spain	1935	Italy attacks Ethiopia
		Nuremberg Laws deprive Jews of German citizenship; purges in Russia

THEATER		SOCIETY, POLITICS, CULTURE
Federal Theater Project (until 1939); *Waiting for Lefty,* Clifford Odets (1906–1963), United States; *Murder in the Cathedral,* T. S. Eliot (1888–1965), England		
	1936	Spanish Civil War (until 1939)
Tyrone Guthrie (1900–1970), director of Old Vic, England	1937	
The Theater and Its Double, Antonin Artaud (1896–1948), France	1938	
	1939	World War II (until 1945)
	1941	*For Whom the Bell Tolls,* Ernest Hemingway (1898–1961)
The Skin of Our Teeth, Thornton Wilder (1897–1975)	1942	
Antigone, Jean Anouilh (1910–) France	1943	*The Myth of Sisyphus,* Albert Camus (1913–1960), France
No Exit, Jean-Paul Sartre (1905–1980), France	1944	Liberation of France
Compagnie Madeline Renaud–Jean-Louis Barrault, founded in France	1946	Nuremburg trials
The Maids, Jean Genet (1910–), France	1947	
A Streetcar Named Desire, Tennessee Williams (1911–1983); Actors' Studio founded, United States		
The Bald Soprano, Eugène Ionesco (1912–), France	1949	Creation of East and West Germany
Brecht opens Berliner Ensemble in East Berlin		*1984,* George Orwell (1903–1950)
Death of a Salesman, Arthur Miller (1916–), United States		
	1950	Korean war (until 1953)
The Queen and the Rebels, Ugo Betti (1892–1953), Italy; Jean Vilar (1912–1971) made director of Théâtre National Populaire	1951	
Waiting for Godot, Samuel Beckett (1906–), France	1953	Death of Stalin
	1954	McCarthy-Army hearings
		Hydrogen bomb tested

THEATER		SOCIETY, POLITICS, CULTURE
Separate Tables, Terence Rattigan (1911), England	1955	
Look Back in Anger, John Osborne (1929–), England	1956	Russia crushes Hungarian revolt; Khrushchev denounces Stalin
The Visit, Friedrich Duerrenmatt (1921–), Switzerland		
	1957	*Sputnik I,* first artificial earth satellite
Biedermann and the Firebugs, Max Frisch (1911–), Switzerland; *The Birthday Party,* Harold Pinter (1930–), England	1958	Fifth Republic of France
Marat/Sade, Peter Weiss (1916–); Polish Theater Laboratory founded by Jerzy Grotowski (1933–)	1959	
The Zoo Story (American premier), Edward Albee (1928–), United States	1960	
Tyrone Guthrie Theater opens in Minneapolis, Minnesota	1961	Berlin Wall
Cafe LaMama opened, off-Broadway theater	1962	Cuban missile crisis
Albee's *Who's Afraid of Virginia Woolf?*	1962	
National Theater established (England's first state-subsidized theater	1963	John F. Kennedy, president of the United States, assassinated; John Glenn orbits earth
		Warfare escalates between North and South Vietnam; Martin Luther King arrested in Birmingham;
Dutchman, LeRoi Jones (Amiri Baraka) (1934–), United States	1964	Resignation of Khrushchev
Tango, Slawomir Mrozek (1930–), Poland	1965	
Viet-Rock, Megan Terry(1932–), United States	1966	
Hair, Ken McDermott, United States	1968	
Towards a Poor Theater, Grotowski, Poland		
Ceremonies in Dark Old Men, Lonne Elder III (1931–), United States	1969	Neal Armstrong walks on the moon, United States

THEATER		SOCIETY, POLITICS, CULTURE
	1970	*The Female Eunuch*, Germaine Greer, England
Sticks and Bones, David Rabe (1940–)	1971	
Peter Brook's (1925–) interpretation of Shakespeare's *A Midsummer Night's Dream*		
N.Y. Shakespeare Festival (Joseph Papp) produces *Two Gentlemen of Verona*, *Sticks and Bones* and *That Championship Season* in New York City	1972	
	1973	Vietnam cease-fire
Equus, Peter Shaffer (1926–), England	1974	Watergate scandal; President Richard M. Nixon resigns
	1975	Francisco Franco dies; Helsinki agreement, recognizing the postwar status quo in Europe, signed
	1976	Mao Tse tung, leader of Communist China, dies; Jimmy Carter becomes president of United States
The Shadow Box, Michael Cristofer (1946–), wins the Pulitzer Prize	1977	Camp David accords reached between Israel and Egypt; the novelist Vladimir Nabokov dies
Buried Child, Sam Shepard (1943–), wins Pulitzer Prize	1979	
Harold Clurman, (1901–1980) Group Theater founder and director, dies	1980	
A Soldier's Play, Charles Fuller (1939–) wins Pulitzer Prize	1982	

Note The preceding historical survey follows the development of theater in western civilization, but another important theater, the Asian theater, was evolving along a path of its own. The following section traces theater in India, China, and Japan. Theater emerged also in such places as Cambodia and Indonesia.

ASIA

THEATER		SOCIETY, POLITICS, CULTURE
INDIA		
Natyasastra, principal critical work on Sanskrit drama	ca. 50–100	
Sanskrit drama highly developed	ca. 320	Gupta dynasty reunites northern India after 500 years division; golden age of classical Sanskrit

THEATER		SOCIETY, POLITICS, CULTURE
The Little Clay Cart		
Shakuntala, Kalidasa, best-known Sanskrit playwright	ca. 400	
	ca. 600	Earliest known use of the zero and decimal
Bhavabhuti, highest-ranked playwright after Kalidasa	ca. 730	
Decline of Sanskrit drama	ca. 1150	
Indian dance drama, puppet and folk plays	ca. 1192	Beginning of Muslim rule
	1526	Mogul Empire (until 1761)
	1790	British power established in India
King of the Dark Chamber, Rabindranath Tagore (1861–1941)		

CHINA

THEATER		SOCIETY, POLITICS, CULTURE
	618	T'ang dynasty founded (until 907)
Academy of the Pear Orchard, school for dancers and singers established by Ming Huang	712	Emperor Ming Huang (r. 712–756), brief flourishing of arts and literature
	ca. 850	Advent of block printing
Development of "northern" and "southern" schools of drama during Sung dynasty	960	Sung dynasty (until 1279), flowering of arts, literature, and scholarship
Development of professional theater companies and urban audiences		
Scholars and artists move south during Yüan dynasty, but a vigorous popular drama flourishes in the North	1260	Yüan dynasty, China ruled by Mongol Khans until 1368
Southern drama becomes predominant during Ming dynasty and develops highly literary and romantic drama	1368	Ming dynasty, Mongol rulers expelled
	1644	Ch'ing dynasty, Manchu rulers (until 1912)
Gradual decline of Southern drama; Peking eventually replaces Soochow as cultural capital		
	1839	Beginning of Opium wars

THEATER		SOCIETY, POLITICS, CULTURE
Kabuki becomes most popular form of theater	1675–1750	
Japanese "doll theater" established in Osaka (Bunraku)	1685	
Chikamatsu Monzaemon (1653–1724), Japan's most famous playwright, wrote for the Bunraku and the Kabuki	ca. 1800	
Kabuki becomes the most popular form	ca. 1853	Japan open to the west, beginning of continuing western influence
	1868	Meiji restoration; New rules in Japan sanctions exchanges with west
Noh, Kabuki, and Bunraku continue, but modern realistic theater (Shingeki) begins	1910	
"Peking opera," a less literary and more theatrical form, becomes dominant	ca. 1875	
	1900	Boxer Rebellion
Spoken drama, based on western models, becomes important	1920	

	JAPAN	
	645	Beginning of great period of cultural infusion and cultural growth (until ca. 800)
Development of traditional dance forms		
	ca. 1020	*The Tale of Genji,* classic Japanese novel, by Murasaki Shikibu
	ca. 1100	Civil strife encourages the rise of military government and feudalism
Zeami Motokiyo (1363–1444), development of the Noh drama	1395	Rule of Yoshimitsu (r. 1395–1408), stable period of artistic and literary creativity, but followed by civil wars
	ca. 1542	First Europeans to visit Japan
	1568	Period of national unification (until 1600)
First appearance of Kabuki, a more popular and theatrical form than Noh	ca. 1600	

THEATER		SOCIETY, POLITICS, CULTURE
	1640	Friction with foreigners and religious disputes leading to cultural and political isolation
Noh drama becomes associated with the aristocracy, and its conventions are rigidly standardized	ca. 1650	

5
REALISM
AND
NONREALISM

Nonrealism on stage.
In this appendix realistic elements of theater are contrasted with nonrealistic elements. Realism means that what we see and hear on stage conforms to observable reality: dialogue, dress, settings, and the actions of characters are like those found in everyday life. Nonrealistic elements depart from this. An example is the masks, costumes, and other fantastical elements in this scene from Shakespeare's *The Merrry Wives of Windsor.*

The distinction between realistic and nonrealistic techniques in the theater becomes clearer when the two approaches to theater are placed side by side. They are present in all aspects of theater, as the following table illustrates.

REALISTIC TECHNIQUES	NONREALISTIC TECHNIQUES
STORY	
Events which the audience knows have happened or might happen in everyday life: Blanche DuBois in Tennessee Williams's *A Streetcar Named Desire* goes to New Orleans to visit her sister and brother-in-law.	Events which do not occur in real life but only in the imagination: Emily in Thornton Wilder's *Our Town,* after she has died, appears alive and returns to visit the earth for one day.
STRUCTURE	
Action confined to real places; time passes normally as it does in everyday life: in *The Little Foxes* by Lillian Hellman, the activity occurs over several days in Regina's house as she takes control of her family's estate.	Arbitrary use of time and place: in Strindberg's *The Dream Play,* walls dissolve, characters are transformed, as in a dream.
CHARACTERS	
Recognizable human beings, such as the family—mother, father, and two sons—in O'Neill's *Long Day's Journey into Night.*	Unreal figures like the Ghost of Hamlet's father in *Hamlet,* the Three Witches in *Macbeth,* or the people who turn into animals in Ionesco's *Rhinoceros.*
ACTING	
Performers portray people as they behave in daily life: Nora Helmer in Ibsen's *A Doll's House* leaves her husband and an unsatisfactory marriage in a believable, forthright manner.	Performers act as ghosts and animals; they also engage in singing, dancing, acrobatics, and gymnastics in a musical comedy or a New Theater piece.

REALISTIC TECHNIQUES	NONREALISTIC TECHNIQUES

LANGUAGE

Ordinary dialogue or conversation: the Gentleman Caller in Williams's *The Glass Menagerie* tells Laura about his future in the language of an optimistic young salesman.	Poetry such as Romeo speaks to Juliet in Shakespeare's play; or the song "Tonight" sung to Maria in the musical *West Side Story*.

SCENERY

The rooms of a real house, as in Chekhov's *The Cherry Orchard*.	Abstract forms and shapes on a bare stage —for a Greek play, for example, such as Sophocles's *Electra*.

LIGHTING

Light on stage appears to come from natural sources—a lamp in a room, or sunlight, as in Ibsen's *Ghosts*, where the sunrise comes through a window in the final scene.	Shafts of light fall at odd angles; also, an arbitrary use of colors in the light. Example: a single, blue spotlight on a singer in a musical comedy.

COSTUMES

Ordinary street clothes, like those worn by the characters in Walker's *The River Niger*.	The bright costumes of a chorus in a musical comedy; the strange outfit worn by Caliban, the half-man, half-beast in Shakespeare's *The Tempest*.

MAKEUP

The natural look of characters in a domestic play such as Hansberry's *A Raisin in the Sun*.	Masks worn by characters in a Greek tragedy or in a modern play like van Itallie's *America Hurrah*.

NOTES

INTRODUCTION

1 Bernard Beckerman, *Dynamics of Drama: Theory and Method of Analysis,* Knopf, New York, 1970, p. 129.
2 Reprinted by permission of the Yale University Press from Eugene O'Neill, *Long Day's Journey into Night.* Copyright 1955 by Carlotta Monterey O'Neill, p. 108.
3 Robert Edmond Jones, *The Dramatic Imagination,* Theater Arts Books, New York, 1941, p. 40.

CHAPTER ONE

1 Jean-Claude van Itallie, *The Serpent: A Ceremony,* written in collaboration with the Open Theater, Atheneum, New York, 1969, p. ix.
2 Walter Kerr, "We Call It 'Live' Theater, but Is It?" *New York Times,* January 2 1972. Copyright 1972 by The New York Times Company. Reprinted by permission.
3 Gustave Le Bon, *The Crowd: A Study of the Popular Mind,* 20th ed., Ernest Benn, London, 1952, p. 23.
4 Ibid., p. 27.
5 Lawrence S. Wrightsman, *Social Psychology,* 2d ed., Brooks/Cole, Monterey, Calif., 1977, p. 579.
6 Ibid., p. 559.
7 B. F. Skinner, *Science and Human Behavior,* Macmillan, New York, 1953, p. 312.
8 Bernard Beckerman, *Dynamics of Drama: Theory and Method of Analysis,* Knopf, New York, 1970, p. 9.

CHAPTER TWO

1 Carl G. Jung, *Man and His Symbols,* Aldus Books, London, 1964, p. 21.
2 J. A. Hadfield, *Dreams and Nightmares,* Penguin, Baltimore, 1961, p. 8.

·CHAPTER THREE

1 Notes on *King Lear* are from G. K. Hunter's edition of Shakespeare's *King Lear,* Penguin, Baltimore, 1972, pp. 243–244.

(There are no notes for Chapter 4.)

CHAPTER FIVE

1 Arthur Miller, *The Theater Essays of Arthur Miller,* Viking, New York, 1978, pp. 3–5.
2 Friedrich Nietzsche, "The Birth of Tragedy," from Nietzsche, *Works in Three Volumes,* Carl Hanser Publishers, Munich, vol. 1, pp. 92, 19.

(There are no notes for Chapter 6.)

CHAPTER SEVEN

1 Alvin B. Kernan, *Character and Conflict: An Introduction to Drama,* 2d ed., Harcourt, Brace & World, New York, 1969, p. 286.
2 Kenneth MacGowen, *A Primer of Playwrighting,* Dolphin Books, Doubleday, Garden City, N.Y., 1962, p. 62.

CHAPTER EIGHT

1 Jean Anouilh, *Antigone,* adapted and translated by Lewis Galantiere. Copyright 1946 by Random House, p. 36.
2 John Gassner, *A Treasury of the Theater (From Henrik Ibsen to Arthur Miller),* Simon & Schuster, New York, 1959, p. 457.

CHAPTER NINE

1 Albert Camus, *Le Mythe de Sisyphe,* Gallimard, Paris, 1942, p. 18.
2 Eugène Ionesco, *The Bald Soprano,* in *Four Plays,* Grove Press, New York, 1958, p. 39.
3 Samuel Beckett, *Waiting for Godot,* Grove Press, New York, 1954, p. 28b.

4   Michael Kirby, "The New Theatre," *Tulane Drama Review,* vol. 10, no. 2, Winter, 1965, p. 27.

5   John Cage, "An Interview," in *TDR,* vol. 10, no. 2, *Tulane Drama Review,* Winter 1965, p. 55.

6   Martin Esslin, *The Theatre of the Absurd,* Doubleday, Garden City, N.Y., 1961, p. 149.

7   Ibid., p. 159.

CHAPTER TEN

1   Michael Kirby, "The New Theatre," *Tulane Drama Review,* vol. 10, no. 2, Winter 1965, p. 31.

2   From Eric Bentley (ed.), *Naked Masks: Five Plays by Luigi Pirandello.* Copyright, 1922, by E. P. Dutton. Renewal copyright, 1950, by Stefano, Fausto, and Lietta Pirandello. Reprinted by permission of the publishers, E. P. Dutton, New York, 1957, pp. 266–267.

CHAPTER ELEVEN

1   From *Death of a Salesman* by Arthur Miller, Copyright 1949 by Arthur Miller. Reprinted by permission of Viking, New York, 1968, pp. 100–103.

2   Erving Goffman, *The Presentation of Self in Everyday Life,* Anchor Books, Doubleday, Garden City, N.Y., 1949, p. 72.

3   Nelson W. Aldrich, Jr., "St. Jacqueline and the Celebritariat," *Horizon,* August 1978, pp. 28–29.

4   Robert Ezra Park, *Race and Culture,* Free Press, Glencoe, Ill., 1950, p. 249.

5   Theodore Shank, *The Art of Dramatic Art,* Dickenson, Belmont, Calif., 1969, p. 36.

CHAPTER TWELVE

1   Richard Findlater, *The Player Kings,* Weidenfeld and Nicolson, London, 1971, p. 25.

2   Constantin Stanislavski, *An Actor Prepares,* Theatre Arts Books, New York, 1948, p. 73.

3   Constantin Stanislavski, *My Life in Art,* Meridian Books, New York, 1946, p. 465.

4   Stanislavski, *An Actor Prepares,* Theatre Arts Books, New York, 1948, p. 92.

5   Ibid., p. 88.

6   Ibid., p. 38.

7   Ibid., p. 136.

8   Harold Clurman, *On Directing,* Macmillan, New York, 1972, pp. 261 ff.

9   Walter Kerr, drama review, *New York Herald Tribune,* January 10, 1961.

10   Jerzy Grotowski, *Towards a Poor Theatre,* Clarion Books, Simon & Schuster, New York, 1968, p. 133.

11   Ibid., p. 147.

CHAPTER THIRTEEN

1 Harold Clurman, *On Directing,* Macmillan, New York, 1972, p. 27.
2 Ibid., pp. 221 and 255.
3 Ibid., p. 30.
4 Ibid., p. 30.

CHAPTER FOURTEEN

1 The Performance Group, *Dionysus in 69,* Noonday Press, Farrar, Straus & Giroux, New York, (n.p.).
2 Material on the first three types of stages was suggested by a booklet prepared by Dr. Mary Henderson for the educational division of Lincoln Center for the Performing Arts.
3 Arthur Waley, *The Nō Plays of Japan,* Grove Press, New York, (n.d.), pp. 10–11.
4 Antonin Artaud, *The Theater and Its Double,* Grove Press, New York, 1958, pp. 96–97.

CHAPTER FIFTEEN

1 Robert Edmond Jones, *The Dramatic Imagination,* Theatre Arts Books, New York, 1941, p. 25.
2 Ibid., pp. 23–24.
3 Reprinted from *The Dramatic Imagination.* Copyright 1941 by Robert Edmond Jones, with the permission of the publishers, Theatre Arts Books, New York, 1941, pp. 71–72.

(There are no notes for Chapters 16 and 17.)

CHAPTER EIGHTEEN

1 Tennessee Williams, *Tennessee Williams: Memoirs,* Doubleday, New York, 1975, pp. 111–113.
2 Ibid., p. 111.
3 Ibid., p. 111.
4 Toby Cole and Helen Krich Chinoy (eds.), *Directors on Directing,* Bobbs-Merrill, New York, p. 364.
5 Ibid., pp. 364–365.
6 Ibid., pp. 366–367.
7 Ibid., pp. 374–375.
8 Ibid., p. 372.
9 Ibid., p. 378.

APPENDIX 1

1 S. H. Butcher, *Aristotle's Theory of Poetry and Fine Art,* 3d ed. Macmillan, London, 1902, p. 23.
2 Arthur Miller, *The Theater Essays of Arthur Miller,* Viking Press, New York, 1978, pp. 3–4.

SELECT
BIBLIOGRAPHY

Aristotle: *Aristotle's Poetics*. Tr. by S. H. Butcher. Introduction by Francis Fergusson. Hill and Wang, New York, 1961.

Artaud, Antonin: *The Theater and Its Double*. Tr. by Mary C. Richards. Grove Press, New York, 1958.

Atkinson, Brooks: *Broadway*. Rev. ed. Macmillan, New York, 1974.

Bay, Howard. *Stage Design*. Drama Book Specialists, New York, 1974.

Beckerman, Bernard: *Dynamics of Drama: Theory and Method of Analysis*. Drama Book Specialists, New York, 1979.

Benedetti, Jean: *Stanislavski: An Introduction*. Theatre Arts Books, New York, 1982.

Benedetti, Robert: *The Actor at Work*. Prentice-Hall, Englewood Cliffs, N.J., 1971.

Bentley, Eric: *The Life of the Drama*. Atheneum, New York, 1964.

————(ed.): *The Theory of the Modern Stage*. Penguin, Baltimore, 1968.

Brecht, Bertolt: *Brecht on Theatre*. Tr. by John Willett. Hill and Wang, New York, 1965.

Brockett, Oscar G.: *History of the Theatre*. 4th ed. Allyn and Bacon, Boston, 1982.

———— and Robert R. Findlay: *Century of Innovation: A History of European and American Theatre and Drama Since 1870*. Prentice-Hall, Englewood Cliffs, N.J., 1973.

Brook, Peter: *The Empty Space*. Atheneum, New York, 1968.

Burns, Elizabeth: *Theatricality*. Harper & Row, New York, 1973.

Clark, Barrett H. (ed.): *European Theories of the Drama*, Rev. ed. Crown, New York, 1965.

Clurman, Harold: *On Directing*. Macmillan, New York, 1972.

Cohen, Robert: *Acting Power*. Mayfield Publishers, Palo Alto, Calif., 1978.

Cole, Toby: *Playwrights on Playwriting*. Hill and Wang, New York, 1961.

————, and Helen Krich Chinoy: *Actors on Acting*. Crown, New York, 1970.

Corrigan, Robert (ed.): *Comedy: Meaning and Form*. Chandler, San Francisco, 1965.

————(ed.): *Tragedy: Vision and Form*. Chandler, San Francisco, 1965.

Corson, Richard: *Stage Makeup*. 6th edition. Prentice-Hall, 1981.

Dukore, Bernard: *Dramatic Theory and Criticism: Greeks to Grotowski*. Holt, New York, 1974.

Emery, Joseph S.: *Stage Costume Technique*. Prentice-Hall, 1981.

Esslin, Martin: *The Theatre of the Absurd*. Rev. ed. Doubleday, Garden City, N.Y., 1969.

Fergusson, Francis: *The Idea of a Theater*. Princeton, Princeton, N.J., 1949.

Gassner, John: *Masters of the Drama*. 3d ed. Dover, New York, 1954.

———— and Edward Quinn: *The Reader's Encyclopedia of World Drama*. Thomas Y. Crowell, New York, 1969.

———— and Ralph Allen (eds.): *Theatre and Drama in the Making*. 2 vols. Houghton Mifflin, Boston, 1964.

Goffman, Erving: *Presentation of Self in Everyday Life*. Overlook Press, New York, 1973.

Goldman, Michael: *The Actor's Freedom: Toward a Theory of Drama*. Viking, New York, 1975.

Grotowski, Jerzy: *Towards a Poor Theatre*. Simon & Schuster, New York, 1968.

Heilman, Robert G.: *Tragedy and Melodrama: Versions of Experience*. University of Washington Press, Seattle, 1968.

Hodge, Francis: *Play Directing: Analysis, Communication, and Style*. Prentice-Hall, Englewood Cliffs, N.J., 1971.

Izenour, George: *Theatre Design*. McGraw-Hill, New York, 1977.

Jones, Robert E.: *The Dramatic Imagination*. Meredith, New York, 1941.

Kerr, Walter: *Tragedy and Comedy*. Simon & Schuster, New York, 1967.

Kirby, E. T.: *Ur-Drama: The Origins of Theatre*. New York University Press, New York, 1975.

Kirby, Michael: *Happenings*. Dutton, New York, 1965.

Lahr, John, and Jonathan Price: *Life-Show*. Viking, New York, 1973.

Langer, Susanne K.: *Feeling and Form*. Scribner, New York, 1953.

Miller, Arthur: *The Theatre Essays of Arthur Miller*. Ed. by Robert Martin. Viking, New York, 1978.

Mitchell, Loften: *Black Drama*. Hawthorn, New York, 1967.

Nagler, Alois M.: *Sourcebook in Theatrical History*. Dover, New York, 1952.

Novick, Julius: *Beyond Broadway*. Hill and Wang, New York, 1968.

Oenslager, Donald: *Scenery Then and Now*. Norton, New York, 1936.

Parker, W. Oren, and Harvey K. Smith: *Scene Design and Stage Lighting*. 4th ed. Holt, New York, 1979.

Pilbrow, Richard: *Stage Lighting*. Rev. ed. Van Nostrand and Reinhold, New York, 1979.

Roberts, Vera M.: *On Stage: A History of the Theatre*. 2d ed. Harper & Row, New York, 1974.

Schechner, Richard: *Environmental Theater*. Hawthorn, New York, 1973.

Schevill, James: *Breakout! In Search of New Theatrical Environments*. University of Chicago Press, Chicago, 1972.

Southern, Richard: *The Seven Ages of the Theatre*. Hill and Wang, New York, 1961.

Stanislavski, Constantin: *An Actor Prepares*. Tr. by Elizabeth Reynolds Hapgood. Theatre Arts Books, New York, 1936.

Wilson, Edwin, and Alvin Goldfarb: *Living Theater*. McGraw-Hill, New York, 1983.

Young, Stark: *The Theatre*. Hill and Wang, New York, 1963.

INDEX

Costumes (*Cont.*):
  resources of designer, 357–359
  responsibilities of designer, 356–
    357
  sketches, 357–358
  symbolic, 353–355
  tone and style, 350–351
Counterpoint, 163
Counterweight, 403
Country Wife, The (Wycherly),
  112, 162, 196, 355
Covent Garden Theater (London),
  282
Coward, Noël, 116
Craig, Gordon, 334, 414
Created or found space, 295–299
  adaptation of space to fit pro-
    duction, 297, 328
  Artaud and, 296–299
  historical precedents for, 299
  multifocus environments, 298–
    299, 328
  nontheater buildings, 296–297
  outdoor settings, 298
  scene designer and, 327–328
  street theater, 21, 38, 298
Creating a Role (Stanislavski), 238
Creative dramatics, 21
Credibility of characters, 226–233,
  236, 238
  (*See also* Realistic theater, act-
    ing)
Crew, 265–266, 403
Crimes of the Heart (Henley),
  228
Critic, 59–61, 263
Critical criteria, 60–61
Criticism, 60–61, 262–263
Cronyn, Hume, 28
Cross, 403
Cross-fades, 341
Crossing Niagara (Alegria), 24–25
Crucible, The (Miller), 133, 259,
  410
CSC Repertory Company, 333
Cue, 403
  lighting, 338, 341
Cue sheet, 403
Culture, link between theater and,
  44–45, 48–51
Curtain, 403
Cutouts, 322
Cycle plays, 288
Cyclorama, 379, 403
Cyrano de Bergerac (Rostand), 94,
  144, 162

Dalí, Salvador, 306
Daly, Augustin, 95
Dames at Sea (film), 410

Dance, actor training for, 240,
  244–245
Dark Ride (Jenkin), 334
Darwin, Charles, 33, 50, 253
Day of Absence (Ward), 361
Dead End Kids (Mabou Mines),
  color plate (fol. 206)
Death of a Salesman (Miller),
  66–67, 89, 90, 162–163, 194,
  214–217, 314, 316–317
Death of Tragedy, The (Steiner),
  397
Defense of Poesy, The (Sidney),
  396
De Hartog, Jan, 360
Delphi, 276–277, 291
Delsarte, François, 227–228
Denouement, 403
Deputy, The (Hochhuth), 416
Desert Song (operetta), 183
Designers, 125, 252, 302
  (*See also* Costume designers;
    Lighting; Scene design)
Desperate Hours, The (Hayes),
  96
Details, importance of in acting,
  231–232
Deus ex machina, 71, 153, 403
Dewhurst, Colleen, 72
Dialectic, 163
Diderot, Denis, 227
Dim out, 403
Dimmer, 339, 403
Dining Room, The (Gurney), 221
Dinner theaters, 57
Dionysus in 69, 177, 178, 279,
  295
Director, 250–272, 403
  audience's point of view and,
    262–264
  casting by, 260–261, 376–377
  central image or metaphor and,
    257
  concept of production and,
    255–257, 371, 375
  designers and, 262, 268, 315,
    338, 374–375
  in historical perspective, 252–
    253
  pace of play and, 265
  playwright and, 255, 262, 374
  in rehearsals, 261–262, 377–
    379, 381
  responsibility of, 252, 268
  rhythm of play and, 265
  script and, 254–255, 375
  style of production, 258–260
  task of, 254–267
  technical rehearsals and, 265–
    266
  tryouts and, 266

Directors on Directing (Kazan),
  375
Doctor Faustus (Marlowe), 191,
  239
Doctor in Spite of Himself, The
  (Molière), 112
Doll's House, A (Ibsen), 91, 140,
  193–194, 446
Domestic drama, 98–102, 411
Doubling, 220–221
Down lighting, 339
Downstage, 321, 403
Dramatic characters, 188–205
  contrasting, 202
  credibility of, 226–233, 236,
    238
  with dominant trait, 196
  exceptional, 89–93, 191–192
  existential, 173, 176
  extraordinary, 86, 190–191
  as images of ourselves, 204–205
  juxtaposition of, 201–203
  major, 202
  minor, 197, 202–203
  in modern theater, 191–194
  nonhuman parts, 200–201, 353–
    355
  orchestration of, 203–204
  ordinary, 193–194
  permanence of, 205
  realistic and nonrealistic con-
    trasted, 446
  stock, 194–196, 362
  variety, 248
Dramatic script (*see* Script)
Dramatic structure, 127–187
  conventions of, 132–137
    balance of forces, 142–143
    conflict, 133–134
    motivation, 143–144
    part of total experience, 386
    space limit, 139–140
    strongly opposed forces, 141–
      142
    time limit, 140–141
  development of, 137–139
    crisis and climax, 138–139
    obstacles and complications,
      138
    opening scene, importance
      of, 137
  in musical theater, 182–186
  nonsense and *non sequitur*,
    170–176
    in avant-garde, 179–182
    in theater of the absurd, 170–
      176
  patterns, 178–179
  plot, aspects of: climactic, 138–
    139, 147–153, 161–163,
    371, 386